GIRLS' TOYS

OF THE FIFTIES AND SIXTIES

Memorable Catalog Pages from the legendary
Sears Christmas Wishbooks 1950 - 1969

Edited by Thomas W. Holland

Windmill Press

Published by Windmill Press, P.O. Box 56551, Sherman Oaks, California 91413
Telephone (818) 995-6410   FAX (818) 995-3590

ISBN: 1-887790-02-0

LC: 96-61343

Publisher's Cataloging in Publication
(Prepared by Quality Books Inc.)

Girls' toys of the fifties & sixties : memorable catalog pages from
the legendary Sears Christmas wishbooks 1950-1969 / edited by
Thomas W. Holland.
p. cm.
ISBN: 1-887790-02-0

1. Toys--Catalogs--History. 2. Manufactures--Catalogs. 3.
Sears, Roebuck and Company--Catalogs. I. Holland, Thomas W.

GV1218.5.G57 1997   790.1'33'0216
                               QBI96-40460

*Front cover photograph: A young girl is amazed by the wondrous toys
available in Sears' 1954 Christmas Wishbook. (Model: Katherine Lapin)
Rear cover photographs: Sears Department Store, Canoga Park, California as it looked in 1964; catalog ad
circa 1956 for tin litho suburban doll house. (Photos courtesy Sears, Roebuck and Co.)*

1950 - Cover plus Pages 160, 174, 212-213, 218, 252-253 © 1950 Sears, Roebuck and Co.
1951- Cover plus Pages 166-167, 228-229, 234-235, 238 © 1951 Sears, Roebuck and Co.
1952 - Cover plus Pages 244-246, 264-267, 440-441 © 1952 Sears, Roebuck and Co.
1953 - Cover plus Pages 231-232, 251-252, 265-266, 280 © 1953 Sears, Roebuck and Co.
1954 - Cover plus Pages 233-234, 247-250, 333 © 1954 Sears, Roebuck and Co.
1955 - Cover plus Pages 232, 244, 266-267, 270-274 © 1955 Sears, Roebuck and Co.
1956 - Cover plus Pages 178, 192-193, 244-245, 352 © 1956 Sears, Roebuck and Co.
1957 - Cover plus Pages 184, 204-209 © 1957 Sears, Roebuck and Co.
1958 - Cover plus Pages 306, 353-354, 397, 408-409, 414 © 1958 Sears, Roebuck and Co.
1959 - Cover plus Pages 388, 396-397, 401, 474-476 © 1959 Sears, Roebuck and Co.
1960 - Cover plus Pages 366-368, 370-371 © 1960 Sears, Roebuck and Co.
1961 - Cover and Back Cover plus Pages 228-229, 314-317, 334-336, 351
         © 1961 Sears, Roebuck and Co.
1962 - Cover plus Pages 348-349, 366, 384-385, 410-411 © 1962 Sears, Roebuck and Co.
1963 - Cover plus Pages 35, 52-55, 75, 103, 116-117 © 1963 Sears, Roebuck and Co.
1964 - Cover plus Pages 16, 59, 66-67, 107, 131, 242 © 1964 Sears, Roebuck and Co.
1965 - Cover plus Pages 559, 562, 575, 583, 588, 615-616, 623-624
         © 1965 Sears, Roebuck and Co.
1966 - Cover plus Pages 574, 580, 598-599, 604-605, 616 © 1966 Sears, Roebuck and Co.
1967 - Cover plus Pages 364, 450, 459, 559, 564-565, 576 © 1967 Sears, Roebuck and Co.
1968 - Cover plus Pages 397B, 465, 474-475, 482, 506, 541, 556, 566, 600-601
         © 1968 Sears, Roebuck and Co.
1969 - Cover plus Pages 461, 470, 505, 509, 573, 586-587, 589, 606-607
         © 1969 Sears, Roebuck and Co.

Sears makes it easy for you...

to make your family's Christmas wishes come true

Have you ever thought what a simple matter it would be to buy ALL your gifts from Sears Catalogs on Sears Easy Terms? You can order everything you want now, before Christmas, and spread the payments over the months ahead. You don't need all ready cash—and you don't have to disturb your savings. It takes only a small down payment to buy for *everyone* on your gift list.

If you have a Sears Easy Payment Account you can "add-on" your Christmas purchases with NO down payment. Your present monthly payment will not be increased unless your new balance requires a larger payment according to Sears Payment Table. (See page 373 for complete details about Sears Easy Payment Plan, or contact the Credit Department of your Sears Catalog Sales Office.)

For Will and Emily

Acknowledgments

Many people worked behind the scenes to bring this book to fruition and I am most grateful for all the help I received.

Most importantly, I want to thank Sears, Roebuck and Company and their archivist Vicki Cwiok. Without their help this book simply would not have been possible.

Thanks also to Doug Roth and Eleanor Holland for their moral support and invaluable advice. Thanks to Paul Holland for his marketing help.

My oldest friend, Frank Thompson, assisted massively to this book with his knowledge of collectible toys and I am forever grateful.

Tracking down all these rare catalog pages was a logistical ordeal and required the kind assistance of numerous people. I want to particularly thank catalog experts Jerry Harrington, Ed Osepowicz, Tim Goss, and Rich Hesson.

Thanks to Betsy Annas for photographing the cover, Katherine Lapin for modeling, and Carolyn Porter and Alan Gadney who helped me with design and the complex job of reproducing the delicate old catalog pages.

Introduction

Although its primary purpose was to sell products, the Sears catalog was also a recorder of the day -- a beautifully illustrated diary of America, it's people and the way we thought about things. Surely the designers who first assembled the wonderful old catalog pages in this book never realized they were compiling an historical document, but these old images show volumes about us and how things were in other times. In many ways the Wishbook tells us about the past better than history books can.

When I began compiling GIRLS' TOYS and its companion book BOYS' TOYS, it was fascinating to see how the items sold in the Sears catalog over the years tracked with events in American history. Postwar catalogs of the Fifties were quite naive -- selling relatively "low-concept" toys like trains, trucks and baseballs to increasingly affluent buyers. The influences in toys made for boys was clearly evident. World War II's effect on the toy world brought plenty of guns and rifles for little cowboys and soldiers. Rocketry and the space race of the early Sixties brought a deluge of high tech toys. The war in Vietnam brought boys G.I. Joe. The Cold War introduced them to spy toys. Even the Beatles had an influence on the Sears catalog with "mod" drum sets and record players.

While societal impact on the toys marketed to girls is not as obvious -- the catalog's influences were just as powerful. Massive changes in the status of women occurred during the decades of the Fifties and Sixties, and toys sold female Baby Boomers helped mold their feelings about themselves and their place in the American culture of the time.

The Wishbooks of the Fifties assumed most girls would follow in their mother's footsteps to become full-time housewives and mommies. While boys toys always had an air of excitement -- even danger -- it is difficult to make a toy ironing board or sewing machine look thrilling. Girls were offered plenty of beautiful dolls, kitchen sets and relatively quiet toys.

Things changed a little as the Sixties began. The fight for equal rights had some impact on the Wishbook. Boys and girls were seen playing with the same toy together, but usually the boy was playing; the girl was standing behind him with an adoring "Isn't he great!" look. Still, boys were sold the Doctor's Kits. Girls could buy the accompanying Nurse's Kit and uniform.

By the late Sixties, the catalog's approach to girls was a bit more even balanced thanks to media coverage of the Feminist cause. Now girls could actually play with a chemistry set! They could explore outer space with Dad, using the Home Planetarium. But the majority of toys targeted to girls were dolls and accessories -- and it remains that way today.

The most important thing I found in assembling this book is that toys go far beyond just their play value. They reflect the times, good and bad. Most toys eventually break and are thrown out. It is the fond memories that remain that are important. Those are more durable, and more fun, than any toy could ever be.

Thomas W. Holland

The Sears Catalog

The roots of the famous Sears Catalog began in 1886 when Richard W. Sears, then a railroad station agent for the Minneapolis and St. Louis Railway in North Redwood, Minnesota, began selling watches and jewelry and later offered them through printed mailers which grew into catalogs. In those years the railroads literally moved America, taking people to work, settlers to new homes and delivering the clothing and supplies they would require. Thanks in large part to the railroad's ability to move things virtually anywhere in the country cheaply and quickly, Sears, Roebuck and Company grew into one of the nation's leading corporations.

In 1896 Sears produced its first large general merchandise catalog featuring 753 pages of merchandise targeted to America's farmers and their families with a variety of items for sale -- from apparel to plows -- watches and jewelry -- even toys and dolls. The specialized Sears Christmas Catalogs -- nicknamed the "Wishbook" -- began in the mid-1930's. It became a holiday staple in virtually every American home.

Not realized at the time, of course, the Sears catalogs were recording the changing scene in America and represented the daily lives and work of thousands of Americans. Edgar Rice Burroughs, author of the famed "Tarzan" series, was at one time a copywriter for Sears catalogs. Jean Arthur, Lauren Bacall, Joan Caulfield, Anita Colby, Susan Heyward, Fredric March, Norma Shearer and Gloria Swanson all appeared on the pages of Sears catalogs as models in years past.

The famous Sears catalogs have been a barometer of the time, reflecting events, the way people lived and how they perceived their surroundings. For example, within months after the destruction of the U.S.S. Maine in Havana harbor in 1898, the catalog offered a complete "stereopticon lecture outfit" on that subject and the Cuban war.

Its easy to forget how far back the Sears catalog really does go. Sears sold the pioneers "Covered wagon covers" and in 1889, before the West was fully settled, the catalog stated: "Cash in full must accompany all orders from points in Washington, Oregon, California, Idaho, Nevada, Utah, Arizona, New Mexico, Montana and Wyoming -- if you live in one of the ten states and territories named." But C.O.D. orders were accepted from the more settled Eastern States.

Even wars and depressions are reflected in the catalog's pages. Song hits sold in the Spring 1918 catalog included "It's a Long Way to Berlin," "Keep the Home Fires Burning," and "Good-Bye Broadway, Hello France." And in the Fall 1942 catalog, Sears announced that its subsidiary, Allstate Fire Insurance Company, sold "the New U.S. Government War Damage Insurance Plan to protect homes and farms against war damage due to enemy attack or resistance by U.S. armed forces." In 1943 the catalog proclaimed: "Silvertone radios have gone to war. Tomorrow they will be back -- better than ever."

For anyone who recalls the Great Depression of the 1930's, perhaps the single most telling proof of its effect appeared in the 1933 Sears catalog which offered a book titled "Understanding the Stock Market" for 87¢. Called "a simple, yet thorough explanation of how the mysterious stock market operates," it had been marked down from $2.50.

Certainly, if anyone wishes to trace the rise of the automobile and the decline of the horse-drawn buggy, the Sears catalog documents the entire process. Taking note of the Tin Lizzie for the first time, the 1894 catalog listed automobile caps and books. But the horse still ruled the roads, with the catalog devoting eight full pages to such items as buggy boots, bridles, cruppers, harness, tops and whips. By 1929 the tables had turned. The buggy offering was down to half a page, and disappeared entirely thereafter. The catalog index, at the same time, listed 266 separate items under auto accessories.

In January 1993, Sears discontinued most of its catalog operation. But the old pages that still exist, such as those reproduced in this book, offer a rare peek through a window to the past, documenting virtually everthing about we Americans and our lives. For readers interested in the wonderful toys of the 1950's and 1960's, the Sears Wishbook documents the era in a visual way no other historical text can.

The little girls who pored over the 1950 Sears Christmas Wishbook made up the first generation of post-War children. Many had been born while their fathers were overseas in the Armed Forces; they grew up with mothers who balanced traditional parenting with the demands of the business world. While this generation -- the youngest of them were the original Baby Boomers -- would have more leisure time, and more disposable income, than any children in history, it's striking to notice how many of their toys weren't meant just for fun. And ironically, since many of their mothers had worked at "men's jobs" during the war, the great majority of their toys seem made only to prepare them for a life of domesticity -- as wives and mothers.

But all of that comes gradually; in fact, it's nearly absent from this Wishbook. The 1950 Christmas catalog is filled with bicycles and rocking horses for play. And for girls with a Western bent ("little Cowgirls"), there are Dale Evans six guns and costumes. In case those little girls want to grow up in the business world, there are toy typewriters, blackboards and adding machines. In short, the 1950 Wishbook seems to offer a relatively diverse future for girls -- if relatively little of the fun their brothers were having.

A NEW, BIGGER THAN EVER STOREHOUSE FOR SANTA

SEARS 1950 *Christmas Book*

SEARS, ROEBUCK AND CO., 925 S. HOMAN AVE., CHICAGO 7, ILL.

Satisfaction guaranteed or your money back . . Index starts on page 279

Sears Christmas
Wishbook

1950

Blackboards encourage creative play . . . bring happy hours of learning

Popular-priced Blackboard

- Sturdy frame and legs 39x19 in. overall **$1.98**
- Improved 6-frame roller chart

Ideal for small boys and girls. Roller chart has extra strength and durability with new fiberboard backing. Composition slate writing surface (both sides)—15¾x12 in. Maple finished wood rack for supplies. Maple finish board has Masonite Presdwood back. Eraser, 2 pieces of chalk included. Allow 10 pounds postage, according to postal regulations.
79 N 01812—Folds flat for easy storage.........$1.98

Better blackboard, hardwood frame

- All-screw construction—41½x19½ in. **$3.98**
- Improved 12-frame colored roller chart

Built for long use. Sturdy, natural-finish hardwood frame. Strength *plus* with steel hinge plates on rear legs and Masonite Presdwood back; roller chart has fiberboard backing. Smooth composition writing surface (both sides) 16x12 inches. Wood rack for supplies. 2 pieces of chalk and an eraser are also included. Folds flat for easy storage. Order one now!
79 N 01819—Shipping weight 11 lbs. Mailable.... $3.98

Super de luxe Blackboard, metal frame

- Tubular steel construction; 41x20 in. **$8.49**
- Improved 12-frame roller chart
- Rubber-tipped legs make board extra steady

Chromium-plated frame . . . built to last for years. Masonite Presdwood trim. Composition slate writing surface 15¾x12 in. on both sides in hardwood frame. Colored roller chart with plastic window, fiberboard backing shows pictures, numbers, alphabet. Rack for supplies. Chalk and eraser included.
79 N 01820—Shpg. wt. 14 lbs. Folds easily. Mailable $8.49

Happi-Time De luxe Blackboard—play clock and animal statuettes **$5.39**

[A] Large composition slate writing surface 18x14 inches wide.

- Improved hardwood frame; 44½ in. high—all screw construction
- Colorful die-cut animals appear in two portholes at top as child turns wood knobs . . . lift out for tracing on board
- Movable hands on clock help teach child to tell the time

Here is a board with many extra features—moderately priced. Opens easily to form a convenient desk . . . just right for junior "students". Roomy 16-inch wood rack for chalk, eraser, books and other supplies. Rear legs have metal hinge-plates insuring extra steadiness and strength. Heavy Masonite Presdwood back. Bright trim. Folds snugly.
79 NM 1811—Eraser, chalk included. Shipping weight 14 lbs. Shipped freight or express. . $5.39

Wall Blackboards

$1.09
24x18 in.

Glareless writing surface with alphabet, numbers and gay figures stenciled on sides and top. Easy to hang or fasten to wall. Made of non-warping Masonite Presdwood, smoothly coated. Chalk marks erase easily. Thorough cleaning with damp cloth won't harm finish. Sturdy maple finished wood chalk rail on both boards. Eraser and 2 pieces of chalk included. Two sizes—two big values!

[B] 79 N 01822—24x18 in. Shipping weight 4 lbs.......$1.09
[C] 79 N 01823—Giant size. 36x 24 in. Please allow 10 pounds postage, according to postal regulations.................$1.89

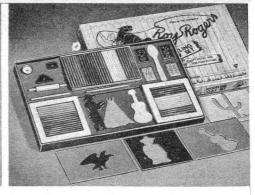

HAPPI-TIME Paint and Coloring Set

Trace, paint, color . . . all with one set. Set features metal tray with 21 paints, 15 paint tablets, 4 plastic animal paint cups. Includes brush, 4-section mixing pan, 6 crayons, 6 pictures to color, tracing paper, color chart. Hinged carrying case (15x 8¾ in.) with metal snap lock and handle. **98c**
49 N 1703—Shipping weight 1 lb. 6 oz. 98c

Big 194-piece Paint and Crayon Set

Extra big set to develop the young artist's creative ability. Includes 26 wood tubs of paint, 46 paint tablets, 6 bottles of poster paints, all in assorted colors. 2 brushes, 2 water pans, palette, 16 crayons, color chart, 10 stencils, 84 pictures. Beautiful box 20x13 in. Another HAPPI-TIME Value! **$1.98**
49 N 1719—Shipping weight 3 lbs. 4 oz. $1.98

ROY ROGERS Modeling Clay Set

Over 1 pound of modeling clay in 6 different colors to work with in this Roy Rogers Set. Use the 3 tin molds, the 4 plastic impression stamps to work the clay . . . or design your own figures. Includes 3 wood tools (rolling pin, 2 pointed sticks), 1 wood spoon, 3 cutouts, 3 stencils. **92c**
49 N 1724—Shipping weight 2 lbs. 6 oz. 92c

Instructive fun with chalk or crayons

Children have great fun writing, drawing and coloring with this chalk and slate set. Includes: 10½x7½-inch *natural slate* wood frame drawing board, black on one side for chalk, white on the other for crayons. With 16 pieces of chalk, 8 crayons in assorted colors, 10 stencils, 1 blackboard eraser, 15 coloring pictures. **98c**
49 N 1701—Shipping weight 2 pounds 8 ounces. 98c

ACTUAL SIZE OF TYPE

Toy Typewriters are Fun!

Easy to operate—Write neat letters

Writing letters, playing secretary or journalist is fun for career-minded youngsters. This well-designed typewriter has 40-character dial instead of keyboard. Complete alphabet, numbers, punctuation marks are found on dial. Dummy keyboard looks like regular typewriter. Carriage, moved by lever, is 11¼ inches wide. Accommodates up to 8½-inch wide paper. Linespacer and plastic roller knobs. Measures 6⅝ inches high to top of dial. Self-inking rolls easily inserted. Two ink rolls included. Order now for a very Merry Christmas! Was $3.49 **$2⁹⁸**
49 N 1915—Shipping weight 2 pounds 8 ounces. $2.98
49 N 1916—Ink Roll Refill. Shipping weight 2 ounces. 10c

NEW! Typewriter with <u>real</u> keyboard

A useful and exciting gift! Looks and works like a real typewriter . . . letters arranged on keyboard same as on a standard typewriter. Types 82 characters including a complete alphabet of capital *and* small letters, plus numerals, punctuation marks. Has ball bearing spacing bar, paper release, shift keys and bell action for margin. Uses standard ½-in. ribbon and takes 8½x 11-in. paper. Rugged all-steel construction with red crinkle finish. Size: 9 inches deep, 11 inches wide, 5½ inches high. **$13.95**
79 N 01842—Shipping weight 9 pounds. $13.95

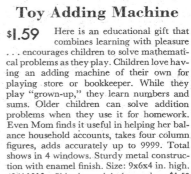

Toy Adding Machine

$1.59 Here is an educational gift that combines learning with pleasure . . . encourages children to solve mathematical problems as they play. Children love having an adding machine of their own for playing store or bookkeeper. While they play "grown-up," they learn numbers and sums. Older children can solve addition problems when they use it for homework. Even Mom finds it useful in helping her balance household accounts, takes four column figures, adds accurately up to 9999. Total shows in 4 windows. Sturdy metal construction with enamel finish. Size: 9x6x4 in. high.
49 N 1810—Shipping weight 1 pound. . . . $1.59
Buy all your Christmas needs on Sears Easy Terms . . . Complete details on page 283

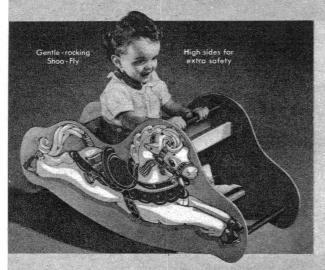

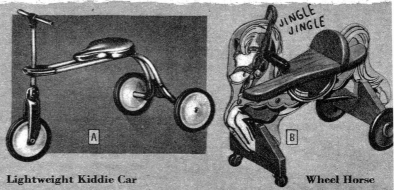

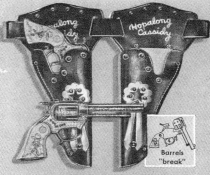

Hopalong Cassidy Set

$3.69

Hoppy, himself, endorses this 2-gun set for his young pals. His picture is on the plastic butt-plates of both guns, and his name is printed on both holsters. Black split-cowhide holsters with white trim, 12 in. overall to top of adjustable belt. Two 8½-in. metal pistols. (Do not shoot.) Order set now.

49 N 2718—Shipping weight 2 pounds 6 ounces. Set..... $3.69

Roy Rogers Pistol and Spur Set

$2.19

Any "hard ridin' young tophand" will be thrilled with this combination. Gold-plated 9-in. metal pistol with plastic butt-plates. Gold-color spurs have adjustable straps with Roy's name and steerhead concha. (Gun does not shoot.)

49N2690—Shpg. wt. 2 lbs. 5 oz. $2.19

NEW—Chap Set

$1.79
3-pc. Set

Adds extra thrills to wild-west games . . . a fine party costume, too. Decorated with typical Western designs. Cotton chaps and vest have leathery feel. Simulated belt band in front, adjustable cloth belt and leg straps on back. Bandanna included. Shipping weight each 1 pound.

49N2705—Small (For 3,4,5) . . $1.79
49N2706—Medium (For 6,7) . . 1.79
49N2723—Large (For 8,9,10) . . 1.79

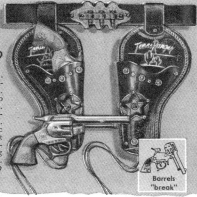

Low-priced 2-gun Set

$2.79

Sure-fire hit at a budget-pleasing price. Two black split-cowhide holsters 11 in. long overall to top of adjustable belt. White and gold-color trim. Two 8-in. metal pistols, plastic butt-plates. (Do not shoot.) Wood "bullets." Shipping weight 2 lbs. 12 oz.

49N2685—Set. $2.79

Single-gun Holster Set

$1.49

Two-tone, split-cowhide holster, 11 in. long overall to top of adjustable belt. Holster front decorated in real Western style. Eight-inch metal pistol with plastic butt plates. (Pistol does not shoot.) Wood "bullets." Always makes a big hit with the little fellows. Shipping weight 1 pound 6 ounces.

49 N 2717—Set. $1.49

★ Wild West Thrills ★

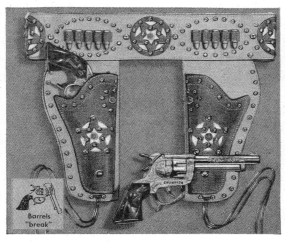

De luxe 2-gun Set, top-grain leather

$6.59

For pride of ownership, give him this extra-fine quality set . . . as flashing and colorful as the Old West itself. Genuine top-grain leather, tan and red holsters and belt have more decoration than most sets. Two 9-in. gold-plated pistols. Holsters 12 in. long to top of adjustable belt.

49 N 2687—Wood "bullets." (Guns do not shoot.) Shipping weight 3 pounds 8 ounces......... $6.59

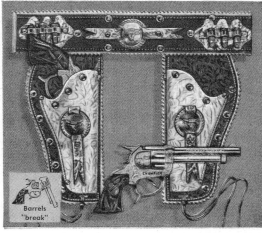

2-gun Set with gold-plated pistols

$4.49

Rarin' for action and built to take hard play. Black and white split-cowhide holsters, 11 in. long overall to top of adjustable belt. They're decorated in Western style and have felt backing. Two 9-in. metal pistols are gold-plated . . . a feature not usually found at such a low price.

49 N 2691—Wood "bullets." (Guns do not shoot.) Shipping weight 3 pounds 10 ounces......... $4.49

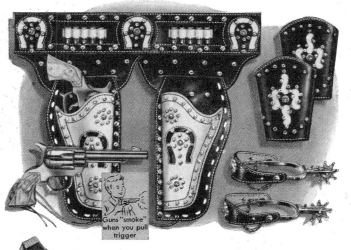

Super de luxe Set with top-grain leather holsters, cuffs and spurs . . . new "smoker" Guns

$8.79
Complete Set

Yippee-ee-ee! Here's the best holster set we've ever offered . . . one that will make your "straight-shootin' young cowpoke" feel just like his favorite Western hero. Why it's so realistic that the guns even puff "smoke" when you pull triggers. ("Smoke" is harmless powder. You get enough for 5,000 shots with each gun.) Holsters, belt, cuffs and spur straps are all genuine top-grain leather. Swing-type holsters with black backs and white fronts are 14½ in. long overall to top of adjustable belt. Nickel-plated, 9½-in. metal pistols have special "smoker" mechanisms with repeater triggers. "Jewels" and "nailheads" add sparkle and color in true Wild West style. Wood "bullets." (Guns do not shoot caps.)

49 N 2688—Shpg. wt. 5 lbs. 3 oz...... Set $8.79

Be sure to see page 283 for Sears Easy Terms

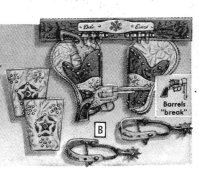

Gifts for Little Cowgirls

A **NEW—Skirt and Vest.** Cotton with suede-like feel. Plastic fringe trim. Skirt adjusts with drawstring. Shipping weight 1 pound per set.

49 N 2715—Small (For 3, 4, 5)........ $2.39
49 N 2716—Medium (For 6, 7)......... $2.39
49 N 2724—Large (For 8, 9, 10)........ 2.39

B **NEW—Dale Evans Holster Set** with cuffs and spurs. Two 7½-in. gold-color metal pistols with repeater triggers. (Do not shoot.) Split-cowhide holsters about 9½ in. long overall to top of belt. Split-cowhide cuffs. Gold-color metal spurs.

49 N 2689—Shpg. wt. 3 lbs. 14 oz...... $4.89

Distinctive J. C. Higgins Bikes

De luxe .. Exciting automotive design, smooth riding spring fork

Streamlined tank has 4 exhaust rings on each side...push button electric horn

Welded tubular steel frame has curved lower bar to increase streamlining

Comfortable Troxel saddle covered with tough, waterproof Vinylite plastic

Jet design luggage carrier has 2 reflectors and die cast chromed nameplate

Heavy duty deep crescent fenders. Rear fender has red safety reflector.

Twinbeam headlight in sleek, streamlined bat-wing case makes night riding safer

Here's how Spring Fork works Front hub and special fork transfer jolts to powerful coil spring. Spring expands, absorbs shocks. You get smooth "flow-motion" ride.

De Luxe Bike without Spring Fork

Same streamlined styling ... same features and accessories as Deluxe with Spring Fork—but this model does not have smooth-riding spring fork. Your choice of same color combinations as De luxe with Spring Fork. *State color.* See Shipping Information at right. Shipping weight 68 pounds.

$47 45 From factory

6 NM 4586F—Boys'. From factory............$47.45
6 NM 4586—Boys'. From mail order house..... 48.45
6 NM 4587F—Girls'. From factory............ 47.45
6 NM 4587—Girls'. From mail order house..... 48.45

[A] Nothing in Santa's bundle of gifts will give your youngster a bigger thrill. The finest J. C. Higgins bike . . . fleetly streamlined with dashing new design.

Streamlined design gives appearance of motion. Exhaust rings in tank . . . just like those in big cars. Massive tank with chrome-plated drop makes bike look bigger. Luggage carrier has sleek jet tube design.

Beautiful. Vivid, gay colors in baked-on enamel. Bright color-flow styling. Gleaming chrome-plated handlebars, truss rods, rims, sprocket, hubs.

Smooth riding. Spring fork eases bumps. Patterned after knee action auto springs. Improved J.C. Higgins coaster brake gives fast, dependable stops.

Durable tubular steel frame is strongly welded and brazed at points of strain for long service. Special weatherproof undercoating protects frame from rust.

Fully equipped with de luxe features and accessories. All shown above and these. 26-in. balloon tires of long-wearing rubber have white sidewalls. Non-skid treads. Synthetic rubber tubes. Exclusive J.C. Higgins pedals with rubber treads, ball bearing action. Steel kick-up park stand. Streamlined chain guard. Girls' have skirt guard too. De luxe J.C. Higgins nameplate.

Register with Pinkerton's. Decal is on rear fender. For youngsters over 9 and adults. Seat to pedal length adjusts from 28 to 32½-in. 6 batteries not incl. **Boys'.** Maroon frame, fenders, guard. Gold tank, color-flow. Maroon and gold carrier, headlight. White, gold, vermilion trims. *OR* Ivy (dark) green frame, fenders, guard. Gold tank, color-flow. Ivy and gold carrier, light. Green, white, gold trims. Shpg. wt. 70 lbs.

6 NM 4588F—*State color.* From factory..........$52.45
6 NM 4588—*State color.* From mail order house.... 53.45

Girls'. Fathom (dark) blue frame, fenders, guard. Strato (light) blue tank, color-flow. Fathom and strato luggage carrier, headlight. White, vermilion trims. *OR* Ivy (deep) green frame, fenders, guard. Seafoam (light) green tank, color-flow. Ivy and seafoam carrier, headlight. White, green trims. Shpg. wt. 70 lbs.

6 NM 4589F—*State color.* From factory..........$52.45
6 NM 4589—*State color.* From mail order house... 53.45

SHIPPING INFORMATION for Full size Deluxe Bikes and for 24-in. De luxe Junior bikes (at lower left of page). Shipped by freight or express from factory in Cleveland, Ohio, or from mail order house. Order from mail order house. Pay shipping charges from shipping point on delivery. Saddle, pedals and handlebars unattached.

Trail Riders .. western-style bikes for young cowpunchers

J. C. Higgins 20-inch Trail Rider
Designed for young Westerners 5, 6 and 7 years old. Seat to pedal length adjusts from 21 to 25 inches.

14-inch Trail Rider
Designed for smaller cow-punchers 4, 5, 6. Seat to pedal length adjusts from 18 to 22 in.

[B] Boy! just like a real "cowpony"! Just the mount your young "bronc-buster" will want for hard-riding posses and for fighting Indian wars. It's a steed every young buckaroo dreams about.

Handsome plastic coated artificial leather gun case with a pop-gun rifle. Saddle bags on rear fenders and dispatch case on handlebars. Gaily trimmed with thongs, brass-plated buttons, brand marks and studs. Welded tubular steel frame for long life. Improved J.C. Higgins coaster brake for fast, dependable stopping action.

Troxel saddle. Streamlined chain guard. Kickup park stand. Red safety reflector. 20-inch Allstate Crusader balloon tires and tubes. Register with Pinkerton's. Decal is on rear fender. *Colors*—"palomino" brown or black. White rims. Chrome-plated handlebars, stem, sprocket and hubs. *State color.*

6 NM 4590F—Boys'. From factory......$41.95
6 NM 4590—Boys'. From m.o. house..... 42.95
6 NM 4591F—Girls'. From factory....... 41.95
6 NM 4591—Girls'. From m.o. house..... 42.95

[C] Smaller wranglers will look forward to countless hours of fun in bandit-chases and round-ups with this smaller Trail Rider. It's a stallion to make them the envy of the gang. Plastic coated artificial leather gun case with toy "pop-gun" rifle. Saddle bags on rear fenders and dispatch case on handlebars. Trimmed with streamers, brass-plated buttons and studs. Troxel saddle. Welded tubular steel frame. Chain guard. 14-inch semi-pneumatic tires. Chain drive. Extra rear wheels make it easy and safe to ride. Set at ground level while child learns. Raise slightly when experienced; take off entirely when expert. *State color* black or "palomino" brown. White rims.

6 NM 6568—Pinkerton registration not included. Shpg. wt. 34 lbs. $26.5

NOTE. Trail Riders shipped freight or express with saddle, pedals, handlebars unattached. 20-in. from factory in Cleveland, Ohio or mail order house. 14-in. from M.O. house. Order from M.O. house. Pay charges from shipping point.

Juvenile Bikes big bike riding thrills with complete safety

NEW! De luxe 24-inch Junior Bike
Designed for youngsters 7, 8, 9 years old. Seat to pedal length adjusts 23½ to 27½ in.

16-inch Sidewalk Bicycle
For youngsters 4, 5, 6. Seat to pedal length adjusts 19 to 23 in.

12-inch Sidewalk Bicycle
For small youngsters 4, 5, 6. Seat to pedal length adjusts 16-20 in.

[D] Imagine this good-looking bike by your Christmas tree. Streamlined tank has 3 chrome exhaust rings, push-button electric horn. Torpedo headlight. Luggage carrier. Boys' is red with black, white trims; girls' light blue with dark blue, white trims. Chrome-plated metal surfaces. 24-in. white sidewall balloon tires. Troxel saddle. Tubular steel frame. J.C. Higgins coaster brake. Register with Pinkerton's. *See shipping information under De luxe bikes at top right.* Shpg. wt. 59 lbs.

From factory. 6NM4592F—Boys'. $41.95 6NM4593F—Girls'. $41.95
From m.o. house. 6NM4592—Boys'. 42.95 6NM4593—Girls'. 42.95

[E] Just the right size and weight for learning to ride. Tyke-Bike-Aid keeps bike balanced while child learns. Raise off ground slightly when experienced; take off entirely when expert. Welded tubular steel frame. Troxel saddle. Coaster brake. Semi-pneumatic tires. Chain drive. Chain guard. Boys' red; girls' blue. White rims, trim. No Pinkerton registration.

6 NM 6562—Boys' Model. Shpg. wt. 47 lbs. ..$27.95
6 NM 6563—Girls' Model. Shpg. wt. 47 lbs. .. 27.95

[F] Here's a bike that's easy and safe for the smaller lad or lass to ride. Extra rear wheel (similar to Tyke-bike-aid on 16-inch model at left) balance bike—help youngsters learn to ride safely. No middle bar . . . makes mounting, dismounting easy. 12-inch hard rubber tires. Streamlined chain guard. Metal seat. Welded tubular steel frame. Chain drive. No Pinkerton registration. *Color*—red with white trim.

6 NM 6567—Shipping weight 23 lbs......$13.95

Sidewalk bikes shipped freight, express from mail order house. Saddle, pedals, handlebars unattached.

Style Leaders .. with eye-catching designs

Dashing design, superb colors combine with extra strong construction to make these fine bikes really great values.

A $52⁴⁵ Cash
$5.50 Down
From Factory

Girls' also come in attractive dark and light blue color combination

REGISTERED WITH
PINKERTON'S
NATIONAL DETECTIVE
AGENCY, INC.
209 West Jackson Blvd., Chicago 6, Ill.

Pinkerton Registration aids in recovery of your bike if lost or stolen. Decal above is on rear fender.

Boys' also come in good-looking green and gold color combination

BIKES SHOWN ARE DESCRIBED ON OPPOSITE PAGE

B $41⁹⁵ Cash
$4.50 Down
From Factory

C $26⁵⁰ Cash
$3.00 Down

D $41⁹⁵ Cash
$4.50 Down
From Factory

E $27⁹⁵ Cash $3.00 Down

F $13⁹⁵

C PAGE 253 .. BIKES

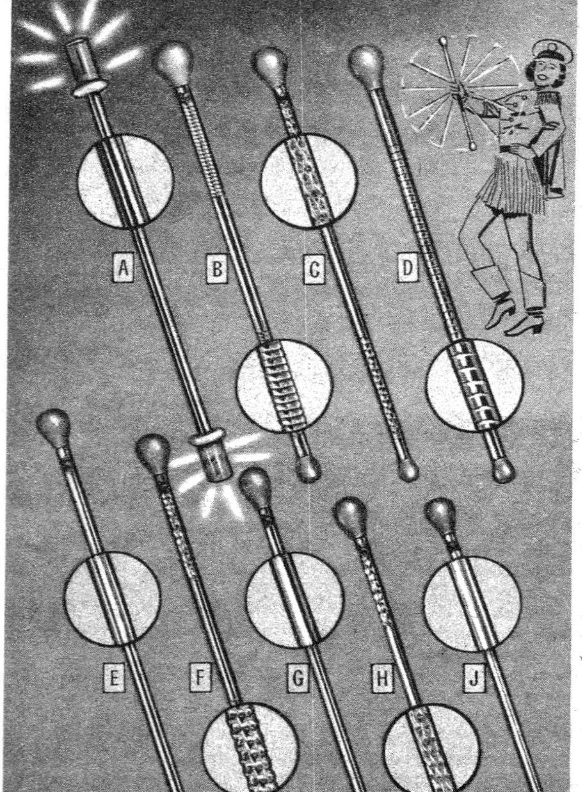

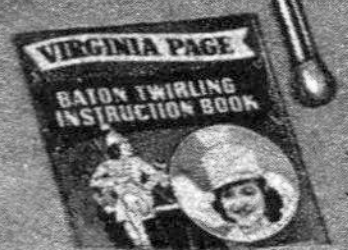

Nick Manoloff Batons

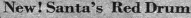

[A] 57 N 3796—**New Lighted Baton.** Lights built in each end . . powered by penlight batteries . . . protected by clear lucite tips that will not break with normal use. Chrome-plated, balanced shaft, 28x5/8-in. Complete with 2 clear lucite tips, 1 red and 1 blue tip, 2 rubber practice tips, 2 bulbs, 8 batteries, instructions. Shpg. wt. ea. 3 lbs. *Buy 5 and save $3.00* . . . . 5 for $26.90 . Ea. $5.98

Lighted baton **$5.98**

[B] 57 N 3773—28x3/4-in. **De luxe Red Spiral Baton Combination.** Red eye-catching spirals. White rubber ball, tip. *With special Twirling instruction book.* Wt. ea. 1 lb. 4 oz. *Buy 5 Save $1.95* . . . . 5 for $12.95 . . Ea. $2.98

[C] 57 N 3771—28x5/8-in. **De luxe Red Star Baton.** Hammered star design. White rubber ball, tip. Instructions. Wt. ea. 1 lb. 2 oz. *Buy 5, save $1.15*. 5 for $8.75 . . Ea. $1.98

57 N 3776–28x3/4-in. **De luxe Red Star Baton.** Similar to (C). Wt. 1 lb. 4 oz. . . . . . *Save $1.15*—5 for $8.75 . . Ea. $1.98

[D] 57 N 3754–28x3/4 in. **Spiral Shaft Baton.** White ball, tip. Wt. 1 lb. 4 oz . . . . *Save $1.15*—5 for $8.75 . . Ea. $1.98

[E] 57 N 3775–28x5/8-in. **Plain Shaft Baton.** White ball, tip. Wt. 1 lb. 4 oz. . . . . . *Save 36c*—5 for $7.89 . . Ea. $1.65

57 N 3752—28x3/4-in. **Plain Shaft Baton.** Similar to (E). Shpg. wt. 1 lb. 4 oz . . . . *Save 36c*—5 for $7.89 . . Ea. $1.65

[F] 57 N 3770–26x5/8-in. **De luxe Red Star Baton.** White ball, tip. Wt. 1 lb. 2 oz. . . *Save $1.15*—5 for $8.75 . . Ea. $1.98

[G] 57 N 3769–24x5/8-in. **Plain Shaft Baton.** White ball, tip. Wt. 1 lb. 2 oz. . . . . . *Save 47c*—5 for $6.98 . . Ea. $1.49

[H] 57 N 3784—22x5/8-in. **Jr. Size Red Star Baton.** Shpg. wt. ea. 1 lb. 8 oz. . . . . . . *Save $1.00*—5 for $8.45 . . Ea. $1.89

[J] 57 N 3783—20x5/8-in. **Junior balanced Baton.** Silver color oxidized *light-weight* aluminum. White ball, tip. Shpg. wt. ea. 1 lb. 4 oz. . *Save 36c*—5 for $5.89 . . Ea. $1.25

57 N 3778—20x5/8-in. **Junior Unbalanced Baton.** Light-weight aluminum. Red rubber ball and tip. Shipping wt. each 1 lb. 4 oz. . . . . *Save 26c*—5 for $3.19 . . Each 69c

57 N 4609—**Twirling Instruction Book.** It's easy and fun to learn the art of baton twirling with this book. Fully illustrated. Shipping weight 4 ounces . . . . Each 79c

New! Santa's Red Drum

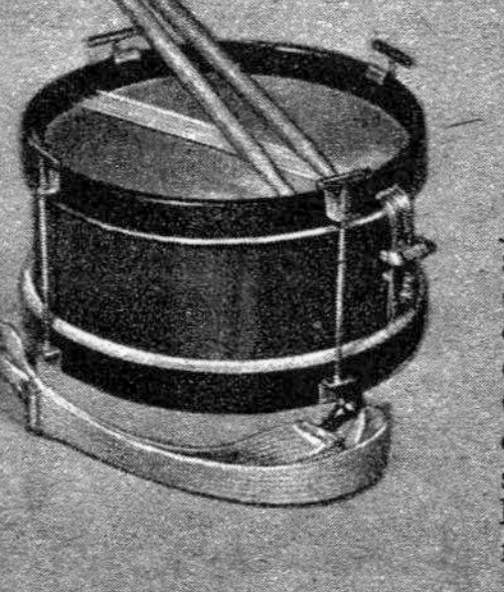

Only **$6.98**

Not just a toy, but *a real drum designed especially for children! Genuine buckskin heads* with adjustable tension rods . . . same as used on orchestra drums. Silk wire wound drum snares. Bright red enameled maple shell. Complete with hickory drum sticks, canvas web sling and instruction book. Drum size, 10 5/8-in. diameter, 5 1/4-in. high.
57 N 2603–Wt. 3 lbs. . $6.98

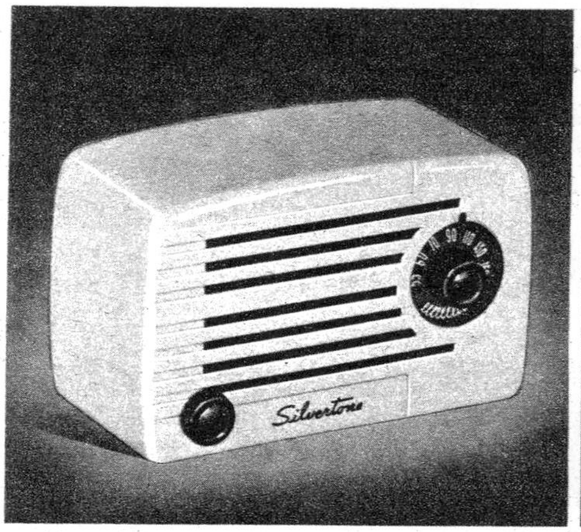

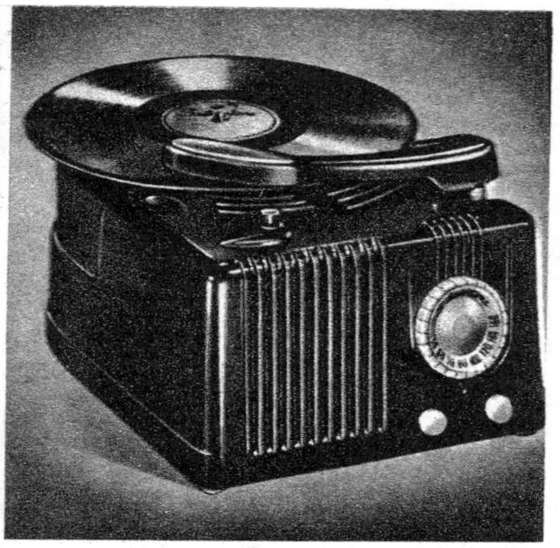

Present your child with a radio of his very own!

Kids love a radio of their very own . . . just like the grownups. And Christmas is the perfect time to give this compact SILVERTONE, too! Easy direct tuning. Gives good local reception. Tunes 540–1600 KC standard broadcast. 3 tubes plus rectifier. 4-inch speaker. Built-on antenna. Non-breakable metal cabinet . . . choice of brown or ivory color. Size, 5x8 3/8x4 in. For 105–125-volt, 25–60-cycle AC or DC. UL approved.

Brown cabinet **$9.95**

57 N 01—**Brown cabinet.** *Mailable.* Wt. 5 lbs. . . . $9.95
57 N 02—**Ivory color.** *Mailable.* Wt. 5 lbs. 10.95

A Radio-Phonograph to delight any youngster

What young fellow or girl wouldn't love to find this compact SILVERTONE in his Christmas stocking? Powerful AM radio plus a *3-speed phonograph!* Plays any size, any speed record singly . . . with one tone arm, one needle, one spindle. Radio has super heterodyne circuit for better reception. 4 tubes plus rectifier. 4-inch speaker. Built-in aerial. Ebony brown plastic cabinet, 7 1/4x9 3/4x12 3/4 inches. Tunes 540–1600 KC. 105–125-volt, 60-cycle AC.

$32.95 Cash
$3.50 Down

57N09073–UL approved. *Mailable.* Wt. 13 lbs. $32.95

Santa Chooses Silvertone

to develop your child's musical interests

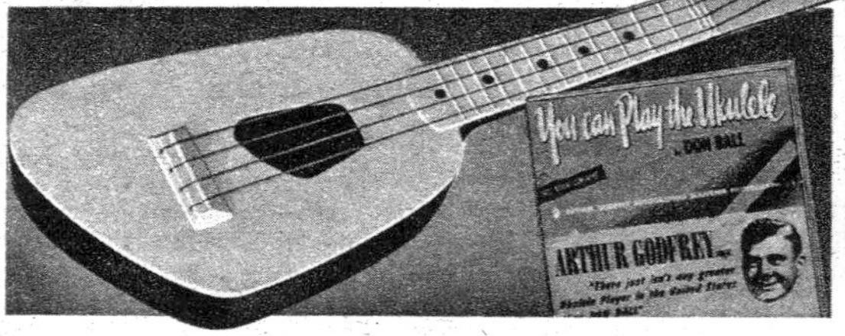

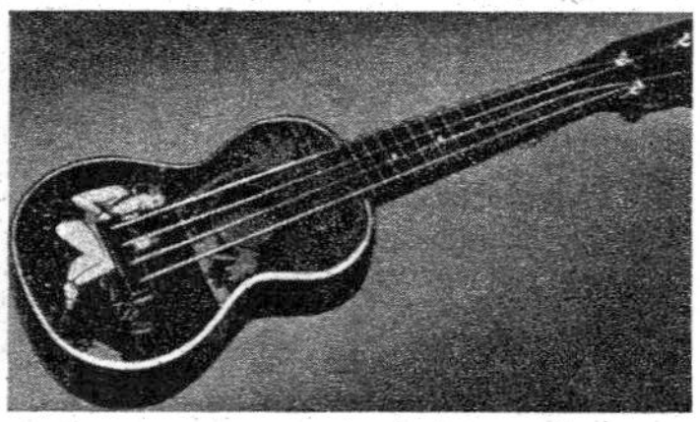

Join in the holiday fun with a Silvertone Ukulele

New! Our lowest priced Ukulele combined with *You Can Play the Ukulele*—a new instruction book by Don Ball, the uke expert whom *the fabulous ARTHUR GODFREY considers to be the greatest player he's ever known!* Modern, functional shaped Lustrex ukulele resists moisture, chipping or fading. Colorful red back and sides, white top. Waterproof nylon strings. Plastic bonded body joints. Size, 21 3/4x6 3/4 in.

Ukulele only **$2.79**

57 NT 828—**Ukulele, Book Combination.** Wt. 2 lbs. 2 oz . . . $3.59
57 N 0827—**Lustrex Ukulele only.** Shpg. wt. 2 lbs. 2.79
57 N 4608—**Don Ball Instruction Book.** Shpg. wt. 2 oz. 95c

Silvertone Hawaiian Scene Ukulele. Capture the enchantment of the islands with this handsome uke. Decorative Hawaiian scene in green and ivory on mahogany finished hardwood body. White stripping around top edge. Waterproof nylon strings. Strong, durable construction. Size, 20 5/8x6 3/8 in. Complete with instruction book, pick.
57 N 0852—Shpg. wt. 2 lbs. $4.98

Only **$4.98**

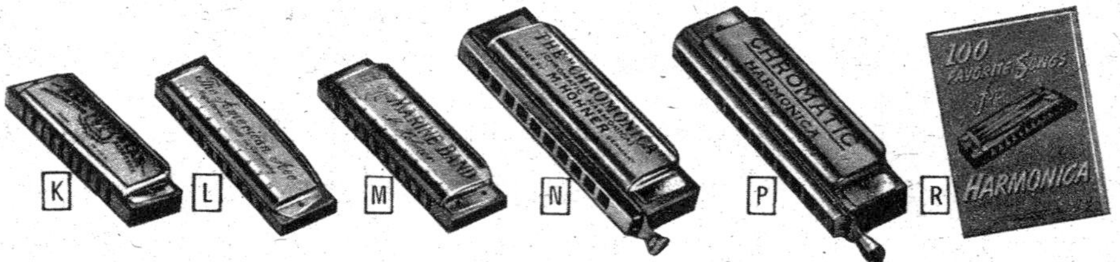

[K] **All Star Harmonica.** Polished metal covers. 20 brass reeds, 10 holes. 4 inches long. Key of C. Complete with instruction book. A perfect gift for the youngsters. **69c**
57 N 1806—Shipping weight 9 ounces 69c

[L] **American Ace Harmonica.** Nickel-plated brassed plates. 10 holes, 20 reeds. 4-in. long. Key of C. Instruction book. **98c**
57 N 1807—Shipping weight 9 ounces 98c

[M] **Hohner Marine Band Harmonica.** Heavy nickel-plated brass covers. 10 holes, 20 reeds. Hinged box. 4-in. long. Instruc. **$1.98**
57 N 1808—*State key of C or G.* Shpg. wt. 9 oz. . $1.98

[N] **Hohner Chromatic Harmonica.** 3 octaves. Nickel-plated. 10 holes, 40 brass reeds. 4 7/8 in. long. Key of C. **$8.98** 3-octave
57 N 1811—(Shpg. wt. 1 lb. 5 oz.) *Postpaid* $8.98
57 N 1812—Like above, except 3 1/2 octaves. 12 holes, 48 reeds. 5 5/8 inches long. Instructions. (Shpg. wt. 1 lb. 8 oz.) *Postpaid* $11.98

[P] **Gretsch Chromatic Harmonica.** 3 octaves. Nickel-plated. 10 holes, 40 reeds. 4 7/8 in. Key of C. Instructions. **$7.98**
57 N 1815—Swiss made. Wt. 1 lb. 4 oz $7.98

[R] 57 N 4621—**Harmonica Song Book.** 64 pages; 100 songs; simple instructions. Shpg. wt. 9 oz. 19c

NOTE: Health rules forbid return of harmonicas. If defective on receipt, replacement will be made. (L), (M) and (N) made in Germany.

Easy Terms, page 283

To judge from the 1951 Wishbook, girls could look forward to two kinds of lives -- they could be Cowgirls like Dale Evans -- with several different authorized costumes in which to do it -- or they could be Mommies. There wasn't much middle ground.

This Wishbook is chock full of dolls, from basic models at $4.79, to elaborate electronic talking dolls at a whopping $23.79. One doll was designed to wear real infant's clothing, in an early form of recycling; others did the basic baby thing -- sleep, wet, coo. In fact, one of the most popular models was Baby Coo: "She coos when you cuddle her. She sobs when you paddle her."

To transport all of these baby dolls, the Wishbook offered a wide selection of doll buggies and walkers, and to make sure they had comfortable places to sleep, wet and coo, there were cribs, bassinets -- even bunk beds.

When little girls weren't taking care of baby, they were serving dinner on Blue Willow China, or cooking on an aluminum baking set, or stocking the toy fridge or baking in the toy oven. All of this exhausting work was, according to the Wishbook, "Fun for your little hostess!"

Sears Christmas

Wishbook

1951

Roy Rogers

NEW OUTFITS
Western-Styled
Colorful New Styles
Fringe Decorated

$4.98

[A] Boys' 9-piece western-style Roy Rogers cowboy outfit

[B] Girls' 9-piece western-style Dale Evans cowgirl outfit

Brother and Sister Combinations

Palomino
COWBOY SETS

[G] $3.98

[H] $3.98

Deluxe 2-Gun Sets

$6.77

[C] Dale Evans 10-pc. set Genuine leather trim

[D] Roy Rogers 10-pc. set Genuine leather trim

Deluxe Frontier Wearing Apparel

$9.70

[E] Girls' 2-pc. Dale Evans Suit Crease-resistant Rayon Suiting

[F] Boys' 2-pc. Roy Rogers Suit Crease-resistant Rayon Suiting

New!
Roy Rogers
Western Style DENIMS

New!
Western Outfit Favorites

[K] Two-piece Frontier Suit $4.89

[J] 8-oz. Blue Denim Jeans or Jacket $1.97 ea.

[L] 2-pc. Leather set $6.77

Complete Western Outfits

ILLUSTRATED IN COLOR ON OPPOSITE PAGE

Colorful ROY ROGERS, DALE EVANS Sets

[A] New! Roy Rogers 9-pc. **$4.98** set. Bat-wing cotton twill chap-front pants. 2-tone cotton shirt, loop tie and leather slide. Cotton hat. Leather belt, holster. Toy clicker pistol, lariat. Shipping wt. 2 lbs. 2 oz.
State size 4, 6, 8, 10, 12. Measure to be sure. See size chart "A" below.
40 N 4552—9-pc. Roy Rogers Set $4.98

[B] New! Dale Evans 9-pc. **$4.98** set. Cotton twill skirt with flannel front, 2-tone cotton blouse; Western loop tie and genuine leather slide. Cotton hat. Leather belt and holster. Toy clicker pistol. Lariat.
State size 4, 6, 8, 10, 12. See chart "A" below. Shipping wt. 2 lbs. 2 oz.
40 N 4553—9-pc. Dale Evans Set $4.98

[C] New! Dale Evans 10-pc. **$6.77** Deluxe cowgirl suit. Leather decorated cotton suede-cloth skirt. Cotton flannel plaid shirt. Western-style loop tie and leather slide. 2 leather holsters, belt. 2 toy pistols, lariat. No hat. Shpg. wt. 2 lbs. 12 oz.
Sizes 4, 6, 8, 10, 12. Chart "A" below.
40 N 4555—10-pc. Dale Evans Set. $6.77

[D] New! Roy Rogers 10-pc. **$6.77** Deluxe cowboy suit. Suede-cloth chap-front pants with leather decorated waistband. Cotton flannel plaid shirt. Loop tie and leather slide. 2 leather holsters, belt. 2 toy pistols, lariat, no hat. Shpg. wt. 2 lbs. 12 oz.
Sizes 4, 6, 8, 10, 12. Chart "A" below.
40 N 4554—10-pc. Roy Rogers Set $6.77

Western Frontier Outfits for Dress wear

[E] New! Dale Evans 2-pc. **$9.70** Frontier Suit of crease-resistant rayon suiting. Matches Roy's suit at right. Western design red and black shirt with embroidered picture of Dale on back. Matching red skirt with zipper closure, 2 snap-fasteners at waist. Shpg. wt. 1 lb. 15 oz.
Sizes 3, 4, 5, 6, 7, 8, 9, 10. Chart "A".
40 N 3295—2-pc. Dale Evans Suit. $9.70

[F] New! Roy Rogers 2-pc. **$9.70** Frontier Suit of crease-resistant rayon suiting. Western decorated red and black shirt with embroidered picture of Roy and Trigger on back. Snap-fastener front, cuffs. Black zip fly pants; snap-fastener at waist. 2 flap pockets. Shpg. wt. 1 lb. 15 oz.
Sizes 3, 4, 5, 6, 7, 8, 9, 10. Chart "A."
40 N 3294—2-pc. Roy Rogers Suit. $9.70

PALOMINO Cowboy, Cowgirl Outfits

[G] 9-pc. Palomino Cowboy **$3.98** Set. Palomino print cotton chap-style pants. Elastic back waist. Matching vest. Plaid cotton flannel shirt. Embossed leather belt, holster. Toy pistol, cowboy hat, lariat, bandanna. Shpg. wt. 2 lbs. 2 oz.
Sizes 4, 6, 8, 10, 12. Chart "A" below.
40 N 4519—9-pc. Cowboy Set. . . . $3.98

[H] 8-pc. Palomino Cowgirl Set. **$3.98** Partner to outfit at left. Palomino print skirt. Matching western-style vest. Plaid cotton flannel blouse. Embossed leather belt and holster. Toy clicker pistol, cowgirl hat, lariat. Shipping wt. 1 lb. 13 oz.
Sizes 4, 6, 8, 10, 12. Chart "A" below.
40 N 4520—8-pc. Cowgirl Set. $3.98

New! ROY ROGERS Western-Style Denims

[J] Super-tough Sanforized 8-oz. blue denim Jeans; max. shrinkage **$1.97 Jeans** 1%. Extra heavy-duty zip fly. 2 sturdy copper riveted front swing pockets. Embroidered Roy Rogers patch on front pocket facing. 2 back patch pockets. Thread bartacks in back won't mar furniture. **$1.97 Jacket**
50 N 9136M—Jeans. State size 4, 6, 8, 10, 12. Chart "B". Wt. 1 lb. 1 oz. $1.97

Western design Sanforized 8-oz. denim Jacket; 1% max. shrinkage. Front pleats, Western action back. Woven Roy Rogers label on chest. 2 copper riveted chest pockets. Snap-fastener front, cuffs. Roy's leather patch on waist.
50 N 9137M—Jacket. State size 4,6,8,10,12. Chart "A" below. Shpg. wt.1lb.1 oz. $1.97

Popular Western Playtime Outfits

[K] NEW! Palomino Kid 2-pc. Frontier Suit. San- **$4.89** forized cotton flannel shirt; max. shrinkage 1%. Button front, cuffs. Pinwale corduroy frontier pants. Half-belt front, elastic back waist, zip fly; 2 pockets, Palomino print flaps. Wash alone. Shpg. wt. 1 lb. 6 oz.
Sizes 3, 4, 5, 6, 7, 8. Chart "A" below.
40 N 3239—2-pc. Frontier Suit. $4.89

[L] NEW! 2-pc. Leather Front Chap and Vest **$6.77** Set. Open seat chaps; leather front, waist, back strap. Cotton twill back, uppers. Bat-wings with leather decorated conches. Leather front vest; cotton twill back, 2 pockets. *Other clothes, gun not included.* Shpg. wt. 2 lbs.
Sizes 4, 6, 8, 10, 12. Chart "A" below.
40 N 4535—2-pc. Cowboy set. $6.77

Chart "A": How to Order PLAYCLOTHES, JACKETS. Measure height without shoes. (Denims: measure height, waist. Chart B.) Measure waist over trousers without belt. Waist sizes are actual garment measurements. Measure chest around body, under arms, over tips of shoulder blades. Order only sizes listed.

If Height is Inches	If Chest is Inches	Order Size	If Height is Inches	If Chest is Inches	Order Size
34½ to 37	21½ to 22	3	48½ to 50	26 to 26½	8
37½ to 40	22½ to 23	4	50½ to 52	26¾ to 27¼	9
40½ to 43	23½ to 24	5	52½ to 54	27½ to 28	10
43½ to 46	24½ to 25	6	54½ to 58	28½ to 29½	12
46½ to 48	25¼ to 25¾	7	58½ to 61	30 to 31½	14
			61½ to 64	31¾ to 33	16

Chart "B": DENIM JEANS. Measuring instructions above.

Height, in.	34½–40	40½–46	46½–50	50½–54	54½–58
Waist, in.	22½	23½	24½	25½	26½
Order Size	4	6	8	10	12

Hopalong Cassidy

Girls' 7-pc. Set
Sanforized (shrinkage 1%) **$4.98** black cotton twill skirt. Sanforized black cotton poplin blouse. Leather belt, holster. Toy pistol. Loop tie and metal tie slide.
State size 4, 6, 8, 10, 12. See chart "A" below. Shipping wt. 2 lbs.
40 N 4583—7-pc. set. . . $4.98

Boys' 7-pc. Set
Sanforized (shrinkage 1%) **$4.98** black cotton twill chap-style pants. Sanforized black cotton poplin shirt. Leather belt, holster. Toy pistol. Loop tie, metal tie slide.
State size 4, 6, 8, 10, 12. See chart "A" below. Shipping wt. 2 lbs.
40 N 4582—7-pc. set. . . $4.98

[M] $2.20 Ea. Jeans or Jacket

[N] $1.98 Ea. Jeans or Jacket

Western Style

[M] Sanforized 8-oz. black denim Jeans **$2.20 Each** 'n' Jacket; 1% max. shrinkage. Zip fly jeans with narrow-cut legs, 4 pockets. Matching pleated jacket with snap-fasteners, 2 pockets. No belt. Wash alone.
Sizes 4, 6, 8, 10, 12. Wt. ea. 1 lb. 3 oz.
50 N 9165M—Jeans. Chart "B" $2.20
50 N 9166M—Jacket. Chart "A" 2.20

[N] Sanforized 7¼-oz. blue denim jeans 'n' Jacket; 1% shrinkage. Zip fly jeans; 4 pockets. Matching jacket; snap-fasteners, 2 pockets. No belt. Wash alone.
Sizes 4, 6, 8, 10, 12. Wt. ea. 1 lb. 1 oz.
50 N 9124M—Jeans. Chart "B" $1.98
50 N 9125M—Jacket. Chart "A" 1.98

Football, Baseball Suits

$4.79

[P] 4-pc. football suit. Heavy cotton duck pants; padded hips, thighs. Leather lace fly front. Leather knee patches. Elastic bottoms. Blue and gold cotton jersey. Cotton footless socks. Press-on alphabet.
Sizes 4, 6, 8, 10, 12, 14. Chart "A" at left. Shpg. wt. 2 lbs. 6 oz.
40 N 4518. . . . . $4.79

$3.98

[R] 6-pc. baseball uniform. Gray cotton flannel shirt; colorful braid trim. Matching Gray cotton flannel pants; hip pocket. Matching cap, cotton footless socks. Leather belt. Press-on alphabet.
Sizes 4,6,8,10,12,14, 16. Chart "A," left. Shpg. wt. 2 lbs. 6 oz.
40 N 4508. . . . . $3.98

Give a Toni Play-Wave Doll!

Dolly has the Toni! Her lustrous hair is Nylon .. behaves beautifully when washed and waved

HELP MAKE THEIR DREAMS COME TRUE

$11²⁹
14½-in. size

Everybody's talking about Toni . . . saying she's a queen among dolls. And she is! Her crowning glory is her soft, shining Nylon hair . . . and it's locked to her scalp to stay. Her little "mother" can try her skill at hairdressing as often as she pleases . . . let Toni keep pace with changing fashions. Toni's "permanent" was specially created to retain its lovely texture, despite frequent shampooing, play-waving and combing.

Toni comes with a complete Play Wave Kit which contains famous Toni creme shampoo, play wave solution (completely harmless), curlers, comb, end-papers and directions. When you want a refill for the play wave solution, all you have to do is mix 1 teaspoon of sugar with ⅓ cup of water . . . it's that simple!

Toni's plastic, so it won't matter if she gets wet during shampooing. Just wipe her dry and go ahead with the "beauty treatment." She's practically unbreakable, too . . . made to be a fascinating companion for active play. Jointed arms and legs move with lifelike grace. Head turns and tilts to all sorts of poses, just like a lively little girl's. Sparkling go-to-sleep eyes are fringed with thick lashes. Toni wears a braid-trimmed bolero-style dress made of fine cotton pique. Cotton half slip and panties, rayon socks, imitation leather shoes.

49 N 3374—14½ inches tall. Shipping wt. 1 lb. 14 oz.......... $11.29
49 N 3375— 16 inches tall. Shipping wt. 2 lbs. 4 oz.......... 12.98
79 N 03380— 21 inches tall. Shipping wt. 6 lbs.............. 18.98

SHE SINGS, TALKS, LAUGHS, AND PRAYS

Hello Mommy

Mary had a Little Lamb

Now I lay me down to Sleep

Her hair can be combed and brushed

You can set her curls

Beautiful Electronic Talking Doll

A wonder-child, truly! Press the magic button and you'll hear Noma perform. (*There's no motor to wind.*) Noma sings, recites, prays and laughs . . . all in a clearly recorded, childlike human voice. You can keep her talking as long as you like. Voice is an electrical unit (encased in plastic) inside doll's body; runs on two ordinary flashlight batteries (incl.). Finely molded plastic head, sparkling go-to-sleep eyes with lashes. Soft vinyl plastic arms and legs. Full-skirted dress made of rich, rustling rayon taffeta. Rayon panties, rayon socks, imitation leather shoes.

79 N 03198—Full 27 inches tall. Shipping weight 8 pounds. $23.79

$23⁷⁹
Cash
$2.50 Down

Has hair you can comb, brush, curl

Cute, cuddly curlylocks . . . with pretty Saran hair that's made to be washed, brushed, combed, curled. She's irresistible to look at . . . but even more fun to care for! Her hard-to-break plastic head turns to many positions; glassene go-to-sleep eyes have real lashes; open mouth reveals small teeth and tongue. Soft rubber-skin arms and legs are softly stuffed; cloth-covered body is cotton stuffed. Tilt dolly back and she cries appealingly. Wears crisp organdy dress and bonnet, lace-edged cotton slip and panties, rayon socks, imitation leather shoes.

49 N 3170—About 20 inches tall. Shipping weight 2 pounds 10 ounces. $6.99

$6⁹⁹

228 .. SEARS, ROEBUCK AND CO. CPB   *Make their Christmas dreams come true .. it's simple, when you use Sears Easy Terms. See page 313.*

Stroke color on gently

Roll curls and pat on color

Blot color with towel

Comb; put up in curlers

Comb and brush hair; Separate into curls

Put it up on curlers

NEW! "Tintair" Glamor Girl Doll

You can shampoo, curl, **change hair color of Tintair Doll!**
A real glamor girl and it's fun to change color of her hair. $11.45
Your little "hairdresser" can color it chestnut brown one
day, carrot top red the next or change it back to natural blonde. Coloring kit
has 2 bottles of *non-toxic* coloring, 2 applicators, plastic dish, curlers. Plastic
body; fully jointed. She has rayon dress and panties; socks, shoes.
49 N 3679—14 inches tall. Shipping weight 2 pounds. $11.45

Mme. Alexander Dolls

Finest quality we've found in all America . . . exquisitely made
dolls, practically unbreakable . . . with painstaking details and finest workmanship. Your little girl's dream of a doll comes to life!

A 18½-in. Bunny-Baby   **$12.98**
- New soft vinyl head
- Wig can be combed and set

Soft molded vinyl arms, legs, head . . .
most lifelike look and feel ever achieved!
Go-to-sleep glassene eyes. Wig can be
brushed, curled, combed. Cloth-covered
body. Organdy dress, bonnet; rayon
slip, panties; suede shoes, curlers, comb.
49 N 3295—Shpg. wt. 3 lbs. $12.98

B Wig can be brushed,   **$9.39**
combed, curled; all   14½ inch
plastic body almost un-
breakable! Betty is pert and perfectly
lovely! Sleeping eyes, plastic fiber wig.
Jointed arms, legs. Head turns. Swishy
rayon taffeta dress. Cotton half slip,
panties; suede shoes, curlers, comb.
49N3387—14½ in. Wt. 1 lb. 4 oz. $9.39
49N3388—17½ in. Wt. 1 lb. 12 oz. 11.67

C Clarabell. Beloved TV   **$4.79**
comic—famous on pop-
ular Howdy Doody show—is fully
equipped, right down to the familiar
trinket box! Floppy cotton-stuffed,
cloth-covered body; mask face. Yarn
nose, hair; felt mouth, ears, eyebrows.
2-tone rayon satin suit has net clown's
ruff, jingle-bell on sleeves. 19 in. tall.
49 N 3581—Shpg. wt. 1 lb. 4 oz. . . . $4.79

D Slumbermate. Drowsy   **$6.69**
dreamer . . . ideal nap
companion. Soft vinyl plastic head is
turned to one side for a sound sleep;
cheeks are rosy-tinted. Soft, jersey-cov-
ered body is stuffed with fine kapok. 2-
piece removable sleeper with real buttons made of best quality jersey. 14 in.
tall. Lace-edged rayon satin pillow.
49 N 3657—Shpg. wt. 1 lb. 14 oz. . . $6.69

$2.87   "Glamor Box" by Mme. Alex-
ander. Plastic comb, brush,
mirror, barrette, compacts for powder and
rouge, lipstick, hairpins, ribbons, curlers,
many other accessories. Plastic fiber braid
to make braided wig, and chignon. Specify
BLONDE or BRUNETTE.
49 N 3501—Shpg. wt. 1 lb. . . 15-pc. set $2.87

She has 6 Stylish Outfits . . Wig you can brush, set

- Now with beautiful wig to comb, brush and set
- Almost unbreakable plastic jointed body, head turns, tilts
- Separate outfit for almost every occasion, play, party, etc.   **$8.98**

Your little girl will have the best dressed dolly with this wardrobe. Plastic
fiber hair can be curled and set to suit her best. Wardrobe includes 4-pc. ski
suit, trousers with knit anklets, plastic belt, cap, jacket. Evening gown with
slip. Shortie coat, hat, pajamas. Cotton play suit. Wears shirt and blouse outfit, panties, socks, imitation leather shoes. Sleeping eyes.
49 N 3382—14 inches tall, 6 outfits. Shipping weight 1 pound. $8.98

BABY COOS wears real-life "hand-me-downs"

$12⁹⁸ Just haul out your own tot's outgrown clothes . . . the ones you've tenderly laid away in the old trunk . . . BABY COOS fits right into them. She's a 27-inch bundle of joy and wears actual size baby clothes, size 6 to 12 months . . . from bonnet to shoes, she's easy to outfit. Extra-big BABY COOS has soft, smooth Magic Skin rubber body . . . she can be sponged off, dried and powdered. Her molded plastic head is very unlikely to break, **ever**. Beautifully realistic, go-to-sleep eyes with lashes . . . babylike coo-type voice makes her seem to come to life, makes it almost impossible to resist hugging her. BABY COOS arrives without a stitch of clothes to her name . . . can be dressed as boy or girl. Whether she wears soft organdy dresses or corduroy overalls doesn't matter . . . we know you're going to love her anyway.

79 N 03070—Full 27 inches tall. Shipping weight 7 pounds. $12.98

Famous "Baby Coos"

Pals! Life-size Baby Coos is almost as big as a 1-year-old child

Pressure applied to legs or body produces babylike cries

Nod her head or press arms against body— she answers with a sob

Brother Coos is big as a real baby!

$19⁹⁸ He's the boy member of the celebrated Coos family . . . and he's certainly no sissy. Why, he measures over two feet tall . . . 27 inches, in fact! His clothes are the size a real, live baby (6 to 12 months) would wear. And of course this young fellow has all the characteristic BABY COOS features . . . makes sounds like a baby when you squeeze him. Magic Skin rubber body is stuffed with cotton and foam rubber; can be sponged off and powdered. Plastic head is practically unbreakable. Go-to-sleep eyes have silky lashes. Wears cotton gabardine trousers, tam to match; sporty jacket, open-collared knit shirt, rayon socks, real leather baby shoes. (For a change, let him wear children's outgrown baby clothes.)

79 N 03071—27 inches tall. Shipping weight 7 pounds. $19.98

This Wee One Wets, Sleeps

$3²⁵
- Popular priced; 13 in. tall
- Fully jointed, molded rubber body; plastic head turns
- Appealing go-to-sleep eyes

Feed her from her bottle and she'll wet her diaper. Then tuck her in bed and she'll close her eyes for a nap. Though very young, she's already learned to sit alone. Her plastic head is almost impossible to break. Her body, arms and legs are soft, molded rubber . . . washable and almost unbreakable. Head turns, jointed arms and legs take all sorts of positions. Young tots will love to bathe and care for this lovable baby . . . she seems *almost* human.

49 N 3611—Shpg. wt. 2 lb. 8 oz. $3.25

Dolldom's favorite for the last 3 years!

$5⁷⁹
14-inch
- She coos when you cuddle her
- She sobs if you paddle her
- She complains if you pinch her
- And she has go-to-sleep eyes

No doubt you've read the success story of BABY COOS in the newspapers or heard it on the radio—and perhaps you saw her on TV. She rates her popularity because she looks—feels—and even makes sounds like a real, live baby. Caress her gently—she coos affectionately. Pinch her—she gives a plaintive sob. Squeeze her roughly—she'll scream to let you know it hurts! Her warm, cuddly Magic Skin rubber body is stuffed with soft cotton and foam rubber. Like any infant, she must be bathed, powdered and dressed. Her head is practically unbreakable plastic. Her lucite eyes sparkle; her lashes are long and silky. BABY COOS wears rib-knit cotton shirt and panties. Outfit includes dainty lace-trimmed organdy dress, bonnet; cotton slip, rayon socks, imitation leather shoes, 3 powder puffs, 6 clothespins.

49 N 3040—14-inch. Shipping weight 2 pounds. $5.79
49 N 3042—18-inch. Shipping weight 2 pounds 8 ounces. 9.77

230 . . SEARS, ROEBUCK AND CO. ©

Buy on Easy Terms
See page 313

Three Popular Buggies . . Thrifty, Easy-on-the-Budget Prices

[A] Low-priced Loom Woven Fiber Buggy. $5.79 Braid trim. Beige color; woven design. 5-inch stamped wheels; 3/8-inch rubber tires. Aluminum-enameled gear; handle (23 in. high). Body 9½x18x 5 in. deep.
79 N 08245—Wt. 7 lbs. $5.79

[B] Town and Country Folding Strollerette. $8.95 Frames; reversible pusher (27½ in. high) of nickel-plated tubular steel. Seat 8½x10 in. has adjustable back, footrest. Plastic pad. Carriage type gear; hand brake. 7-in. wheels; rubber tires. 12x11x9 in. deep.
79 N 08275—Wt. 12 lbs. $8.95

[C] Happi-Time Folding Buggy. $4.98 Spanish grain washable leatherette: light gray, red trim. 3-bow folding hood; sun visor. Steel handle 23½ in. from floor. 6-inch stamped wheels; 3/8 inch rubber tires. "L" type foot brake. Collapsible aluminum-finish steel frame. Body 19x9x7 in. deep.
79 N 08265—Shpg. wt. 6 lbs. . . .$4.98

22-inch Folding Happi-Time Buggy

Little "doll mothers" will have grand fun taking dolly for a stroll in this trim HAPPI-TIME $7.98 buggy. Washable Spanish grain vinyl leatherette in maroon and gray. Fiberboard insert. Toe extension. Four-bow folding hood; sun visor. Tubular aluminum handle is 29 in. high. 7-in. wire wheels; ½-in. rubber tires. "L" type foot brake. Folding steel frame. Aluminum paint finish.
79 N 08266 — Body 22x11x9 inches deep. Shipping weight 9 pounds. $7.98

Doll Buggies

Give proud little girls more make-believe fun with their dolls

HELP MAKE THEIR DREAMS COME TRUE

Our Finest . . famous Boodle Buggy

All these wonderful features . . . just like Mother's favorite Boodle buggy. Body lifts $18.98 right out to form cradle or play pen for dolly (see small view). Full shackle type duchess gear. Luxuriously padded sides; upholstered half-draft rail. Storm shield. Single wheel spring action foot brake. Two-tone body (blue and gray) with white piping in washable leatherette. Fiberboard insert. Folding toe extension. 5-bow folding hood; sun shield. Chrome-plated pusher 29½ in. from floor. Large 8-in. wire wheels; thick 1-in. rubber tires. Folding steel frame. Body 25½x13x12 inches deep. Shipping weight 25 pounds.
79 N 08220 . . . .$18.98

Folding Buggy with Duchess Gear

Lucky dolly rides in style in this handsome HAPPI-TIME buggy. $9.98 Full shackle type duchess gear assures smooth riding. Two-tone body (Royal blue and gray) in washable Spanish grain artificial leather. Fiberboard insert. Foot extension. Four-bow folding hood with sun visor. ½-inch tubular aluminum-finished handle 29½ in. high. 7½-inch wire wheels; ⅝-inch rubber tires. Double action foot brake. Folding steel frame; aluminum paint finish. Body is 24x12x9 inches deep. Shipping weight 12 pounds.
79 N 08267 . . . .$9.98

Upholstered Half-draft Rail

Collapsible buggy has shackle-type duchess gear; spring-actuated leg lock. Washable Spanish grain leatherette—French blue and light gray. Fiberboard insert. Toe extension. Storm curtain. 4-bow folding hood, sun shield. Chrome-plated handle 30 in. high. 7½-in. wire wheels; ¾-in. rubber tires. 2-wheel, double action foot brake. Steel frame, aluminum paint finish. Body 24¾x13¾x11 inches deep. Shipping weight 15 pounds.
79 N 08268—(Doll not included) $13.95

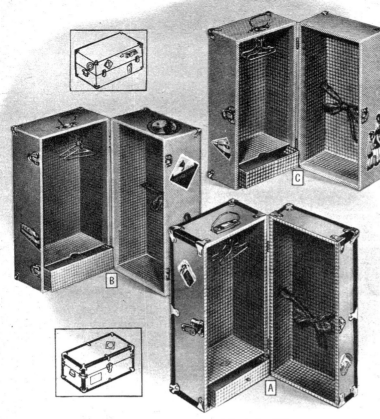

Doll Suitcase

NEW! Can be used as suitcase for "traveling" dolls . . . and children will find many other uses, too. Wood and fiberboard construction, striped paper outside, houndstooth inside. Clear plastic handle with plated hardware, hasp. 11x7x3⅞ in. 49N7953—Shpg. wt. 1 lb. 7 oz. $1.00 — **$1.00**

Doll's Vanity Case

It's brand new and it's a lovely gift . . . a vanity case to keep dolly clean, neat and pretty through hours of play. Fitted with nylon bristle hairbrush, plastic comb, mirror . . . with gay nursery circus patterns. Red imitation alligator (plastic) cover. Paper lined. 11x8x4 in. deep. 49 N 7944—Shpg. wt. 2 lb. 4 oz. . . . **$2.89**

Sturdy wood trunks . . for dolls who like to travel in style . . for storing clothes and accessories

[A] **Metal-over-wood Trunk.** Strong, blue-enameled metal over sturdy wood . . . makes one of the nicest looking, most durable trunks dolly could own. Has a rack and hangers for hanging doll clothes . . . a convenient drawer for storing accessories and little "extras." Metal binding, brass handle. Brass hasp holds trunk shut. Travel stickers on sides. Handsome houndstooth paper lining inside. 79 N 07902—About 15⅝x8x7½ inches overall. Shipping weight 8 lbs. . . . . $3.98 — **$3.98**

[B] **Tough wood and fiberboard trunk.** Striped paper outside gives canvas effect. Lined with houndstooth pattern paper. Drawer in bottom for accessories; rack and clothes hangers. Travel stickers on sides. Corners bound in metal. Metal hasps, hinges, handles. Trunk closes securely . . . keeps dolly's clothes fresh and clean . . . prevents their being lost. 79N07960—Measures 18x10x9½ inches overall. Shipping weight 5 lbs. . . . . $2.98 — **$2.98**

[C] **Wood and fiberboard trunk** similar to 79 N 07960 but slightly smaller. Same sturdy construction. Shipping weight 4 pounds. 79 N 07906—Measures 14x7½x7 inches. . . . . 1.98 — **$1.98**

Take Dolly Traveling

Versatile Doll's Chair or High Chair
$379

A wonderfully useful toy for busy little mothers . . . it's easy to feed dolls and keep them in place with this attractive high chair. Easily converted into a regular doll's chair by removing lower portions of legs. All metal with shaped seat, backrest. Feeding tray moves up and down just like a real high chair. Footrest. Rubber feet won't scratch floors. Leg spread at base 12x12½ in. Overall height 29½-in. Two-tone enamel finish with colorful decal. Easy to assemble, hardware included. Mailable. 79 N 07940—Shpg. wt. 8 lbs. $3.79

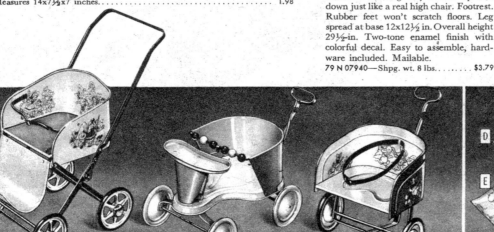

$3.81 $2.27 $2.10

Handsome New Doll Stroller

Dolly will have a pleasant trip when riding in this brightly lithographed, all metal stroller. Has a leatherette-covered 9½x9-in. seat. Folding under-carriage, adjustable footrest and safety strap. Handle 24 in. from floor. 5½-in. stamped spoke wheels, rubber tires. 79 N 08270—Shpg. wt. 6 lbs. **$3.81**

Jaunty Doll Walker

Every smart young lady with a doll family needs a walker for strolling about the neighborhood. All metal with 4-in. double disc wheels. Finished in pink and blue enamel. 7¾x 6½-in. cream colored seat. Play beads on tray. Handle 21½ in. from floor. 79 N 08297—Shpg. wt. 5 lbs. . . **$2.27**

Inexpensive Doll Sulky

Make-believe homemakers will love to wheel their dolls around in this gaily colored little sulky. Made of heavy gauge metal. Blue and red baked-on enamel, colorful trim. 8x7-in. cream color seat. 4-in. steel disc wheels with molded rubber tires. Plastic safety strap is adjustable. 49 N 8261—Shpg. wt. 3 lbs. **$2.10**

Bedding for Dolly's Crib

[D] **Comforter and Pillow Set.** Quilted cotton cover. Cotton stuffed. Pillow 7½x9½ in. Comforter 21x16 inches. 49 N 3530—Shpg. wt. 1 lb. . . . . . . Set **$1.29**

[E] **Doll Bed Mattresses.** Cotton or tufflex stuffed. Bright patterns. 49 N 3517—11x21 in. Shpg. wt. 8 oz. . . **86c** 49 N 3524—14x25 in. Shpg. wt. 12 oz. . . **$1.14**

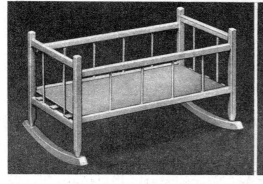

Rock dolly to sleep in this Cradle

When Mr. Sandman comes around, it takes just a tiny bit of rocking and a soft lullabye to put baby dolls to sleep. And there's never a bump from the smooth wood rockers. All wood, beautifully finished in blue enamel. Removable slat bottom. Dowel joinings for extra strength. 20 in. long, 10¼ in. wide, 11¼ in. high. Shipped partly assembled. Easily assembled; no hardware needed.

49 N 7908—Shipping weight 2 pounds............98c

98c

Bassinet for wee mothers

At nap time and night time, dolly will slumber peacefully in her own little bed. Finished in lovely light blue enamel with colorful play beads on foot, decal on head. Made of sturdy wood, snug-fitting dowel joinings. Strong corrugated cardboard bottom. Takes up to 22-in. doll. Mattress not included . . . order from opposite page. Easily assembled, no screws needed. 22½x12½x15½ in.

79 N 07920—Shipping weight 4 pounds.........$1.79

$1.79

Drop-side Crib . . storage drawer

A beautifully finished, comfortable bed for her favorite doll. Drawer makes convenient storage place for doll clothes or bedding. Selected wood, rounded corners. Head is fiberboard with colorful decal. Play beads on foot and head. Bed, drawer have sturdy cardboard bottoms. Blue enamel finish. Snug fitting dowel joints, easy to set up. 22½x12½x15½ in.

79 N 07925—Shipping weight 8 pounds........$2.98

$2.98

.. Bathe her, put her to bed

Combined Bath and Dressing Table

Completely equipped with washcloth and soap for dolly's bedtime bath

$3.98

Dolls, like children, do get dirty . . . and it's fun to bathe them in this leakproof vinyl plastic tub. Handy tray below bath for accessories. Splash-guard has pockets for soap and washcloth. Wash dolly in tub, then slide dressing table top over tub. Safety strap holds doll securely. Easily cleaned tub has drain hose with clip. Tubular aluminum frame folds easily . . . will *not* rust. 20x11½x 22½ in. high. 25 inches to top of frame. Legs are rubber tipped. Doll not included.

79 N 07938—Shipping weight 5 pounds................$3.98

Happi-Time Drop-Side Doll Crib

Dolly will snuggle down to pleasant dreams in this beautifully finished crib that's built just like a real baby bed

$4.98

A wonderful gift for any little mother . . . she'll love tucking them away when day is done. Mellow maple finish with decal decorations. Sturdy wood frame, tough fiberboard end panels. Colorful play beads. Rounded corners and edges. Rails doweled into legs for added strength. Wood slat bottom; side can be raised or lowered. Smooth-rolling casters. Shipped partly assembled, easy to assemble. Order bedding from opposite page.

79 N 07954—20½x14½x26 in. long. Shipping weight 12 lbs............$4.98

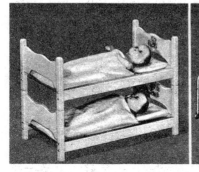

Double-Deck Beds

Two dolls can sleep comfortably at same time; one in upper bunk, other in lower. Or set them side by side for a set of twin beds. Pastel enameled wood, decal trim. Heavy cardboard bottom. 21½x12x16 in. 15-in. wood ladder. Shipped flat, easily set up. Bedding not included.

79 N 07932—Shpg. wt. 4 lbs....$3.59

$3.59

Metal Doll Bed with springs

A comfortable, bouncy bed for dolly . . . an ideal gift for any little girl. All steel construction with link-type springs. Finished in blue baked-on enamel with colorful decal. Embossed panel headboard, detachable side panels. Hard rubber swivel casters. 25¾x13¾x12¾ in. high. Shipped partly assembled. Easy to assemble, hardware included.

79 N 07919—Shipping weight 6 lbs.......$3.19

$3.19

Roomy Doll Basket, Stand

Made to look like a real baby's basket . . . same fine quality woven fiber and construction. Enameled pure white with soft pastel trim. Folding legs have easy-rolling swivel casters. 20 inches high. Basket is 23x13x8 inches high.

79 N 07958—Shpg. wt. 6 lbs.....$5.47

$5.47

Plastic basket liner and pad to fit above basket. White with pastel pattern.

49 N 7962—Shpg. wt. 8 oz.....$1.85

Imported China Sets

Deluxe Dinner Service for Six. Every young hostess needs just the right equipment for entertaining. She'll be extra proud of this set. Made of real china; floral pattern with luster tan finish. Just the thing for make-believe meals and tea parties. It's a wonderful way to teach children to care for possessions, too—for any little girl will take extra good care of her "best" china. Teach her all the rules of gracious dining, how to set the table properly. Imported from occupied Japan. Larger

pieces than set at right. Set includes 6 cups, 6 saucers, 6 plates. Also, there's a teapot (with cover) in which the little hostess can really make tea; sugar bowl with cover, creamer, meat platter, vegetable dish, footed gravy boat, casserole with cover—everything she'll need for a complete meal. Plates have 4½-in. diameter; other pieces in proportion. Shipping weight 6 lbs.

49 N 879. . . . . 28-piece set $3.29

$329
28-pc. set

Blue Willow China Tea Set for Six

A traditional old pattern that's a favorite with grown-ups . . . now comes in a smaller size for small homemakers. Complete as mother's own tea service . . . in real sparkling china. Any young make-believer will swell with pride when she serves her doll family or playmates from such a beautifully detailed set. Made in occupied Japan of delicate china . . . finished in popular blue willow pattern. Set consists of 6 cups, 6 saucers, 6 plates. There's a cake plate for tea parties, a perky little teapot and sugar bowl with covers; creamer . . . everything she needs to set a lovely table. Plates are 3 13/16 inches in diameter, others in proportion.

$1.79
24-piece set

49 N 878—Shipping weight 3 lbs. 12 oz. . . . . 24-piece set $1.79

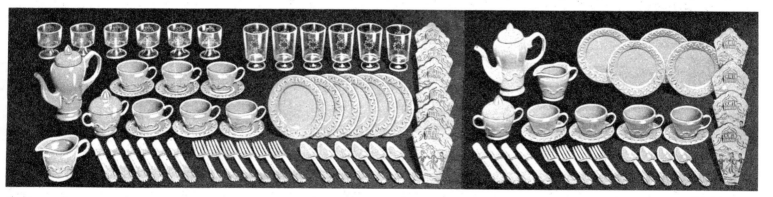

Complete Plastic Table Service for Six . . 53 pieces!

Toy dishes are wonderful for teaching children the use of dishes and utensils. Set has about every type of dish needed. Heavy pastel blue plastic with a delicate scroll design. Little girls have fun entertaining playmates at make-believe banquets and tea parties. Fine for children with large doll families. Set consists of 6 each of the following: cups, saucers, plates, knives, forks, spoons, napkins; teapot and sugar bowl with covers; also creamer. 6 crystal-clear plastic goblets, 6 sherbets. Plates 5 in. in diameter, other pieces in proportion.

$3.79

49 N 828—Shipping weight 2 pounds 14 ounces. $3.79

Plastic Tea Set . . . Complete Service for Four

A little girl's Christmas wish come true . . . Pastel blue plastic tea set that's modeled just like mother's. Now she can serve tea to friends that come to play . . . or neighbors who drop in to visit. Set consists of 29 pieces made of extra-heavy, durable plastic that's almost unbreakable . . yet lightweight. There are 4 each: cups, saucers, plates, knives, forks, spoons. Also sugar bowl and teapot with covers, creamer, and napkins. Plates are 5 inches in diameter, other pieces in proportion.

$2.29

49 N 823—Shipping weight 1 pound 13 ounces. $2.29

Handloom . . just like big ones

A real handloom on which youngsters can really make things. It weaves beautiful fabric in endless variety of patterns, yet it's simple enough for children to operate. Constructed of hardwood 12x8¼x5 in. wide. Illustrated book on weaving, 3 skeins of colorful wool yarn, 3 plastic shuttles included.

$5.59

49 N 1215—Shipping weight 2 lbs. 10 oz. $5.59

Colorful Indian Beadcraft Kit

Children can design and make belts, rings, and many useful articles with this kit. Includes metal bead loom frame 11½x2¾ inches, 6 vials of brightly colored Indian seed beads, 2 special needles, wire, bead thread, center stones, wax, everything needed to start right in weaving. Illustrations of various designs are included. It's a grand toy to stimulate creative imagination, encourages constructive play.

$2.29

49 N 2010—Shipping weight 1 lb. 5 oz. $2.29

Make useful items with Tilecraft

Keep little hands busy with constructive play. This kit is the perfect outlet for children who like to make things. Keeps them occupied on rainy days or when they have to stay indoors. With the bright colored beads, they can make table mats, coasters, plaques, or even a basket. Assorted colored porcelain beads. Cord and 2 needles included. Easy-to-follow instructions show how to make a variety of designs.

$1.79

49 N 2028—Shipping weight 1 lb. 12 oz. $1.79

Metal Tea Set for 6

Make a tiny hostess happy on Christmas morning with this bright little tea set . . . she'll be proud as punch to show it off to her playmates. 29 pieces in all . . . bright, lithographed design on metal that takes lots of hard wear and positively won't break. Tea-time will come often for the proud owner of these lovely dishes. Complete set consists of 6 each of the following: 4⅛-in. plates, cups, saucers, and butter plates. For tea parties, there's a gay little teapot and sugar bowl with covers; matching serving tray 8x10 inches, and creamer.

49 N 925—Shpg. wt. 1 lb. 8 oz......95c **95c**

Tea for Two

[A] Tea parties will be far more fun with this delightful little 15-piece set. Two-tone plastic—almost unbreakable. Includes 2 each: 3⅜-in. saucers, cups, knives, forks, spoons; also teapot, cover, teapot stand, sugar bowl, creamer.
49 N 825—Shpg. wt. 1 lb. 6 oz.....$1.15 **$1.15**

Beverage Tray Service

[B] Beautifully colored heavy quality plastic. Set contains large scalloped tray (9¼-in. diameter) with removable handle. Pitcher, 2 goblets, 2 sherbets.
49 N 821—Shpg. wt. 2 lbs. 6 oz...$1.15 **$1.15**

Soda Fountain Set

[C] Big 6-in. plastic dispenser serves liquids through spigot. 3 sundae dishes and 3 soda cups with holders, 2 banana split dishes, 6 spoons, ice cream scoop; all in colorful plastic. Straws in plastic holder. 20x12-in. box.
49 N 1204—Shpg. wt. 1 lb. 12 oz..$2.19 **$2.19**

Soft drink mixer

[D] Wind the spring motor, watch your drink being mixed. Sturdy metal, about 9½ in. high. Plastic mixing tumbler. 4 plastic tumblers and straws.
49 N 1213—Shpg. wt. 1 lb. 4 oz...$1.79 **$1.79**

Ice Cream Freezer

[E] Make ice cream in 5 to 6 minutes! Blue plastic outer tub 4¾ in. high, 3½-in. diameter. Aluminum freezing container, plastic mixer. Instructions, ice cream mix included. 5¾ in. high overall.
49 N 1745—Shpg. wt. 10 oz.......89c **89c**

"Silverware" Chest

[F] Plastic with metalized finish to look like silver. 4 knives, 4 forks, 4 spoons, salt and pepper shakers, pie server, butter knife. 8¾x6-in. cardboard chest. Knife 5 in. long, others in proportion.
49 N 824—Shpg. wt. 10 oz........89c **89c**

Magnetic Paper Doll

Magic Mary is a paper doll with a very special quality that will thrill your little girl. She can be dressed in an instant because her clothes cling like magic, due to magnetic attraction. She comes with a wardrobe of 14 dresses to be cut out. Cardboard doll is on metal base . . . she stands alone. Mary is about 10 inches tall, and she's about the most colorful paper doll we've seen.
49 N 1251—Shipping weight 1 pound..................$1.05 **$1.05**

Fun for your little hostess

Real, workable Weaving Loom

Keep little ones busy, happily weaving hot-pan holders, coasters and other useful items. You'll be surprised at how easy it is to weave. Even small children can learn in a short time. Metal loom is adjustable from 4 to 8 inches, square or rectangular. Two skeins of yarn, loopers, hook and needle included . . . so they can start right in. A Christmas present to keep them busy all year round. Meets the child's instinctive desire to be constructive and imitate mother. Shipping weight 1 pound 7 ounces.
49 N 1250....................98c **98c**

40-piece toy Percolator Set

The little percolator really "perks" . . . has standard sieve-type coffee basket and lid with glass inset. Since it's aluminum, this set has extreme durability. Plates and saucers have embossed Bo-Peep decoration. Set includes percolator, 6 cups, 6 saucers, 6 plates, 6 forks, 6 knives, 6 spoons, round serving tray, 6 paper napkins. Percolator about 4½ in. high, other pieces in proportion. Service for 6.
49 N 906—Shipping weight 1 pound......$1.39 **$1.39**

Aluminum Cooking, Baking Set

Includes 4-in. pie plate (other pieces in proportion), tube cake pan, measuring cup, 6-cup muffin pan, biscuit pan, skillet with enameled handle, cookie cutters in 4 animal shapes, cookie sheet, mixing bowl, double boiler, colander, canister and scoop, 2 measuring spoons. Set stays clean, bright, smooth.
49 N 921—Shipping weight 1 pound.......$1.39 **$1.39**

17-piece Kitchen Set

Little girls have grand fun helping mother cook or bake on a set of their very own cooking utensils . . . just the right size. Designed for real use, these miniature utensils will make her want to try her hand at baking delicious cakes, cookies and other pastries. Set includes pastry board, rolling pin, meat grinder, potato masher, egg beater, plastic scoop, cookie cutter, 4 metal pans, pie plate, plastic cake server, plastic mixing bowl, spoon, colorful plastic apron and recipe booklet. **$1.19**

49 N 924—Shipping weight 1 lb. $1.19

New .. Big Double-Oven Stove

Big, modern non-electric stove chuck full of play value. Perfect equipment for beginning homemakers. See all you get . . . 2 oven doors that open and close, 8 multicolor plastic play push buttons that push "on" or "off" just like a grown-up stove, convenient recessed base. 8-piece plastic utensil set. Sturdy steel construction with white baked-on enamel finish, bright red handles and lithographed trim. 14x7¾x14½ inches high. **$3.69**

79 N 01132—Shipping weight 6 pounds . . $3.69

New economy-priced Play Stove

Designed especially for little beginner cooks. Styled just like Mother's. Hinged oven door opens and closes, adds to stove's play value. Four vari-colored plastic play push buttons actually "push in". Dummy timer. Colorful plastic utensils. Bright red handles, heavy gauge steel. Non-electric stove is 11x6½x12 inches high. Wonderful gift for such a low price. Every little girl needs a stove of her own to practice on . . . order one today. **$1.95**

49 N 1128—Shpg. wt. 4 lbs. 2 oz. $1.95

HELP MAKE THEIR DREAMS COME TRUE

For "Cooking Fun"!

ELECTRIC TOY RANGES that actually cook things

Large Size Electric Range with twin top, glass window oven, toy utensils. Has 4 burners, 2 at left and 2 at right for handier "cooking." Separate heating elements for burners and window oven. Steel with baked-on white enamel. Plastic play switches, chrome-plated door handle. Oven has spring-lock door. Insulated cord with plug. UL approved. For 110-120 volt AC-DC. 15x7¾x12¾ inches high overall. 9 utensils and cook book included. **$769**

79 N 01136—Shipping weight 10 pounds $7.69

Electric Range with glass window oven, toy utensils. Warm meals are best for dolly, so naturally doll mothers prefer an electric range. Steel model has 4 burners on top, separate heating element for oven. Baked-on white enamel finish; plastic play switches and handles. Oven has spring-lock door. Insulated cord with plug. UL approved. For 110-120 volt AC or DC. Eight cooking utensils and cookbook included. 12½x6¾x11 in. high overall. **$498**

79 N 01135—Shipping weight 7 pounds $4.98

Toy Refrigerator with Freezer Compartment

$1.98 Preparing meals for dolly can be twice as much fun when she has a miniature toy refrigerator just like Mother's to help keep dolly's food "fresh". She'll be so proud of the "freezer compartment" with a separate door like newest, big refrigerators. 2 removable plastic ice cube trays. Both doors open . . . bright red handles. Heavy gauge metal enameled white. Six colorful cutouts of food items are included to give extra play appeal. Non-electric refrigerator, 8x5½x13½ inches high. Shipping weight 2 lbs. 9 oz.

49 N 1129 . . . . $1.98

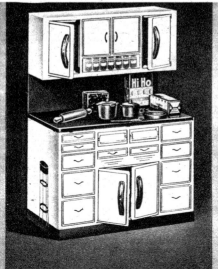

Modern Metal Kitchen Cabinet .. 6 utensils

$1.98 Her kitchen isn't complete without a roomy cabinet to store cooking supplies for "dolly's dinner." She'll love to imitate mother's kitchen chores at this miniature cabinet. Shelves are stocked with play packages of famous grocery brands . . . such fun when planning make-believe menus. 4 doors open with colorful plastic handles. 6 plastic cooking utensils in assorted colors plus tiny rolling pin. Lithographed in white and red with "painted-on" spice shelf and kitchen stool at side. About 11x6½x15¾ inches high.

79 N 01124—Shpg.wt.4 lbs. $1.98

While their little brothers were having exciting shootouts in their backyard O. K. Corrals or spending hours setting up their Marx playsets, little girls were having _real_ fun in 1952 -- sewing, knitting, sweeping, vacuuming, ironing.

Some of the toy kitchens in this Wishbook put many a real kitchen to shame; some of the electric toy ranges actually worked, if you could find pots and pans small enough to fit. But then, of _course_ you could -- they were for sale, too.

For leisure time, girls had electric phonographs, drum sets, accordions and toy pianos, as well as puzzles, balloons, bubble pipes and play tents. And for all the pent-up frustration of taking care of a tiny make-believe home and family, there was a smiling "Punch Me" toy.

Medical kits were also big. Those aimed at boys were called "Tinytown Family Doctor." Girls could aspire only to be "Tinytown Visiting Nurse." However, the contents of each set were similar, if not identical.

Sears Christmas
Wishbook
1952

Castle Home Movies

See your Hollywood favorites at home
Over 80 titles for the whole family

Titles available in 8mm silent, 16mm silent, 16mm sound editions. Silent movies in complete or short editions; complete editions only for sound.

HOW TO ORDER: Catalog numbers with "F" shipped from New York factory. *State catalog number, title and title number.* Example for 8mm silent short edition: 3 N 8600—Midget Car Maniacs (818). *Sent postpaid.*

3N8600—8mm Silent Short Ed. About 50 ft. (Wt. 3 oz.).ea. $1.79
3N8602F—8mm Silent Complete Ed. About 150 ft. (Wt. 6 oz.).$5.65
3N8601—16mm Silent Short Ed. About 100 ft. (Wt. 6 oz.).ea.$2.79

3 N 8603F—16mm Silent Complete Edition. About 250 ft. for cartoons; others 350 ft. (Wt. 1 lb.) Ea. .$9.49
3 N 8604F—16mm Sound Complete Edition. About 250 ft. for cartoons; others 350 ft. (Wt. 1 lb.) Ea. $19.95

ABBOTT AND COSTELLO
Midget Car Maniacs (818)
High Fliers (816)
Riot on Ice (814)
Kitchen Mechanics (812)
Fun on the Run (811)
Oysters and Muscles (809)
No Indians, Please (808)

HOPALONG CASSIDY
Prairie Vengeance (568)
Heart of the West (563)
Bar 20 Rides Again (562)
Three on a Trail (561)
Danger Trail (567)
Border Justice (566)
Rustler's Valley (573)
Trail Dust (574)

WESTERNS
Terror Trail—Tom Mix (572)
Guns of Vengeance—Tom Mix (571)
Prairie Pirates (570)
Cheyenne Cowboy (565)
West of Laramie (564)
Desperate Trails (569)
Western Feud (560)
Lawless Frontier (558)
Code of Courage (556)

SPECIALS
Alice in Wonderland (1005)

W. C. FIELDS
Hurry, Hurry (817)
The Great Chase (813)

SPORTS PARADE
Junior Bronc Busters (367)
Water Devils (369)
Babes in Sportland (370)
Living Dangerously (361)
Sports 'Round the Globe (359)
Snow Speed (357)
Fishing Fun (354)
Thrills on Wheels (352)
Spills and Thrills (340)

WORLD PARADE
Caribbean Holiday (241)
Yellowstone (240)
Florida Holiday (239)
Grand Canyon (238)
Bermuda (236)
America's Wonderland (234)
Glacier National Park (231)

ADVENTURE PARADE
Chimp Steps Out (633)
Carnival at the Zoo (632)
Circus at the Zoo (630)
Chimp the Sailor (625)
Ten Fathoms Deep (634)

LANTZ CARTOONS
Brat Cat (488)
Love Sick (487)
Keeper of the Lions (486)
Happy Scouts (441)
Beachcombers (442)
Cheese Napers (443)

WOODY WOODPECKER
Well Oiled (493)
Solid Ivory (494)
Smoked Hans (492)
Coocoo Bird (491)

FAIRY TALE CARTOONS
Jack and the Beanstalk (765)
Simple Simon (764)
Puss in Boots (762)
Big Bad Wolf (760)
Sinbad the Sailor (759)
Little Black Sambo (757)
Mary's Little Lamb (756)
Old Mother Hubbard (753)
Aladdin's Lamp (752)

CHRISTMAS SPECIALS
Howdy Doody Christmas (824)
Night Before Christmas (807)
Woody Plays Santa Claus (819)
Dickens Christmas Carol (830)

Complete list of Castle Movie Titles sent with your order on request from your mail order house.

MELTON MOVIE VIEWER

$4.79 Here's a pocket-size way to see all 8mm movies . . . without a projector or screen! Just turn knob at any speed you want and watch movies through brilliant optical lens. Show your home movies off at work or at friends' homes. You can also edit home movies scene by scene. Servicemen can see movies of loved ones at home. Children will like it too—they can see their favorite cartoon friends come alive. Black plastic. Uses any 8mm movies up to 50 ft. length. Ideal gift for movie fans.
3 N 8551—*Postpaid.* (Wt. 2 lbs.) $4.79

View-Master Magic!

ILLUSTRATED ON OPPOSITE PAGE

More fun than a circus parade! See color scenes of cartoons, your favorite vacation spots in 3 dimensions. View-Master scenes thrill young and old alike. Stereoscope scenes stand out in true color and depth . . . some objects appear close, others far away—just as your eyes see. Over 400 entertaining, educational reels available for use in View-Master stereoscope and projector. A perfect gift for any age. You'll give hours of enjoyment . . . years of pleasure. Order one for every person on your list.

[A] Stereoscope. For viewing View-Master reels. Lever changes scenes. Black plastic. Uses reels below or your own made with new View-Master camera.
$2.00 Stereoscope only
3 N 6450—*Postpaid.* (Wt. 1 lb.) $2.00

[B] Light Attachment. Fastens easily on back of stereoscope to light scenes anywhere. Order 2 batteries below.
3 N 6457—*Postpaid.* (Wt. 1 lb.) . . . $2.00

[C] Transformer. Use stereoscope light attachment without batteries. 10-ft. cord. Uses 115-volt, 60-cycle AC only. *UL listed.*
3 N 6470—*Postpaid.* (Wt. 12 oz.) . . . $3.00
Batteries for Light Attachment. *Postpaid.*
3 N 6880—(Wt. 8 oz.) . . . . 2 for 23c

Model S-1 Projector. For home, classroom or commercial use. Projects non-stereo images of View-Master reels up to 36x36 in. Metal body. Simple to operate. Any 110–120-volt AC-DC. *UL listed.* (Wt. 7 lbs.)
3 N M6458T—*Exp. prepaid.* $47.50

[E] Junior Projector. Uses View-Master reels to project non-stereo color pictures up to 16x18 in. Any 110–120-volt AC-DC. *UL listed.* (Wt. 4 lbs.) . . $10.95

[F] Bible Reels. How to Order: *State catalog No.* 3 N 6456, *reel number and title.* Bible Story Reels. *Postpaid.*
3 N 6456—(Shpg. wt. 4 oz.) . . . . 4 for $2.00
CH6A—Savior's Birth I   CH47—Good Samaritan
CH6B—Savior's Birth II   CH49—Good Shepherd
CH1—Angel Gabriel   CH55A—Prodigal Son I
Visits Zacharias   CH55B—Prodigal Son II
CH8—The Wise Men Find Jesus
CH15—Jesus Turns Water into Wine
CH37—Herod Kills John the Baptist
CH40—Jesus Answers Prayer of a Mother

[G] Library Box. Holds Viewmaster Stereoscope and 100 reels (not incl.). Two-tone plastic.
3 N 6451—*Postpaid.* (Wt. 2 lbs.) $1.85

[H] Screen for table or wall. Glass beaded. 18x24 in. Compact and collapsible. Not postpaid.
3 N 8608—Shpg. wt. 2 lbs. $2.79

View-Master Outfit. Consists of Viewer (A), Light attachment (B) with bulb and 2 batteries, and choice of 6 reels (D) below.
3 N 06485—*Postpaid* (Shpg. wt. 3 lbs.) $6.23

DeLuxe View-Master Outfit. Has viewer (A), light attachment (B), transformer (C) and choice of 6 reels (D) below.
3 N 06453—*Postpaid* (Shpg. wt. 3 lbs.) $9.00

Thrill to Magic of View-Master Color Pictures
Fairy Tales, Animals, Cowboys, Travel Scenes

View-Master Reels shown as (D) on opposite page. Choose from over 175 reels. Seven color scenes per reel. View pictures in true-to-life depth in Stereoscope. Show non-stereo pictures on screen with projector. *State catalog No., reel No. and title.* (Example: 3N6452 FT5 Cinderella.)
$2.00 6 reels
3 N 6452—*Postpaid.* (Shipping wt. 4 oz.) . . . . 6 reels $2.00

Fairy Tales
FT5—Cinderella
FT1—Little Red Riding Hood
FT2—Hansel and Gretel
FT3—Jack and the Beanstalk
FT4—Snow White and 7 Dwarfs
FT6—Goldilocks and 3 Bears
FT7—The Three Little Pigs
FT8—Little Black Sambo
FT9—The Ugly Duckling
FT25—Rudolph, The Red-Nosed Reindeer
FT30—Night Before Christmas
FT50A—Aladdin's Lamp I
FT50B—Aladdin's Lamp II
FT51—The Magic Carpet
SP9058—Santa's Workshop

Alice in Wonderland
FT20A—White Rabbit
FT20B—Mad Tea Party
FT20C—Croquet Game

Christmas Story
XM1—Mary and Joseph
XM2—The Shepherds
XM3—The Wise Men

Easter Story
EA1—The Resurrection
EA2—The Appearances of Jesus
EA3—The Ascension

Adventures of Sam Sawyer
SAM1—Sam Flies to the Moon
SAM2—Sam Finds a Treasure
SAM3—Sam in Land of Giants
SAM4—Sam in Darkest Africa
SAM5—Sam in the Land of Ice
SAM6—Flying Saucer Pirates

Circus
701—A Day at the Circus I
702—A Day at the Circus II
703—A Day at the Circus III

Cowboys
940—The Rodeo
942—Cattle Roundup
945—Roy Rogers and Trigger
950—Gene Autry, Champion
955—Hopalong Cassidy, Topper
960—Cisco Kid and Pancho

Wild Animals in Captivity
910—Animals of Africa I
911—Animals of Africa II

Wild Animals (Cont'd.)
912—Animals of India
913—Animals of North America
914—Animals of South America
925—Performing Elephants
926—Performing Chimpanzees
927—Performing Lions
901—Wild Animals in Africa
975—Tarzan Rescues Cheta

Mother Goose Rhymes
MG1—Miss Muffet to Jack, Jill
MG2—Boy Blue to King Cole
MG3—Bo-Peep to Cat and the Fiddle

Cartoons
800—Bugs Bunny and Elmer
810—Tom and Jerry
820—Woody Woodpecker

National Parks
21—Crater Lake, Oregon I
26—Grand Canyon, S. Rim I
27—Grand Canyon, S. Rim II
30—Grand Canyon, Bright Angel Trail, Arizona
31—Grand Canyon, Kaibab Trail, Arizona
32—Grand Canyon, Havasu-pailand, Ariz.
36—Grand Canyon, N. Rim
126—Yellowstone, Grand Canyon Area, Wyoming
127—Yellowstone, Mammoth
128—Yellowstone, Old Faithful
129—Yellowstone, Lower Basin
131—Yosemite, California I
132—Yosemite, California II
176—Petrified Forest, Arizona
251—Carlsbad Caverns, N.M. I
252—Carlsbad Caverns, II
336—Great Smoky Mountains I
101—Rocky Mt. Trail Rd., Col.
337—Great Smoky Mts. II
339—Mammoth Cave, Ky. I

United States Travel
51—Garden of Gods, Colorado
76—Mount Vernon
96—Scenic Coast of Oregon
111—Redwood Highway I
112—Redwood Highway II
124—Dells of Wisconsin River
136—Washington, D.C. I
137—Washington, D.C. II
151—Columbia River Highway

United States Travel (Cont'd.)
156—New York City I
157—New York City II
158—Rockefeller Center and Empire State Bldg., N.Y.
160—St. Augustine
161—Silver Springs
162—Daytona Beach to Key West, Fla.
163—Miami Beach, Florida
165—Miami, Florida
164—Cypress Gardens, Florida
166—Marine Studios, Florida
175—Navajo Indians
177—Painted Desert, Arizona
198—San Francisco, California
203—Black Hills of S. Dakota
206—Sun Valley in Winter
8—Hoover Dam Tour
11—Hoover Dam
219—Hollywood, California
220—Homes of Movie Stars
238—Royal Gorge, Colorado
245—Pike's Peak, Colorado
286—Indian Tribal Ceremonial
309—The Eskimos
332—Mardi Gras, New Orleans
333—Chicago, Ill.
338—Lookout Mountain, Tenn.
174—Monument Valley
81—Niagara Falls, New York
82—Niagara Falls in Winter
234—Cave of the Winds, Col.
342—Blue Grass Country, Ky.
SP9071—Tulip Time in Holland, Michigan
370—Oklahoma, Sooner State
221—Los Angeles, Calif.

Foreign Travel
4000—Jerusalem, Holy City
319—Lake Louise, Canadian Rockies
523—Mexican Bullfight, Mex.
1401—Paris, France I
1402—Paris, France II
2001—Matterhorn, Switz.
1410—Palace of Versailles
1420—Battlefields of World War II, Normandy
375—Niagara Falls, Ontario
388—Gaspe Peninsula, Quebec
3303—Great Pyramids and Sphinx
1001—London, England I
4871—Tokyo, Japan
4872—Mt. Fujiyama, Japan
4873—Festival of Japan
4302—Maharaja's Festival

Hawaii
61—Hula Dancers I
63—Honolulu
68—Tropical Flowers I
66—Hawaii, Orchid Island
73—Waikiki, Island of Oahu

Complete title list of View-Master Reels sent with each order or upon request from your Sears Mail Order House.

Kodachrome full-color pictures "Come to Life" in 3 Dimensions

ITEMS A–H DESCRIBED ON FACING PAGE

FUN FOR EVERYONE WITH
View-Master
REELS, PROJECTORS, KITS

Junior Projector

Handsome Library Box

Light attachment fits on stereoscope to light scenes

Roy Rogers and Trigger   Bugs Bunny   Niagara Falls   Wild Animals

PERSONAL STEREO CAMERA

- Now take your pictures in 3 dimensions ... it's easy to do and a thrilling experience

- Two lenses see the same as your eyes ... in depth and beautiful natural colors.

- See your pictures in the stereoscope ... they look real enough to walk right into.

Keep your pictures as real as the day you snapped them with View-Master's Stereo camera. Two lenses—that see just as your eyes see—take pictures not only in 3 dimensions but also beautiful color! Easy to operate ... complete with instructions, you can make your own reels too. Uses regular 35mm color film. Gives 37 pairs on 20-exposure film; 69 pairs on 36-exposure film.

$149.00
Camera only
$15.00 Down
Cash or Terms

"Expo-sure" calculator automatically adjusts lens opening and shutter speed. Coated anastigmat f:3.5 lenses stop down to f:16. Shutter speeds from 1/10 to 1/100 sec., and bulb. Focused from 7 ft. to infinity. Flash synchronized. Eye level optical view-finder.

3NM6134MT–*Express prepaid* (Wt. 3 lbs.) . $149.00
3 N 6410MT–*Case. Ppd.* (Wt. 1 lb. 8 oz.) . 14.75
3 N 6438M–Flash Unit. With batteries. Order No. 5, 25 or SM bulbs. *Ppd.* (Wt. 1 lb.) . . $19.75

Personal Stereo Camera ACCESSORIES

For fullest enjoyment of your stereo camera order these useful accessories

J Metal View-Master Film Cutter die-cuts stereo pairs for the Personal Reel (below) to .001 inch accuracy. Fit proper film perforations on sprocket—press down—an accurately die-cut stereo pair falls from the machine.
3 N 6411T–*Postpaid*. (Shipping wt. 3 lbs. 4 oz.) $19.50

K Personal Reels. Mount pictures on reels—then see them in the $2.00 viewer. Die-cut stereo pairs slip easily into reel pockets.
3 N 6412M–*Postpaid*. (Shipping wt. 1 lb.) . . . . 6 for $1.00

L Matched Type "A" Filters. Color corrected so you can use Type A film inside or outdoors. Coated.
3 N 6413M–2 orange filters. *Postpaid*. (Weight 8 oz.) $4.50

Double-oven Play Stove

De luxe modern, non-electric. 2 oven doors open and close, 8 multicolor plastic buttons push "on" and "off," 8-pc. plastic utensil set. Sturdy steel construction, white baked-on enamel finish, bright red handles. 14x7¼x14½ in. high.
79 N 01132—Shpg. wt. 6 lbs.........$3.55

$3.55

Economy-priced Stove

Non-electric play stove—styled like Mother's. Hinged oven door opens and closes, 4 vari-colored plastic buttons actually "push in." Dummy timer. Colorful plastic utensils. Red handles. Sturdy steel construction. 11x6½x12 in. high.
49 N 1126—Shpg. wt. 4 lbs. 2 oz. $1.98

$1.98

ELECTRIC TOY RANGES that actually cook and bake

Large-sized Electric Range with twin top, glass window oven, toy utensils. Has 4 burners, 2 at left and 2 at right for handier "cooking." *Separate heating elements for burners and oven.* Steel construction with shining white enamel finish. Plastic play switches go "on" and "off." Red door handles. Oven has spring-lock door. Insulated cord with plug. UL approved. For 110-120-volt AC-DC. 15x7¾x12¾ inches high overall. 10 utensils and cook book included.
79 N 01136—Shipping weight 10 pounds.........$7.69

$7.69

Electric Range with glass window oven, toy utensils. For pies and cakes like mother makes, for good warm meals for dolly. *Two separate heating elements* for burners and oven. Steel with baked-on white enamel finish; plastic play switches; red handles. Spring-lock oven door. Insulated cord with plug. UL approved. For 110-120-volt AC or DC. 8 cooking utensils; cook book. 12½x6¾x11 in. high.
79 N 01135—Shipping weight 7 pounds.......$4.98

$4.98

Dolly's Laundry Set

$1.59 Complete laundry set to wash the baby's bunting in. Every little mother will have the time of her life keeping dolly's clothes fresh and clean. Just turn the handle and the cups gently beat up and down. Special glass tub lets her see it all. Adjustable wringer makes it easy. Washer stands on sturdy metal base. About 9 inches high overall. Rinsing tub, revolving dryer, clothes pins complete the set. Shpg. wt. 3 lbs. 9 oz.
49 N 1005...............$1.59

Play-House Fun

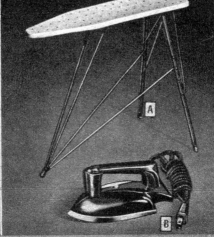

4-piece Cleaning Set

Junior size for every tiny tot who wants to help mother with the housework. Streamlined metal sweeper has 6⅝x5¼-in. base, 18-in. wood handle. Brightly colored dust pan 5x5¼ in. Multicolored dust mop, 18-in. handle. Colorful plastic apron to keep her clean.
49 N 1307—Shpg. wt. 1 lb........89c

89c

Super De Luxe 5-piece Sweeper Set

She'll dust and sweep sparkling clean with this de luxe equipment. Special Happi-Time set is realistically designed for the most fun ever. Bigger and better, it includes streamlined enameled metal sweeper with 8x7-in. base. Special fiber bristle broom and fluffy dust mop will help her do a "professional" job. All have 21-in. enameled handles. Matching dust pan. Sparkling plastic apron for that extra "grown-up" feeling.
79 N 01329—Shipping weight 4 pounds.........$1.97

$1.97

New Ironing Board .. Play Iron

[A] Metal ironing board with superior safety features. Sturdy legs lock in place; rubber tips. Folds. Top 7x27 inches.
79 N 01001—22 inches high. Shpg. wt. 6 lbs....$2.07

$2.07

[B] Electric Play Iron . . *actually heats!* Enameled base, black handle. UL approved for 110-120-volt, AC-DC current. 6¼ inches long overall.
49 N 1004—Shipping weight 1 lb. 10 oz.......$1.79

Order today .. add Play House Fun Toys to your Easy Terms order. See page 353 for complete details

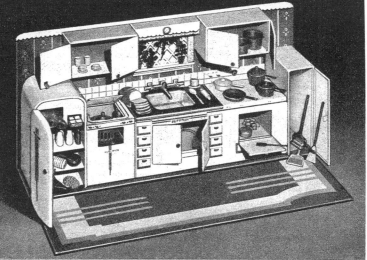

2-door Toy Refrigerator

She'll be so proud of her miniature refrigerator with *separate "freezer compartment"* that has its own door. Both doors open . . . bright red handles. Heavy-gauge metal enameled white. Removable plastic ice cube tray. Six colorful cutouts of food items give extra play appeal. Non-electric. 8x5½x13½ inches high. **$1.98**

49 N 1129—Shpg. wt. 2 lbs. 9 oz......$1.98

Metal Kitchen Cabinet

Fully stocked with "supplies" and utensils. 4 doors open with colorful red handles. 6 plastic cooking utensils plus tiny rolling pin. Variety of play packages of famous grocery brands. Cabinet is white and red with "painted-on" spice shelf and kitchen stool at side. About 11x6¼x15¾ inches high. **$2.14**

49 N 1124—Shpg. wt. 4 lbs. 12 oz....$2.14

New, complete modern Kitchen . . 6 basic units
Perfect miniatures with "real" working parts

A complete, metal kitchen all her very own. Includes: refrigerator, stove, dishwasher and washing machine combination, sink, broom closet, 2 cabinets. All doors open and close. Every piece with fascinating "real" working parts. Complete set of miniature plastic accessories such as pots, pans, cleaning set, etc. 23¾x10½x11 inches high. Easy to complete partial assembly. **$3.59**

49 N 1102—Shipping weight 5 lbs. 12 oz. $3.59

New Sewing Kit—make dolly a complete outfit

Ideal for all little girls who want to learn to sew. Fascinating, entertaining . . . easy, too, to make dolly a complete wardrobe. Kit contains everything she'll need. 7½-inch plastic doll. Pretty materials, cute patterns for an entire outfit. Metal scissors, needle, thimble and 4 bobbins of thread; buttons, rick rack in assorted colors. Packed in 11¾x18¼x2½-inch carrying case with snap lock and handle. **$1.79**

49 N 1235—Shipping weight 2 lbs. $1.79

Special De luxe
TOY SEWING MACHINE
Sews neat, even chain stitch . . makes fine seams

- De luxe model has felt pads on bottom to protect the surface of your table.
- Has two sturdy metal clamps . . holds the machine more securely . . it can't slip
- Safe, too! Body completely housed . . precision built . . . no exposed moving parts
- Scientifically built of heavy-gauge steel . . . handsome baked-on enamel finish

Finest in appearance, superb in performance . . . superior in every way. Your little seamstress will quickly learn to turn out a fine seam. She'll spend many busy hours making dresses for her dolls. Tension disc adjusts to fabric thickness for tight, even chain stitch. Uses No. 14 Torrington sewing machine needles. 8x4x6½ inches high.

49 N 1201—Instructions, needle, thread included. Shpg. wt. 3 lbs..............$5.49

$5⁴⁹

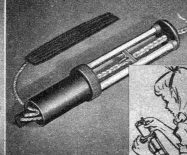

Sewing Machine

Economy-priced toy sewing machine to delight each little maid. Easy to operate . . . ideal for beginning seamstresses. Sews in chain stitch. Clamp holds machine firmly to table. Tension disc adjusts to fabric thickness. Made of good-looking enameled metal. Size 7¾x4x7¾ inches. Sure to be on top of every little girl's Christmas list. **$2.59**

49 N 1203—Shpg. wt. 1 lb. 4 oz..$2.59

New Magic Knitter

Automatic knitting device. With a simple twist of the wrist, you can spin out knitted yarn that has a "professional" look. Make beanies, pot holders, scatter rugs, mittens now—*no practice necessary.* Of metallic plastic. Two safely concealed steel knitting machine needles. Yarn included. Ideal for young and old alike. **$1.05**

49 N 1241—Shpg. wt. 6 oz...$1.05

Miniature Electric Organ

Sounds just like a big organ with its deep, full tone. Scientifically designed reeds respond with perfectly-pitched tone to the lightest touch. 25 keys—15 white, 10 black—play 2 full chromatic octaves . . single tones or chords. Smooth finish plastic case 11½x6½x5½ in. For 110–120-volt AC only. UL approved. Cord attached. Song folio incl. On-off switch.

79 N 0563—Shipping weight 7 lbs.....$17.95

$17.95

Electric Player Organ

NEW! No skill needed. Just turn switch . . it plays rich, mellow organ tones with rolls similar to those used in mechanical pianos. Has range of 2 chromatic octaves. Comes with 3 rolls, each with 3 songs, including old favorites, popular and religious music. Sturdily built. Bright red plastic case about 13x9x8 in. For 110–115-volt AC only. UL Approved.

79 N 0534—Shipping weight 10 lbs...$17.95

$17.95

Insert roll with 2 fingers; automatic re-roll. Off and On switch.

NEW! 11-inch Snare Drum

Here's just the gift for the youngster with rhythm in his system. He'll love beating time on this big 11-inch snare drum. It has two strong cloth heads, convenient neck cord for carrying, 2 drumsticks. Metal shell is lithographed in bright red, green, blue, white diamond design.

49 N 589—Shipping weight 2 lbs..........89c

89c

Musical Storybook

A musical toy that will keep youngsters happy for many hours. They love to look at the colorful pictures of "The Farmer in the Dell", as the pages are turned and the book's song is played. Ideal for children whether they read or not. Size 7x1x5 in.

49 N 527—Shpg. wt. each 10 oz.......89c

89c

NEW! Music-maker Man

Action! Surprise! And plenty of music! Colorful organ grinder moves his head and shoulders while he and the children play a gay tune on the Hurdy Gurdy together. Then, surprise! Up jumps the bell-ringing Jocko. Brightly lithographed. *Size 10¾x5⅞x5 in.*

49 N 521—Shpg. wt. 1 lb. 4 oz........$1.79

$1.79

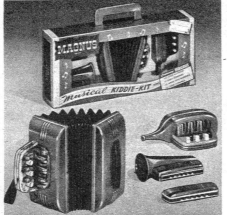

NEW! Musical Kiddie Kit

The perfect gift for the versatile youngster. It's a kit complete with 4 different plastic instruments. The bright colored "travel bag" holds a toy accordion, a keymonica, a horn harmonica, and a harmonica. A wide choice of musical toys for the child who likes variety . . . and so convenient to carry in their colorful carrying case.

49 N 599—Shpg. wt. 1 lb........$2.69

$2.69

DISCOVER HIDDEN TALENT WITH MUSICAL TOYS THAT CAN ACTUALLY BE PLAYED

Electric Toy Phonographs . . Records

[A] **Electric Toy Phonograph.** A real acoustic phonograph built just for children. Self-starting induction motor has on-off switch. Aluminum diaphragm gives rich, clear tones. Plays up to 12-in. 78 rpm. records. 2 packages of needles included—for soft or loud playing. Extra-strong pressed steel body, 13x8x7 in. Baked-on enamel finish. For 110-volt 60-cycle AC.
79 N 0577—UL Approved. Record not incl. Shpg. wt. 6 lbs.....$8.79 **$8.79**

[B] **Our BEST—Portable Electric Phonograph . .** with balanced tone arm and NEW built-in tone chamber for clearer tone. Youngsters . . even teen-agers . . thrill to this clear-voiced acoustic-type phonograph. Good-looking case of vivid red imitation leather inside and out. Sturdy wood frame has straight lock joint corners, reinforced inside. Outer edges all rounded smooth. Self-starting electric motor; on-off switch. Plays up to 12-in. 78 rpm records. 2 pkgs. of needles included—for soft or loud playing. About 13x11x5⅝ in. Plastic handle, metal lock, hinges. 5-ft. cord attached. For 110–120-volt, 60-cycle AC only.
79 N 0552—UL Approved. Record not included. Shpg. wt. 9 lbs.$11.79 **$11.79**

[C] **Children's Records—Nursery songs, Christmas songs.** Each assortment contains four 7-inch records (8 playing sides) of fine quality, sturdy plastic—almost unbreakable. Fine reproduction, minimum surface noise. **69c Set of 4**
49 N 601—Nursery Songs. Old King Cole, Humpty Dumpty, Jack and Jill, 3 Blind Mice, 15 other favorites. Shpg. wt. 11 oz...........Set of 4, 69c
49 N 602—Christmas Songs. Silent Night, Adeste Fidelis, Little Town of Bethlehem, Jingle Bells, 5 others. Shpg. wt. 11 oz..........Set of 4, 69c

Musical Toys You Can Really Play

[D] **8-key Xylophone.** Has extra pleasing tone because of its metal tone chamber. Heavy metal tone bars cushioned on felt. Enameled case has lyre-shaped ends. 2 mallets—rubber for mellow tones, wood for sparkle. About 12½ in. long.
49 N 505—Instructions included. Shipping weight 2 lbs. 14 oz.....$2.49 **$2.49**

[E] **Cowboy Ge-tar.** Anyone can play this Ge-tar because it plays 2 ways. Turn the crank for a real western song or play with the pick. Sturdy plastic with western design, cord.
49 N 569—About 13¾x4½ inches. Shipping weight 8 ounces.....$1.29 **$1.29**

[F] **Toy Piano-key Accordion.** Many hours of musical fun. Made of colorful, glossy finished plastic. Plastic coated bellows. 16 tuned reeds produce 8 full notes with rich mellow tone. 8 plastic keys really work. Songs played by numbers.
49 N 593—Instructions included. Shipping weight 1 lb. 8 oz.....$2.98 **$2.98**

[G] **Toy Finger Button Accordion.** Precision built for real musical value. Full, resonant tone. 20 carefully tuned plastic reeds. 10 quick-acting plastic buttons. Plastic case; pyroxylin-coated bellows. Size: 4x4½x8½ in. Plays in key of C.
49 N 520—Instructions included. Shpg. wt. 1 lb. 4 oz............$3.39 **$3.39**

[H] **3-drum Trap Set.** Beat out peppy rhythms. Ivory-color metal shells, red rims. 16-in. bass drum has steel foot beater; front head has hillbilly design. Drummer side, 6¼-in. snare and tom-tom have cloth heads. "T" holds triangle, cymbal. 2 nickel-plated bells. Two 8-in. drum sticks. Easy to set up.
79 N 0566—Instructions included. Shipping weight 5 pounds.....$2.69 **$2.69**

Toy Pianos that make real music

[J] **8-key Piano.** True pitch, pleasing tone. Feather-touch, standard width keys prepare youngsters for big pianos. Sturdy metal body, no sharp edges. Turned wood legs, removable music stand. Bright enamel finish. About 10⅞x8⅜ in.
49 N 506—16-page music book included. Shpg. wt. 2 lbs.........$1.98 **$1.98**

[K] **NEW 17-key Toy Piano.** All wood construction. Heavy masonite presdwood top, bottom; enameled red. 10 white, 7 black plastic keys have positive key action, play easily.
49 N 597—Size 11¼x9¾x5 in. Shipping weight 3 lbs. 8 oz.....$3.29 **$3.29**

[L] **NEW 29-key Table Model Baby Grand Piano.** Just like concert pianos . . sized for youngsters. Sturdy wood, glossy mahogany finish. Special key action for easy playing. 17 white keys, 12 black keys of long-wearing plastic.
79 N 0598L-About 18¼x18x10½ in. Shipping weight 13 lbs.....$8.98 **$8.98**

[M] **New! 36-key De Luxe Spinet with Stool.** Finest quality; develops real musical talent. Designed just like full-sized spinet with high gloss mahogany finish. Has 36 plastic keys including sharps and flats. Key action is regulated for smooth, responsive touch. Measures 21⅞x16½x22¾ in. Matching stool, 14½x7¼x10¼ in. A gift your child will treasure many years.
79 N M555—Shipped freight or express. Shpg. wt. 36 lbs.....$23.69 **$23.69**

A Electric Phonograph $8.79

C Nursery, Christmas Records 4 for 69c

THIS CHRISTMAS GIVE YOUR CHILD

Musical Toys

HELP STIMULATE HIS INTEREST IN MUSIC

B Electric Portable $11.79

H 3-drum Trap Set $2.69

D 8-key Xylophone $2.49

E Cowboy Ge-tar $1.29

F Toy Piano Accordion $2.98

G Toy Accordion $3.39

J 8-key Piano $1.98

K 17-key Piano $3.29

L 29-key Baby Grand $8.98

M 36-key Deluxe Spinet $23.69

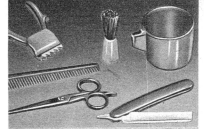

Toy Barber Shop Set

Every little boy likes to "make believe" and this set will make him a first-class "barber" in one easy lesson. 6-pc. set of durable, pliable plastic. 6-inch scissors, play razor, clippers (do not cut), comb, brush, mug. **$1.08**
49 N 1841—Shpg. wt. 6 oz...... $1.08

Popular Joke Assortment

Complete practical joker kit provides lots of fun for everyone. Includes dribble water glass, snow storm tablets, economical teaspoon, ink bottle and ink spot, suction cup joke, magic soap, hot toothpicks, bitter "cigs," dummy matches and others. 12 tricks in all. **$1.79**
49 N 1945—Shpg. wt. 1 lb. 2 oz.. $1.79

Walt Disney Puzzles

Set of 3 brilliantly-colored puzzles showing favorite Disney characters: Three Little Pigs, Mickey Mouse, and Snow White. Over 400 pieces per puzzle. Each puzzle 19x14 inches. **83c** Set of 3
49 N 1707—Shpg. wt. 1 lb. 12 oz.. 83c

It's fun to "treat" little playmates with this equipment

Play Kit for Make-believe Doctors

More realistic than ever .. because the bandage strips and adhesive tape included are genuine .. just like doctors use. Kit includes 12 bandage strips; adhesive roll, ½-inch x 1 yard; Kleenex; gauze pads; stethoscope that really works; plastic microscope; hypo needle; ear tester; eyeglass frames; thermometer; play watch; head reflector; reflex hammer; medicine spoon; intercom system with talking tape—plus accessories as signs, shingle, diploma and prescription blanks. Shpg. wt. 1 lb. 8 oz. **$1 59** Complete
49 N 1711—Incl. cardboard carrying case, 9x14 inches. $1.59

Play Kit for Make-believe Nurses

Kit now includes 12 real bandage strips and genuine adhesive roll, ½ inch x 1 yard .. just like nurses use in hospitals. 24 Kleenex tissues, 2 gauze pads, apron, stethoscope, eyeglass frames, thermometer, play watch, comb, sterilizing pan, soap, hypo needle, ear tester, medicine spoon, play scissors. Accessories include shingle, eye chart, diploma, health certificate, needed for efficient nursing. Complete in cardboard carrying case, 9x14 inches, with metal snap lock and handle. **$1 59**
49 N 1712—Shipping weight 1 pound 8 oz.......... $1.59

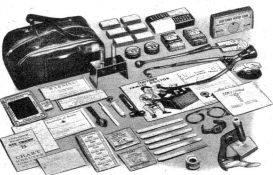

De Luxe Doctor Kit in zipper bag

Little doctors are proud to make "calls" with this professional-looking kit. Zip bag of black pliable plastic contains all the items in 49 N 1711 (above) plus 2 ointment cans, test tubes with stand, arm band, fluoroscope and films, pressure gauge, pill boxes. **$2.85**
49 N 1722—Kit 5½x8½x4 in. Shpg. wt. 1 lb. 6 oz..... $2.85

De Luxe Kit for Visiting Nurses

For efficient little nurses .. a handy zip bag with shoulder strap .. of red pliable plastic. Includes all items in 49 N 1712 (above) plus larger stethoscope that carries sound, fluoroscope, film, pressure gauge, bottle, nipple, intercom system, pill boxes. **$2.85**
49 N 1723—Kit 3x4x9½ in. Shpg. wt. 1 lb. 6 oz....... $2.85

Four Scenic Adult Puzzles

Brazil, Mt. Etna, Waikiki Beach, Statue of Liberty, each 17x11 in. Over 300 pieces each. Shipping weight 2 pounds. **98c**
49 N 1706 ....Set of 4, 98c

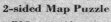

2-sided Map Puzzle

Map of U.S. on one side, world map on other. Durable Tekwood (3-ply fiberboard, wood center). Colorfully lithographed. 24x14 inches. Shipping weight 1 lb. 8 oz. **$1.29**
49 N 1889 ....$1.29

8-piece Lead Cowboy Outfit

Children love to play "cowboy." Five standing cowboys, 2¼ in. high; others in proportion. Two crawling; one 2-gun kneeling cowboy. Hand decorated .. made in England. Shipping weight 14 ounces. **79c**
49 N 5973 ....8-piece set 79c

8-piece Lead Indian Set

Colorful Indian band. Six standing Indians, in various poses, each 2¼ inches high; others in proportion. One kneeling; one crawling. Hand-decorated .. made in England. Shipping weight 14 ounces. **79c**
49 N 5972 ....8-piece set 79c

"Punch Me" Toy

Knock him down, he bounces right up again .. floats upright in water

Punch him .. knock him down .. he bobs right back with a great big smile. Strong vinyl plastic with electrically welded seams. Weighted base, so he can't stay down. Easy to inflate by mouth. Inflating stem tucks under flap .. needs no tying. Gay water-resistant colors. Floats upright. About 23 in. high, inflated.

$1.30

49 N 2525—Shpg. wt. 1 lb. 6 oz........ $1.30

Funny-face Juggle Head

Loads of laughs for everyone . . . adults will enjoy it, too. 20 colored plastic features attach magnetically to molded plastic head . . to make many amusing faces. Includes sets of rolling eyes; noses; ears; mustaches; paper cutouts of clothing; hats; bow tie; etc.

$1.79

49 N 1920—Shpg. wt. 1 lb. 2 oz......... $1.79

Tots' Inlay Picture Puzzles

[A] Mother Goose. Easy-to-assemble fiberboard pieces fit into border that holds puzzle. Each puzzle 8½x5½ in. Peter Pumpkin, Simple Simon, Mary and Lamb, etc., gaily colored.

89c set

49 N 4832—Set of 8   Shpg. wt. 2 lbs... 89c

[B] Set of 4 Furry Inlaid Puzzles, each 12½x9½ in. Red Riding Hood, Jack in Box, etc. Flocked bright colors, on cardboard.

$1.15 set

49 N 4829—Shpg. wt. 2 lbs. 12 oz... Set $1.15

HOURS OF FUN
The Toy
MAKES 54 MODELS

Build a real "play-in" size house, airplane, canopy... take it apart, put it together .. a toy for endless fun

$3.19

Large enough to play in and around .. children can assemble it
Sensational assembly toy opens up a whole new world of play

A PROVEN SUCCESS! IT'S SO BIG! SO DIFFERENT! Builds a house, an airplane, a tent .. almost anything a child's imagination can dream up. Tots love to play inside large structures . . remember the fascination of old boxes and crates? Now, with these colorful panels and connecting pieces, THE TOY enables children to satisfy their desire for king-size structures.

THE TOY consists of extra-heavy kraft paper panels, in assorted bright colors, and coated with water-resistant plastic. Included are 4 panels, each 29 in. square; 4 panels, each 29 in. triangular; more than the necessary number of dowels for connecting and bracing the panels, and a supply of pliable connectors. It's easy to assemble, no tools needed. Easy to take apart .. stores in compact container. Illustrated instruction sheet shows some of the many toys that can be made. Older boys and girls will find THE TOY ideal for party decorations, floats, festivals.

THE TOY is terrific! It gives such a lot of play value for so little money. Give your child this exciting, versatile toy .. for year around fun and fascination.

79 N 01942—Shipping weight 3 pounds........... $3.19

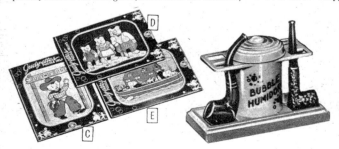

Judyette Inlay Puzzles

Large pieces fit in 5/16-inch thick board with back to hold puzzles. Each puzzle is 8½x11½ inches, made of sturdy hard-to-bend Tekwood and Masonite Presdwood. Shpg. wt. 1 lb. 2 oz.

[C] 49 N 4930—Cowboy.......... 89c
[D] 49 N 4931—Three Bears.......... 89c
[E] 49 N 4933—Noah's Ark.......... 89c

Plastic Bubble Pipe Set

It's fun to blow soap bubbles with this grown-up looking set. Set of two pipes (3¾ inches long), humidor to hold bubble solution, pipe rack. 2¾x5½x3½ inches high. All of plastic.

59c

49 N 5069—Shpg. wt. 8 oz..... 59c

18-Balloon Assortment

Roy Rogers or Dale Evans motif on six, twelve others plain. Varied sizes and shapes. Some inflate to 4 in. diameter, some to 18 in. long.

55c

49 N 5018—Shpg. wt. 8 oz..... 55c

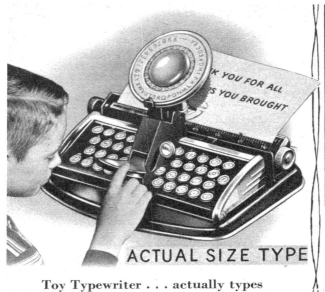

ACTUAL SIZE TYPE

Toy Typewriter . . . actually types

Has 40-character dial with alphabet, numbers, punctuation marks. Dummy keyboard. Carriage, moved by lever, is 11¼ in. wide . . . takes up to 8½-in. wide paper. Line spacer, plastic roller knobs. 6⅝ in. high, to top of dial. Self-inking rolls. Develops word-interest and spelling ability. **$3.69**

49 N 1915M—2 ink rolls included! Shpg. wt. 2 lbs. 6 oz. . . . $3.69
49 N 1916M—Ink Roll Refill. Shipping weight 1 ounce . . . 14c

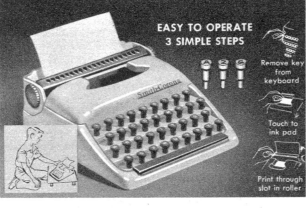

EASY TO OPERATE 3 SIMPLE STEPS

Remove key from keyboard
Touch to ink pad
Print through slot in roller

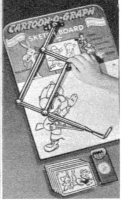

Brand New! Stamp Pad "Typewriter"

Youngsters will spend many busy hours writing to their friends on this new printing set. Molded in plastic to look just like a Smith-Corona typewriter. Paper rolls around roller just like big typewriter. Young "typists" just take a letter from the keyboard . . touch it to the built-in ink pad, and print through the slot in the roller. Child can always see what has been printed! Package makes portable case. A wonderful Christmas surprise for your child. **$1.79**

49 N 1710—7x8x2½ inches overall. Shpg. wt. 1 lb. 4 oz. $1.79

Cartoon-O-Graph

Enlarges cartoons and pictures *exactly!* Develops drawing skill. 8 cartoons, pencil, thumb tacks, sketch pad, crayons included. Metal enlarging arm. 19x14 inches overall. **$1.79**

49N1901–Wt. 2 lbs. 14oz $1.79

STIMULATE YOUNG MINDS WITH Educational Toys INSTRUCTIVE . . LOTS OF FUN

Toy Adding Machine..adds to 9999

Youngsters enjoy playing store or bookkeeper with their own adding machine. Helps them learn to add. Older children can use it to check homework . . adults to help balance accounts. Takes 4-column figures; adds accurately up to 9999. Sturdy metal construction; enamel finish. Order your adding machine today. **$1.75**

49 N 1810—9x6x4 in. high. Shpg. wt. 1 lb. 9 oz. $1.75

Roy Rogers Modeling Clay Set

Over one pound of modeling clay in six different colors. Youngsters can design their own figures or use the three tin molds; four plastic impression stamps. Set also includes wood rolling pin, pointed stick, spatula and 3 stencil cards with 3 cutouts. Lots of fun with this big modeling set . . . order today. **92c**

49 N 1724—Shipping weight 2 pounds 6 ounces 92c

Chalk and Crayon Slate Set

Three-in-one set . . for writing, drawing, coloring. *Natural slate*, wood frame drawing board, black on one side for chalk, white on other side for crayons. Set includes 14 pieces of chalk, 8 crayons, 3 stencil cards with 9 animal cutouts, blackboard eraser, 12 coloring pictures. 10⅛x7½-inch board. **98c**

49 N 1701—Shpg. wt. 2 lbs. 8 oz. 98c

Happi-Time Paint Sets develop creative ability

159-piece set has 26 wood tubs of paint, 46 paint tablets, 6 bottles poster paints . . all in assorted colors. Brush, 2 water pans, 16 crayons, palette, color chart, 10 stencils, 50 pictures to color. Box 20x13 in. A big set for a big Christmas surprise. **$1.98**

49 N 1732—Shpg. wt. 3 lbs. 4 oz. $1.98

72-piece set . . everything the young artist needs. Trace, paint color. Set has metal tray with 21 paints, 15 paint tablets, 4 plastic animal paint cups. Also brush, 4-section mixing pan, 6 crayons, 6 pictures to color, tracing paper, color chart, 4 stencil cards with 12 animal cutouts. Hinged-carrying case 15x8¾ inches. **98c**

49 N 1703—Shpg. wt. 1 lb. 7 oz. 98c

Molding, Coloring Set

Make your own models of Tom Corbett, Roger and Astro . . . famous space cadets. Set includes 5 rubber molds of Tom, Roger, Astro, a space control board and space respirator; 4 paint tabs, paint brush, ½ lb. molding powder, wood spatula, talcum powder and instructions. Models shown not included. **$1.79**

49 N 1714—Shpg. wt. 2 lbs. $1.79

Frontier Molding Set

Make up a real western drama . . . then mold your own figures to act it out. Set includes 5 rubber molds of Hero Cowboy, Badman, Lady hostage, Indian, Horse. Also 4 paint tabs, brush, talcum powder, molding powder. Easy-to-follow instructions for molding and painting. Models shown not included. **$1.79**

49 N 1715—Shpg. wt. 2 lbs. $1.79

The "Little Homemaker" had a lot to choose from in the 1953 Wishbook, but Gals of the Golden West preferred the Cowgirl's skirt and vest set, made from "suede-like cotton." She had to make do with Roy Rogers or Gene Autry six-guns, but there was a selection of Dale Evans watches; and she could drive around in a miniature version of Roy and Dale's jeep Nellybelle.

Girls in a more fairy-tale frame of mind might prefer the official Disney Snow White or Cinderella watches (the latter came in a "glass slipper"). Or they might have fun with Howdy Doody or Peter Pan marionettes.

The Marx Happi Time Farm playset was also a popular item. It was a real bargain, too, with its large lithographed metal barn and 100 pieces including animals, tools, tractors and farm family. Auburn Rubber Toys also offered an attractive farm set -- no barn, but detailed figures, animals and vehicles. It's easy to see how girls might have preferred playsets like these -- running a farm is hard work -- but it's got to be better than ironing all the time.

Sears Christmas
Wishbook
1953

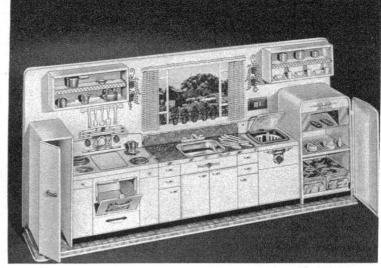

NEW! Little Girl's Vanity Set

$449

Give your daughter a vanity table all her very own . . . where she can play "grown-up" to her heart's content. Wood frame and stool, Masonite Presdwood kidney shaped top . . . 20½x23½x12¾ in. Printed plastic skirt. Sturdy vanity stool 9¾x9x5½ in. Mirror 9x6¾ in. Set includes perfume bottle, plastic powder case, mirror, comb, compact, brush, powder, lipstick, coin purse, memo pad and pencil, and many others. Shipped partly assembled.
79 N 01281—Shpg. wt. 7 lbs. $4.49

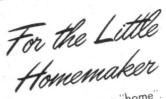

For the Little Homemaker

She'll keep her own "home" . . . cooking, sewing, taking care of baby

FOR A MERRY CHRISTMAS

NEW! Modern Kitchen

All perfect miniatures with "real" working parts . . includes dishes. **$298**

A complete kitchen with all appliances for little homemakers. Sturdy steel construction with attractive lithographed design depicting kitchen window, radio, etc. Includes refrigerator, washing machine, sink, stove, broom closet and wall cabinets with miniature plastic accessories; griddle, pressure cooker, washing tub, ice cube trays, etc. Includes dishes, tableware for three. 25½x5¼x11¾ in. high. Shipped partly assembled.
79 N 01105—Shpg. wt. 6 lbs. $2.98

NEW! 32-pc. Formula Set

Everything for doll feeding. Contains sterilizer and cover in all-metal, blue enamel finish; rust resistant bottle rack; 6 Evenflo baby bottles, nipples, discs, caps; blue plastic funnel, formula cup, spoon; bottle brush; bottle cleanser. **$1.79**
49 N 1268—Shpg. wt. 2 lbs. $1.79

Metal Loom Weaving Set

Keep your little girl happily busy weaving hot pan holders, coasters and other useful items with this handy kit. She'll find it's easy to weave. Metal loom adjusts from 4 to 8 in. square or rectangle. 2 yarn skeins, loopers, hook, needle. **89c**
49 N 1250—Shpg. wt. 1 lb. 7 oz. 89c

NEW! 19-pc. Utensil Set

Gleaming metal set with plastic handles. Includes sauce pan, frying pan, grinder, grater, 2 pie plates, 2 spoons, 2 strainers, potato masher, egg beater, mixing spoon, potato peeler, ladle, turner, spatula, 2 mixing bowls. **$1.79**
49 N 933—Shpg. wt. 1 lb. $1.79

"Silverware" Set

New . . designed like Mother's real silver. Durable plastic with metalized finish to look real. 4 each of knives, forks, spoons, plus pie server, butter knife, salt and pepper shakers. In cardboard hinged box with window fronts. 15x10x1¼ in. **89c**
49 N 834—Shpg. wt. 8 oz. 89c

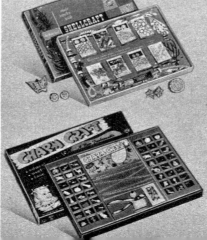

Stitch a Story

Embroidery kit for the young "Miss." It's fun . . practical. Toy today, treasured possession tomorrow. With needle, thimble, thread, scissors, 4 frames and easy-to-embroider subjects. **$1.85**
49 N 1282—Shpg. wt. 1 lb. $1.85

NEW! "Jewelry" Chest

Sixteen sparkling pieces of "make-believe" jewelry for every costume . . bracelets, earrings, pendants, rings and clips. Metalized finish, 8 gold color, 8 silver color. Cardboard jewelry chest with drawer. 7x7x2¾ in. A bright jewelry accent for every outfit. **89c**
49 N 1269—Shpg. wt. 10 oz. 89c

Shellcraft Set

$1.85 For fun . . for gifts . . an old craft made easy. Turn seashells into eye-catching colored earrings and brooches. Eight exciting projects . . shells for each packed separately. Set includes easy-to-follow instructions, pictures of finished items and tube of cement.
49 N 1210—Shpg. wt. 14 oz. . . . $1.85

Charm Craft Jewelry Kit

$1.79 Hours of fun! Forty-eight colored plastic beads, charms, clasps, plus jewelry chain, pliers, thread for necklaces, bracelets, earrings, lapel pins and other jewelry items. Develops child's handicraft skill . . . lets her make her own gifts. Attractive 14½x11½-in. box. Instructions included.
49 N 1207—Shpg. wt. 1 lb. 12 oz. $1.79

Roy Rogers
[A]
With 10-in. Pistols $8⁷⁹
Official Holster Set

[B]
With 12-in. Pistols $9⁸⁵
Our finest Six-Shooter Set

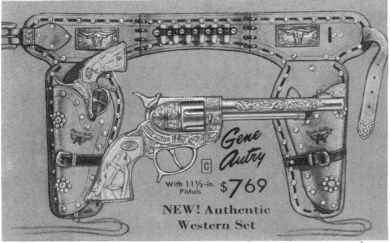

Gene Autry
[C]
With 11½-in. Pistols $7⁶⁹
NEW! Authentic Western Set

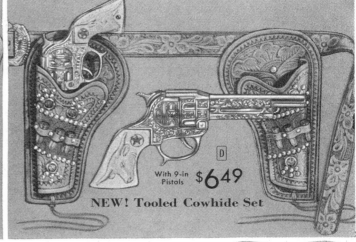

[D]
With 9-in Pistols $6⁴⁹
NEW! Tooled Cowhide Set

$1.98 $4.98 $2.49

Holsters, guns not included

[E]
With 9-in. Pistols $4⁸⁹

Roy Rogers
[F]
With 10-in. Pistols $3⁹⁵

Notice: Residents of Col., Del., D.C., Idaho, Iowa, Miss., N.J., N. Mex., Ohio, Wash. order non-firing guns.

[H]
Single Holster set $1³⁵

[G]
With 8¼-in. Pistols $2⁸⁹

Economy Chap Set. Durable 2-tone suede-like cotton with fancy fringe trim. Steerhead concha. Adjustable cotton belt; leg straps in back. Kerchief included.
49N2779-Small(age3-5). Waist sizes 18-30 in.
49N2780-Medium (age 6-9). Waist sizes 20-33 in.
49N2781—Large (age 10-12). Waist sizes from 22 to 35 inches. Shipping weight each 1 lb. . . Each **$1.98**

Leather Chap Set. Split cowhide chap and vest. Colorful fancy trim. Leather belt; Western buckle. Cotton leg straps on back. Chrome studs, and sunrise conchas. Kerchief included.
49N2810—Small (age 3-5). Waist sizes 18-30 in.
49N2811—Med. (age 6-9). Waist sizes 20-33 in.
49N2812-Large (age 10-12). Waist sizes 22-35 in. Shipping wt. ea. 1 lb. 12 oz. .Each **$4.98**

Cowgirl's Skirt and Vest Set. Attractive suede-like cotton. Drawstring adjusts skirt. Suede fringe on vest and skirt. Western conchas on skirt. Kerchief included.
49N2715—Small (ages 3, 4, and 5).
49N2716—Medium (ages 6, 7, 8, and 9).
49N2724—Large (ages 10, 11, and 12). Shpg. wt. each 1 lb. . . . . Each **$2.49**

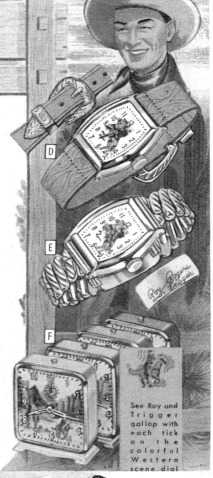

Roy Rogers

DOUBLE R BAR RANCH

DALE EVANS
Queen of the West

Good-looking "Rodeo" Watches for Girls . . in Dial Styling that's Brand-New this season!

[A] **Dale Evans and Pal,** her spirited Western horse, pictured on the dial of this small, thin watch! Chrome-plated case has stainless steel back. Non-shatter crystal. Dependable Ingraham movement. Silver-color metal buckle and tip. **$4.95**
4 N 1882E—With Texas-style "saddle tooled" genuine leather strap.... $4.95

[B] **All-new model for this book.** Case is 10-karat rolled gold plate, with stainless steel back. Dale Evans and Pal pictured on the dial . . and it's an extra-thin watch. Has non-shatter crystal and dependable Ingraham movement. **$5.95**
4 N 1884E—With Texas-style "saddle tooled" genuine leather strap.... $5.95

[C] **Our finest Dale Evans watch!** Shows Dale Evans and Pal, her Western horse, on the handsomely colored dial. Dependable Ingraham movement. Highly-polished chrome-plated case is extra-thin; has stainless steel back. Non-shatter crystal. **$6.95**
4 N 1883E—Has all stainless steel expansion band in *cactus flower* motif; right size for small wrists...... $6.95

ROY ROGERS
King of the Cowboys

Handsome *He-Man* "Rodeo" Watches for Boys . . Extra-Thin . . Roy and Trigger on the Dials

[D] **Roy Rogers and Trigger,** his golden palomino horse, are pictured on the dial in exciting colors. Sturdy *made-to-last* chrome-plated case; stainless steel back. Non-shatter crystal. Has dependable Ingraham movement. **$4.95**
4 N 1860E—Has Texas-style "saddle tooled" genuine leather strap.... $4.95

[E] **Our best Roy Rogers watch.** Roy and Trigger pictured in color on the dial. Highly polished chrome-plated case; stainless steel back. Non-shatter crystal. Dependable Ingraham movement. **$6.95**
4 N 1865E—Has small extra-thin case, movement. "Lariat Link" expansion band has stainless steel plate engraved with Roy's own signature...... $6.95

[F] **Roy Rogers "Movie" Alarm Clock** . . at cut price. Roy and Trigger gallop with each tick. Ingraham movement. Metal case; 4½ in. high. *Case Colors* Desert Sand (tan), pale Cactus Green, Sky Blue (light), or Dark Saddle Brown. Shpg. wt. 1 lb. 6 oz. Was $3.49 **$2.99**
4 N 7306E—State color wanted..... $2.99

See Roy and Trigger gallop with each tick on the colorful Western scene dial

Many More Youngsters' Watches in this catalog . . see index

Snow White for Girls $7.65
"Pretty as a picture" *Snow White* watch for girls. Dependable U. S. Time movement. Strap just right size for small wrists. Chrome-plated case, stainless back. Easel for standing up mirror. Seven dwarfs pictured on the "Magic Mirror" gift box.
4 N 1881E...................... $7.65

Cinderella for Girls $7.65
Thrilling *Cinderella* watch for girls . . with dainty plastic "glass slipper". Dial shows Cinderella dressed in blue for Prince Charming's ball. U. S. Time movement. Chrome-plated case; stainless back. Strap right size for small wrists.
4 N 1868E—With Disney gift box.. $7.65

Hopalong Cassidy

FOR A MERRY CHRISTMAS

Young America!
Watches, Field Glasses Featuring Famous-Name Radio and TV Stars!

Space Ranger

Space Cadet

Look, Fellows! Hoppy!
"Hopalong Cassidy" wrist watch with old "Two Gun" Hoppy's picture on the dial . . and "Good Luck from Hoppy" engraved on back of case! Small chrome-plated case; stainless steel back. Black leather Texas-style strap. **$7.65**
4 N 1866E—U. S. Time movement.. $7.65

"Hoppy" Field Glass!
"Hopalong Cassidy" 3-power field glass. Center focus. Official "Hoppy" insignia on metal frames. Artificial leather case; Vinyl neck strap. **$2.98**
4 N 6284E—Shpg. wt. 1 lb. Gift boxed.$2.98

Space Ranger Watch!
Rocky Jones, Space Ranger . . a watch colorfully designed to thrill youngsters. Dial pictures Rocky (dressed in space suit), famous space hero, and his space ship. Chrome-plated case; stainless back. With right-size genuine leather strap. **$3.95**
4 N 1915E—Ingraham movement.. $3.95

Space Cadet Watch!
Z-o-o-m! Tom Corbett, Space Cadet, with Polaris, his supersonic space ship, pictured on dial of this extra-thin watch. Genuine Tom Corbett leather strap—rocket ship and other interplanetary insignia pictured. Chrome-plated case; stainless back. **$4.95**
4 N 1916E—Has Ingraham movement.$4.95

Space Cadet Field Glass
Tom Corbett 3-power field glass. Official insignia on the metal barrels. Artificial leather case; strong vinyl neck strap. Non-glare *amber* lenses. **$2.98**
4 N 6285E—Shpg. wt. 1 lb. Gift boxed.$2.98

Watches (shpg. wt. ea. 4 oz.) on this page sent postpaid. Bands and straps specially made to fit small wrists. Watch and clock prices include 10% Fed. tax; field glasses, 20%. Watches shown ¾ actual size; all gift boxed.

$12⁹⁸

IMPORTANT:
All wheel toys
shipped partly
assembled to
save you money

$24⁸⁵ $2.50
Cash Down

Chain drive

$29⁹⁸ $3.00
Cash Down

Low Priced, slick-styled Auto

Has many features of higher priced autos . . . quick
turning, easy pedaling ball bearing drive. Heavy
gauge steel; seat pad. Ball bearing drive mechanism,
rear axle hanger. 8-in. double-disc steel wheels; ⅝-in.
rubber tires. Adjustable rubber pedals. Enameled
blue with white and silver color trim.
79 N 08910L—36x17 inches. Shpg. wt. 28 lbs......$12.98

NEW! Super Deluxe "Torpedo"

Ball bearing drive for easy pedaling, no dead centers,
provides smooth, constant drive action. New,
"FREE Steering." 8-in. double disc ball bearing
steel wheels; 1-in. rubber tires. Chrome-plated radi-
ator and trim. Plastic bulb-type horn. Heavy gauge
steel body. Enameled grey, red trim.
79 N 08934L—39x17 inches. Shpg. wt. 39 lbs.....$24.85

One-pc. Steel Body "Kidillac"

Has speedy, easy-to-operate chain drive that develops more power with less foot pressure. Ball bearings
on rear axle and pedal crank; 2-pc. pedals. Has
spare wheel, rear view mirror. 8-in. double disc
wheels; 1¼-in. rubber tires. Enameled chartreuse
with black, red and aluminum color trim.
79 N M8953—45x20 in. Shpg. wt. 51 lbs........$29.98

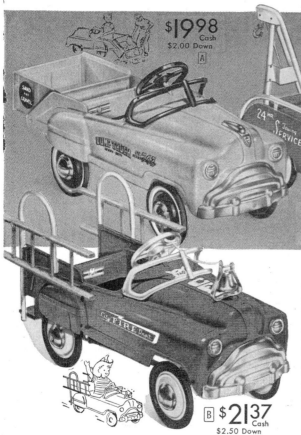

$19⁹⁸ $2.00
Cash Down
A

$19⁷⁹
Cash
$2.00 Down

$22⁹⁵
Cash
$2.50 Down

Roy Rogers

"NELLYBELLE"

B $21³⁷
Cash
$2.50 Down

NEW Realistic Tow Truck

Thrilling action . . . little mechanics speed to
the scene of the "accident" for repairs. Simple to operate self-locking winch raises or
lowers on genuine gears that work with professional smoothness. Has tool box on rear.
White enameled hand rails. Heavy gauge
steel throughout. Ball bearing rear axle and
push rods for easy riding. 7-inch double disc
wheels, ¾-inch tires. Two seat levels and 3
pedal adjustments. Heavy duty bumper. Enameled bright red with white trim.
79 N 08930L—47½ in. long. Wt. 33 lbs..$19.79

Roy Rogers' "Nellybelle"

An authentic reproduction of Roy's famous
jeep . . filled with play features children
can't resist. Tow hook on rear . . folding
windshield . . removable overhead rack . .
tail gate opens and closes . . gun port in front
. . realistic license plate. Lots of extra room.
Made of heavy gauge steel. Has smooth ball
bearing rear axle, push rods for easy pedaling. Seat and pedals adjustable. Big 10-in.
wheels have 1¼-in. semi-pneumatic tires.
Gun metal gray enamel finish; white trim.
79 N 08931L—40¾ in. long. Wt. 40 lbs...$22.95

NEW! Ball bearing Dump Truck

A Big dump box is easily dumped with steel handle at side of
driver's seat. Locking device holds box in carrying position.
Tail gate raises or lowers. New steering mechanism permits
shorter turns with little effort. Heavy gauge steel body and undergear. Smooth pedaling, no "dead center," ball bearing drive. 8-
inch double-disc ball bearing steel wheels, ⅝-inch rubber tires.
Enameled yellow; black and silver color trim.
79 N 08933L—47x17 inches overall. Shipping weight 36 lbs.....$19.98

Ladder Fire Truck . . room for two

B Full ball bearing wheels and driving mechanism for easy
pedaling without dead center. New "FREE steering" permits
tighter turns. Plenty of sitting or standing room. Has hand rails,
rear step and rear deck. Heavy gauge steel body, undergear. 8-in.
double disc steel wheels; ⅝-in. rubber tires. Fiber type seat pad.
Adjustable rubber pedals. Removable wooden ladders. Chrome-
plated bell. Enameled red; white and silver color trim.
79 N 08923L—47x17 inches overall. Shipping weight 37 lbs.....$21.37

NEW! "Hot-Rod" Racer for pint-sized Speed Drivers

Easy-to operate Chain Drive

Chain
drive

$19⁴⁵
Cash
$2.00 Down

Just like real hot-rods . . .
built to take all the rough,
bruising treatment your
youngsters can give. Heavy
gauge steel throughout. Has
simulated cut-out noise for
authentic engine action.
Easy-rolling ball bearings on
rear axle and pedal crank.
Speedy chain drive mechanism like bicycle. 2-piece rubber pedals. 10-inch artillery
wheels have big 1.75-inch
semi-pneumatic tires. En-
ameled orange; black, white
trim. 35 inches long. Shipping weight 38 lbs.
79 N 08950L........$19.45

*Orders of $20 or more can be purchased on Sears
Easy Terms . . . see page 369 for complete details*

Realistic Farm Sets

Complete equipment
Just like big farms

FOR A MERRY CHRISTMAS

Big NEW Farm Set with Barn, Silo. Now has over 100 pieces $4.99

Hoist plastic bales of hay

Litter carrier slides on rail

Rear view . . . stall for stock, big hayloft

Always something to do on this little farm . . . hundreds of chores to keep little farmers busy for months.

Big hipped-roof metal Barn. Realistically lithographed sheet steel. Edges turned for strength, safety. Open at back; animals can be put in stalls. Barn is 10¾ in. high, 9¼ in. wide, 13⅝ in. long. Has haylift and litter carrier that slides on rail.

Big 10-in. Silo of sturdy lithographed steel with plastic roof. 2 plastic cupolas. Plastic implements hitch to plastic tractor. Authentically detailed; everything a real farmer uses. Tractor, corn planter, plow, stone boat, spike-toothed harrow, hi-lift scoop, wagon, scraper. 55 colorful plastic farm animals, fowl, horses, cows, calves, colts, dogs, lambs, kids, little pigs, goats, sows, roosters, hens, ducks etc., plus 12 tiny birds. Horse 2⅜ in. high, others in proportion.

Plastic Milk Pick-up Platform: 3 milk cans, 11 sections of plastic interlocking white board fence; each section about 6 inches long.

Plastic Barn Accessories: Include feed bags, feedbox with movable cover, block and tackle with hook; litter carrier that slides along overhead rail, garbage can with lid, and many other farm "necessities." Implement and animal content may vary slightly. Easy-to-follow instructions.
79 N 05951—Shipping weight 5 pounds . . . . Complete set $4.99

12-Piece Set of Extra Animals and Trough for Stock Farm (not illustrated). All soft vinyl plastic. In variety of positions. Horses, cows, others.
49 N 5983—Shipping weight 10 ounces . . . . Set 87c

Implements hook to tractor

Hitch horses to implements

Roomy shed; doors open

17-piece Molded Rubber Farm Equipment Set

Perfectly scaled miniature farm implements add exciting realism to "play farming." All realistically molded rubber . . . a work-saving feature for Mom because they can't mar or scratch furniture. Washable too. Easy-rolling wheels. Two-horse team (3½ in. high); other pieces in proportion. Includes heavy duty tractor, farm wagon, manure spreader, and many others. All implements attach to either tractor or horses. Whiffle-tree attachment permits hitching team to implements without unharnessing horses. Packed in corrugated cardboard shed; shed doors open. Shipping weight 3 lbs.

$1.98 17-pc. set

49 N 5275—Complete 17-piece set $1.98

19-piece Animal Set

Get more fun out of your HAPPI-TIME farm and implement set. Add these detailed miniature animals and fowl. Soft, washable vinyl appropriately enameled. Practically unbreakable. Add to your farm set. Big 19-pc. Set includes colts (2½ in. high) sheep, pig, and many others. All stand on solid bases.

98c 19-pc. set

49 N 5239—Shpg. wt. 8 oz. . . . . 19-piece set 98c

"Color" Television. You can enjoy your own "color television" this year. Pull the lever and watch Donald Duck and three other Disney favorites on 4 separate action strips. Operates on long running keywind motor . . easy to wind. Set in plastic case 5¼ inches high. **$1.79**
49 N 5522—Shpg. wt. 1 lb. 8 oz.....$1.79

Kiddy Projector. Give the fascination of a real projector. Plastic; about 4¾ in. high. Easy for a child to use. One 20-picture color comic film disc included; no threading or rewinding. Easy-to-focus lens. Cardboard box converts to screen. 7 watt lamp, 6-ft. cord. **$2.59**
49 N 5550—UL approved. 110–120 volt AC-DC. Wt. 2 lbs. $2.59
49 N 5549—4 film discs; 3 black and white, 1 color. Red Riding Hood, 3 Bears, Sinbad, Lion & Mouse. Wt. 2 oz....Set of 4 89c

Flash Camera. Takes 12 clear 2¼x2¼-in. pictures on 620 film. Plastic case and sight. Film, 2 penlight batteries, bulb not included. (See index for No. 5 bulbs.) **$3.98**
49 N 5525—Wt. 1 lb...$3.98

3-power Binoculars. Bring distant objects close. Ground lenses. Adjustable focus and eye separation. Made of metal and plastic. 4¾x5 inches. 20% Fed. Tax included. **$2.79**
49 N 5072E—Wt. 1 lb...$2.79

NEW 5-piece Metal and Plastic Set

All with rubber wheels. **Hook and Ladder.** Ladder moves up and down and complete circle. 11 in. long. **Auto Transport** with 4 plastic cars. Detachable trailer. 10 in. long. **Moving Van:** detachable trailer swivels. 8¾ in. long. **Steam Shovel Truck:** crank-operated; 8½ in. long. **TV Repair Truck.** 5 in. long. **$1.79**
49 N 5265—Shpg. wt. 2 lbs. 4 oz.................$1.79

NEW Fix-It Modern Convertible

• Hood opens . . reveals plastic motor
• Fill battery with water, removable oil gauge **$2.79**
Mechanical moppets can really go to work on this car! Jack car up, use wrench to remove wheels, repair and put back on. Rear luggage compartment opens, holds complete set of tools, spare tire, emergency gas can. 13 in. long.
49 N 5378—Brightly colored plastic. Shpg. wt. 2 lbs.....$2.79

Optically Ground Lens Bright, Clear Pictures

Famous 16 mm. Keystone Electric Moviegraph Projector. Easy to operate. Shows 16x12-in. pictures, 7 ft. from screen. UL approved constant speed fan-cooled electric motor for 110–120-volt, 60-cycle AC. Sturdy steel frame. Pleasing neutral finish. Complete with empty 400-foot capacity reel, "On-Off" switch, cord, plug. Big, 140-watt tubular projection lamp in vented housing. 14 inches high. Film not included. See index for films.
$22.75
Cash
$2.50 Down
79 N 05572—Shpg. wt. 10 lbs........$22.75

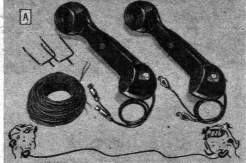

NEW Bomber . . Exploding Ship

"Fly" airplane over target, press release, bomb drops. If target is hit, battleship (with wheels) explodes into 8 parts. Easy to put battleship together again. 4-motor atom bomber has tricycle-type landing gear; 4 spinning propellers, wing spread 9 in. Durable plastic. Battleship molded of high impact plastic to withstand heavy bombing. Shpg. wt. 1 lb. **$1.79** Battleship 13 in. long.
49 N 5262—Battleship 13 in. long.........$1.79

NEW Walkie-Talkie

[A] You can talk and listen at the same time. Press button on one phone, other phone buzzes for incoming call. 50 feet double wire. 2 metal hangers included, can be screwed into post, tree, etc. to hold head set. Head set 8½ inches long. 2 batteries incl. **$5.79**
49 N 5399—Shpg. wt. 2 lbs.....$5.79

Pliable Tools

[B] Popular with Mom . . won't mar or scratch furniture. 7½-in. rubber saw. Flexible vinyl plastic: wrench, screwdriver, hammer, hatchet, pliers. Wood handles on hammer, hatchet; bright colors. **75c**
49 N 5310—Wt. 12 oz....75c

Jet Roller Coaster for exciting action

Different, fascinating action with the accent on high speed performance. Car is elevated to upper track by motor-driven lift arm. With breathtaking speed, it coasts down to lower track speeding to the top at the end; then reverses its direction, coasting underneath the tracks to be elevated again. Action repeated many times. Shipping weight 1 pound 8 ounces. **$1.45**
49 N 5848—Lithographed metal; keywind motor. 21 in. long.........$1.45

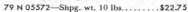

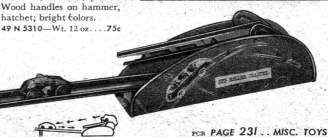

NEW! Livestock Hauler with Animals

Drop ramp at rear of trailer, drive herd in like a real farmer. Cab $2.39
snaps off easily from chassis, revealing dummy plastic motor, steering
wheel and seat; plastic cab. Lithographed metal trailer with dual rear wheels.
14 detailed, molded vinyl animals. Dummy air horns on top of cab. Figures include cows, horses, colts, and many others.
49 N 5641—Cab and trailer 17 in. long overall. Shpg. wt. 2 lbs. 8 oz. $2.39

NEW! Trick Action Bank

A barrel of fun, saving money! $1.79
Put any size U. S. coin in dog's
mouth; press lever, dog jumps through
hoop held by clown, drops coin in barrel. Heavy plastic. Overall 8⅞ in. long.
49N5330—Bright colors. Wt. 1 lb. 6 oz. $1.79

4 New Whirling Tops

Round and round they go . . 79c
a fascinating marvel of bright
whirling action. Set of 4: 3-in. bounc-
ing top, 3-in. whistling, 1¾-in. "snappy," 4-in. humming. Bright metal.
49 N 2583—Wt. 12 oz. Set of 4 . . . . . 79c

$2.79

Pirate Ship

Man the sails . . hoist the anchor!
We're off for pirate gold. Sail on
water . . pull it on land. Detailed
replica on wheels. Flies the authentic "Jolly Roger" flag. 6 ferocious
vinyl plastic pirates. Cannon shoots
mock cannon balls. Pirate plank,
dinghy with oars. Tough, brightly
colored plastic. 11 in. high.
49 N 5281—Shpg. wt. 1 lb. $2.79

"Ring 'N Buzz" Set
A direct line for fun

• 3 children can play at one time $4.69
• Rings . . buzzes . . dials click
Kiddies "buzz" with excitement to the buzz-
ing of this big switchboard. Just like the one
in Daddy's office, it has a clicking dial, attached receiver, 4 insert plugs, and 2 plastic
phones attached with snap back dials. 2
"Ring 'N Buzz" levers . . push, it buzzes,
pull, it rings. Yank cords from board just like
real operators . . plug snaps back into place.
Enameled metal board 4⅞x8x9⅝ in. high.
Uses standard flash light battery; battery included. Enough fun to keep 3 children happy,
and switchboard busy for hours.
49 N 5095—Shpg. wt. 3 lbs. $4.69

Simple one-piece hand control
operates mouth and body action

Fun for the entire family with these lifelike Marionettes. Simple one-
hand movement controls mouth and body action . . . real lifelike movement as you make them "dance", "walk", "talk." Costumes are authentically designed cotton with composition parts. Just follow the simple
instructions, and you, too, can skillfully operate these marionettes.
   TWO NEW favorites are added to your marionette collection this year.
From "Never Never Land" comes lovable PETER PAN and the villainous
CAPTAIN HOOK. Peter Pan is an authentic replica from his famous wide-
eyed expression to his colorful clothes. Captain Hook wears boots, plastic
hook, and a jaunty plumed hat. ALL WITH ONE-HAND CONTROL!

[A] Howdy Doody©—Wt. 1 lb. 4 oz.
   49 N 5161—16½ in. tall. . . $2.98
[B] Clarabell ©—14½ inches tall.
   49 N 5160—Wt. 1 lb. 4 oz. . $2.45
© Kagran

[C] Peter Pan—16½ inches tall.
   49 N 5093—Wt. 1 lb. 4 oz. . $2.45
[D] Captain Hook. 15 inches tall.
   49 N 5094—Wt. 1 lb. 4 oz. . $2.45

$2.79

Cash Register . . NEW Special Key

STURDY STEEL. More realistic than ever before. 14 keys: 12
show denominations, 1¢ to $1.00, 1 "No Sale." Press keys,
amount visible in window. Hit special key . . partitioned drawer
opens, bell rings. Play money included. Enamel finish.
49 N 5280—7¼ x6½ x7¼ in. Shpg. wt. 4 lbs. $2.79

3-coin Register Bank

[E] Deposit coins, bell rings. Registers nickels, dimes, quarters.
Computed dollar, cent totals visible. Locks when 25c is deposited.
Opens automatically at $10.00.
Rear slot for other coins, hole for
bills. Holds about $50.00. Enam-
eled heavy-gauge metal. 6x5x4½ in.
49 N 5349—Shpg. wt. 2 lbs. . . . $3.69

Now Reduced

[F] Musical Carrousel. Pull lever,
(self winding motor), release
. . . round and round she goes,
flags waving, merry tune tinkling.
Lithographed metal. 11x12½ in.
high. Shpg. wt. 5 lbs.
79 N 05794—Was $3.58. Now $2.98

[E] $3.69

[F] Was $3.58
Now $2.98

In addition to a staggering array of toy dishes, silverware, pots and pans, and baking goods, the 1954 Wishbook offered little girls an escape from the drudgery of housework. She could apply her makeup at a tiny vanity table, or sort out the booty in her jewelry case. She could even make her own costume jewelry with a set that promised to "keep small hands busy."

Some lucky girls found a giant 6 room colonial doll house under the tree that Christmas. This lithographed metal palace came with a full assortment of interior and patio furniture, as well as a slide, sand box, see-saw and wading pool for the baby of the house -- all for $5.98.

It is interesting to note the beginnings of a promotional campaign directed toward young girls that continues to this day. Aunt Jemima pastry products, made in scaled down boxes, were included in a set that allowed kids to bake just like Mommy — and hopefully buy the products in full size boxes when they grew up.

Sears Christmas
Wishbook

1954

Picture these beautiful skates under your tree . . J. C. HIGGINS Best Sidewalk Roller Skates—with longer-wearing *Quiet Wheels!*

$1.98

$3.19

$498

8 Ball Bearings Per Wheel

- Rubber shock absorbers on both trucks
- Toe Clamps curved to fit foot
- Long leather ankle strap with buckle

Eight steel ball bearings in each case-hardened steel wheel. Steel girder chassis shiny plated to fight rust. Reinforcing flanges on foot plates add extra strength. Rubber shock absorbers on front, rear trucks reduce vibration, improve steering action. Long leather ankle strap with buckle. Curved toe clamps shaped for right and left side, fit snugly without scuffing shoes. Skate size adjusts 7½ to 10½ inches. Skate key included.
6 N 2303—Shpg. wt. 3 lbs....... $1.98

16 Ball Bearings Per Wheel

- Rubber shock absorbers on all trucks
- Curved right and left toe clamps
- Heavy Duty 500 Mile Steel Wheels
- Ankle strap has sponge rubber pad

Heavy duty 500 mile wheels . . 16 ball bearings per wheel. Stronger steel girder chassis gives miles of extra wear. Foot-plate is beaded, has flanged sides for added strength. Shiny plated to fight rust. Rubber shock absorbers on front, rear trucks. Leather ankle strap has ¼-in. thick felt-backed sponge rubber pad across instep. Skate size adjusts 8 to 10¾-in. Key included.
6 N 2301—Shpg. wt. 4 lbs....... $3.19

Case hardened steel rims provide outer shell .. 16 double race ball bearings per wheel .. Neoprene rubber core absorbs noise

For Beginners to 7 years of age

Teach 'em how with J. C. HIGGINS Beginner's Roller Skates. Sleeve bearings in wheels do *not* build up dangerous speeds . . they're safer for youngsters to age 7. Child has plenty of fun with less chance of a fall. Steel wheels. Shiny plated steel girder chassis. Red leather toe strap, web ankle strap. Size adjusts 6½ to 8½ inches.
6 N 2361—Shipping weight 2 lbs........ $1.29

Our Laboratory tested 'Quiet Wheels' actually outwear standard steel wheels 4 to 1. These skates passed the 700 mile mark . . . still going strong. 16 ball bearings in each wheel. Inner cushion of Neoprene rubber cuts noise in half. Reduced vibration makes skating easier on young feet. Axle and housing resist wear because wheels roll free on ball bearings. Tubular steel frame. Brightly plated to resist rust.
Heavy duty steel wheel rims absorb sidewalk punishment. Working with rubber shock absorbers, they give the right side-slip on turns. Cowhide ankle strap has ¼-in. thick sponge rubber pad. Skate size adjusts 8 to 11 inches. Toe clamps.
6 N 2364—Quiet Wheel Roller Skates with Key. Shipping weight 6 pounds.........$4.98
6 N 2300—As above except has rugged blued steel rim wheels. Shipping weight 5 lbs... 4.39

Official Roller Derby Rink Skates

$15.95

Top grain, elk-tanned cowhide shoes. Sponge rubber padded 2-pc. shaped tongue. Built-in steel arch support. 10° Truck Action. Chrome-plated to resist rust. Double rubber shock absorbers. 16 ball bearings in each wheel. Non-binding, adjustable cones. Rock maple, kiln dried wheels. Chrome-plated struts, foot-plates. Wrench included. *State size* Men's—6, 7, 8, 9, 10, 11, 12. Women's—3, 4, 5, 6, 7, 8, 9, 10. Wt. 7 lbs. See How to Order.
(A) 6 N 2391—Men's $15.95
(B) 6 N 2393—Women's   15.95

$14.95

Here's why we feel J. C. HIGGINS is YOUR GREATEST RINK SKATE VALUE

1. **16 BALL BEARINGS** per wheel, steel cups, bearings, cones
2. **10° ACTION TRUCKS** . . the same action found on the finest skates
3. **SHOCK ABSORBERS** .. a ¾-in. thick rubber cushion
4. **MALLEABLE STEEL AXLE** bracket .. stronger than cast steel

$12.85

Our Best J. C. HIGGINS Rink Skates

- Skate shoes are top grain, elk-tanned leather .. fully cloth lined
- Sponge rubber padded shaped tongue .. laces tight without binding
- Your choice of semi-jumbo rock maple or longer wearing fiber wheels

Flexible, foot-soothing select leather shoes. Full cloth lining. Goodyear double-stitched 2-ply soles. Built-in steel arch support. Snug fitting heel counters. Full length leather reinforcement of rear seam. 10° Pivot action trucks. Action screw adjusts steering and action of rubber shock absorbers. Machined cups, bearings, cones. 16 ball bearings per wheel. Men's sizes 5, 6, 7, 8, 9, 10, 11, 12. Women's sizes 3, 4, 5, 6, 7, 8, 9, 10. *State size.* Wrench included. See How to Order.
(C) 6 N 2353—Men's. Black. Fiber wheels. Shpg. wt. 7 lbs......$14.95
  6 N 2354—Men's. Black. Maple wheels. Shpg. wt. 7 lbs....... 14.95
(D) 6 N 2306—Women's. White. Fiber wheels. Shpg. wt. 7 lbs.... 14.95
  6 N 2305—Women's. White. Maple wheels. Shpg. wt. 7 lbs.... 14.95

Low-Priced Rink Skates

- Top grain, elk-tanned leather shoes, felt-padded tongue
- 10° Pivot Action with standard size rock maple wheels
- Lock-stitched 2-ply sole .. built-in steel arch support

Top grain, elk-tanned leather shoes. Compare with the many skates sold near this low price made of split leather. Felt padded 1-pc. tongue. Lock-stitched 2-ply sole. Built-in steel arch support. Snug-fitting heel counters. Leather reinforcement at rear seam. 10° action trucks. Action screw adjusts steering action, rubber shock absorbers. Standard size maple wheels. 16 ball bearings per wheel. Machined cups, bearings, and cones. Adjustable non-binding cones. Shiny plated steel axle brackets. Shiny plated steel foot plate and struts. Wrench included. Men's sizes 6, 7, 8, 9, 10, 11, 12. Women's 4, 5, 6, 7, 8, 9, 10. See How to Order.
(E) 6 N 2387—Men's. Black. *State size.* Shipping weight 7 lbs.... $12.85
(F) 6 N 2388—Women's. White. *State size.* Shipping wt. 7 lbs.... 12.85

Bright metal Skate Cases, Rubber Toe Stops

Rinkster Toe Stops. Fit on frame, attach it yourself with just a skate wrench. 3 positions. Fits all skates. Instructions included.
6 N 2383—Shipping weight 1 lb..... Pair $2.29

Rubber Toe Stops. Give fast brake action. Will not mark floor or scuff skates. Nails incl.
6 N 2382—Shipping weight 1 lb....... Pair 79c

HOW TO ORDER ALL RINK SKATES. If you wear full size shoe, order same size rink skate. If you wear half-size shoe, order next larger full size rink skate.

Stronger, aluminum alloy skate case. A real lightweight, easy to carry. Snap hasps, center lock. Key included. Palm fitting plastic handle. Large 14½x10½x5¼-in. size. No federal tax required on this case.
6 N 2352—Shipping weight 3 lbs........ $4.49

Colorful, Riveted Skate Case. Strong steel over wood frame. Top and bottom fiber reinforced. Two snap closures. 15x11x5½-in. *State color* red, green, blue. Shpg. wt. 5 lbs. 8 oz
6 N 2381E—Price includes 10% Fed. Tax. $3.98

Completely Furnished

Modern 6 Room Colonial
is Now ready
for Christmas occupancy

$5⁹⁸

Two story suburban completely furnished with over 65-pieces of detailed plastic furniture and accessories. Easy to assemble without tools; sturdy metal construction, all windows, edges turned, floor sections ribbed, walls double turned for additional strength. Lithographed stone and white clapboard exterior landscaped with flower bed and low cut bushes. "See-through" cut out windows trimmed with bright painted shutters and flower boxes. Interior decorated in latest colors with beautiful draperies and picture groupings. Living room has fireplace, built-in shelves. Child's room abundant with nursery design. Den complete with pennants, shuffle board and trophy shelves. Furniture includes: **Living room;** Club sofa, club chair, barrel chair, coffee table, end table, lamp, T.V. . . **Dining room;** table and 4 chairs, hutch cabinet, buffet . . **Kitchen;** table, 4 chairs, sink, stove, refrigerator . . **Bedroom;** double bed, vanity, bench, chest on chest, nite stand, chair . . **Nursery;** crib, play pen, chest, potty chair . . **Bathroom;** sink, commode, tub, hamper . . **Den;** curved sofa, milk bar, 2 stools, piano, bench, juke box, table, coffee table, table tennis, 2 tavern chairs . . **Utility room;** washer, mangle, iron ing machine, double wash tub, chair, ladder, basket . . **Patio;** umbrella-table, 2 chairs, chaise lounge . . **Playground;** slide, pool, sand box, etc. 3 plastic figures. 4 secs. plastic fence. 79 N 01409—38x9½x15½ in. high. Shipped flat. Wt. 9 lbs. **$5.98**

FOR SALE New 4 Room Ranch with side porch

All-Metal Doll Houses

$3⁸⁹

Just move in . . . completely furnished, even to rugs and pictures on the wall. Over 38 pieces of detailed plastic furniture and accessories. Sturdy metal construction with edges and cut out windows rolled smooth. Lithographed flagstone and clapboard type exterior. Big floor to ceiling picture window and door that opens and closes. Plastic bird roost and weather vane on roof. Interior finished in modern decorator colors sets off smartly styled furniture. Furniture includes: **Living room;** overstuffed chair, sectional sofa, end table and lamp, coffee table, occasional table and chair, floor lamp, T.V. set and table . . **Dining room;** table, 4 chairs, buffet, hutch cabinet . . **Bedroom;** dresser, double bed, vanity and bench, chair, crib, chest, potty . . **Bathroom;** tub, commode, washstand, hamper . . **Kitchen;** stove, refrigerator, sink, table and 4 chairs . . **Porch;** play pen, double chair, single chair. Shipped flat. Easy to assemble without tools.
79 N 01408—33x9x10 inches high. Shipping weight 6 pounds **$3.89**

DE LUXE STYLING . . Just like full-sized Buggies Real Mothers have

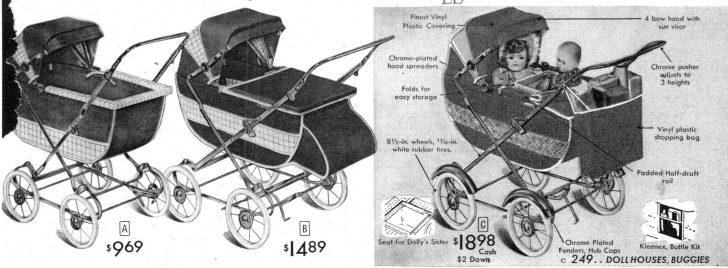

[A] $9⁶⁹

[B] $14⁸⁹

Finest Vinyl Plastic Covering

Chrome-plated hood spreaders

Folds for easy storage

8½-in. wheels, ¹⁵⁄₁₆-in. white rubber tires.

Seat for Dolly's Sister

4 bow hood with sun visor

Chrome pusher adjusts to 3 heights

Vinyl plastic shopping bag

Padded Half-draft rail

[C] $18⁹⁸ Cash $2 Down

Chrome Plated Fenders, Hub Caps

Kleenex, Bottle Kit

c 249 . . DOLL HOUSES, BUGGIES

Our Finest Imported China Service for Six

A little hostess needs a "best" china set for entertaining, just the way Mother does. For very special occasions give her this beautiful 28-piece set with dainty floral pattern, made of real china imported from Japan. Includes 6 plates, 6 cups, 6 saucers, teapot and sugar bowl with covers, creamer; platter, vegetable dish, gravy boat, casserole with cover. 4¼-in. diam. plates; others in proportion.

$2.98 28-pc. set

49 N 844—Shipping weight 5 pounds 8 ounces.........28-piece set. $2.98

Blue Willow China Set

She'll set such a lovely table with her real china service for six, imported from Japan! 26-piece set decorated with ever-popular Blue Willow pattern contains 6 plates; 6 cups; 6 saucers; platter; casserole, teapot and sugar bowl with covers; and creamer. 3⅞-in. diam. plates; others in proportion.
49N827—Wt. 3 lbs. 8 oz.$1.79

$1.79 26-pc. set

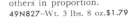

Little Hostess Sets — everything she needs to make miniature tea parties a success

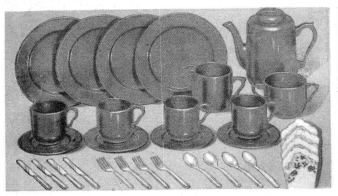

Ruby-tone Plastic Service for Four

Graceful modern design in a rich ruby hue. Practically unbreakable plastic set includes 4 each of the following pieces: plates, cups, saucers, napkins; silver-color plated knives, forks, spoons. Teapot with cover, sugar bowl and creamer complete set. 6⅛-in. diam. plates; others in proportion.

$1.89 28-pc. set

49 N 808—Shipping weight 1 pound 8 ounces.....28-piece set $1.89

Plastic Service for Six with "Wheat" motif

Tea parties are such fun, especially when you have this beautiful service of ivory-color plastic with gold-color trim. Contains 6 each plates, cups, saucers, knives, forks, spoons, napkins; clear plastic sherbets and goblets. Also, shakers, tea urn with cover, sugar bowl and creamer. Plates are 6 in. in diam.—others in proportion.

$4.89 54-pc. set

49 N 855—Shipping weight 2 pounds 6 ounces............................54-piece set $4.89
49 N 856—28-pc. Set for 4. As above, but no goblets, sherbets, shakers. Wt. 1 lb. 12 oz........ 2.98

New Tableware Chest

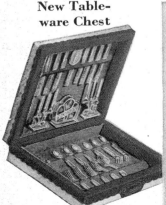

Plastic "Silver"

New "silver" has six each of knives, forks, spoons, plus cake knife, shakers, napkin holder, 2 candelabra. Cardboard "chest," 15x10x1¼ in.

$1.98 25-pc.

49 N 857—Wt. 12 oz..$1.98

New Aunt Jemima Pastry Mix Sets make Delicious Real Foods

23-mix set. Here's everything your petite pastry cook needs to make delectable pancakes, popovers, cornbread, or devil's food cake, etc. In fact, all she has to do to make delicious pastry is add milk or water to tasty prepared mixes. Set includes cake, cookie, pancake, biscuit, pudding mixes; pie filling, crust; frostings; chocolate chip, and many others. 20 utensils include cake pan, pie tin, bread tin, spoon, cookie sheet, rolling pin, muffin tin, mixing bowl, pancake grill, turner, ginger man cutter, decorator, 2 decorator nozzles, 4 cookie cutters, funnel, recipe book. See refill mix set at right.

$3.89 23-mix set

49 N 1292M—Shipping weight 2 pounds 6 ounces.................$3.89

12-mix set. When baking day arrives, little girls can bake for playmates while Mother bakes for the family. Ready-mixed pastry is easy to use—simply add milk or water. Includes white, yellow and devil's food cake, frostings; gingerbread, white bread, chocolate and vanilla cookie mix; pie crust and filling. Muffin tin, cake pan, pie tin, bread pan, cookie sheet, rolling pin, spoon, cookie cutter, recipe book.

$1.79 12-Mix Set

49 N 1291M—Shipping weight 1 pound 4 ounces......... $1.79
49 N 1264M—Refill Set. 8 ready-mixed foods. Wt. 12 oz...89c

Charm Craft Jewelry

For hours of fun! Forty-eight colored plastic beads, clasps, charms, plus chain, pliers, thread for bracelets, lapel pins, earrings, etc. Develops child's handicraft skill. Provides many pleasant hours. In 14½x11½-inch box. Easy-to-follow instructions included for making many items. **$1.79**

49 N 1207—Shpg. wt. 1 lb. 12 oz. $1.79

"Jewelry" Chest

NEW! 21-piece Jewelry and Vanity Chest. "Make-believe" bracelets, earrings, pendants, rings, etc., plus powder and rouge compacts, lipstick cases, combs . . . all of metalized gold and silver color plastic. 4-drawer cardboard chest 14¼x7x3 in. **$1.89**

49 N 1293—Wt. 1 lb. 4 oz. $1.89

Costume Jewelry Craft

Offers craft lovers an exceptional variety of designs for brooches, earrings, necklaces, bracelets, pins, ties, belts, etc. Contains assorted simulated pearls, rhinestones, sequins, seed beads, rocailles, bugles and thread. Wire and clasps, designs and instructions for making items included. Excellent to keep small hands busy. **$2.69**

49 N 1294—Shpg. wt. 1 lb. 4 oz. $2.69

Cork 'N Pom-Pom Jewelry

New, unusual craft that's fascinating for all ages. Contains a big assortment of beads, sequins, spangles, simulated pearls, cork balls, sequin pins, earring backs, velvet tubing, etc. Everything to make cork and pom-pom jewelry items such as necklaces, bracelets, hat ornaments, etc. No needles or thread required. Instructions for making these attractive pieces. **$2.69**

49 N 1296—Shpg. wt. 1 lb. 12 oz. $2.69

For Little Homemakers
toys for sewing, housekeeping, jewelry making, personal care

Little Girl's Vanity Table and "Make-up" . . Save 51c! Was $4.49, now $3.98

A Vanity Table all her very own—where your "little lady" can play grown-up to her heart's content. Kidney-shaped table is just like the adult ones, with printed plastic skirt. Top is strong Masonite Presdwood, 20½x23½x12¾ inches. Wood table frame and stool. Mirror for table is 9x6¾ in. Stool 9¾x9x5½ in. Sized just right for particular little misses who want to keep their grooming ever-so-neat. Set includes all the extras so dear to small girls . . . plastic powder case, mirror, comb, compact, brush, powder, lipstick, coin purse, memo pad and pencil and many other items. Shipped partly assembled. **$3.98**

79 N 01281—Shipping weight 7 pounds $3.98

Modern Miniature Kitchen .. working parts .. complete with Dishes, Tableware

A complete kitchen with all the appliances for little homemakers. Sturdy steel construction with attractive lithographed design showing kitchen window, radio, etc. Includes refrigerator, washing machine, sink, stove, broom closet and wall cabinets with miniature plastic accessories; griddle, pressure cooker, washing tub, ice cube trays, etc. All perfect miniatures with "real" working parts. Includes dishes and tableware for three. 25½x5¼x11¾ in. high. Partly assembled. **$2.89**

79 N 01105—Shipping weight 7 pounds $2.89

New! Dishwash Set

The newest equipment to make dishwashing for doll dishes a pleasure. Steel dish pan and rack, rubber drain board, plastic sink strainer, plastic apron, dish towel, polishing cloth, dish mop and bottle brush. Sponge, Suz soap powder, SOS pads. **$1.69**

49 N 1118—Shpg. wt. 2 lbs. $1.69

32-piece Formula Set

Everything for dolly's feeding. Set contains all-metal sterilizer and cover in blue enamel finish; rust-resistant bottle rack; 6 Evenflo baby bottles, nipples, discs and caps; blue plastic funnel, formula measuring cup, spoon; bottle brush; bottle cleanser. **$1.79**

49 N 1268—Shpg. wt. 2 lbs. $1.79

Vanity Kit for Travel

Beautiful padded lizard-effect vinyl plastic case to delight little girls. Made like Mother's, looks very expensive! Case is 9⅜x5¼x4½ in. Contains a treasure-trove of safe, harmless cosmetic and vanity items . . ideal for "dress-up" games, too. Keeps Mother's cosmetics safe. **$2.69**

49 N 1308—Shpg. wt. 1 lb. $2.69

Miniature Furniture

3-piece set—each piece lights up when switched on! TV screen lights; Fireplace log glows; lamp on chest lights. 3 batteries incl. TV 2½ in. high. **$1.25**

49 N 1414—Wt. 14 oz. . . . $1.25

Doll Carriages
styled like real baby buggies

Ever Popular Woven Fiber Buggy

$5.59

Low-priced, yet a beautiful buggy that will make your little girl's dreams come true. Fancy 3-color design in loom-woven, pearl gray fiber with handsome braid trim. 5-in. stamped spoke wheels; 3/8-in. rubber tires. Aluminum enamel finish undercarriage. Handle 23 in. high. Body 18x9½x11⅛ in. Wt. 8 lbs.
79 N 08245................$5.59

$2.89

A perfect "first" buggy. Beautiful red, 17x8x5 in. Washable vinyl plastic body. Folding aluminum finish steel undercarriage. Three-bow folding hood. Handle 21 in. from floor. White 4-in. stamped spoke wheels with 3/8-in. rubber tires.
49 N 8204—Shpg. wt. 4 lbs.........$2.89

$4.79

NEW! 20-in. Folding Doll Carriage. Forest green and gray body 20x9x7½ in. deep. Vinyl plastic, fiberboard insert. Aluminum finished folding steel frame. 3-bow hood, sun visor. L-type foot brake. 5 in. stamped spoke wheels, 3/8-in. rubber tires.
79 N 08205—Shpg. wt. 6 lbs.........$4.79

NEW! 22-in. Folding Carriage—Duchess Gear

$7.89

First time shackle-type duchess gear offered on 22-in. buggy at this low price. Gives "floating cradle" ride. Washable gray vinyl leatherette body 22x10x8¼ in. deep. Maroon trim, stencil decoration. Fiberboard insert. 3-in. toe extension. Four-bow folding hood. Tubular steel pusher 28 in. high. 6½-in. wire wheels, ½-in. tires.
79 N 08206L—Shpg. wt. 9 lbs.......$7.89

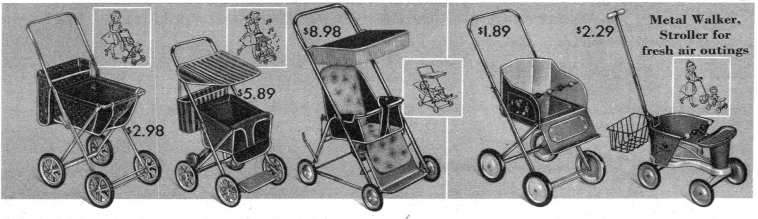

$2.98 $5.89 $8.98 $1.89 $2.29

Metal Walker, Stroller for fresh air outings

Three Doll Strollers for "Little Mothers"

Shopping Stroller
Wonderful folding stroller is complete with attached shopping bag. Covered in green plastic material. 9x10-in. seat provides room for almost any size doll. Handle 24 in. from floor. 5-in. spoke wheels with 3/8-in. rubber tires. Assembled, except wheels.
79N08292—Wt. 6 lbs. $2.98

Musical Stroller
Pert red and white candy striped hood and shopping bag; red seat 6½x7½x5¾ in. deep—all vinyl plastic. Music box plays gay tune as "she" strolls with dolly. Aluminum finished steel frame. White wheels, black tires. Handle 23 in. from floor.
79N08214—Wt. 5 lbs. $5.89

New DeLuxe Stroller
Stroller body converts to horizontal position so dolly can sleep. Royal blue cotton twill body, with white trim, fringed hood. White vinyl plastic cover inside. Seat 8½x7½ in., 11-in. back. Chromed tubular handle 27 in. from floor. 4½-in. disc wheels, ½-in. tires. Metal foot rest.
79N08225L—Wt. 12 lbs. $8.98

Gaily lithographed all metal stroller. Adjustable footrest, safety bar, play beads. Blue and ivory enameled with picture trim. 4½-in. wheels. Handle 20 inches from floor. Folds for storage. Shipping weight 4 pounds.
79 N 08210.................$1.89

Metal walker with wire basket for parcels. 4-in. rubber tired wheels roll smoothly and noiselessly. Colored play beads on doll guard. Blue, pink and ivory enameled finish. 12½ inches long, 8 inches wide.
49 N 8201—Shpg. wt. 4 lbs. 8 oz.. $2.29

Beautiful Carriage Sets

D $1.89   E $2.89

[D] Reversible comforter, pillow for "baby's" buggy. Comforter 18x24 in. for average size buggies. Quilted in rich, soft rayon satin. Pink and blue, matching 7x10-in. pillow.
49 N 8276—Shpg. wt. 10 oz. Set $1.89

[E] NEW reversible satin cover and pillow set. Cover 21x27 in. with ruffle, 3½-in. blue edge, beautiful vari-colored pastel embroidered 9½x15¼ in. insert. Reverse side blue with 2-in. pink ruffle. 11x14-in. pillow with ruffle; matches cover.
49 N 8226—Shpg. wt. 14 oz. Set $2.89

Our finest HAPPI-TIME Buggies styled to adult specifications make any dolly's "Mother" happy!

[A] Sparkling 3-position chrome-plated handle adjusts from 27½ to 29½ in. from floor. Large 25½x12x9¾-in. deep body of washable maroon leatherette with off-white quilted plastic. Half draft rail. Four-bow folding hood, sun visor. Full shackle-type duchess gear. Foot brake. 7¼-in. white spoke wheels, ⅝-in. white coated rubber tires. Sturdy steel frame.
79 N 08207L—Shipping weight 11 pounds........................$9.69

[B] NEW Deluxe Folding Baby Carriage. 27x13½x11 in. deep body in forest green vinyl leatherette, off-white quilted plastic. Chrome-plated hood spreaders and tubular steel pusher that adjusts from 27½ to 30½ in. Kleenex and bottle in inside pocket. PLUS: storm curtain, shackle type duchess gear, foot brake, 8¼-in. white spoke wheels, ¾-in. white coated rubber tires.
79 N 08208L—Shipping weight 19 pounds...........................$14.8?

[C] NEW Super Deluxe Folding Carriage. Royal blue and gray quilted vinyl plastic body with embossed designs is 27x13½x11 in. deep . . made of finest quality material available. Extra dolly seat fits on half draft rail. Chrome-plated hood spreaders, fenders, 2¾-in. hub caps, tubular steel handle that adjusts from 28 to 31 in. PLUS: full shackle-type duchess gear, storm curtain, 4-bow hood, visor, inside Kleenex and bottle pocket, plastic shopping bag, foot brake, white 8½-in. wheels, 15/16-in. rubber tires.
79 N 08209L—Shipping weight 20 pounds. Dolls not included.....$18.98

Happi-Time first .. they'll look-alike in "Mom and Daughter" Honeysuckle dresses

$9⁷⁹

$8⁹⁷

$9⁹⁸

Order the Same Dress for "Mom"

Now! HAPPI-TIME Babies in HONEYSUCKLE dresses that you can order in "little girl" sizes 3 to 6x for your little "mom." See page 199 for a complete description of these beautiful little girls' dresses

So lifelike! Baby-soft vinyl with rooted hair

..more fun than ever to play "mother and daughter" .. in dresses that look -alike! And, any mom would be proud of this ever-so-soft all-vinyl baby. Her -wing complexion can be sponged clean from head to toe .. and her ROOTED -ran hair can be combed, brushed, set again and again on her own plastic curl-s. Bright glassene go-to-sleep-eyes are edged with thick lashes. Jointed arms, -ovable head. Coo voice. So adorable in her HONEYSUCKLE dress .. a light -ue acetate taffeta tiered party dress, lace trim (girl's dress described on page -99). Complete with undies, socks and "baby-doll" vinyl plastic shoes, curlers.

79 N 03685—Doll 24 inches tall, in Hon- eysuckle dress. Wt. 5 lbs..........$9.79
29 N 5526—Dress for little girl. State size 3, 4, 5, 6, 6x. Shpg. wt. 12 oz.....$3.98

New!'Almost-as-real as little "sis"

A 24-inch bundle of fun, molded of softest vinyl plastic. Her glowing Saran hair is ROOTED, each strand implanted so you can comb, brush and set it just like little sister's. She loves to be sponged with soap 'n' water, too. Movable head, jointed arms. Pretty go-to-sleep eyes and a sweet coo voice. She and "mom" will make quite a pair in their navy blue "school-day" cot- ton dresses, with net petticoat flounce (described on page 199). Doll wears socks, undies, vinyl shoes.

79 N 03334—24-in. Doll in Honeysuckle dress. Shpg. wt. 4 lbs..........$8.97
29 N 5514—Dress for little "Mom." State size 3, 4, 5, 6, 6x. Wt. 12 oz. $2.98

New! Hard Plastic Doll WALKS with you

This beautiful 23-inch miss walks hand in hand with you, tilts her pretty head coyly. Thick Saran tresses frame her delicate little features .. can be combed, brushed, set, on her own plastic curlers. Gay flowers nestle in her curls. Fully jointed. Wonder- wide eyes close in sleep. Can be wiped clean with a damp cloth. A real vision of loveliness in her pucker nylon HONEY- SUCKLE dress. A rose and blue print confection that's as flattering to "mom" as it is to her tiny "daughter"—needs no ironing (details on page 199). Doll wears rayon undies, socks, plastic shoes.

79 N 03337—23-in. Doll in Honeysuckle dress. Shpg. wt. 4 lbs...............$9.98
29 N 5571—Dress for "Mom." State size 3, 4, 5, 6, 6x. Shpg. wt. 10 oz..........$3.98

Baby-soft vinyl

Rooted hair

Adorable in her 3-piece Ensemble

$5.95

Her gleaming feathery-soft curls are ROOTED .. can be combed, brushed, set on her own curlers. Molded of vinyl plastic from top to toe .. so carefully detailed she looks, feels, "almost-real." Her one-piece body is cotton stuffed to make her extra huggable. Has coo voice. Loves to be sponged clean. So cute in her hat, coat and dress of lace- trimmed rayon taffeta, with cotton panties, socks and vinyl shoes.

49 N 3657—17 inches tall. Shpg. wt. 2 lbs. 8 oz. $5.95

Happi-Time Wardrobe Doll WALKS with you

$8.95

Walks hand in hand with her "mom" .. just as smart as any model. She's ready for any occasion, with her 5 different outfits. Her wardrobe consists of a cotton play dress, formal party dress, shortie coat and hat set, 3-piece skiing outfit, sunsuit, sunglasses, and 2 coat hangers. She wears panties, socks and vinyl plastic shoes. Lustrous long Saran hair frames her face, can be dampened, combed, brushed, set. Fully jointed, in hard-to-break plastic. Head turns when she walks; eyes close for bedtime.

49 N 3384—14½-inch Doll, Wardrobe. Shpg. wt. 2 lbs. Was $9.49 .... $8.95

Add these items to your Easy Terms order, see page 371

Soft vinyl head

"Rooted" hair

Save 91c
Was ~~$9.89~~
$8.98
22 in. tall

Press legs or body and she'll cry

Nod head, press arms against body, she'll sob

$499
With layette

Priced Lower Than Ever Before!

So realistic .. so wonderfully economical! Lifelike vinyl head with baby bright complexion, lustrous ROOTED Saran hair you can comb, brush, set over and over again. Her tiny little features are accented with shiny thick-lashed glassene eyes she closes at naptime. Her legs and arms are delicately detailed in soft-as-baby vinyl .. her cotton-stuffed body is vinyl coated, so you can sponge her clean. Cries softly when you cuddle her. Wears organdy dress, with flocking and lace trim, bonnet, flowers in her hair, sheer cotton undies, rayon socks, vinyl shoes.

49 N 3174—18-inch Baby.
Shpg. wt. 2 lbs. 8 oz. Was $7.98...$7.39

79 N 03184—De luxe 22-inch Baby.
Shpg. wt. 4 lbs. Was $9.89...now $8.98

Soft and Cuddly "Magic Skin" Baby Coos

She's such a little darling you'll almost think she's real! Her tiny baby features are perfectly formed. Her head is made of kitten-soft vinyl plastic .. her body cuddly Magic rubber skin, stuffed with cotton and foam rubber to make her feel oh-so-real. Baby Coos loves to be sponged clean. Her sparkling go-to-sleep eyes are edged with long lashes. She loves to be loved, too, and coos when you cuddle her .. cries and sobs when you squeeze her too hard. She's dressed in a colorful print, lace and rick-rack trimmed sunsuit .. but she's got her whole wardrobe with her. You'll love her sheer organdy dress with the pique weskit-effect and lace trim, the matching bonnet, cotton slip, knit bootees, soap, washcloth, clothespins, 3 powder puffs, diaper, sunsuit and dress in assorted styles. Shipping weight 1 pound 6 ounces.

49 N 3041—13½ inches tall. With complete layette........................$4

Pert Pony Tail

"Rooted" hair

Walks with you, turns her head, sits

$3.89

$4.99

ONLY
$1.98

All Vinyl
ONLY $4.89

Pert "Pony-Tail" Doll

Now she walks .. yet costs no more than last year! **$9.79** Her glossy Saran hair is ROOTED firmly in her soft vinyl head. Can be dampened, combed, brushed, set time and again. Eyes are long-lashed, close when she sleeps. Hard-to-break plastic body is carefully proportioned, fully jointed. In a rayon taffeta dress with metallic braid and lace trim, ruffled collar. Flouncy under slip has net ruffling. Undies, socks, metallic-type shoes.
49 N 3339—19 in. Wt. 3 lbs.. $9.79

Caressable Molded Hair Babies—Priced to Please

All latex rubber body can be sponged clean just like Baby. Cotton stuffed to make her huggable. Composition head, molded with soft-looking baby curls, turns. Her go-to-sleep eyes are edged with thick lashes. She's a real little dream, dressed in a perky embossed cotton dress, trimmed with embroidery, lace and braid. Matching sun-bonnet. Cotton undies, rayon socks and leather-effect shoes. 14 in. tall.
49 N 3115—Wt. 1 lb. 4 oz. $1.98

Baby-like features and tiny molded curls are beautifully molded in real-life vinyl plastic. One-piece rubber latex body makes her easy to clean from head to toe. Cotton stuffed and cuddly. Bright glassene eyes close. She cries when you squeeze her. Sheer ninon dress with braid trim and lacy embroidered collar, bonnet. rayon slip, panties; and leather-effect shoes. 16 in. tall.
49N3619—Shpg. wt. 2 lbs. $3.89

So adorable in her pink and blue cotton knit cardigan and matching bonnet. As cuddly as a baby can be, with her pretty vinyl plastic head, arms and legs. Has soft-as-life vinyl-coated, cotton stuffed body. Soft crying voice and big go-to-sleep eyes. Wears an organdy dress with embossed cotton and lace trim, slip, panties, socks, and vinyl shoes. 16 in. tall.
49N3250—Wt. 2 lbs. 6 oz. $4.99

19 inches tall .. and a real bundle of joy! Made of ever-so-soft vinyl plastic from her tiny molded curls to her little pink toes. You can keep her glowing baby complexion bright by sponging her clean from top to toe. Soft coo voice, big go-to-sleep eyes. So pretty in her sheer ninon dress with lace inset and satin ribbon, bonnet, crisp cotton slip, cotton panties, socks and vinyl shoes. 19 in. tall.
49 N 3637—Wt. 3 lbs. 4 oz. $4.89

The Davy Crockett Craze of 1954-55 didn't offer much to girls. There was a white "Polly Crockett" coonskin cap and other costume items, but by and large, this fad was left to the boys. But who needed Davy Crockett when there was such a vast variety of dolls to choose from? There was Toodles, "the first all-jointed action doll" who "kneels, drinks and wets." There was Magic Lips, whose lips moved as she cooed "Mama." And there was Ricky Jr., straight from the hit TV show "I Love Lucy."

For girls on the go, the Wishbook offered scooters, bicycles and velocipedes (that's tricycles, to you), and all manner of baby carriages, ranging from a "gaily lithographed" stroller at $1.89 to an adjustable carriage in blue leatherette for $13.79. And, since home is where the heart is, Marx added a new five room metal doll house complete with furniture and picket fence -- the suburban American dream.

Sears Christmas
Wishbook
1955

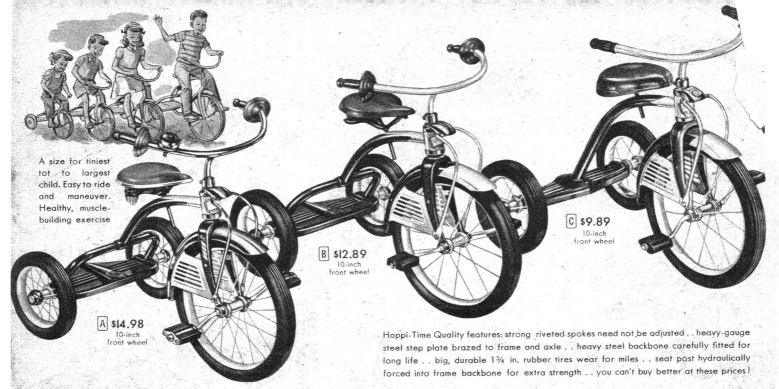

A size for tiniest tot to largest child. Easy to ride and maneuver. Healthy, muscle-building exercise

A $14.98
10-inch front wheel

B $12.89
10-inch front wheel

C $9.89
10-inch front wheel

Happi-Time Quality features: strong riveted spokes need not be adjusted .. heavy-gauge steel step plate brazed to frame and axle .. heavy steel backbone carefully fitted for long life .. big, durable 1¾ in. rubber tires wear for miles .. seat post hydraulically forced into frame backbone for extra strength .. you can't buy better at these prices!

SEARS HAPPI-TIME VELOCIPEDES

Our Best, Strongest Velocipede

Chrome-plated front fender, handlebar, truss rods and seat springs .. heavy U-bar frame .. all wheels ball bearing for easy-rolling rides, longer wear

A **Our Best!** Rugged 1¼-in. back, 1-in. U-bar tubular steel frame. All wheels ball bearing. Riveted multiple spoke wheels. Heavy-duty cap bearing in head. 1¾-in. semi-pneumatic rubber tires. Chrome-plated fender, adjustable handlebar, truss rods. Heavy-gauge steel step plate. Adjustable vinyl top saddle; chrome-plated body springs. Vinyl knuckle guards. Double block rubber pedals. Metallic maroon finish, white trim. Bell.

79 N 08750K—10-inch front wheel. 14 to 17-inch leg reach. Shipping weight 22 pounds $14.98
79 N 08751K—12-inch front wheel. 16 to 18-inch leg reach. Shipping weight 24 pounds $16.45
79 N 08752L—16-inch front wheel. 18 to 20-inch leg reach. Shipping weight 28 pounds $17.98
79 N 08753L—20-inch front wheel. 20 to 22-inch leg reach. Shipping weight 34 pounds $19.75

B **Fine Quality Happi-Time Velocipede.** All wheels have ball bearings. Extra-strong 1¼-in. hydrogen-brazed back, 1-in. U-bar tubular steel frame—the strongest made, to take the roughest wear. 1¾-in. semi-pneumatic rubber tires. Heavy-gauge steel step plate brazed to frame, axle. White enameled adjustable steel handlebar, truss rods, fender skirts. Shaped vinyl top spring saddle adjusts. Vinyl knuckle guards. Molded rubber pedals. Metallic blue finish, white trim.

79 N 08725K—10-inch front wheel. 14 to 17-inch leg reach. Shipping weight 22 pounds. $12.89
79 N 08726K—12-inch front wheel. 16 to 19-inch leg reach. Shipping weight 23 pounds. $13.98
79 N 08727L—16-inch front wheel. 18 to 20-inch leg reach. Shipping weight 27 pounds. $15.79
79 N 08728L—20-inch front wheel. 20 to 22-inch leg reach. Shipping weight 32 pounds. $17.35

C **Good Quality Happi-Time Velocipede** at the lowest price we've seen for all of these features. Strong 1¼-in. tubular steel frame, 1¾-in. head. 1¾-in. solid rubber tires (all except rear tires of 10-in. size which are 1½ in.). Shaped steel saddle with adjustable post. White enameled adjustable handlebar, fender skirts, truss rods. Easy-rolling ball bearing front wheel, plain bearings on rear wheels. Rust-resistant baked-on red enamel finish, white trim. Order now for Christmas.

79 N 08708—10-inch front wheel. 14 to 17-inch leg reach. Shipping weight 19 pounds $9.89
79 N 08709K—12-inch front wheel. 16 to 19-inch leg reach. Shipping weight 22 pounds $11.59
79 N 08710L—16-inch front wheel. 18 to 20-inch leg reach. Shipping weight 26 pounds $12.98

New Streamlined "Falcon" Velocipede

D As streamlined as a space ship, as much fun to ride. Roomy step plate. Guard rail, big safety styled bucket seat. 12-in. front, 7-in. rear wheels with nylon bearings. Semi-pneumatic rubber tires: 1¾-in. front, 1½-in. rear. Heavy ⅞-in. tubular steel frame; 2-in. head. Adjustable handlebar, bronze bushing in fork. Rubber pedals. 22 in. wide at rear. 17 to 20-inch leg reach. Bittersweet (reddish brown); ivory trim.
79 N 08551L—Shipping weight 29 lbs. $17.75

Economy-Priced Velocipedes

E Easy-rolling ball bearing front wheel, sleeve bearing rear wheels, 1¼-in. strong tubular steel frame. Shaped seat adjusts. Truss rods. Rubber hand grips, pedals. Enameled red, white trim.

49 N U8656—10-in. front wheel. ⅝-in. tires. 14-17-in. leg reach. Shpg. wt. 13 lbs. $6.98
79 N 08658L—13-in. front wheel. ¾-in. tires. 16-18-in. leg reach. Shpg. wt. 14 lbs. $7.89

NOTE: For leg reach on all velocipedes, measure child from crotch to foot

All Steel Scooters for Speedy Sprouts

F G Self-oiling "Congo" wood bearings. Double disc wheels; semi-pneumatic rubber tires. Rubber hand grips. Parking stand. Enameled bright red. Easy to assemble. Thrifty gifts—and fun!

F 79 N 08825—10-in. wheels. 38x34 in. high. Brake. 1¾-in. tires. Shipping weight 15 pounds. $4.49
G 49 N U8810—7-in. wheels. 33x30 in. high. 1¼-in. tires. Shipping weight 9 pounds. $2.98
H 49 N U8814—3-wheel Scooter for tots. Wide platform. 5-in. wheels. ½-in. rubber tires. Enamel finish. Size 24x25 in. Shipping weight 6 pounds $2.49

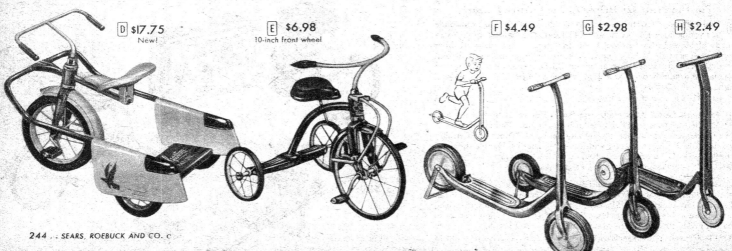

D $17.75
New!

E $6.98
10-inch front wheel

F $4.49

G $2.98

H $2.49

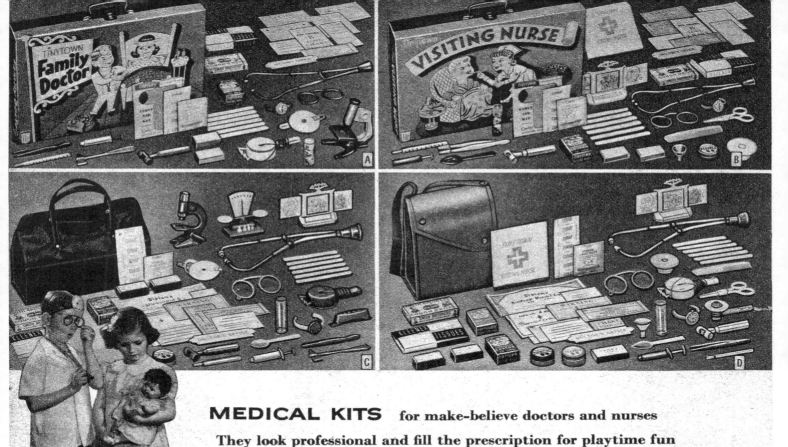

MEDICAL KITS for make-believe doctors and nurses
They look professional and fill the prescription for playtime fun

A Doctor Kit and Case for mite-sized medics. Is there a "doctor" in *your* house? If your young "doc" is just hanging up his shingle, this professional-looking kit is just what he needs. Brightly colored heavy cardboard carrying case holds blunt edged plastic instruments en route to case. Upon arrival he'll pull out his real stethoscope, make-believe hypo, or one of his many other instruments to aid the patient. Includes real adhesive, gauze, cotton and printed medical forms. Instruction booklet included. 8½x13¾-in. cardboard case.
49 N 1805—Shipping weight 1 pound 4 ounces $1.49

B Visiting Nurse Kit and Carrying Case. No wonder nurse's patients always make a quick recovery! She seems just like a real registered nurse with her medical equipment at her finger tips. Blunt-edged plastic instruments include real stethoscope, earoscope, play hypo and many others. Colorful cardboard carrying case measures 8½x13¾ inches. Snowy-white apron. Real gauze, adhesive strips, cotton—everything needed to give patient the best in bedside care. Instructions, printed medical forms—sick charts, "diploma," etc., are included.
49 N 1806—Shipping weight 1 pound 4 ounces $1.49

C Our Best Doctor Kit. It's just what your little M. D. ordered! Pint-sized doctors, just starting to practice, will glow with professional pride at the sight of this authentic-looking black plastic bag with snap closing, handles. Over 16 blunt edged plastic instruments including a real stethoscope to pick up heartbeat, Vue scope germ finder and many others. Real adhesive, gauze, cotton to treat minor wounds, etc. "Wonder working" candy pills. Complete with instructions, sick charts, printed matter. 5½x9⅜x4⅜-inch plastic bag.
49 N 1807—Shipping weight 1 pound 4 ounces $2.69

D Our Best Nurse Kit. When your little nurse goes out on a case, she'll have everything she needs to follow up doctor's orders. Smart snap bag with shoulder strap for visiting nurse realism. Over 14 blunt plastic instruments help care for pains in dollie's tummy. Real stethoscope finds heartbeat and pulse, play hypo, and many others. Nurse's apron for crisp appearance. Real adhesive, gauze, cotton for binding cuts. Soap and comb freshen up "bed cases." Complete with instructions, medical forms. Plastic bag measures 4x6x7½ inches.
49 N 1808—Shipping weight 1 pound 2 ounces $2.69

$1.79

89c

$2.25

New Coloring Toy. A revolutionary idea to spark child's imagination. Object is for child to color assorted dolls, animals, fish, and other "shapes," outlined on heavy-duty die-cut paper, and assemble pieces to form anything his imagination creates. Parts are joined together with clips. Set contains 8 20¾x7-in. sheets of paper, 16 crayons, clips.
49 N 1708—21x7½x1-inch box. Shipping weight 1 lb. 6 oz. $1.79

Meet Mr. Potato Head. He's loads of fun for *all* the family. 28-pc. kit transforms any ordinary fruit, vegetable, or the Styrofoam® head (incl.) into many silly, funny-faced characters. Plastic features—eyes, noses, ears, mustaches, pipe, hats, mouths, glasses, body, hands, feet included. 9x7x3-in. box.
49 N 1773—Shipping weight 10 oz. 89c

New Winky Dink Television Game Kit. Contains Magic plastic window for use during Winky Dink TV program; game book plus 40 plastic "doodles" in assorted colors, shapes for playing games, and illustrated stories for tot to color; 8 crayons; erasing mitt; die-cut jigsaw puzzle.
49 N 1843—Shipping weight 2 lbs. $2.25

D $7.79

E $4.59

F $2.89

G $5.59

H $6.59

A $9.59

C $13.79

B $17.49

Buggies A, B, C have de luxe styling
... just like real baby buggies

Kleenex and bottle
inside pocket

Knee action full
shackle-type gear

Handle adjusts
to 3 heights

J Completely furnished six-
room doll house with light $4.89

FOR DOLLYS' OUTINGS .. Color-bright Happi-Time Buggies
and Strollers .. sturdy rust-resistant steel frames, rubber tired wheels

◄ BUGGIES DESCRIBED BELOW SHOWN ON OPPOSITE PAGE

Handles on A, B, C Adjust for Added Years of Fun

A Set chrome-plated handle at lowest position—next year, raise it. (Adjusts from 27 to 31 in.). Extra strong leatherette body in cherry red with off-white quilted plastic trim. Large chrome-plated hub caps. Half draft rail on full steel frame. Full shackle-type Duchess gear for cradle-smooth rides. ⅝-in. gray rubber tires on 7½-in. wire spoke wheels. Folding steel frame, aluminum enamel finish. 4-bow hood folds. Sun visor. Foot brake. Kleenex, bottle in pocket. Fiberboard insert. Wt. 12 lbs.
79 N 08234L—24x12¼x9½ in. deep. Bedding, doll not incl..............$9.59

B Our Finest Happi-Time Buggy. Storm curtain with clear plastic shield. Chrome-plated fenders, 3½-in. hub caps, handle adjusts (27–32½ in. high). Metallic blue leatherette, gray quilted plastic trim. Biggest wheels—8½ in., wire spokes. Thickest ¹⁵⁄₁₆-in. white rubber tires. Shackle gear. Steel frame folds. Brake. 4-bow hood folds. Kleenex, bottle in pocket. 27x13½x11 in. deep.
79 N 08236L—Shpg. wt. 19 lbs.$17.49

C Big 27x13¼x10-in. size! Fold-up toe extension. Chrome-plated 2¾-in. hub caps, handle adjusts (26–32 in. high). Bright blue leatherette, off-white quilted plastic trim. Half-draft rail on full steel frame. 8¼-in. wheels, ¾-in. white rubber tires. Duchess gear. Aluminum enameled steel frame folds. 4-bow visored hood folds. Brake. Kleenex, bottle in pocket.
79 N 08235L—Shpg. wt. 15 lbs.$13.79

D 22-in. Folding Buggy. Duchess gear for smooth "big buggy" rides. Washable green, ivory leatherette. 22x10x8¼ in. deep. Tubular chrome-plated handle 28 in. high. 4-bow hood folds. 6½-in. wire wheels, ½-in. gray rubber tires. L-type brake. Steel frame. Large plated hub caps.
79 N 08233L—Shpg. wt. 9 lbs..$7.79

E 20-in. Folding Buggy. 2-tone blue vinyl plastic body. 20x9x7 in. deep. Fiberboard insert. 3-bow folding hood, visor. Tubular steel handle easy for little hands to hold, 23¾ in. high. Aluminum finish steel frame. Foot brake. 5-in. wheels, ⅜-in. rubber tires, push-on hub caps.
49 N U8232—Shpg. wt. 6 lbs...$4.59

F Our Lowest Priced! The perfect "first" buggy. Washable red vinyl plastic body, white trim. 17x7½x5 in. deep. Aluminum finished steel frame folds. 3-bow hood folds. Handle 21 in. high. 4-in. wheels. ⅜-in. rubber tires.
49 N U8231—Shpg. wt. 3 lbs..$2.89

G Ever Popular Woven Fiber Buggy. Fancy 3-color design in loom-woven, white fiber with braid trim. 5-in. stamped spoke wheels; ⅜-in. rubber tires. Aluminum finish steel frame. Reversible hood. Tubular steel handle 23 in. high. 18x9½x11⅛ in. deep.
49 N U8245—Shpg. wt. 7 lbs...$5.59

H Our Finest Doll Stroller. Victoria blue embossed plastic body, detachable hood and shopping bag. Big 9x10-in. seat. Chrome-plated handle 29½ in. high. Footrest. Brake. Sturdy 6-in. wire wheels, ½-in. rubber tires. Aluminum finished steel frame.
79 N 08241—Shpg. wt. 8 lbs..$6.59

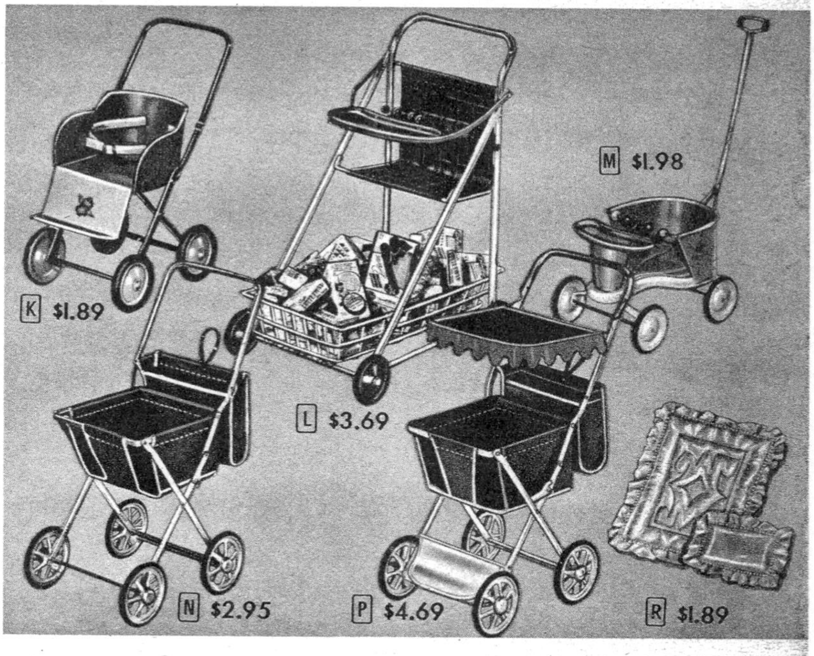

K $1.89 — **M** $1.98 — **L** $3.69 — **N** $2.95 — **P** $4.69 — **R** $1.89

K Gaily Lithographed Metal Stroller. Footrest adjusts. Blue and pink. Folds 7¼x9x5 in. deep. Handle 20 in. high. 4½-in. wheels.
49 N U8247—Shpg. wt. 4 lbs....$1.89

L New Tubular Steel Shopping Cart. 11x21x4-in. wire basket removes. Plastic seat with strap. Handle 26 in. high. Assorted miniature brand packages.
79 N 08250—Shpg. wt. 9 lbs...$3.69

M Metal Walker. Blue, pink, ivory enamel finish. 8 in. wide. Rubber tired 4-in. wheels. 12½ in. long.
49 N 8200—Shpg. wt. 4 lbs... $1.98

N Folding Stroller with Removable Shopping Bag. Green plastic body. 9x10-in. seat. Handle 24 in. high. Rubber tired 5-in. spoke wheels. Steel frame.
49 N U8239—Shpg. wt. 5 lbs....$2.95

P Folding Stroller with Detachable Shopping Bag, Canopy. Footrest. Red plastic body, gray trim. 9x10 in. seat. 26-in. chrome pusher.
79 N 08240—Shpg. wt. 6 lbs.....$4.69

R Carriage Set. Quilted 18x24-in. reversible comforter, 7x10-in. pillow. Pink and blue rayon satin.
49 N 8276—Shpg. wt. 10 oz....$1.89

◄HOUSE ILLUSTRATED ON OPPOSITE PAGE

Our Biggest Happi-Time Metal Doll House with beaming light, ringing doorbell

J Ting-a-ling goes the doorbell! Someone's here to see Sister's spacious new 6-room colonial doll house. It's modern as can be with its cool breezeway. Completely furnished—over 48 pieces of detailed plastic furniture. Beaming light in living-dining room operated by battery. Big 31½x15½x9-in. size. Sturdy metal construction. All windows, edges safety turned. Floor sections ribbed, walls double turned for strength. Finely lithographed stone and clapboard exterior, bright painted shutters, flower boxes. Cupola and weather vane. Interior decorated in bright modern colors with beautiful lithographed draperies, paintings. Den complete with pennants, shuffle board, trophy shelves. Break-resistant finely molded plastic furniture: **Living Room;** Club sofa, club chair, barrel chair, coffee table, end table, floor lamp, TV set. **Dining Room;** Table, 4 chairs, hutch cabinet, buffet server. **Kitchen;** Table, 4 chairs, refrigerator, sink, stove. **Bedroom;** Double bed, vanity dresser, bench, chest, night table, boudoir chair. **Bathroom;** Toilet, bathtub, washstand, hamper. **Child's Room;** Crib, play pen, chest, potty chair. **Den;** Curved sofa, milk bar, 2 stools, piano, piano bench, juke box, round table, coffee table, ping pong table, 2 chairs. House shipped flat. Easy assembly.
79 N 01405—Battery not included. Shpg. wt. 8 lbs........$4.89
34 N 4650—Battery for above. Shpg. wt. for 2, 8 oz.. .2 for 28c

$2.98

5-Room Metal Doll House Complete with Furniture

Just move in—completely furnished, even to lithographed rugs and pictures on the wall. 36 pieces of break-resistant molded plastic furniture. Sturdy metal construction. All windows, edges safety turned, rolled smooth. Floor sections ribbed, walls double turned for additional strength. "See through" cut-out windows. Brightly lithographed stone and clapboard exterior. Interior decorated in modern colors. Measures 19½x15½x9 in. deep. Easy to assemble, no tools needed.
49 N U1410—Shipped flat. Fence not included, see below. Shpg. wt. 5 lbs....................$2.98
49 N 6022—6 sections Green Metal Fence. 2 in. high, 10 ft. long overall. Shpg. wt. 1 lb........$1.69

A $11.79
24-inch

B $9.79
24-inch

C $18.95
20-inch

D $4.98
16½-inch

E Was
~~$5.69~~
$4.99
16-inch

F $7.95
21-inch

G $5.39
17-inch

OUR BEST HAPPI-TIME DOLLS with Saran hair

Comb, brush and set their shiny, springy locks in party-pretty styles

[A] **Lively Happi-Time Walker now has jointed knees.** A similar 24-inch doll without hat and coat was $14.95 last year. She walks, she sits, she kneels to pray, she rolls her big eyes and cries too —she's as peppy as her young "mother." She can strike almost any pose a little girl thinks of. She seems alive as she toddles through toy town tilting her pretty head from side to side and rolling her thick-lashed eyes flirtatiously. She closes her eyes at naptime to dream. Play beauty shop; comb, brush and re-do her gleaming Saran pigtails. Molded of almost unbreakable plastic, she takes rough play right in stride. Fashionably dressed in an embossed cotton dress with matching sewed-in panties, lace-trimmed cotton gabardine coat and hat, socks, vinyl plastic shoes.

De Luxe 24-inch Doll. Eyes flirt and close.
49 N U3392—Shpg. wt. 5 lbs. $11.79

17-inch Doll. Eyes close, do not flirt.
49 N U3323—Shpg. wt. 3 lbs. $8.89

[B] **Fun-loving 24-inch Teen-ager** is all dressed up for a Saturday night date in a red puckered nylon dress with a sheer lace-trimmed blouse attached. An elfish red felt hat sits jauntily atop her long curls. Bright just-pretend blooms add spice to her enchanting outfit. Sweet voice when hugged. Comb, brush and set her rooted Saran locks in all the ways you can dream of. All vinyl plastic skin, feels so warm and real, wipes clean with a damp cloth. Jointed arms. Long-lashed go-to-sleep eyes. Wears rayon panties, socks, vinyl plastic shoes. 3 curlers included.
49 N U3338—Shipping weight 5 lbs. $9.79

All of the Happi-Time Dolls shown on these two pages have shimmering Saran hair that little mamas can comb, brush and set over and over. Saran locks stay springy and lustrous and easy to manage. We believe you can't find better quality at these low prices.

[C] **Happi-Time Walking Wardrobe Doll with a Big Steel Trunk.** Enough clothes in her trunk for a trip around the play world! She walks gayly, tilting her head from side to side. Comb, brush and set her shiny Saran wig in all the latest styles. Fully jointed. Made of hard-to-break plastic. Go-to-sleep eyes. Wears a bonny Scotch plaid rayon dress frosted with lace, cotton underskirt, panties, socks, vinyl plastic shoes. In her trunk you'll find a fluffy net trimmed rayon taffeta formal with panties, a denim coat and hat, 2-piece cotton pajamas, cotton housecoat, embossed cotton print play dress, comb, brush, mirror, sunglasses, 6 plastic hangers, extra pair of socks and vinyl plastic shoes. All steel trunk with steel reinforced corners, hinges and snap locks.

20-inch Doll with big 3-drawer trunk, 20¼ x11x11 in. Shpg. wt. 12 lbs.
79 N 03325. . . . . . $18.95

16-inch Doll with one-drawer trunk, 16¼ x9x9 in. Shpg. wt. 8 lbs.
49 N U3324. . . . . $14.89

[D] **Demure Baby Doll** in her Sunday best; lace-trimmed organdy dress with cotton pique panel, matching bonnet. Short Saran curls are rooted in; comb, brush and set them over and over. Vinyl plastic head, skin. Go-to-sleep eyes; coo voice. Undies, socks, shoes, curlers.
49 N U3224—16½ inches tall. Shipping weight 3 lbs. $4.98
49 N U3227—18½ inches tall. Shipping weight 4 lbs. $5.98

See our big selection of doll furniture and buggies in this section

[E] **Reduced! Pigtailed Walking Playmate** turns her head coyly as she toddles. Thick, glossy Saran braid wig can be dampened, combed and set like a real little girl's hair. Sweet molded plastic face. Fully jointed, hard-to-break plastic body wipes clean. Go-to-sleep eyes. Lacy cotton and rayon taffeta dress (Assorted styles), shoes, 2 curlers.
49 N U3356—16 inches tall. Shipping weight 2 lbs. Was $5.69 . . . . $4.99
49 N U3357—21 inches tall. Shipping weight 3 lbs. Was $7.95 . . . . $7.49

[F] **Adorable in her three-piece ensemble.** New "Super-flex" in her shapely legs—she can sit, kneel and bend her knees. Baby-soft vinyl plastic from head to toe. Go-to-sleep eyes; soft coo voice. Rooted Saran curls to comb, brush, set. Rich heather-mix cotton coat, bonnet, lacy ninon dress, rayon slip, knit panties, socks and shoes.
49 N U3638—17 inches tall. One-piece body. Shpg. wt. 3 lbs. $5.95
49 N U3639—De luxe 21-in. with jointed arms for more poses. Wt. 5 lbs. . . . $7.95

[G] **Lovable Baby Doll,** a 17-inch bundle of joy at a low price. A shimmering Saran pony tail accents her delicate little girl features. Comb, brush, set her hair—it's rooted to stay in. Soft vinyl head. Cuddly cotton-stuffed body has soft latex skin that wipes clean. Jointed arms. Coo voice; go-to-sleep eyes. Lace-trimmed ninon dress in bonbon pastels, rayon slip, knit cotton panties, socks, imitation leather shoes and 2 curlers included.
49 N U3229—Shpg. wt. 3 lbs. $5.39

[H] **21-inch Teen-ager** with pert pony tail and bangs, like the girl next door. Perfect proportions, delicate features. Life-like vinyl plastic skin wipes clean. Rooted Saran hair to comb, brush, set. Pick her up, she cries when cuddled. Go-to-sleep eyes. Jointed arms. Dressed for a party in costly nylon dress with printed nylon tea apron, dainty lace-trimmed cotton half slip, panties and vinyl plastic shoes, 21 in. tall.
49 N U3321—Shpg. wt. 4 lbs. $7.98

[J] **19-inch Happi-Time Princess** walks with her mama. Her pony tail bobs merrily as she turns her head from side to side. Comb, brush, set her rooted Saran hair. Fully jointed plastic body. Vinyl plastic face; go-to-sleep eyes. Wears aqua-blue party dress of shimmering rayon trimmed in gold color rick-rack and fluffy net ruffles, gold color belt, floral spray; slip, undies, vinyl plastic shoes. Curlers included.
49 N U3349—Shpg. wt. 3 lbs. $9.79

[K] **New 17-inch Baby** with perky poodle cut hair and a big butterfly bow. She coos with delight at your caresses. Comb, brush and set her short, springy ringlets; her Saran hair is rooted in. Soft-to-touch latex skin feels smooth as baby sister's; keep her clean with damp cloth. Plump one-piece cotton stuffed body. Go-to-sleep eyes. Lace trimmed sheer ninon dress, full slip, knit panties, imitation leather shoes.
49 N U3621—Shpg. wt. 2 lbs. $3.79

[L] **Happi-Time Wardrobe Doll** walks with you. She's smart as a model with her 4 outfits. Her wardrobe includes a cotton play dress, shortie coat and hat (assorted styles), three-piece skiing outfit, sunsuit, sunglasses, 2 coat hangers. She wears panties, socks, vinyl plastic shoes. Saran hair wig to comb, brush, set. Fully-jointed hard plastic body wipes clean. Head turns, eyes close. 14½ inches tall. Shpg. wt. 2 lbs.
49 N 3384—Doll Wardrobe $7.98

[H] $7.98
21-inch

[J] $9.79
19-inch

[K] $3.79
17-inch

[L] $7.98
14½-inch

$9.79 Doll and bath

Was $3.59
$2.79 For 11½-in. doll

Tiny Tears .. Ding Dong School Bath!

11½-in. **Tiny Tears** cries real tears, wets her diaper, blows bubbles. She loves tubbings in her own 21x 11½x29-in. bath; tub holds water, has a drain hose. Change her on the fold-away vinyl dressing table. Heavy gauge steel frame has folding tray, pockets for soap, diapers, etc., rubber-tipped legs. Dainty Tiny Tears has twinkly go-to-sleep glassene eyes, molded hair, hard plastic head, molded rubber body. Layette: diaper, bootees, plastic bubble pipe, pacifier, soap, sponge, Kleenex, bottle. In assorted style cotton pajamas.
79 N T3086L—11½-in. tall doll. Wt. 7 lbs.........$9.79

For Tiny Tears

Reduced! Layette has sheer embroidered cotton dress, bonnet, panties, lacy rayon taffeta jacket, diaper, knit bootees, pacifier, bubble pipe, nipple bottle.

49 N 3450—For 11½-in. doll Wt. 1 lb. Was $3.59... $2.79
49 N 3451—For 13½-in. doll Wt. 1 lb. Was $3.77... $2.89
49 N 3452—For 16-in. doll Wt. 2 lbs. Was $4.49... $3.69

NEW JOINTED WALKERS

Jointed at knees, hips, elbows, shoulders

Sweet Sue—fully jointed walking dolls. They're one of America's most life-like playmates. Sue does almost everything a real little girl can do—bends her knees, kneels to pray, bends elbows to fold hands, sits; assumes 101 poses. And she walks right along with her new "mama," turning her head as she goes. She has rooted Saran hair that can be dampened, combed, curled, and waved—just like your own—and it won't pull out. No special shampoo or pins needed. Sue's vinyl arms are beautifully detailed to show off her gracefully tapered little fingers. There's a flush of spring in her delicately tinted cheeks. Her thickly-lashed glassene eyes close at naptime. Finely molded head, legs and body are made of highest quality break-resistant plastic. You've seen Sweet Sue, an American character doll, on Television—now you can have one of your very own.

[A] Sweet Sue Coed, dressed for school days

This pertly dressed miss is the sweetheart of the campus. She wears a fashionable felt skirt laced with contrasting ribbon, and cotton print blouse. The white rayon taffeta ruffle under her skirt rustles as she strolls along with her little mother. Her felt hat and purse match. She wears rayon panties—little stylish shoes and stockings.

18-inch size	22-inch size
49 N U3301—Shpg. wt. 3 lbs... $10.95	49 N U3302—Shpg. wt. 5 lbs... $12.95

[B] Sweet Sue "Cotillion," the prettiest girl at the dance!

The Queen of the Ball .. she's a picture of grace and elegance in her exquisite evening gown with imported lace bodice and sleeves—ruching and lace trim—and full nylon tulle skirt with dust ruffle. Her hooped petticoat makes her gown stand out. She wears pretty silver-color evening slippers, imitation pearl necklace and 2 dainty flowers in her hair.

18-inch size	25-inch size
49 N U3303—Shpg. wt. 3 lbs... $12.95	79 N 03304—Shpg. wt. 7 lbs... $18.95

A National Broadcasting Co., Inc., Service and Trademark

$9.39
11½-in. tall with Fur Wig

TINY TEARS CRIES, WETS, BLOWS BUBBLES

She's just as lovable and lifelike as a real baby!

Tears roll down her cheeks when she's sad

She blows bubbles with bubble pipe

She loves to bathe in neck-high water

She's as lovable and lifelike as baby sister! Big wet tears well up in her eyes and roll down her cheeks to melt the heart of the sternest young mom. She cries lustily, closes her thick-lashed glassene eyes at naptime, drinks her bottle, wets her diaper and blows bubbles .. even comforts herself with her pacifier like any real infant. And she loves to be bathed. Her pretty head is molded of hard-to-break plastic. Jointed body of soft molded rubber. Embossed cotton romper suit, with layette that includes lovely cotton pique dress, panties and bonnet, flannelette nightie, soap, Kleenex, 2 clothespins, wash cloth, bubble pipe, nipple bottle, stockings, shoes, diaper, sponge and pacifier. *See sizes below.*

"Tiny Tears" with Curly Wig, Suitcase, Big Layette

Loves to have her tousled curls combed, brushed, washed. Exactly as described above (11½-inch size has bootees instead of shoes and socks), she's a favorite with tiny moms everywhere. Ready to go anywhere in her "ready-for-hard-play" fiberboard suitcase. Smart leather-effect finish, with snap lock, sturdy handle. Easy to store.

11½-inch size	13½-inch size	16-inch size	New 20-in. size
49 N U3032	49 N U3037	49 N U3044	49 N U3047
Shpg. wt. 3 lbs.	Shpg. wt. 4 lbs.	Shpg. wt. 6 lbs.	Shpg. wt. 9 lbs.
$9.39	$11.29	$13.98	$16.98

"Tiny Tears" with Molded Hair

As pert and pretty as can be, with realistic molded hair. (Not illustrated.) She has all the features described above, except her layette includes: lovely cotton pique dress, matching bonnet and panties. Soap, Kleenex, wash cloth, bubble pipe, nipple nursing bottle, diaper, sponge and pacifier. Comes in colorful display box. A favorite with little mothers everywhere.

13½-inch size	16-inch size
49 N U3031—Shpg. wt. 3 lbs. $7.45	49 N U3033—Shpg. wt. 4 lbs. $9.45

WITH SARAN HAIR
Comb, brush, set their hair

Jointed at knees, shoulders, and elbows

Kneel to say their prayers alongside "mama"

Saran hair can be combed, brushed, set

A $10.95
18-inch

B $18.95
25-inch

Press mechanism to move lips

MAMA

$13.95

$5.59
13-inch

$15.89

$9.75

New! Ricky, Jr. He sits, stands, bends his knees

Ricky Junior is the most active little fellow you've ever seen. He can stand, sit, bend his legs in any position. A wire inside his cuddly body makes these tricks possible. He's a true-life replica of his TV counterpart. All vinyl, sponges clean, is almost unbreakable. Molded hair. He wears corduroy overalls in bright pastel color, cotton shirt, corduroy beanie; shoes, socks.
49 N U3021—13 in. tall. Wt. 2 lbs. $5.59
49 N U3025—17 in. tall. Wt. 3 lbs. 7.49

Toodles, the action doll kneels, drinks and wets

The first all-jointed vinyl doll. Jointed at knees, hips, shoulders, elbows. She's soft and cuddly; does all the things real babies do—sits, drinks, wets, crawls, plays with her fingers and toes. Her head moves in any direction; her molded hair always stays in place. She has beautiful detailed fingers, wears sandals to show off her pretty toes. Easy to sponge clean. Wears nylon playsuit, rayon taffeta bonnet, has bottle. 21 in. tall.
49 N U3048—Shpg. wt. 6 lbs.... $15.89

Baby Big Eyes .. 23-inch baby with big sleeping eyes

She'll steal your heart away the minute you look into her beautiful big eyes. And when her new Mama hugs her cuddly body, she'll find her irresistible. Her rooted Saran hair resembles that of a six months old baby. Tiny fingers and toes are so real-looking, they're made of a new type plastic. Vinyl head, arms, legs; vinyl-coated cotton stuffed body. Sponges clean. Cry voice. In flannelette snowsuit.
49 N U3260—Shpg. wt. 5 lbs... $9.75

New! "Magic Lips" moves her lips as she "talks"

Press gently on her back, she closes her lips; release pressure and her mouth opens cooing softly to her "Mama." Life-like vinyl head, arms, legs; cotton stuffed vinyl-coated body. Eyes close. Rooted Saran hair to brush, set, comb. Wears pretty flocked organdy dress, rayon slip, panties, socks, vinyl shoes. 24 in. tall. Tiny tooth brush for her 3 teeth.
79 N 03358—Shpg. wt. 6 lbs... $13.95

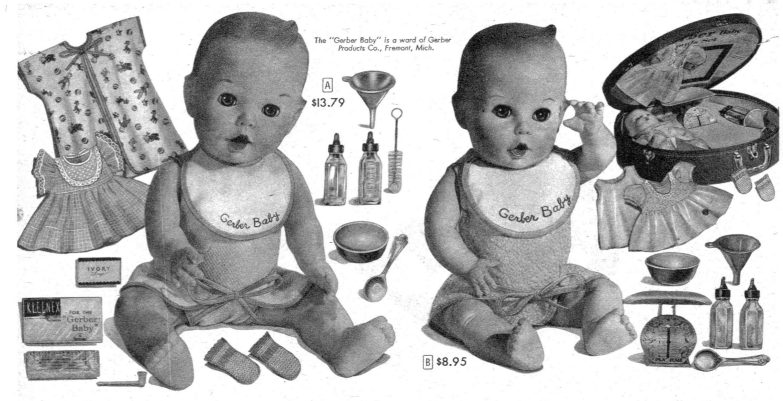

The "Gerber Baby" is a ward of Gerber
Products Co., Fremont, Mich.

[A] $13.79

[B] $8.95

TUBBABLE BABY DOLLS that drink .. wet .. cry

Our finest 18-in. All-Vinyl Gerber Baby with wardrobe

[A] So big, so cuddly! Baby-soft vinyl body and head finely molded from the dimples in her cheeks to her graceful little fingers. Delicately tinted features, rounded arms, legs. Heavy-lashed go-to-sleep glassene eyes. Fully jointed arms and legs make diaper changing, dressing easy for little mommies. Loves to splash in tub. She turns her head, cries, drinks, wets, sleeps, even blows bubbles with her own bubble pipe! Finely made wardrobe: Barred dimity dress, cotton flannel kimono, cotton romper, bib, bootees. Silver-plated spoon, bottles, brush, dish, soap, funnel, kleenex, bubble pipe, swabs, picture.

79 N 03568—Shipping weight 6 pounds..$13.79

13-in. Gerber Baby with Scale, Traveling Case, Dress

[B] Beautiful heavy-lashed glassene eyes close when she naps. Delicately molded vinyl plastic head. Rubber body is fully jointed. She loves to splash in the tub, drink from her bottle, (and wet her diaper, too.) Weigh baby on her very own metal "Pla-Scale." Squeeze baby and hear her cry. She blows bubbles with her own bubble pipe. Complete with bright red plastic-bound carrying case that locks securely with 3 metal clamps. Plastic contour handle for easy carrying—sized right for little fingers. Pretty lace-trimmed cotton and ninon dress. Cotton slip, romper, bib, bootees. Bottles, funnel, dish, silver-plated spoon, picture.

49 N U3565—Shipping weight 6 lbs...$8.95

Gerber Baby, Formula Set, Case

[C] Smallest version of the famous Gerber Baby—for tiny tots. 12 in. tall, she cries, drinks, wets, blows bubbles with her own bubble pipe! Fully jointed to have variety of real-life poses. Finely detailed vinyl head—even to wispy molded curl and dimpled cheeks. Stationary glassene eyes. Molded rubber body. 3 bottles in wire rack, funnel, dish, bottle brush, silver-plated spoon, bubble pipe. She wears cotton romper, bib. Sturdy, leather-effect snap-lock carrying case. Picture of Gerber Baby.

49 N U3506—Shpg. wt. 4 lbs...................$5.49

18-in. lovable "Bannister Baby"®

[D] 18-inch Bannister Baby inspired by Constance Bannister, famous baby photographer. Molded of all vinyl, jointed arms, legs. Head turns. And when it's naptime her glassene eyes close in sleep. Drinks from her bottle (incl.), wets panties, cries, blows bubbles with plastic pipe. Her fine wardrobe includes lace-trimmed pink ninon dress, cotton slip, bootees, knit panties, cotton flannel robe.

49 N U3564—Shpg. wt. 4 lbs..........$9.29

12-in. Betty Bows

[E] Lovable Betty wears a perky bow in her molded hair. Turnable vinyl head, molded rubber body, jointed arms, legs. She drinks, wets, cries, sleeps, and blows bubbles. Thick-lashed go-to-sleep glassene eyes. Entirely workable. She wears cotton romper, bootees. Pipe, bottle.

49N3505—Shpg. wt. 1 lb. 4 oz.$2.69

10-in. Tiny "So-Wee"

[F] Made especially for the tiniest doll mommies. Loves to splash in tub, drink from her bottle. Cries lovingly when squeezed. Wonder-wide stationary plastic eyes. All rubber from head to toe. So-Wee wears a cotton diaper and wears a cotton terry cloth bib. Nursing bottle included.

49 N 3514—Shpg. wt. 1 lb...$1.75

[E] $2.69

[D] $9.29

[C] $5.49

[F] $1.75

As proof positive that the toy pages in the Sears Wishbook were written by adults, not kids, check out the headline on a page of grooming toys -- "It's fun being neat!" Well, if that's true, little girls could have a real blast with the full assortment of combs, brushes, barrettes, and mirrors offered. Toy horses wore "saddles" that held toothbrushes, combs and nail clippers; and even Jiminy Cricket lent a hand, by holding onto your toothbrush.

Girls who already had cribs and baby carriages for their broods could now add a four-drawer chest, a hutch cupboard and a maple high chair to the nursery. But when she just had to get away from it all, there was the Western convertible bike. Complete with saddle bag and rifle with case, this bike, with the addition or removal of a top bar, easily converted from boy's bike to girl's, and back again. "It's fun sharing a bike with your bratty brother!"

Sears Christmas

Wishbook

1956

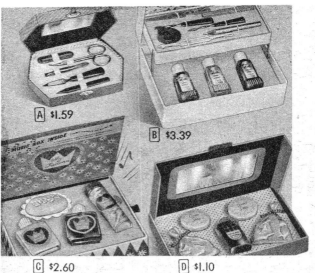

[A] $1.59 [B] $3.39

[C] $2.60 [D] $1.10

[E] $2.15 [F] $1.00 [G] $1.00

[H] $2.98 [J] $3.98 [K] $1.98

[L] $1.10 [M] $1.10 [N] $1.98 [P] $1.59

Trimmer tresses for playtime Western glamour gals

$2.98

Beautiful "My Lady Fair" Horse. An easy answer to the problem of rounding up would-be "cowgirls" at tidy-up time. 7½x8½-inch white plastic horse is break-resistant, has gold-color fittings. This "white prancer's" black plastic saddle holds six gold-color barrettes (three pairs in various designs) and a white nylon comb.

"My Lady Fair" makes grooming fun; any little girl will be pleased to have it "decorate" her dresser. Mother will be pleased with the new found interest in hair-do neatness, too. A gift that's different.

8 N 9528—Shipping weight 8 ounces...................$2.98

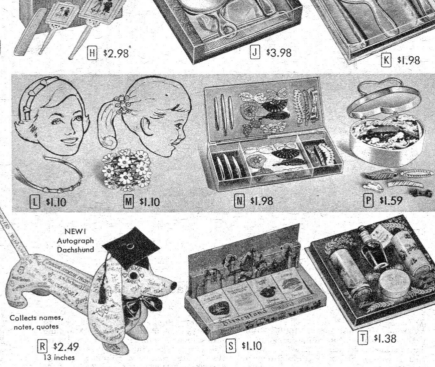

NEW! Autograph Dachshund

Collects names, notes, quotes

[R] $2.49 13 inches

[S] $1.10

[T] $1.38

It's fun being neat..

when Santa brings these grooming aids for little girls

[A] **Vanity Manicure Set** in red and gold-color case. Emery board, tweezer, cuticle scissors, file, cleaner-pusher . . . gay red plastic handles. She'll love her own set. Mother will like her new neatness. (9c Fed. tax incl.)
8 N 9525E—Shpg. wt. 6 oz...$1.59

[B] **Junior Miss Manicure Set.** Pink plastic jewel box has self-rising tray, contains ½ oz. ea. natural polish, remover, cuticle remover; file, emery boards, pusher, cuticle knife, nail white, 2 others. (7c Fed. tax incl.)
8 N 9023E—Wt. 1 lb. 4 oz...$3.39

[C] **My Treasures by Wrisley.** A fragrant set of bath cosmetics in a musical treasure box. Delicately scented pink soap; 1½ oz. ea. hand lotion, cologne; 2 oz. talcum powder. Music box plays "Alouette." Ppd. (Wt. 1 lb. 4 oz.)
8 N 9009E—(10c Fed. tax incl.) $2.60

[D] **Little Trav'ler bath cosmetics by Wrisley.** Makes little girls sweet as cherubs at bath time. Red tartan "suitcase" box holds 2 tiny pink guest soaps, 2 bath-size packets bubble bath, ½-oz. refreshing Wrisley cologne.
8 N 9548E—Ppd. (Wt. 8 oz.) $1.10

[E] **Hidden Charm Young Toiletries by Dorothy Gray.** An adorable choice for a sweet little girl. 3 rosebud-shaped soaps; 1 oz. ea. of hand lotion, bubble bath, cologne, 3 gold-plated charms. (15c Fed. tax incl.)
8 N 9554E—Ppd. (Wt. 1 lb.) $2.15

[F] **My Merry Beauty Shop.** "Pretend" powder, lipstick, nail polish, perfume. Bobby pins, 2½-in. comb, mirror; wash cloth, nail white, emery board, manicure rest, rubber curlers, shampoo. All harmless.
8 N 9489—Shpg. wt. 8 oz...$1.00

[G] **Scented Knit Wit**—a comical creature from outer space to intrigue young sophisticates and small fry alike. Foam rubber covered with pink knit material . . cuddly, safe for tiniest tots. Yarn, felt, ribbon trim. 7 in. high.
8 N 9547—Shpg. wt. 8 oz... $1.00

[H] **Tiny Tripper.** Wood and fibre-kraft vanity case. 12x8½x 5 in., fitted with 7¼-in. brush, 10-in. mirror, 6¾-in. comb . . all of white plastic. Brush, mirror have charming old-fashioned design. (11c Fed. tax incl.)
8 N 9483E—Shpg. wt. 3 lbs. $2.98

[J] **Famous Hughes Jr. Miss 3-pc. Blue Lucite Vanity Set** in gift box. 3½-in. diam. hand mirror, 7-in. comb, 6¾-in. brush with Tynex nylon bristles. Sure to be treasured by any little girl. *State color crystal, rose, blue.*
8 N 9482—Wt. 1 lb. 8 oz... $3.98

[K] **Little Miss Vanity Set.** Something nice for the pigtail set! Transparent pink plastic 7-in. contour-shape hair brush, 4-in. diameter double-faced mirror, 7-in. comb. A set she'll be proud to use. Rayon-lined gift box.
8 N 9481—Wt. 1 lb. 8 oz...$1.98

[L] **Beauty Head Band.** Gold-color plastic headband with pastel heart trim. For "little-girl" glamour. Keeps locks in place, looks party-special.
A pretty accessory that makes even hair-combing time fun!
8 N 9539E—Shpg. wt. 2 oz... $1.10

[M] **Expansion Pony Trailer** . . . Perky plastic pony tail holder decorated with dainty white daisies. Holds her hair securely, prettily. Dresses up her clothes, can be worn as a bracelet. Fits in her Christmas stocking.
8 N 9538E—Shpg. wt. 2 oz...$1.10

[N] **26-pc. Barrette Set.** High fashion for her hair. Hinged plastic box holds 26 barrettes, gaily colored, different shapes. 3 pr. aluminum, 7 pr. plastic novelty, 3 pr. jeweled. Pink plastic comb, 4½ in. Wt. 8 oz.
8 N 9549E—(6c Fed. tax incl.)$1.98

[P] **Junior Carry-all with Barrettes.** Heart-shaped, handled plastic purse holds 28 (14 matched pairs) plastic barrettes in assorted colors, shapes and sizes. She'll love choosing the right colors to accent her dresses.
8 N 9545—Shpg. wt. 8 oz...$1.59

[R] **Otto and Super Otto, the Autograph Dachshunds.** Lovable, comical pets that become "living diaries" for the collection of signatures of classmates and chums. Adults will love these floppy-eared friends, too, when used as a guest log in game room, cottage, etc. Yellow heavy cotton poplin skin; firm, smooth stuffing presents a perfect writing surface for pen or pencil. Eyes have movable pupils.
8 N 9513—Otto. 13 inches long. Shpg. wt. 10 oz............$2.49
8 N 9141—Super Otto. 22 inches long. Shpg. wt. 1 lb. 12 oz...$3.49

[S] **Disneyland Bubble Bath Set.** Thrill the youngsters with these twenty ⁹⁄₁₆-oz., gaily illustrated packets of such intriguing fragrances as King Arthur Carrousel, Tomorrowland Speedboats, Dumbo Ride and Autopia.
8 N 9546E—Ppd. (Wt. 1 lb.) $1.10

[T] **Shulton Early American Friendship Garden set for the Junior Miss.** ¾ oz. toilet water, 1 oz. talc, ¼ oz. body sachet, 1¼ oz. bubbling bath crystals . . all charmingly gift packaged. Delightful as a colonial bouquet.
8 N 9559E—Ppd. (Wt. 1 lb.) $1.38

NOTE: All prices of catalog numbers ending in "E" include 10% Federal Excise tax unless otherwise stated

A $1.00	**B** $1.00
C $1.00	**D** $1.49
E $1.60	**F** $1.49
G $1.00	**H** $1.00
J $1.49	**K** $1.80
L 2 for 98c	**M** $1.98
N $1.98	
P $2.98	**R** $1.00
S $2.98	**T** $4.98

Gifts for good Grooming

Especially designed with the younger set in mind

Hop in the Saddle, Pardners; it's Spruce-Up Time

$2.98

Palomino Groomer spurs youngsters to tidy up. You'll be amazed to find miniature cowhands brushing teeth, combing hair, filing nails without prompting from you. Plastic palomino horse has gold-color fittings, is break resistant. Measures 7½x8¼ inches. Tan plastic "saddle" holds nail clipper, nail file, SEARS APPROVED toothbrush, and comb.
8 N 9123—Shipping weight 12 ounces....................$2.98

Giant Palomino Groomer. Almost 3 in. taller! Size 10¼x11¼ in. Tan plastic saddle, grooming accessories as above.
8 N 9529—Shipping weight 1 pound....................$4.98

Playtime Heroes Military Brush and Comb Sets. Rugged idols colorfully adorn the mirror-finish metal brush tops. Military brush has strong nylon bristles . . . measures 4¾x2½ inches. 4½-inch plastic comb fits into special slot on brush top. Choose his favorite for Christmas. He'll be so proud of it in his room.

A 8 N 9543—Daniel Boone.
Shpg. wt. 6 oz......$1.00

B 8 N 9473—Robin Hood.
Shpg. wt. 6 oz.......$1.00

C **Junior Mr. Holster Comb and Brush Set.** Imitation leather holster has western motif, fits on belt. Holds 5½-inch plastic club brush with nylon bristles and 4⅜-inch plastic comb. Makes better grooming fun!
8 N 9480—Shpg. wt. 8 oz. $1.00

D **Clean Hit Kit.** A gift that bats 1000 in any league of young ball-playing enthusiasts. 7½-inch wood back brush in baseball bat shape with white nylon bristles, 5-in. comb, yellow terry cloth bath mitt, ball of Castile soap. Gaily printed acetate-covered gift package.
8 N 9588—Shpg. wt. 14 oz. $1.49

E **Seaforth Wee Scot Set.** Especially for bonnie young laddies. Contains 1¾ ounce shampoo, 1¾ ounce hair groom, 1¼ ounce talc. With 4 novel "movie strips" for him to view. (10c Federal tax included.) Postpaid.
8 N 9078E—(Shpg. wt. 1 lb.) . .$1.60

F **Texas Pete Western Trio.** 3 pure castile soaps on a rope . . . six shooter, Tricky the horse, and Texas Pete. Convenient cord goes around neck. A wonderful way to round up straight-shooting playtimers for clean up time.
8 N 9016—Wt. 1 lb. 8 oz.. $1.49

G **Sports Trio.** He'll really scrub and enjoy bath time, too. Soap-on-a-rope features 3 sports motifs: baseball, football and boxing gloves. Pure castile shower soap has handy round-the-neck cord. Shpg. wt. 1 lb. 6 oz.
8 N 9443....................$1.00

H **My Merry Rise and Shine Kit .** . like Dad's shaving kit, but for young pretenders. 13 items including make-believe plastic razor, .35-ounce Ipana toothpaste, toothbrush, shave brush, hair groom, shoe shine cloth.
8 N 9488—Shpg. wt. 8 oz.. $1.00

J **Mickey Mouse Club "Brush Up" Kit** . . . in Mouseketeer 5¾x6-in. Club House of ivory-color plastic. Hangs on wall, has nylon bristled nail brush, toothbrush, toothpaste holder and 5-in. comb . . . all plastic.
8 N 9520—Shpg. wt. 9 oz.... $1.49

K **Junior Shaver Clean-Up Kit** contains "electric razor" molded of soap with shower rope, sponge, 5-inch comb, talcum, bubble bath, shampoo. He'll have fun imitating Dad! (5c Fed. tax incl.)
8 N 9556E—Shpg. wt. 1 lb... $1.80

L **Colorful Jiminy Cricket Tooth Brush Set by DuPont.** This "Mouseketeer" character encourages youngsters' regular brushing. Plastic holder hangs on wall, holds 5¼-in. child's toothbrush with Tynex nylon bristles.
8 N 9541—Shpg. wt. 10 oz. 2 for 98c

M **Imported from Japan . .** cabinet for precious "treasures." Blonde wood covered with Mosaic-designed parchment. 2 sliding doors reveal two 2¾x2-inch drawers. Bottom drawer 4⅞ x 2⅝ inches. Folding mirror.
8 N 9515—Shpg. wt. 1 lb.. $1.98

N **3-drawer Plastic Playtime Cosmetic Chest.** An exciting gift for any little girl. Has miniature compact, rouge box, lipstick, comb, brush, mirror, barrettes. Pink or blue (sorry, no choice). 4½x6½ inches.
8 N 9377—Shpg. wt. 1 lb.... $1.98

P **8-piece Plastic Dresser Set.** Ivory color with antique gold-color trim. Vanity tray, 2 powder jars, 5¼x3¼-inch jewel box, 8-in. comb, 7¾-inch professional-style brush, 2 picture frames.
8 N 9351—Shpg. wt. 2 lbs.. $2.98

R **5-piece Dresser Set** in feminine pink transparent plastic. Two 4½x5½-inch picture frames, 10⅛-inch hand mirror and 6⅜-inch nylon bristled brush (both with lovely garden scene on back), 6½-inch comb.
8 N 9486—Wt. 1 lb. 9 oz... $1.00

S **Rocky Mountain Mineral Kit with genuine Uranium Ore!** A truly educational gift for sprouting geologists.
16 extra-large specimens of rare minerals, semi-precious stones and ores are carefully mounted.
Order this kit now for your boy or girl . . . it's guaranteed to provide hours of fun!
8 N 9514—Wt. 1 lb, 10 oz.... $2.98

T **Boy Scout Rocks and Minerals Kit.** An ideal gift because it helps youngsters to learn . . . to locate mineral deposits, recognize precious metals and identify geologic formations.
Kit contains 60 selected specimens, including gold- and silver-bearing ores, all beautifully mounted and with detailed descriptions of the specimens.
Perfect for birthday presents and other remembrances, too!
8 N 9542—Shpg. wt. 3 lbs...... $4.98

A $8.59

B $3.69

C $7.69
crib only

D $3.79

E $5.98
basket only

F $5.98

G $4.79
crib only

H $1.98
crib only

J $1.89

K 98c

L $10.95
bed only

M $4.59

N $5.95

P $4.59

R $4.69

Doll Furniture .. all the comforts of home!

Bathe dolly, put her to bed, keep her clothes tidy

◄ ITEMS DESCRIBED BELOW ILLUSTRATED ON OPPOSITE PAGE

[A] De Luxe Doll Bath with Dressing Table. Big for large dolls, yet folds flat to put away. Full square steel frame construction, ivory color finish. Lovely blue Masland Duran plastic tub electronically sealed. Gay decorations. Folding metal tray for accessories. Plastic hammock, drain hose with "on-off" clamp, safety belt. Nursing unit has bottle, nipple, sealing disc, cap. Soap, washcloth, apron. 14½x27¾x30½ in. high. Doll not included.
79 N 09286L—Shipping weight 15 pounds.........$8.59

[B] New Metal High Chair. Feeding tray moves up and down. Rubber feet on legs. Sturdy tubular steel frame, firmly braced. Shaped metal seat, back. Seat 9½x8 in. deep. 29 in. high overall. Easy to assemble.
49 N 9224—Shipping weight 7 pounds............$3.69

[C] Our Best Metal Doll Crib. Finished in pastel blue enamel. Drop side makes it easy for little mothers to put dolly to bed. Color play beads keep dolly amused; animal pictures on full end panels. Swivel casters. 15¼x25¼x21½ in. high. Mattress, doll not included.
79 N 09240—Shipping weight 14 pounds.........$7.69
Tufted Plastic Mattress wipes clean with damp cloth. Inflates to 1½ inches thick. Size 14x24 inches.
49 N 9242—Shipping weight 8 ounces............$1.25

[D] New Doll Bath with dressing table, safety strap. Wheels on 2 legs. Vinyl tub with hammock; metal accessory tray; folding tubular steel frame. Splash guards with pockets; drain hose with clip. Sponge, comb, soap. 25½x12½x20½ in. high. Doll not included.
79 N 09250L—Shipping weight 5 pounds.........$3.79

[E] Fiber Doll Basket with Hood looks like one used for babies! Firm woven fiber construction takes lots of tough wear. Movable hood keeps sun out of little dolly's eyes. Folding legs lock in place. Rolls on casters. Enameled white, pastel trim. 26 in. high.
79 N 09255—Basket only, no liner. Shpg. wt. 7 lbs...$5.98
Pad and Liner. Plastic print liner; Tufflex* pad.
49 N 9253—Shipping weight 7 ounces............$1.89

[F] New! Wood Drop Side Crib. Beautiful, rugged birch and beech woods in natural finish. Side lowers to let dolly's little mother tuck her in easily. Pastel pink end panels of tough Masonite Presdwood. Nursery print at head and foot. Play beads. Swivel casters. Painted hardboard "mattress".
79 N 09239—24½x14½x20¼ in. high. Wt. 11 lbs..$5.98

[G] New Metal Drop Side Crib. All steel crib with full end panels. One side lowers to put dolly to bed. Bright blue enamel finish; gay nursery decorations. Swivel casters. Mattress not incl., see below.
49 N 9225—19¾x12x17 in. high. Shpg. wt. 7 lbs....$4.79
Tufted Plastic Mattress for above. 1 inch thick.
49 N 9226—Inflates. Shipping weight 6 ounces......89c
*Reg. U.S. Pat. Off. (cellulose fiber)

[H] Economy Doll Crib. Wood construction, Maple finish. Snug dowel joints; removable slat bottoms. Mattress not incl. 22½x12½x15½ in. high.
49 N 9283—Shipping weight 4 pounds...........$1.98
Tufflex* Mattress. Soft; covered with easy-to-clean plastic. Brings dolly sweet dreams.
49 N 9251—Shipping weight 7 ounces..............89c

[J] Doll Bedding Set has everything you need to keep dolly comfortable all through the night. Pink cotton blanket, 17x24 in.; cotton flannel receiving blanket, 17x27 in. sheet; embroidery-edged pillow slip; pillow; clothes pins and safety pins. Fits all beds.
49 N 9275—Shipping weight 8 ounces...........$1.89

[K] Tufflex* Mattress is soft to help dolly sleep better. Plastic cover wipes clean with damp cloth. Fits cribs C and F described at left.
49 N 9252—Shipping weight 9 ounces.............98c

[L] Maple Bunk Bed perfect for big doll families, and for big dolls, too. Use as a double decker, 27 in. high; or convert to 2 twin beds, each 14x28 in. long. Real maple with turned corner posts in authentic colonial style. Slat bottom. Mattresses not included (see below). Easy assembly.
79 N 09272—Shipping weight 15 pounds.........$10.95
49 N 9279—Mattress for above bunk bed. Shipping weight 12 ounces............................Each $1.39

[M] Four-Drawer Chest, Hardwood finish in maple. Holds a large wardrobe for your well-dressed doll. Four big drawers let you neatly stack dresses, bonnets, underthings. Copied from adult styles in the popular colonial fashion. 11¼x7x17 in. high over all. Drawers are 9¾x6x2¾ inches deep.
49 N 9298—Shipping weight 9 pounds............$4.59

[N] Roomy Maple Finish Wardrobe. A place for everything dolly wears—hat shelf, hangers for dresses, drawer for socks, underthings, etc. Gay animal decals on doors. Colonial style with shaped gallery top, front apron. Sturdy hardwood construction with Masonite Presdwood back, shelf drawer bottom. Rod under shelf. 14x7x21 in. high.
79 N 09276—Shipping weight 11 pounds.........$5.95

[P] Hutch Cupboard faithfully copied from adult styles in colonial maple finish hardwood. Colorful wallpaper in a charming provincial pattern makes a lovely background to show off dolly's prettiest dishes. Doors open to hold "everyday" dishes, cooking utensils, accessories. Two grooved plate shelves. Size 13½x7x20 inches high.
79 N 09299—Shipping weight 7 pounds..........$4.59

[R] Maple Highchair like mother used when she was little. Makes it easier and more fun for little mamas at dolly's feeding time. Tray swings up to put dolly in, comes down again to hold her dinner. Spindle back copied from true colonial styles. Over all height 26½ in.; seat 9x9 in.
79 N 09291L—Shipping weight 7 pounds..........$4.69

New 12-inch Walking Doll loves to dress up

[S] A real model, she walks, sits, kneels and poses so prettily. Made of hard plastic with turning head, jointed arms, legs, knees. Saran wig to comb and brush. Go-to-sleep eyes. Dressed in lovely lace undies, high-heeled plastic shoes and long sheer hose.
49 N 3476—Shipping weight 14 ounces..............$2.79

[T] 3-pc. Suit Outfit. Cotton felt with imitation fur.
49 N 3477—Shipping weight 10 ounces...........$1.79

[V] Afternoon Dress Outfit. Decorated cotton shantung.
49 N 3478—Straw hat incl. Shpg. wt. 10 oz........$1.79

[W] Ballerina Outfit. Nylon net tu-tu, rayon bodice.
49 N 3479—Shipping weight 10 ounces...........$1.79

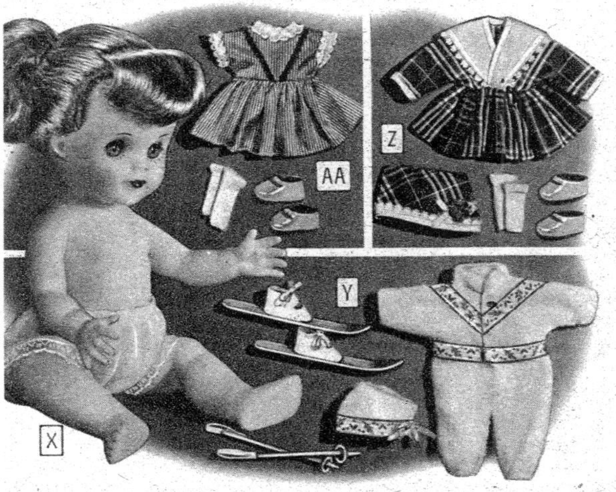

10-in. Vinyl Baby to dress

[X] Beautifully molded all-vinyl baby looks and feels real. Pert pony tail is rooted Saran so you can comb, brush and set it. Head turns; jointed arms and legs. Lashed go-to-sleep eyes. Dressed in lace-trimmed panties. Order clothes below.
49 N 3480—Shpg. wt. 1 lb......$2.69

[Y] Snowsuit Outfit. Cotton flannel jacket, long pants, hat. Shoes mounted on skis, tiny poles.
49 N 3481—Shpg. wt. 8 oz.......$1.79

[Z] Coat Outfit. Scotch plaid rayon coat, hat. Shoes, socks.
49 N 3482—Shpg. wt. 8 oz.......$1.79

[AA] Street Dress Outfit. Striped dress with lace and velvet trim. Shoes and socks.
49 N 3483—Shpg. wt. 8 oz........87c

Petite 8-in. Walker to dress

[BB] Low priced! See her move her head as she walks, comb and brush her Dynel hair. Go-to-sleep glassene eyes. Hard plastic; jointed arms, legs. Wears panties, shoes, socks.
49 N 3457—Shpg. wt. 14 oz.....$1.29

[CC] Bridal Outfit. Pretty bridal gown, veil, bouquet. Panties.
49 N 3473—Shpg. wt. 8 oz......87c

[DD] Majorette Outfit. Rayon dress, bright trim. Hat, boots, baton.
49 N 3474—Shpg. wt. 8 oz......87c

[EE] Negligee Set. Sheer lace-trimmed negligee, chemise.
49 N 3475—Shpg. wt. 8 oz......87c

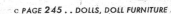

$18.45

$19.45

A boy's and girl's bike .. all in one

View at left shows convertible bike with bar removed for girls. No need to buy a bike for each child—can be passed on from child to child

$23.95
cash
$2.50 down

They're Convertible
Like getting two bikes for the price of one

J. C. HIGGINS 16-inch Convertible Bike for boys and girls ages 4, 5 and 6. When used as a boy's bike, the top bar is firmly attached to frame. You can remove easily to convert to girl's model. The training wheels balance the bike for safety while the youngster is learning to ride. Watch your children progress to 2-wheelers with the same bike. Steel braces. Bike has chain guard. Beautifully enameled colors. Red frame with white trim on fenders and bar. Chrome-plated fork crown and handlebars. White enameled wheel rims and hubs. Coil spring saddle with embossed plastic covered top. Riveted spoke wheels with 16x1¾-in. semi-pneumatic rubber tires. Handlebar grips. Treaded rubber pedals. Strong welded tubular steel frame is reinforced at points of strain to give you a bike that will last for years. Seat to pedal length adjusts from 19 to 23 inches. Shipped freight, express or truck. Order one for your youngster today.

6 N M6571—Shipping weight 34 pounds............$18.45

New! J. C. HIGGINS Equipped Model 16-inch Convertible Bicycle. Can be used by both boys and girls and passed from child to child. Tank type top bar is firmly attached to frame; can be removed easily to change bike from a boy's to a girl's model. Bike has training wheels too, for helping tots learn to ride. Watch your youngsters' progress to 2 wheelers with the same bike. Remove after child has gained confidence, replace for younger child. Training wheels have molded rubber tires.

Strong tubular steel frame is built to last through years of hard wear. Streamlined tank type bar. Easy rolling wheels have 16x1¾-inch semi-pneumatic tires, ball bearings. Seat to pedal length adjusts from 19 to 23 inches. Plastic covered coil spring saddle. Bright red enameled bike frame with attractive white trim. Chrome-plated handlebars, fork crown, truss rods. Plastic handle grips. Steel chain guard. Shipped freight, express or truck. For ages 4, 5, 6.

6 N M6566—Shipping weight 38 pounds.............$19.45

New Western 16-inch Convertible Sidewalk Bike. A wonderful "mount" for your range riding bucka. The comfortable coilspring saddle has a water resistant vinyl plastic top. Handlebar has rubber g with plastic streamers. Saddle bags on the rear of are made of vinyl plastic with white plastic t. Steel chain guard. Bike has attractive Palomi colors—beige and cream. You can remove the to bar to convert from boys' to girls' model. Tubular steel frame. The training wheels balance the bike while child is learning to ride. 16x1.75-inch semi-pneumatic tires. Seat to pedal length adj. from 19 to 23 in. Treaded rubber pedals. Included is a western style rifle with flintlock action. Rifle is 24¾ inches long. There's even a special compartment in the stock. Smart looking gun case is attached to the front of the bike. Gun is plastic, case is vinyl plastic with metal trim. Shipped freight, express or truck.

6 N M6567—Shipping weight 38 pounds...........$23.9

$24.95
cash
$2.50 down

$27.95
cash
$3.00 down

$16.45

A Bike Even The Youngest Can Ride

J. C. HIGGINS 16-inch Convertible Sidewalk Bike has training wheels to help your child learn to ride safely. Easily removed and replaced later for a younger child. Top bar removes easily to convert bike from boy's to girl's model.

You can pass it from child to child, use it for years, and save money in the long run. Bike has coaster brake, just like on full size bicycles for quick, sure stops, controlled coasting. Coil spring saddle has water resistant vinyl plastic cover. Rubber handlebar grips. 16-inch semi-pneumatic tires. Treaded rubber pedals. Brightly enameled bike is red with white trim. Strong welded tubular steel frame for years of riding fun. Chain guard. Seat to pedal length adjusts from 19 to 23 inches. Bike is designed for boys and girls ages 4, 5, 6. Shipped freight, express or truck.

6 N M6588—Shipping weight 36 pounds.........$24.95

New! J. C. HIGGINS 16-inch Standard Sidewalk bicycle (not convertible) with coaster brake and bright, enameled colors. Welded reinforced tubular steel frame has regular bike construction. The coaster brake gives smooth stops—the controlled coasting operates on rearward pressure of foot against pedal. The boys' model is sparkling red and royal blue with white trim. Girls' is royal blue and light blue with white trim. The truss rods and handlebars are chrome-plated. The tan vinyl plastic covered coil spring saddle is water resistant. Plastic handlebar grips .. red on boy's model, white on girl's. Crank and wheels have ball bearings for smoother ride—less pedaling effort. Chain guard. The training wheels balance the bike while child learns to ride safely. Wheels are enameled with molded rubber tires. Steel braces. You can remove training wheels after youngster gains confidence—replace for younger child. Bike has 16x1.75 inch semi-pneumatic tires. Seat to pedal length adjusts from 19 to 23 inches. Shipped freight express or truck.

6 N M6598—Boy's model. Shipping wt. 35 lbs...........$27.95
6 N M6599—Girl's model. Shipping wt. 35 lbs.............27.95

J. C. HIGGINS 13-inch Sidewalk Bike for boys and girls age 2½, 3, 4. Training wheels balance bike while child is learning to ride. You can remove them after tot gains confidence. Bike can be passed on from child to child. Training wheels have rubber tires. Bike has nylon bearings in front, rear wheels and crank hanger. Welded tubular steel frame is built to last for years. 13x1¾-inch semi-pneumatic tires. Streamlined steel chain guard. piece sprocket and crank. Chain tension adjustable. Treaded rubber pedals keep feet from slipping off. Chrome-plated handlebars with handle grips. Enameled wheel rims. Baked on enamel colors. Red frame and fork, red chain guard and fenders with white trim. Large padded coil spring saddle. Seat to pedal length adjusts from 14 to 17½ inches. Bicycle is mailable. Don't disappoint your youngster—order today.

6 N 06579L—Shipping weight 32 pounds. ...$16.4

A little girl in 1957 could spend hours cooking pretend food in her pretend kitchen. But when she ran out of pretend supplies, where could she go? Why, to a pretend store, of course. The Deluxe Supermarket ($2.97) came with grocery bags, packages of groceries and pretend money. Made of corrugated fiberboard, the Supermarket was "loads of fun for enterprising young business people."

The variety of toy kitchen appliances continued to expand. Now there was a sink and stove set -- with running water. There was an electric washer, with cranked wringer. And a toy mixer, that really worked. There were even boxes of food mix scaled down to kid size, so little girls could make real cakes, pancakes and bread.

After all this pre-pubescent housework, girls must have thought of college as a much-needed break. And to make sure that their dorm rooms were properly decorated, the Wishbook offered stuffed animals, college pennants and "novelty signs" like "No Loitering" and "Don't Feed the Animals," guaranteed to provide "laughs" and "kicks" for teens.

Sears Christmas

Wishbook

1957

Sew for Dolly!

Teach her grooming, too, with these toys

Trim-your-own Dresser Set $2.54

She can decorate gold-color plastic set herself with imitation jewels. Handbrush, hand mirror, 2 combs, rouge compact, lipstick, tweezers, powder compact, powder bowl, photo frame. 8 packages assorted play jewels and package of glue. Plastic tray has places for each piece.
49 N 1351—Gift boxed. Shipping weight 1 pound 8 ounces.............................. $2.54

Cosmetic Bag $2.62

Light blue vinyl plastic studded with make-believe pearls is washable. Full of harmless cosmetics and grooming aids. Ideal for "dress-up" games. Case is 4x9x5 in. high.
49 N 1374—Shipping weight 1 pound........... $2.62

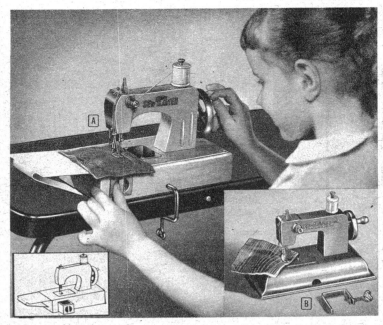

Sewing Machine with Extension Table and Drawer (A) $6.97

[A] Sews strong chain stitch. Hand wheel controls speed. Thread tension adjusts to fabric thickness, pressure foot holds material firmly. Safety guard and enclosed gears protect fingers. Die-cast head, pink enamel finish, plated trim. Hardwood base has metal clamp fasteners. Uses 12x1 number 14 size needles; extra needle, thread included. 12x4¾x6¾ inches high. Imported from West Germany.
49 N 1221—Shipping weight 2 pounds 12 ounces................................... $6.97

[B] Toy Sewing Machine sews in chain stitch. Hand wheel operation. Adjustable thread tension, pressure foot. Safety guard, enclosed gears. Precision-built steel, metallic finish. 12x1 needles. Clamps to table. 8½x4¾x6 in. high. From W. Germany.
49 N 1250—(Extra needle incl.) Shipping weight 1 pound 14 ounces.................... $3.97

Smart, Modern Vanity Table and Bench $8.97
where pretty young ladies learn good grooming

Keeping herself neat is fun at her very own vanity table. Handsomely styled to delight the modern little miss. Natural finish formica top is edged in steel, wipes clean with the swish of a damp cloth. 12x24 inches long, with plenty of room for her personal "beauty aids." Ample 7x9½-inch mirror is set at just the right height. Bench has comfortable padded seat covered with washable pastel-colored vinyl plastic. Bench and table have sturdy, black enameled tubular steel legs, plastic tips. Table is 21 inches high, stool 12½ inches high. Easy to assemble. Cosmetics not included. Fun for playing "dress-up" too. Avoid the crowds .. make Christmas shopping fun .. buy gifts to please the whole family from the Sears catalog. Satisfaction guaranteed or your money back.
79 N 01447—Shipping weight 17 pounds......................... $8.97

Sewing Kit makes complete Wardrobe for Plastic Doll $1.84

All materials for outfitting 7½-inch plastic doll. Doll has movable arms, sleeping eyes, hair. Scissors, needle, thimble, 4 bobbins, thread, buttons and assorted color rickrack. 11x18x2-inch carrying case.
49 N 1357—Shipping weight 1 pound 8 ounces.................................... $1.84

Metal Loom adjusts 4 to 7 in. square. Enameled blue. 4 bags loops, 6 hanks cotton yarn, hook needle. Gift boxed. Shpg. wt. 1 lb. 8 oz.
49 N 1368.............$1.76

Indian Beadcraft. Leather wrist strap, beads, thread, beeswax, wire, imitation jewels for making rings, belts, bracelets. Designs.
49 N 1369—Wt. 1 lb. 8 oz.$2.72
Extra 12 bottles of beads.
49 N 1375—Wt. 7 oz.......93c

Plaid Plastic Purse in little girl size with wallet, hanky, change purse, comb and mirror in cases, cosmetic bag with lipstick, compact, rouge. Make-believe money. Shipping weight 1 lb. 6 oz.
49 N 1362.............$1.76

Snap-Link Kit. Over 170 plastic pieces .. round, square, flower design .. in a variety of sizes for making pretty belts, bracelets, chokers, etc. Assorted colors. Shipping weight 1 pound.
49 N 1367.............$2.64

Betsy McCall Hat Box. Zip lid. Tray. Lotion, lipstick, nail polish, toothbrush, toothpaste, soap, brush, comb. Plastic; 10 in. diam. Shipping weight 2 pounds.
49 N 1270.............$3.42

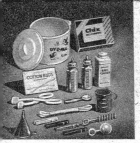

Doll Care Set $1.77
Everything for dolly's care. 4-in. high unbreakable pail, lid; 2 each bottles, caps, nipples, Chix diapers. Cotton buds, baby powder, clothespins, tongs, clothesline, rattle, bottle brush, cup, funnel, spoon.
49 N 1370—Wt. 1 lb. 4 oz....$1.77

7-pc. Diaper Bag Set 92c
Here's a pretty blue plastic bag that holds everything dolly will need when she goes visiting with her new mama. Shoulder strap for carrying. Bag comes complete with 2 plastic bottles, quilted plastic bottle holder, diaper, clothespin, plastic apron. Bag size 8x7x3 in.
49 N 1371—Shpg. wt. 10 oz.........92c

14-pc. Diaper Bag Set $2.64
8x7x3-inch diaper bag has shoulder strap. Receiving blanket, bottle holder. Zippered bottle carrier. Drawstring laundry bag. 3 bottles, 3 nipples. Bib, fancy plastic pants, gold-color safety pins, absorbent diapers. Gift boxed.
49 N 1372—Wt. 1 lb. 10 oz.....$2.64

31-piece Sterilizer and Feeding Set $1.84
Everything a new mama needs to feed her dolly, all in dolly's size. 5 polyethylene bottles with caps, nipples. Enameled metal sterilizer with cover, plastic bottle rack, tongs. Measuring cup, spoon, funnel. Orange juicer with strainer, feeding dish, spoon, teething cup, rattle. For cleaning up, bottle brush, soap powder, sponge. Pastel colors.
49 N 1373—Gift box. Shipping weight 1 lb. 11 oz... $1.84

For the Little Homemaker
Small size housekeeping needs

[A] $3.94   [B] $3.27

Sturdy Fiberboard Cupboard and Stove in little girl size $6.97
for make-believe housekeepers' streamlined kitchen Set (A), (B)

Pennsylvania Dutch design in red and blue on white background. Reinforced corrugated fiberboard, shipped unassembled. Interlocking sections for sturdy construction.

[A] **Dish Cabinet** has three shelves for dishes, pull-out cutlery drawer and big storage compartment with door that opens for pots and pans. Blue work surface.
79 N 01136—16½ x11¼ x40 in. high. (Dishes not included.) Shpg. wt. 5 lbs............$3.94

[B] **Play Stove** has red knobs that turn burners and oven "on" and "off." Pull-out drawer at bottom, oven with shelf, clear plastic look-in oven window. Make-believe burners, timer for pretend cooking.
79 N 01137—16x11x26½ in. high. (Utensils not included.) Shpg. wt. 5 lbs.........$3.27
79 N 01139—Save 24c. Buy the combination of Cabinet and Stove. Shpg. wt. 10 lbs......6.97

Let's play store .. Deluxe Supermarket $2.97
has miniature packages, play money

Loads of fun for enterprising young business people. Outfit includes play money to complete the transaction, make change. Good for lemonade stands too. Colorfully printed in red, black and tan, with realistic tile effect on outside, "free bags," just like a real supermarket. 34x20¼x61 inches high .. lots of room for several junior clerks. Assorted packages fit on spacious shelves. Reinforced corrugated fiberboard. Shipped unassembled, interlocking sections for sturdy construction. Makes a fine low-cost gift for both boys and girls. Order early and get delivery in plenty of time for Christmas.
79 N 01138—Shipping weight 9 pounds $2.97

Toy Ironing Board and Iron for the little mother to keep her dolly's clothes neat

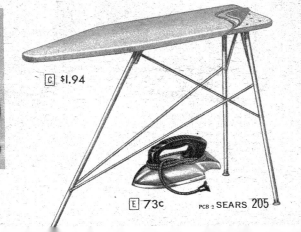

[C] $1.94

[C] **Ironing Board.** 8x30-inch perforated steel top. Steel legs fold. A thrilling gift for tiny housekeepers.
79 N 01002—22 inches high. Shpg. wt. 4 lbs..............$1.94
49 N 1008—Cover and pad for above. Shpg. wt. 4 oz.......67c
79 N 01021—Ironing board, pad and cover. Wt. 5 lbs......2.47

[D] **Electric Iron** really heats. Chrome-plated hood, cast metal base. Black Bakelite handle. 20 watts. *UL approved.* 110-120-volt, 60-cycle AC. Save 34c. Order combination listed below .. get ironing board, pad, cover and iron together.
49 N 1018—Iron. 6¼ inches long. Shpg. wt. 1 lb. 2 oz......$2.27
79N01039—Elec. Iron (D), board (C), pad, cover (49N1008). Wt.6lbs.4.54

[D] $2.27

[E] **Non-electric Iron.** Chrome-plated steel hood with streamlined Bakelite handle. Heavy cord with imitation plug.
49 N 1012—6¼ inches long. Shipping weight 8 oz..........73c

[E] 73c   PCB 2 SEARS 205

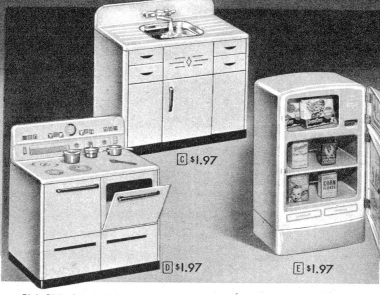

[A] $6.94

[B] $11.97

[C] $1.97

[D] $1.97

[E] $1.97

Pink Sink, Stove, Refrigerator .. heavy gauge metal, lithographed

[C] **Sink** has swivel type faucet. Actually starts, stops running water from reservoir in rear. Large basin with adjustable stopper. Hinged door opens. Pink, trimmed in black. 11½x7x10¾ inches high.
49 N 1127—Shpg. wt. 3 lbs. 4 oz.....Ea. $1.97

[D] **Non-Electric Stove**—Play timer, plastic push buttons. Hinged oven door. 6 plastic utensils. 11x6½x12 in. high. Pink.
49 N 1126—Shpg. wt. 3 lbs. 8 oz.....Ea. $1.97

[E] **Perfect replica of newest refrigerator.** Freezer compartment door and refrigerator door .. both open, close. Plastic ice cube tray and miniature packages of well known products add extra play value. Pink. 8x5½x13½ inches high.
49 N 1133—Shpg. wt. 3 lbs. 12 oz....Ea. $1.97

Complete Ensemble. Save on all 3. Sink, stove, refrigerator (C, D, E).
79 N 01134—Shipping weight 11 lbs.....$5.60

They really bake .. Electric Ranges, Glass Oven Doors
Both complete with 11-piece utensil set

[A] **Toy electric range actually bakes.** Oven door window. Metal with pink baked-enamel finish. Aluminized burner plate and handles. 3 colored play switches. Oven rack .. 4 burners. Cook book of tested recipes .. prepared to fit aluminum utensils included. Sauce pan, lid, pie plate, cake pan, loaf pan, cookie sheet, cookie cutters (2 cats, 2 roosters), measuring spoon. 12½x7x11½ in. high.
49 N 1123—UL appr. 110-120-volt, 60-cycle AC. Shpg. wt. 8 lbs....Each $6.94

[B] **De Luxe Electric Range.** Fiberglas insulated oven has thermostat. Automatically controls heat. Constant heat for better, faster baking. 2 lights illuminate top of stove. Oven door window. Metal with pink baked-enamel finish .. white trim. 4 aluminized burner plates. Cook book of tested recipes for aluminum utensils: measuring spoon, saucepan with lid, 3 cookie cutters, cookie sheet, pie plate, cake pan, angel cake pan, mixing spoon. 15x7½x13¾ in. high.
49 N 1125—UL appr. 110-120-volt, 60-cycle AC. Wt. 11 lbs. 8 oz. Each $11.97

The Littlest Homemaker
loves modern appliances in her kitchen

Piston-Action Toy Refrigerator
Battery operated

Open the door .. light goes on, 2 center shelves go round and round, pistons in "motor" move up and down. Clear plastic window, 2 shelves on door. Removable ice cube tray. Bottom drawer pulls out. Beautifully constructed of durable metal .. finished inside and out in pastel pink enamel. Pastel blue shelves. All smooth edges to prevent cutting little fingers.

Operates on 2 Type C flashlight batteries (not included, see below). 5x5¼x9¾ in. high. Imported from Japan.
49 N 1038—Shpg. wt. 2 lbs. 7 oz....Ea. $3.46
34 N 4659—Batteries. Wt. 4 oz......2 for 35c

[F] $2.54

[G] $2.56

Tappan Toy Gas Range .. has the Visiminder and Visiguide .. adjustments for "cooking" perfection. 4 make-believe plastic burners regulated by knobs that turn. Transparent oven and broiler windows. Separate oven and broiler compartments, each with its own tray. Plastic utensils included. Pastel green metal.
79N01116-15x9½x19 in. high. Wt. 11 lbs. $5.53

Double Oven Non-electric Stove. The little cook will love preparing make-believe meals for dolly and her friends. Doors open and close. Lithographed top shows pretend electric burners and cooking well. Eight multicolor controls at back of top .. really push "on and off". 12-piece plastic utensil set included; scaled to fit tiny hands. Made of steel with glistening white enamel finish. 14x7x15 inches high.
49 N 1132—Shipping weight 6 lbs.......$3.57

[F] **Toy Washing Machine.** Actually washes. Lid lifts to fill tub. Rubber hose drains water. Watch action through plastic window. Red light glows when washer runs. On-off switch. Metal .. pink and blue enamel finish. Battery operated (battery sold below). Imported from Japan.
49 N 1028—6½x5x4½ inches high. Shpg. wt. 1 lb. 7 oz.................$2.54

[G] **Ironer.** Metal; same finish, red light as above. Lever controls shoe pressure against roller. Shelves fold. 12 in. long. Imported from Japan.
49 N 1029—Batteries sold below. Shpg. wt. 1 lb. 9 oz...................$2.56
34 N 4650—2 Standard Flashlight Batteries for above. Wt. 8 oz. ..2 for 35c
49 N 1037—2-Pc. Set (Washer, Ironer above). Shpg. wt. 3 lbs.........$4.70

Toy Mixer .. Really works! $3.77

Actually mixes; won't cut fingers. Mixer unit tilts .. can be detached, used anywhere. Stainless steel beater removes for washing. Aluminum bowl. Operates on 2 standard flashlight batteries (not incl.). White enameled steel. 10 in. high over-all. Gift box.

49 N 1296—Shpg. wt. 1 lb. 13 oz....$3.77
34 N 4650—Batteries. Wt. 8 oz...2 for 35c

4-piece Play "Lectric" Appliance Set $2.47

4 aluminum toys for the modern kitchen in one gift box. Each has make-believe "Lectric" cord and red indicator. *Percolator* with lid, strainer .. 5½ in. high. *Pressure cooker* 4x3¾-in. diameter. *2-"Burner" Hot plate* (switches turn!). 8x4 in., 1¾ in. high. *Modern design square frying pan* with cover and legs. 9x5 in. incl. handle. No heat! No Electricity!

49 N 1135—Shipping weight 1 lb. 8 oz.....Set $2.47

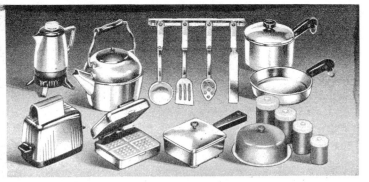

Little Helper's 33-piece Plastic Kitchenware Set $4.67

Adorable miniature appliances and kitchenware .. make-believe bacon and eggs, cake, waffles, toast. All coppertone teakettle, percolator with cover, pop-up toaster, waffle iron with removable grids, modern covered skillet, saucepan, and frying pan. All plated in silver color, coppertone combination. 4-piece plated utensil set with hanging rack (slotted spoon, turner, spatula, soup ladle .. all 5 in. length). 4 white canisters with red covers; cake tray with cover. Toaster is 2⅛x4 inches long .. other items in proportion. Detailed copies .. just like mother's!

49 N 1119—Shipping weight 1 pound 8 ounces.....................Set $4.67

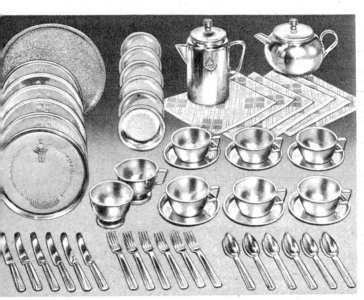

Happi-Time Aluminum Tea and Coffee Set .. 49 Pieces $1.92

Sturdy, rust-resistant aluminum .. all edges smoothly turned to protect little fingers. Percolator and teapot have red knob and handle, size ½ pint. Plates, saucers embossed with Bo-Peep decoration. You're ready for a party for 6. Six each of cups, saucers, plates, knives, forks, spoons, paper napkins, and sauce dishes. Teapot, coffee pot with lids, 6-inch diameter hammered tray, creamer, sugar bowl. Plates are 4½ inches in diameter; other items are in proportion. Gift boxed and ready to give to your little hostess.

49 N 920—Shipping weight 1 pound 4 ounces.....Set $1.92

Housekeeping's Fun
with your playtime utensils and appliances

Happi-Time 27-piece Aluminum Cook and Bake Set $1.82

Kitchen fun galore with your very own set! Contains 2 measuring spoons, 1 each measuring cup, mixing spoon, mixing bowl, scoop, flour canister; 4 animal cooky cutters (friendly dog, cat, rabbit, chick), 1 each cooky sheet, cooky canister, muffin pan (6 cups), biscuit pan, pie pan, cake turner; 2 round layer cake pans, 1 each angel food cake pan, lip saucepan, fry pan, covered saucepan, double boiler. Fry pan is 4 in. in diameter .. others in proportion. Some items trimmed with gay red handles, knobs. Gift boxed.

49 N 921—Shipping weight 1 pound 3 ounces.....................Set $1.82

Doll's Laundry, Linen Closet Set .. 41 pcs.

4 clothespins, 4 hangers, 2 sock stretchers, laundry bag, basket, spoon, clothesline, sprinkler bottle, 7 boxes soap, 4 diapers, 4 safety pins, 2 towels, 4 wash cloths, 1 box cleanser, baby powder, paper towels, toilet and facial tissues. Boxes form 8-in. closets.

49 N 1036—Wt. 14 oz..Set $1.82

Toy Electric Washer.

Battery-operated, actually washes. Metal agitator .. on-off switch at side. Clear plastic lid. Hand-cranked wringer, safe rubber rollers. Washer moves on roller bearings. White with red trim. 7x12¾ in. high. No batteries.

49 N 1003—Wt. 3 lbs.....$4.84
34 N 4650—Batteries.
Shipping wt. 8 oz........2 for 35c

10-piece Laundry Set.

Washer has removable metal agitator with real wash-machine action. Just turn crank at side to actually wash. Adjustable wringer with safe, hard rubber rollers. Clear plastic lid. Pink metal .. no sharp edges. 7½x12 inches high. Also revolving dryer, woven basket, 6 wooden clothespins, clothesline.

49 N 1033—Shipping weight 3 pounds.....................Set $2.87

Sink and Stove Set .. Water really runs!

Automatic pump action. Primed with water, water runs continuously through faucet, into sink, out faucet again. Battery operated (Batteries not incl.). Red light shines under stove burner giving a make-believe electric glow. Doors open. 2 metal pots incl. Metal .. enameled pastel tones. 11¼ in. long. Imported from Japan.

49 N 1366—Shpg. wt. 1 lb. 13 oz...............$2.87
34 N 4650—Batteries. Shipping weight 8 oz......2 for 35c

40-pc. Plastic Tea Set
$2.87

Tea urn has pour spigot. Unbreakable pink and turquoise polyethylene tea urn, creamer, sugar bowl, 6 each cups, knives, forks, spoons. 6 each metal plates, saucers with floral design. Plates 6-in. diam., other pieces in proportion. Gift boxed.
49 N 872—Wt. 1 lb. 12 oz.$2.87
49 N 884—Service for four, 28-piece set. Wt. 1 lb. 8 oz. . $1.97

28-pc. Metal Tea Set
96c

The little hostess will fall in love with the dainty Swiss figures on this unbreakable service for six. Bright red, blue and green flower border. 6 each of plates, cups, saucers and butter plates. Teapot, sugar bowl, creamer. Tray 8x10 in. long. Plates 4 inches in diameter, other pieces in proportion.
49 N 923—Wt. 1 lb. 4 oz...96c

Plastic Play Food
$1.47

A delicious make-believe dinner to serve on her new dishes. 31-piece set includes colorful plastic tablecloth 17x14 in. wide, 2 each of turkeys, loaves of bread, 4 each of sirloin steaks, sweetcorn, carrots, peas, biscuits, slices of pie. Salt and pepper shakers. Gift boxed.
49 N 1122—Wt. 9 oz. . $1.47

Punch Bowl Set
$2.76

27-pc. Styrene plastic in burgundy, cleartrim. Cutlery has silver-like finish. Bowl 7-in. diam., other pieces in proportion: 6 cups, plates, knives, forks. Ladle, platter. Wt. 1 lb. 8 oz.
49N879—Gift boxed $2.76

Bead-A-Basket Kit
$2.73

Make 6-pc. matched set—basket, table mat and coasters. Includes material for sunburst pattern serving basket (top diam. 10 in.), round table mat (9-in. diam.) and 4 coasters (4-in. diam.). Wood. Colored beads.
49 N 1262—Wt. 1 lb. 12 oz.$2.73

Friction Vacuum Cleaner
$1.80

Just push down and forward, hear motor hum, see "cold" sparks in window. Actually picks up dirt by suction and a revolving brush. Vinyl plastic bag inflates; slide off top to empty. Sweeper 6x6½x3 in. high. Overall height 27 in. From Japan.
49 N 1203—Shpg. wt. 2 lbs. . $1.80

Happi-Time Cleaning Set
Works Just Like Mom's
$1.80

A pint-size housekeeper's dream! Metal sweeper really sweeps! It has a fiber bristle brush and bottom that opens for emptying. 24 inches long with wood handle; 9½x7½x2-inch base. Metal dust pan. 24-inch long red plastic bristle broom with wood handle. 26-inch long multi-color yarn dust mop with wood handle. Ruffled plastic apron 12x9 inches. Gift boxed. An exciting gift for mother's little helper.
79 N 01302—Shpg. wt. 3 lbs.. $1.80

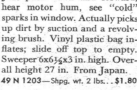

Let's Have a Tea Party
Serve homemade dainties
on miniature dishes

ITEMS BELOW SHOWN ON FACING PAGE

[A] **Russel Wright American Modern Tea Service for 6.** Especially created to delight modern little misses by leading designer, Russel Wright. Strong plastic in modern, mottled, pottery colors. 6 each of plates, cups, saucers, knives, forks, spoons, napkins. 6 clear goblets with etched-type design. Creamer, teapot and sugar bowl with covers. Turned-edge plates are 6¼ inches in diameter, other pieces in proportion. Gift boxed.
49 N 851—Shipping weight 2 pounds 4 ounces.................$3.76

[B] **Beautiful 28-piece Imported China Dinner Set.** Young hostesses love these real china dishes because they're so like Mom's. Dainty floral pattern on each piece. 6 plates, 6 cups, 6 saucers. Teapot, sugar bowl, casserole with cover. Creamer, platter, vegetable dish and gravy boat. Plates measure 4½ inches in diameter, saucers 3¾ inches in diameter, other pieces in proportion. Imported from Japan. Gift boxed.
49 N 842—Shipping weight 5 pounds 8 ounces................$2.77

[C] **32-piece Plastic Tea Set.** How proud she'll be to serve her little guests on this elegant service. Durable styrene plastic and metal in beautiful burgundy. Plates, saucers trimmed in gold color on ivory. 4 cups, plates, saucers, napkins. 4 knives, forks, spoons with silver-like metallic finish. 4 sparkling clear plastic goblets. Creamer, sugar bowl, teapot with cover. Plates 6-in. diameter, other pieces in proportion. Gift box.
49 N 880—Shipping weight 1 pound 12 ounces................$1.97

[D] **Blue Willow Pattern Imported Tea Service.** She'll set such a lovely table with her real china service for 6. And how thrilled to know that its beautiful design is a traditional favorite with grown-ups too. Imported from Japan, set includes 6 cups, saucers and plates. Casserole, teapot and sugar bowl with covers, platter and creamer. Plates are 3¾-inch diameter, other pieces in proportion. Just right for tiny hands. Gift box.
49 N 827—26-piece Set. Shipping weight 3 pounds 8 ounces.....$1.67

[E] **Big 63-piece Food Mix Set with 33 name brand mixes.** 8 Swansdown cake mixes, 4 Aunt Jemima mixes, 8 Flako mixes, 12 Junior Chef Pudding, pie mixes and frostings, bottle Log Cabin syrup. 30 utensils, including 2 each of cake pans, pie tins, spoons, cookie sheets, mixing bowls. Decorator with 3 nozzles. 7 cookie cutters. Bread pan, rolling pin, muffin tin, pancake grill, turner, funnel, egg beater, cookie pan, recipe book. Gift box.
49 N 1179—Shipping weight 4 pounds 6 ounces...............$5.87
49 N 1264—Set of 8 refills. Shipping weight 12 ounces..........87c

[F] **49-piece Food Mix Set with 26 name brand mixes** for a beginning cook. 7 Swansdown cake mixes, 2 Aunt Jemima mixes, 4 different Flako mixes, 13 Junior Chef pudding, pie and decorator mixes. 23 real junior-size utensils including 2 each of cake pans, pie tins and cookie sheets. Decorator with 3 nozzles and 7 various cookie cutters. Bread tin, spoon, rolling pin, muffin tin, pancake turner and recipe book. Decorated box.
49 N 1178—Shipping weight 3 pounds 2 ounces...............$3.87
49 N 1264—Set of 8 refills. Shipping weight 12 ounces..........87c

[G] **35-piece Food Mix Set with 18 name brand mixes.** 4 Swansdown cake mixes, 2 Aunt Jemima mixes, 5 Flako mixes, 7 Junior Chef mixes. 17 utensils: 2 each pie tins, cake pans. 7 cookie cutters, bread pan, muffin tin, cookie sheet, spoon, rolling pin, recipe book. What fun to learn to bake with her very own utensils . . . serve what she makes on her own dishes! Gift box. Order early in time for Christmas.
49 N 1177—Shipping weight 2 pounds 5 ounces..............$2.67
49 N 1176—24-piece set. 12 mixes and 12 utensils. Shipping weight 1 pound 10 ounces...1.77
49 N 1264—Set of 8 refills. Shipping weight 12 ounces..........87c

[H] **Miniature Dining Room and Kitchen.** Box opens up to form colorful room setting. Detachable metal sidewall contains cabinets, sink, stove, refrigerator. Doors open . . . plenty of room for tiny accessories. Equipped with toaster, coffee pot, broom, dust pan, 2 saucepans, 2 cups, saucers, plates. Metal wall for dining unit that includes breakfront cabinet, table with 4 chairs, bowl, 2 candlesticks, 4 cups, saucers, tumblers.
49 N 1121—Shipping weight 1 pound 7 ounces...............$1.80

Save Santa's budget . . buy on Sears Easy Terms. Only 10% down on orders of $20 or more

A $3.76

C $1.97

E $5.87

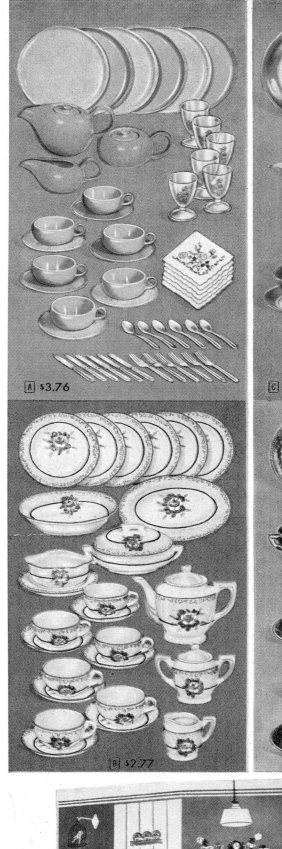

B $2.77

D $1.67

F $3.87

G $2.67

H $1.80

Campus Favorites Brighten Teen Rooms

[A] **Mr. Cool, the Musical Wolf** . . "coolest cat" from junior high to the ivy league. Handsomely attired in black and white from his top hat to his spats. He "digs" rock and roll, and grins as a lively song plays from his Swiss music box. Flexible limbs for many poses. Top-quality rayon plush and wool felt. 22 in. tall.
8 N 9312—Shpg. wt. 2 lbs **$10.97**

[B] **Professor Owl**, wise one, about to deliver lecture. Graduation cap, solemn expression are proof of his great wisdom. Brown-gray with light yellow rayon plush. Deep tan cotton felt accents (webbed feet, nose and ears) brighten his appearance.
8 N 9311—13 in. tall. Wt. 1 lb. 8 oz. **$5.97**

[C] **Musical Calypso Donkey** rakishly dressed, entertains with "Mary Ann" by means of his Swiss music unit. Soft gray rayon plush set off by his bright yellow, flower-trimmed straw hat and colorful saddle. Tinkly bell at his neck to gain further attention. Donkey stands upright, 13 in. tall.
8 N 9300—Shpg. wt. 1 lb. 8 oz. . . **$7.74**

[D] **Musical Joe College Pup.** Collegiate pup sports green freshman's beanie and cutest expression you've ever seen. He's so anxious to get off on the right track. Swiss musical unit plays "Boola-Boola", his favorite song. Brown and white rayon plush, red plastic collar. 10 in. tall.
8 N 9310—Shpg. wt. 1 lb. 8 oz. . . **$7.74**

[E] **Musical Puppy Play Pillow.** Snuggle against his lovable, floppy-eared face. Listen to his version of "Doggie in the Window" (Swiss music box). Impish brown eyes add to his appeal. Ideal novelty throw pillow. Adorable playmate in white and black rayon plush, high-grade cotton stuffing.
8 N 9313—13-in. diam. Wt. 2 lbs. **$7.97**

[F] **Pajama Cat Pillow.** Curl up with Kitty for a nap . . her drooping eyelids show how sleepy she is. Such a cute conversation piece. And, she has a large zipper section for pajamas. Rayon plush in beige and brown.
8 N 9316—21 in. long. Wt. 2 oz. **$5.97**

[G] **Li'l Squirt, the Atomized Skunk** is irresistibly sociable. He's designed to melt teen hearts (grown-ups', too). The sweetest scented skunk you'll ever know. Holds atomizer bottle between his paws. Squeeze tail for a generous spray of desirable scent (not incl.). Cuddly black rayon plush with snow-white stripes. Perky pink pompom nose, cotton felt. Flower trim.
8 N 9319—7½ in. tall. Wt. 12 oz. **$4.77**

[H] **Felix, the Frankfurter Hound.** Wears exaggerated middle of red percale . . *giant yard long* for autographs, special events. Even has his own collar and leash . . you'll love to lead him. Firm stuffing . . fine writing surface for pen or pencil. Rest of body is of buttery-soft black rayon plush.
8 N 09299—1 yard. Wt. 4 lbs. Only. **$4.77**

[J] **Otto, the Autograph Dachshund.** Perky pet with graduation cap . . ready to serve as a permanent record of signatures and sayings you'll want to remember. Yellow heavy cotton poplin skin. Firm, smooth stuffing presents a perfect writing surface for pen or pencil. Movable eye pupils.
8 N 9513—13 in. Shpg. wt. 10 oz. **$2.40**

Musical Super Otto (not shown). Plays rock and roll tune; otherwise, similar to Otto. Also, much longer, full 22 in.
8 N 9426—Shpg. wt. 2 lbs. **$5.97**

Cheer Up and her lovable Canine Family. "The sad sage of dogdom" and "heirs" promote laughter wherever they go. Patty sits "pat" and Perky stands alert. Tailored of wool and cotton felt in white and brown, artfully and permanently airbrushed. Stuffed with ground cork; wired legs, riveted button noses.
8 N 9382—Family of 4. Save $1.41 over individual prices, total $11.38. Shpg. wt. 2 lbs, 8 oz. . . **$9.97**
(K) 8 N 9321—Cheer Up. 13 in. Wt. 1 lb. . . **3.97**
(L) 8 N 9326—Perky. 9 in. Wt. 8 oz. **2.47**
(M) 8 N 9322—Peppy. 9 in. Wt. 8 oz. **2.47**
(N) 8 N 9325—Patty. 9 in. Wt. 8 oz. **2.47**

[P] **Novelty Signs** provide "laughs" and "kicks" for teens. Enliven any room. Package of 5, identical to those illustrated on wall above. Each sign in 2 bright colors . . all of durable plastic. Special pressure-sensitive adhesive tape included for hanging. Sizes in group 8x10, 9x9 and 5x15 in.
8 N 9327—Package of 5. Wt. 2 lbs. 8 oz. . . **$1.97**

College Pennants emphasize the campus motif. Pennants in authentic colors for all schools listed below.

Big Ten
Illinois, Indiana, Northwestern, Iowa, Mich. State, Michigan, Minnesota, Ohio State, Purdue, Wisconsin

Southeastern
Kentucky, Tenn., Tech., Ga., Fla., Miss., Miss. State, Ala., Tulane, L.S.U., Auburn

Ivy League
Brown, Dartmouth, Cornell, Harvard, Princeton, Pennsylvania, Columbia, Yale

Atlantic Coast
Clemson, Duke, N.C. State, Md., N.C., S.C., Va., Wake Forest

Big Eight
Iowa State, Kans. State, Colo., Mo., Kans., Nebr., Okla., Okla. State

Southwest
Texas A. & M., Baylor, Rice, Ark., Texas, Texas Tech., S.M.U., T.C.U.

Pacific Coast
California, U.C.L.A., Idaho, Oregon, Ore. State, U.S.C., Wash., Wash. State, Stanford

Independents
Air Force, Army, Boston College, Holy Cross, Miami, Syracuse, Navy, Notre Dame, Pitt., Penn. State

[R] **Conference Pennants.** String holds 8½-in. pennant for each school in group. Cotton felt. State choice from 8 college groups above.
8 N 9317—Shpg. wt. 1 lb. . . . Each **$1.00**

[S] **Individual College Pennants.** High quality felt (70% wool, 30% cotton). School name, mascot in authentic colors. Giant 29x11½ in. Wt. 6 oz.
8 N 9318—State College above. Ea. **$1.97**

The car culture of the Fifties even filtered down to the tiniest citizens. With just the right pedal cars you could be a mail carrier, a police officer, or a soldier. If you were feeling wild and crazy, you could drive your hot-rod ($18.95) to the Drive-In Playhouse ($12.74) for a little curb service. And if you were feeling wealthy, you might want to cruise about in your Cadillac ($32.95) with electric headlights and horn -- and spare tire.

Budding scientists had a variety of chemistry sets to choose from, starting with a Junior Set for $4.69, all the way up to the Chemcraft Master Deluxe Lab at $27.50. Note that this catalog, for the first time, shows a little girl playing with these science kits!

Musicians-in-training had spinets, trumpets, saxophones and xylophones to help soothe the savage beast.

And, of course, after a busy day in the Chemistry Lab, you could come home and play dress up with a "hat like Mother's" and a "chic chemise." Who says the modern girl of 1958 couldn't have it all?

Sears Christmas

Wishbook

1958

Our Best Bike

Special Buy! Save $7.57

J.C. HIGGINS Equipped Tank Model Bike .. a Christmas "bike dream" come true

Boys' or Girls' 26-inch size	Boys' or Girls' 24-inch size
Normally our price would be ~~$46.45~~	Normally our price would be ~~$45.45~~
$38.88	**$37.88**
Only $5 down	Only $5 down

- Chrome-plated handlebars, truss rods, sprocket, hubs
- Coil spring vinyl plastic covered saddle
- 1.75-inch easy rolling mid-weight tires

J. C. HIGGINS 26 and 24-inch equipped Tank Model Bikes. When your youngster sees this shiny beauty parked by the tree on Christmas morning, it's going to be "love at first sight." A bicycle is the one gift your child will cherish above all others. Check these outstanding features: Torpedo headlight takes 2 batteries (not included); sturdy luggage carrier; safety coaster brakes for sure stops and effortless coasting; strong tubular steel frame reinforced at points of strain to stand years of rigorous use; full ball-bearing head and steering action; ball-bearing pedals.

Bright baked on enamel colors resist scratches and rust. Boys' models are bright red; Girls' are rich blue. Both have white and gold-color trim. Shipped freight, express or truck. See our General catalog for deluxe equipped models.

26-inch for ages over 9. Seat to pedal length adjusts from 28 to 32½ inches. Shipping weight 64 pounds.
6 N M4750—Boys' 26-in. **$38.88**   6 N M4751—Girls' 26-in. **$38.88**

24-inch for ages 7, 8, 9. Seat to pedal length adjusts from 23½ to 27½ inches. Shipping weight 58 pounds.
6 N M4752—Boys' 24-in. **$37.88**   6 N M4753—Girls' 24-in. **$37.88**

Special Buy! Save $3.57

26-in. Normally our price would be ~~$35.45~~ **$31.88**   24-in. Normally our price would be ~~$34.45~~ **$30.88**

Buy now and save on these 26 and 24-inch Middleweight bikes. Shiny chrome-plated handlebars, sprocket, hubs. Safety coaster brake for sure stops and effortless coasting. 1.75-inch midweight tires. Strong tubular frame ruggedly built to give years of service. Metallic-enameled colors resist scratches and rust. Comfortable coil spring saddle with black vinyl plastic cover. Chain guard, kickstand, black tread pedals, red rear reflector, white-enameled tire rims. Boys' models are solid red color; Girls' are blue. Shipped by freight, express or truck.

26-inch for ages over 9. Seat to pedal length adjusts from 28 to 32½ in. Shpg. wt. 52 lbs.
6 N M4674—Boys' model.............$31.88   6 N M4675—Girls' model.............$31.88

24-inch for ages 7, 8, 9: Seat to pedal length adjusts from 23½ to 27½ in. Shpg. wt. 46 lbs.
6 N M4676—Boys' model.............$30.88   6 N M4677—Girls' model.............$30.88

for Sidewalk Speedsters

smooth ball-bearing, chain or pedal drive

Rear door opens to store toys and equipment

AIR MAIL — No 7
U.S. MAIL TRUCK
B
$19.87 cash
$2.00 down

RADAR PATROL
POLICE — CHAIN DRIVE
A
$23.50 cash
$2.50 down

USA — USA 0052I
D
$17.95

HOT-ROD — 5
E
$18.95

"Drive-in" Play House
G
$12.74

Ranchero
C
$19.98 cash
$2.00 down

All vehicles on this page—except (B)—are equipped with Chain Drive for more power with less effort

ATOMIC MISSILE
F
$23.98 cash
$2.50 down

with smooth-rolling rubber tires and many extras

A **Police Cycle.** Red spotlight. Ball-bearing chain drive. Ball-bearing 8-inch double-disc wheels; 1¾-in. semi-pneumatic front tire, 1⅛-in. solid rears. Rear compartment with door. Blue enameled steel; white and red trim. 36x22x 20 in. high. Uses 2 batteries (not incl.).
79 N 08966L—Shpg. wt. 38 lbs.......$23.50
34 N 4659—Batteries. Wt. 4 oz....2 for 35c

B **Mail Truck.** Pedal drive. Adjustable ball-bearing pull straps. Rubber pedals. 8-in. double-disc wheels, nylon bearings; 1-in. rubber tires. Red, white and blue enameled steel. Door latches. 18x42 in. long. Freight, exp. or truck.
79 N M8945—Shpg. wt. 37 lbs.......$19.87

C **New! Ranchero.** Easy-operating ball-bearing chain drive. Motor-tone gear shift. Ball-bearing 8-in. wheels; ⅞-in. rubber tires. Spotlight uses 2 batteries (not incl.); windshield. Gold-color finish on steel; red, white trim. 17x36 in.
79 N 08954L—Shpg. wt. 32 lbs.......$19.98
34 N 4659—Batteries. Wt. 4 oz....2 for 35c

G **Tots' "Drive-In" Refreshment Stand.** Use indoors or out. Gaily colored cotton tent sheeting with screened designs on panels. Plastic mesh side door and front window. Brightly striped roof. Strong tubular steel and metal rod supports.
79 N 08934—3½x3½x4 ft. high over-all. Shipping weight 10 pounds.................$12.74

D **Army Jeep.** Steel. Ball-bearing chain drive. Realistic markings on olive-drab enamel finish. Large 8-in. wheels. 1¼-in. semi-pneumatic tires. Windshield folds down. Two seat levels. Front and rear bumpers. 16x20x43 in. long.
79 N 08955L—Shpg. wt. 36 lbs......$17.95

E **Ball-bearing Chain-drive Racer.** Heavy gauge steel. Nylon-bearing 10-in. steel artillery wheels. 1¾-in. semi-pneumatic rubber tires. Rubber block pedals. Bright yellow baked enamel; black, red trim. 20x35 in. long.
79 N 08951L—Shpg. wt. 38 lbs......$18.95

F **"Atomic Missile."** Enclosed ball-bearing chain drive. Realistic dual controls, simulated instruments, motor-tone gear shift. Rubber pedals. Ball-bearing double-disc 8-in. front wheel . . swivels 360°; 1¾-in. semi-pneumatic front tire; 1⅛-in. solid rears. Gold-color finish; white, vermillion trim on steel. 25x45 in. long. Freight, express or truck.
79 N M8970—Shpg. wt. 41 lbs......$23.98

BEEP BEEP
Kidillac
New! Chain-drive Luxury "Kidillac"
$32.95 cash $3.50 down

Electric headlights, horn . . removable spare

Easy-to-operate chain drive . . enclosed for safety. Ball-bearing rear axle supports, pedal cranks. Nylon-bearing double-disc 8-in. wheels; 1¼-in. semi-pneumatic tires. Plated hub caps, aerial, rear view mirror. Rubber pedals. Red plastic hood ornament. All-steel construction. Flamboyant 2-tone finish: golden dust color with gardenia white. Headlights and horn operated from dash on 6-volt battery (not included).
79 N M8991—20x45 in. long. Freight, express or truck. Wt. 49 lbs.......$32.95
34 N 4702—6-volt Battery for above. Shipping weight 1 lb. 6 oz............95c

Exciting Microscope Sets
See the "invisible world" come to life

Chemcraft Lab Outfits
Unlock the exciting magic world of Science

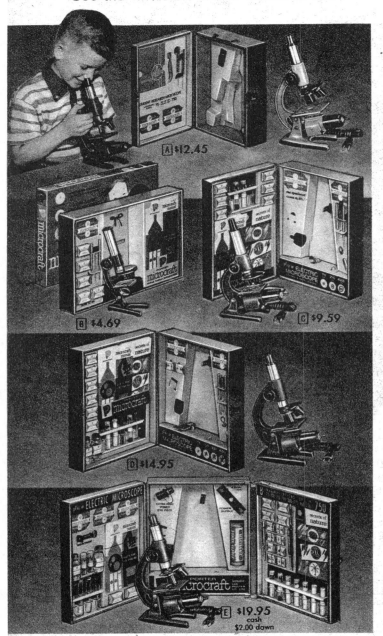

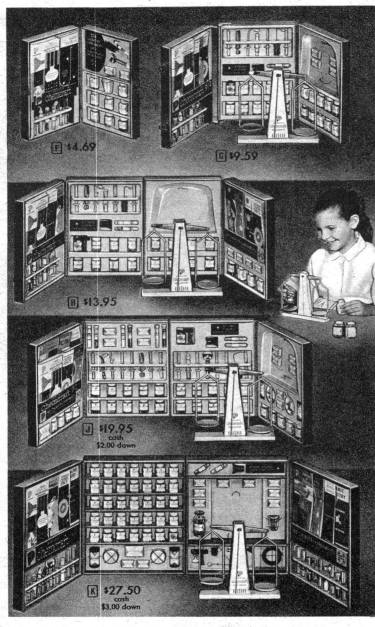

A Student Research Microscope. 11-in. 8-power precision-built 4-turret metal electric microscope magnifies 75 to 750 times. Extra eyepiece, glass slides, dissecting equipment. Case with handle opens to 17x11½ in. Plug, cord.
49 N 2087—Shipping weight 5 lbs. $12.45

B Microcraft Junior Set ideal for beginners. 3-turret microscope magnifies 40-75-150 times. Set packed in 16½x11-inch box, includes manual, glass slides, specimens, dissecting equipment. 8-in. microscope.
49 N 2081—Shipping weight 3 lbs. . . $4.69

C Microcraft Collegiate Set. 3-turret 9½-in. metal electric plug-in microscope magnifies 70-210-425 times. With dissecting equipment, slides, dropper, manuals. In sturdy 21½x 13½-inch metal cabinet.
49 N 2084—Shipping weight 6 lbs. . . $9.59

D Microcraft Lab-Master. Electric plug-in sub-stage lamp gives clear field for easy viewing. 11-in. 4-turret metal microscope magnifies 75-150-300-450 times. Test tube rack, glass slides, dissecting, slide mounting apparatus and living specimens. Microscope and "Secrets of Nature" manuals. Open metal cabinet 23x13½ in.
49 N 2085—Shipping weight 8 lbs. $14.95

E Microcraft Senior Lab-Master has electric plug-in sub-stage lamp to bring out detail. 11-in. 4-turret metal microscope with extra eyepiece gives 8 magnifications up to 750 times actual size. 3-panel strong steel cabinet holds test tubes, living specimens, dissecting and slide mounting equipment, microtome and electronic microscope stage. Cabinet opens to 32x13¾ in.
49 N 2086—Wt. 10 lbs. $2.00 down . . $19.95

F Chemcraft Junior Set with equipment for 374 experiments. Analyze and break down substances like air, water and fuels . . make ink and soap. With removable test tube rack, "Inside the Atom" and instruction manuals. In permanent plastic lab.
49N2076—Cab. 19x13½ in. Wt. 5 lbs. $4.69

G Chemcraft Collegiate Set. 612 exciting experiments in atomic energy, outer space chemistry, chemical magic. 3-panel metal lab holds precision balance, alcohol lamp, test tubes, chemicals, 4 instruction books.
49N2077—Cab. 32x13½ in. Wt. 10 lbs. $9.59

H Chemcraft Senior Lab. 720 experiments—chemistry, glass blowing, chemical magic, atomic energy, and outer space. 4-panel metal lab opens to 42x13¾ in. Balance, alcohol lamp.
79 N 02078—Shipping weight 12 lbs. $13.95

J Chemcraft Master Lab. Big laboratory with 825 experiments in plastics, magic, outer space, atomic energy, glass blowing and many other fields of chemistry. Four-panel colorful metal cabinet opens to 47x13¾ in. Holds Spinthariscope, balance, alcohol lamp, test tubes, racks and brush, huge supply of chemicals, 6-manuals.
79N02079—Wt. 14 lbs. $2.00 down $19.95

K Chemcraft Master De luxe Lab. Finest professional equipment . . 915 fascinating experiments. Organic and inorganic chemistry, qualitative analysis, magic, plastics, atomic energy, outer space, glass blowing. Charts show structure of matter . . with illustrations. Big wood lab opens to 56x16 inches. Huge supply of chemicals and testing apparatus, 8 manuals.
79N02080K—Wt. 21 lbs. $3.00 down $27.50

60-cycle AC, UL Approved. Sets have no dangerous poisons or explosive chemicals

354 SEARS PCBKMN

Sears Easy Terms . . 10% DOWN on orders of $20 or more

Miniatures of Actual Instruments

$23.95 cash
$2.50 down

Beautiful 41-key Piano .. plays over 3 full octaves

One of the finest-looking toy pianos we've seen .. a baby grand with a high gloss ivory finish. Bright red fall board. Hardwood construction. 41 large sized plastic black and white keys. Chromatically tuned tone bar. Positive action. Lift-up top to form music rack. Song book and magic key chart. Piano is 29 in. high, 26¾ in. long; bench is 14¼ in. high, 17¾ in. long.
79 N M684—Shipped freight, express or truck. Shipping weight 27 lbs..........$23.95

$36.95 cash
$4.00 down

OUR FINEST .. 49-KEY SPINET

Plays 4 full octaves .. beautiful walnut finish

A lovely piece of furniture that will fit right in your living room .. piano and bench constructed of finest quality plywood, beautifully finished in simulated walnut. 49 plastic keys, ⅞ in. wide (same as on all standard large pianos). Tone rods are all high carbon precision ground to produce the proper tone. Color chart for keys and music book with notes in color included. Piano 23¾ in. high, 31 in. long; matching bench 10 in. high, 14 in. long.
79 N M685—Shipped freight, express or truck. Shipping weight 32 lbs............$36.95

8-key Xylophone	Keyboard Konsole	New! Tap-A-Song	Plastic Kampanile	Silver Sax and Golden Trumpet
$2.69	$6.98	$2.59	$3.98	Saxophone $2.49 Trumpet $3.29

[A] Plays entire C-major scale .. 8 rich tones. Heavy steel tone bars mounted on felt base .. absolutely true-toned. Enameled metal case, lyre-shaped ends. One rubber mallet, 1 wood mallet, 12 page music book included. Size 12½ inches long, 5½ in. high. Wt. 2 lbs. 8 oz.
49 N 531..........$2.69

[B] A real musical treat for tots. 17 brilliantly colored bells, beautifully tuned to produce harmonious melodies .. all mounted on handsome ivory console. Tones in key of C produced by tapping tops of bells. Color-keyed song booklet included. 26x4½x 6½ in. high. Wt. 5 lbs.
79 N 0561—Ivory.....$6.98

[C] It's brand new and almost as much fun as a regular calliope. As youngster squeezes or taps the rubber bulbs mounted on top of base, this full octave plastic musical instrument gives forth genuine calliope sounds, to the delight of tots. 15½x5x5½ in. high. Shipping weight 1 lb. 6 oz.
49 N 571..........$2.59

[D] A tower of musical bells that tolls beautiful music far and wide. At the softest touch of the keyboard, each precision tuned bell swings and rings one note in the scale. Bells and keyboard color-keyed to children's song book. 14 in. wide, over 12 in. high. Wt. 2 lbs. 11 oz.
49 N 560..........$3.98

[E] **Beautifully made Saxophone**, molded in durable plastic. 8 tuned reeds produce full scale of mellow tones. Packed in a long-wearing carrying case. 15 in. long.
49 N 586—Silver color. Wt. 1 lb. 9 oz... $2.49

[F] **13-inch Trumpet.** Four valves control full scale. Gold-color plastic. Brass-tuned reed notes. Case, stand and mute are included.
49 N 538—Shpg. wt. 1 lb. 8 oz.......$3.29

B 3-piece Set $11.49

D 3-piece Set $18.98

Use Sears Easy Terms . . only 10% down on orders of $20 or more

A 5-piece Enameled Folding Set **$19.95** $2.00 down cash

C 5-piece Chrome Folding Set **$26.50** $3.00 down cash

E 3-piece Set $9.69

F 3-piece Set $13.94

G 20x30 in. 3-piece Set $19.95 $2.00 down cash

H $8.98

J $4.98

K $5.97

M $3.49

LITTLE FOLK LOUNGE PIECES

N $18.95

2-piece Set $12.44 **P**

ROOMY TOY CHESTS

$9.95 **T**

L $7.49

R $8.98

S $6.98

Sturdy Furniture from Santa's Shop

Settee
$17.98

V Roll-top Desk and Chair
$34.95 cash $3.50 down

Northern Hardwood Desk Sets

Golden maple finish. Panel backs, sides. Two deep side drawers, slide-out arm rest, center drawer. Swivel chair has 12½x13-in. seat that adjusts from 13 to 16 in. high; 30 in. high. Fully assembled. Freight, express or truck.

V Roll-top Desk and Chair Set. Five pigeonhole compartments and pigeonhole drawer. 30x15-in. top, 27 in. from floor. 36½ in. high overall.
79 N M9121—Shipping wt. 60 lbs. $34.95

W Flat-top Desk and Chair Set. Desk 30x15½x27 in. high overall.
79 N M9124—Shipping wt. 48 lbs. $27.95

Desk and Chair
$18.95

Reversible Desk and Chair Set

Natural-finish birch plywood; gold-tone-enameled ⅝-in. tubular steel, plastic-tipped legs. Desk 18x32x26 in. high. 9½x4x17½-in. drawer slides in either side for right or left-handers. 9½x8x18-in. shelf. Chair 25 in. high; 13½x12-in. seat. Easy to assemble. Shipping weight 32 pounds.
79 N 09076L. $18.95

Our Best 5-piece Dinette $44.50 cash $4.50 down

A truly luxurious children's ensemble .. with all the beauty and craftsmanship of adult-size furniture. Made of select hardwood with a rich, 6-coat walnut finish. Sturdy, comfortable seats are hand-woven rush cord. Table 26-in. diam., 20½ in. high. Chair seats 14 in. wide, 12 in. from floor. Easy to assemble.

79 N MT9065—5-piece Set: table, 4 chairs. Freight, express or truck. Shipping weight 47 pounds. $44.50
79 N 09066L—Table, 2 chairs. Shpg. wt. 29 lbs. 28.95
79 N 09067L—Extra chairs. Shpg. wt. each 9 lbs. Each 8.98
79 N M9068—Matching Settee. Seat 28 in. wide, 24 in. high. Assembled. Freight, express truck. Shpg. wt. 12 lbs. $17.98

ITEMS DESCRIBED BELOW SHOWN ON OPPOSITE PAGE

A B Bronze-enameled Tubular Steel Folding Sets. Vinyl seats, removable table tops. Chairs Non-slip locks. Chairs 23¾ in. high, seats 11x11¼ in. Assembled. 5-pc. set freight, express or truck.
(A) 79 N M9002—24½ x36 x20 ½ -in. high table, 4 chairs. Wt. 33 lbs. $19.95
(B) 79 N 09001L—24½ x24½ x20½ -in. high table, 2 chairs. Wt. 20 lbs. $11.49
79 N 09003—Extra chairs. Shipping weight pair 12 pounds. Pair $6.49

C D Chrome-plated Tubular Steel Folding Dinettes. Mar-resistant plastic table top. Vinyl chair seats. Baked enamel back rests. Vinyl-capped legs. Table 24x24x20¼ in. high. Chairs 22¼ in. high, seats 12½x12½ in.
(C) 79 N T9104—Table, 4 chairs. Assembled. Shpg. wt. 39 lbs. $26.50
(D) 79 N 09102L—Table, 2 chairs. Assembled. Shpg. wt. 25 lbs. $18.98
79 N 09103—Extra chairs. Shipping weight pair 14 lbs. Pair 8.98

E F Combination Dinettes. Gold-tone-enameled metal legs, spindles; natural-finish birch plywood table tops, chair seats, backs; plastic-tipped legs.
(E) 79 N 09074K—17x24x19-in. high table. Chairs 20 in. high; seats 10½x8½ in. ⅝-in. tubular legs. Easy to assemble. Shipping weight 22 lbs. $9.69
(F) 79 N M9075—25x20½-in. high table. Seats 13x11 in. ¾ -in. tubular legs. Easy to assemble. Freight or truck. Shipping weight 32 pounds. $13.94

G 3-pc. Chrome-plated Tubular Metal Dinettes. Plastic table tops. 10½x13-in. padded vinyl seats. 24-in. high chairs. Mar-proof leg tips. Easy to assemble.
79 N 09057L—20x30x20-in. high table, 2 chairs. Shpg. wt. 32 lbs. $19.95
79 N 09052L (not shown)—18x24x20-in. high table, 2 chairs. Shipping weight 25 pounds. $17.95
79 N 09054—Extra chairs. Shipping weight pair 10 lbs. Pair $9.95

H Cricket Rocker. High-gloss black-finished hardwood frame. Supported, upholstered seat with removable pillow back. Print cover. Pleated skirt. Seat 15¼x14 in. 27¾ in. high. Assembled.
79 N 09062—Shpg. wt. 15 lbs. $8.98

J Colonial Rocker. Golden-finish maple. 12x11-in. padded seat, 11 in. from floor. 23 in. high. Assembled.
79 N 09006L—Shpg. wt. 10 lbs. $4.98

K Musical Rocker. Natural-finish solid oak. Built-in imported musical movement. Seat 11½x 10½ in. 21 in. high. Assembled.
79 N 09023L—Shpg. wt. 10 lbs. $5.97

L TV Swivel Chair. Swivels completely around. Chrome-plated frame. Padded vinyl seat. Matches (G). Seat 13x15 inches. 18½ inches high. Assembled.
79 N 09061—Shpg. wt. 10 lbs. $7.49

M Step-'n'-Chair. Use as chair or step stool. Varnished oak. Seat 6¾x11 in. 14½ in. high.
79N09105—Assembled. Wt. 6 lbs. $3.49

N P Cherry red plastic covers. Blonde lacquered wood frames. Freight, express or truck.

(N) Sofa. 6 no-sag springs. Cotton and Tufflex® padding. Seat 36x14 in. 43x25 in. high overall.
79 N M9016—Shpg. wt. 36 lbs. $18.95

(P) Platform Rocker and Ottoman. 2 full-size coil springs. Rocker has 15x14-in. seat; 24 in. high. Ottoman 12x10x7 in. high.
79 N M9127—Shpg. wt. 25 lbs. $12.44

R Knotty Pine Toy Chest. Walnut stain. Simulated burned-in designs. Rope handles. 30x14¼x14¼ in. high. Easy to assemble.
79 N 09063—Shpg. wt. 19 lbs. $8.98

S Roy Rogers Toy Wagon. Cloth covered wood wagon. 27x16x 12½ in. high to top of rail. 22 in. high overall. Easy to assemble.
79 N 09064—Shpg. wt. 8 lbs. $6.98

T 3-way Toy Chest. Has shelves for books .. sliding doors double as blackboard. Masonite Presdwood over natural wood frame. 36x18x32 in. high. Easy to assemble. Freight, express or truck.
79 N M9011—Shpg. wt. 26 lbs. $9.95
79 N 09040L—No shelves—Shipping weight 21 lbs. $6.79

3-piece Set
$7.69

Metal Table and Chair Set

Red with white ⅝-in. tubular legs. Wood arm rests. Table 23x17x18½ in. high. Chair seats 10½x12 in., 10 in. from floor.
79 N 09106—Easy to assemble. Shipping weight 18 pounds. $7.69

"Dress-up Fun" Outfits

"Dress-up" Delights for the Fashionable Modern Miss

A **Smart Vanity Table and Bench** teaches young ladies good grooming. Pleated wipe-clean vinyl plastic in feminine floral print encircles both vanity and padded stool. 20¾-in. high wood vanity with swing-out arms for extra room. Big 7x9-in. bracket-supported mirror in wood frame. 13x23½-in. easy-to-clean enameled Masonite top holds matched accessories: brush, comb, compact, lipstick and hand mirror.
79 N 01377—Shipping weight 9 pounds.................Complete set **$6.98**
See page 383 for beautiful bride's costume shown above

B **A Hat like Mother's.** White straw hat has wide 2½-in. brim. Gaily trimmed with colorful rayon satin sash and matching plume.
49 N 1328—In candy-striped hat box. Shipping weight 1 lb............... **$1.67**

C **Chic Chemise** of red rayon shantung with gold-color loop trim. 34-in. string of multi-color snap beads. Red nylon hose with elastic tops.
49 N 1080—State: small (age 3-5); med. (age 5-8); lg. (age 8-11). Wt. 5 oz.. **$1.84**

D **Red High Heels.** Safe high-impact plastic sole and heel, tapered no-trip toe. Elastic strap tops with silver-color studs. Wt. 7 oz.
49 N 1081—State: small (age 3-5); med. (age 6-7); large (age 8-10) **87c**

E **Glamorous Red Gown and Accessories.** Tulle and sequin-trimmed rayon taffeta gown sweeps to floor . . filmy net stole drapes shoulders. Shimmering metallic white cotton-jersey mitts. Crowned by silver-color tiara sprinkled with glistening "jewels". Wt. 1 lb.
49 N 1082—State: small (age 3-5); med. (age 6-7); large (age 8-10) ... Set **$5.98**

$1.97

De luxe High Heels

$2.77

"Imitation mink" Stole Outfit

Snap-Link Kit $2.72

Model's Hat Box $3.42

Cosmetic Bag $2.62

F Real high-heeled sandals have flexible composition soles that won't break or slip. Steel shanks support the arch; steel rod prevents heel breakage. Silver-color glitter heels, chic plastic vamp and silver-color straps. *State size:* small (age 3-5); medium (age 6-7); large (age 8-10).
49 N 1084—Shpg. wt. 1 lb. **$1.97**

G For milady's formal evenings . . a 42-inch long "fake fur" stole of the softest deep pile rayon yarns shaded to look like real mink and luxury-lined with shiny rayon satin. Her jewels: a sparkling "diamond" ring which adjusts to fit any finger and an elegant choker of snap-type "pearl" beads. To complete her ensemble she'll wear an "orchid" corsage; comes in a clear plastic "florist's" box. Shpg. wt. 1 lb.
49 N 1072.........Complete set **$2.77**

Approximately 200 colorful plastic pieces . . round, oval, square and flower shapes . . in a big variety of sizes. Design fashion jewelry by merely snapping any combination of pieces together. Pretty for bracelets and chokers . . big enough for belts and long necklaces. In assorted colors. Shpg. wt. 1 lb.
49 N 1367............ **$2.72**

Betsy McCall packs all the young lady's good grooming needs into this plaid plastic hat box. High style case contains lotions, lipstick, nail polish, toothbrush, toothpaste, soap, brush and comb . . specially designed for lovely little girls. Strong zippered lid . . lift-out tray. 10-inch diameter. Shipping weight 2 pounds.
49 N 1270............ **$3.42**

Sturdy vinyl plastic bag is washable . . has pert teenage pony tail design. It's filled with good grooming aids and harmless cosmetics. Ideal for "dress-up" games. Case is 4x9x5 in. high.
49 N 1396—Shpg. wt. 1 lb. **$2.62**

Make this the gayest Christmas ever! Build your order to $20 or more . . pay only 10% down on Sears Easy Terms.

Most little girls like to play dress-up and the 1959 Sears Wishbook offered all kinds of outfits, not all of them entirely logical. The Glitter Gown makes sense, if the little girl wants to pretend she's going to the prom. But The Gibson Girl? Did somebody believe that girls in rock 'n' roll 1959 longed to dress up like characters from the Gay 90s?

Girls who wanted to pretend to be grownups had fake fur ensembles, high heels ("like Mother's"), luggage and "Fancy Pants" lingerie.

And girls who wanted to remain kids had colorful record players and board games based on TV shows like "Concentration" and "The Price is Right".

But the biggest toy news of 1959 is noticeably missing from this Wishbook. Barbie, the shapely doll phenomenon made by Mattel, was introduced this year. However, Barbie did not officially appear until a full year later in the 1960 Christmas catalog.

1959 CHRISTMAS BOOK

SHOP BY PHONE . . See pages 290-292 for number to call
Index starts on page 287 . . Satisfaction guaranteed or your money back
SEARS, ROEBUCK AND CO., CHICAGO 7, ILLINOIS

Sears Christmas
Wishbook
1959

Delight a Junior Sophisticate

[1] **The Gibson Girl.** Top of dress is white organdy, lacy trim, red rose decoration; puff sleeves have elastic. Black and white checked rayon taffeta skirt, black rayon satin ruffle. Veiled straw hat with black and white checked ribbon and bow, red rose. Black plastic belt, gold color buckle. Shoes not incl. *State size* Small (age 3–5), Medium (age 6–8), Large (age 8–10). 49N1020—Wt. 1 lb. 4 oz. **$5.97**

[2] **Balloon Dress Ensemble.** White rayon taffeta bodice bound in black velvet; overskirt of flocked nylon sheer, puffed out and tucked into and under white rayon taffeta underskirt. Black velvet high waistband, removable rhinestone pin. Nylon hose included. Styled for "grown-up" misses. Shoes not included. *State size* Small (age 3–5), Medium (6–8), Large (age 8–10). 49N1027—Shpg. wt. 12 oz. **$3.57**

[3] **Sophisti-Kit Set.** Red rayon satin gown; metallic white cotton jersey mitts; rayon silver color lame clutch bag, sequin trimmed veil; rhinestone ring. Necklace; "orchid" corsage. *State* Small (age 3–4), Medium (age 5–7), Large (age 8–10). 49 N 1045—Shpg. wt. 1 lb. **$3.97**

[4] **Red Shoes.** No-trip design. Plastic strap tops, silver-color studs. *State* Small (age 3–5), Medium (age 6–7), Large (age 8–10). 49 N 1081—Shpg. wt. 7 oz. **87c**

[5] **Glitter Gown.** There'll be stars in her eyes when she sees herself in this glamourous evening gown .. what fun she'll have draping and styling it in a dozen different ways. Gown of blue mylustra jersey highlighted with Lurex. Glitter mitts of white mylustra. Sparkling imitation rhinestone pin included. *Please state size* Small (age 3–4), Medium (5–7), Large (age 8–10). 49N1046—Shpg. wt. 1 lb. **$4.80**

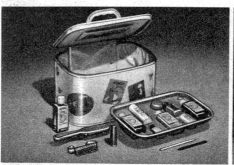

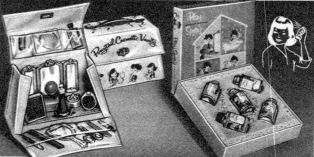

Give her a Train Case

White vinyl case with travel motif decorations. Fitted with high quality non-toxic cosmetics. Lift-out tray, bubble bath, sachet and talcum powder, shampoo, cologne, toilet water, atomizer, hand lotion, nail brush, hair brush, lipstick, emery board, orange stick. Case is 6⅞x9¾x5½ inches high. 49N1047—Shpg. wt. 2 lbs. 10 oz. **$4.70**

Cosmetic Vanity

Sturdy, washable vinyl plastic bag decorated with pert teenage pony tail motif . . . filled with good grooming aids and harmless cosmetics. Includes pretend lipstick, 2 powder puffs, perfume bottle and atomizer, 3-way vanity mirror, powder and rouge compacts, hand mirror, comb, cuticle scissors, emery board, nail buffer and white nail pencil. 4x9x5 inches high. 49 N 1396—Shpg. wt. 1 lb. **$2.62**

Play Spray Set

Easy-to-use non-toxic glamour aids for little ladies . . encourage cleanliness and make bath-time luxurious. Set consists of 2 cans of clean-scented bubble bath, one can of delightfully fragrant cologne foam which soothes and smooths the skin, one can of beauty cream skin softener with dainty fragrance, one can of hair spray just like mother uses. All cans contain 2 oz. 49 N 1048—Shpg. wt. 2 lbs. **$2.87**

Fashion Snap-Link Kit

Compact clear plastic container packed with approximately 200 colorful plastic pieces . . . square and round shapes in a big variety of sizes. Design fashion jewelry by merely snapping together any conbination of pieces . . . make pretty bracelets and chokers, belts and long necklaces. An endless number of designs and items are possible. Kiddies will love showing off the "jewelry" they've designed. Children will create their own "jewelry" styles and shapes. Unbreakable plastic pieces in bright assorted colors. 49 N 1367—Shipping weight 1 pound **$2.58**

Little Luxuries for "grown-up" fun

Every accessory she needs for dressing-up

 [1] $8.60

$1.67 [3]

[2] $2.82

[5] $1.87

$2.90 [6]

[4] $2.99

$1.97 [8]

[7] 87c

[9] $1.97

3-piece Fake Fur Cape Ensemble

[1] For little girls who dream of being grown-up ladies. Sheared red rayon plush cape, 32 inches across. White plush collar, sweater guard, 7x6-inch muff of same red fabric with a gray cord loop. Matching red pocketbook with a button lock. All pieces are fully lined.
49 N 1050—Shpg. wt. 2 lbs. 3 oz. $8.60

"Paris Design" Hat for chic misses

[3] Pretty white straw sailor has wide 2½-inch brim. It's gaily trimmed with colorful rayon satin sash, matching plume.
49 N 1328—In candy-striped box. Wt. 1 lb. $1.67

Handbag Set for Day and Datetime

[5] Black and white daytime bag with net design, white roses on lid; 4⅝x2¾ inches. Black evening clutch; zipper pocket, 8½x4 inches. Both of plastic.
49 N 1014—Shipping weight 15 oz. $1.87

Formal Stole Outfit of Fake Fur

[2] Shaped stole of deep piled rayon yarns, 40 in. long, shaded to look like fur, lined with rayon satin. "Diamond" ring, "pearl" choker of snap-in beads, gold-color plated metal chain with "locket," Earrings. Artificial orchid corsage.
49 N 1005—Shipping weight 1 lb. 2 oz. $2.82

Smartly Designed Musical Purse

[4] Music as she goes. Metal filigree purse with gold-color plating. Mirror, plastic top and bottom. 5⅛x3¼x3 in. high.
49 N 1052—Shipping weight 1 lb. $2.99

"Fancy Pants" Lingerie Set

[6] Pair of 15 denier seamed nylons, garters; stretch girdle, elastic straps, snap fasteners; red lace trimmed acetate panties with bells. *State* Med. (3-5 yrs.), Large (6-8 yrs.)
49 N 1053—Shipping weight 12 oz. $2.90

High Heels Like Mother's . . Safely constructed for growing feet

[7] **Red Shoes.** No-trip design. Elastic strap tops, silver-color studs. *State* Small (age 3-5), Medium (age 6-7), Large (age 8-10).
49 N 1081—Shpg. wt. 7 oz. . .87c

[8] **Black Shoes.** Steel shank; innersole; elastic heel strap, rosebud decoration. *State* Small (age 3-5), Med. (age 6-7), Large (age 8-10).
49 N 1054—Wt. 11 oz. . . .$1.97

[9] **Silver-color Sandals.** Composition non-slip soles; steel shank. Innersole. *State* Small (age 3-5), Med. (age 6-7), Large (age 8-10).
49 N 1084—Wt. 11 oz. . . .$1.97

Her own Adult Jewelry and Case

No need to borrow mama's—now she has high fashion jewelry all her own. 12 assorted items, an exciting array of jewelry including: full size necklaces, bracelets, pins, earrings, rope and a ring. And because a young lady of fashion needs a jewelry box to keep her "treasures", she'll love the light blue simulated leather case. Imitation suede lined. Heraldic gold color tooling motif. Removable tray. Case measures 8½x5½x2½ inches. Price includes 18c Federal Excise Tax.
4 N 4400E—Jewelry and case. Shpg. wt. 3 lbs. .$2.98

Flower Art Handcraft Kit

Kit contains finely detailed polyethylene plastic parts for making six beautiful long-stemmed roses of luscious assorted colors. Provides a wealth of entertaining fun and satisfaction . . . so easy for anyone to do—simply follow the easy directions; the result is a bouquet of real-looking roses, so lovely you'll be proud to keep it as a long-lasting decoration for your home . . . ideal centerpiece for tables . . will look beautiful anywhere in your home. Included are realistic plastic fern and glass vase designed to set off flowers to best advantage.
49 N 1210—Shipping weight 2 lbs. 4 oz. $2.84

5-piece Bobbysox Assortment

A handsome matched set for the young school girl. All white vinyl plastic with 5-color bobbysox design. Includes travel case with 2 compartments, 1 with mirror, has metal turn fasteners, loop carrying strap; measures 9½x8¾x4½ in. deep; Loot Box for her most precious treasures, 7¾x3¾ in.; Heart Shaped Diary for recording those school-day memories . . has padlock, 2 keys, 6x5½ in.; Autograph Book 6½x4½ in.; Photo Album 3¾x3 in., vinyl photo holders.
49 N 1233—Shipping weight 2 pounds 12 ounces. $3.96

Electric Organs

Rich professional tones .. sized for children

$49.95 [1]

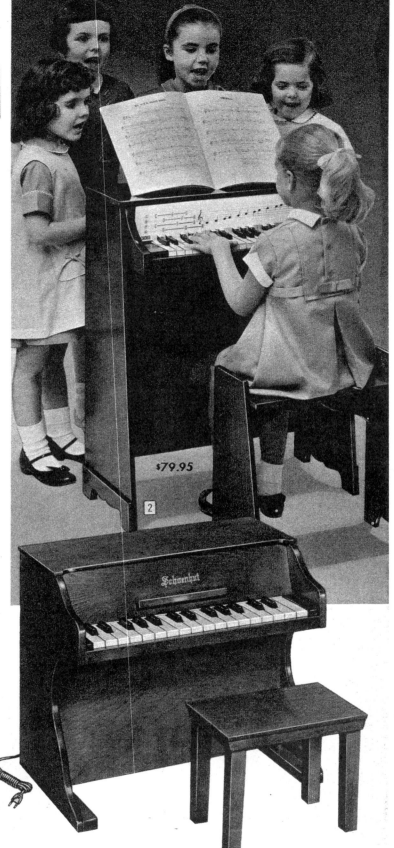

$79.95

[2]

[1] Emenee Table-top Studio Organ .. fine, full tone. 37 black and white full size plastic keys .. 3 full chromatic octaves. Plays sharps, flats, chords. Easily portable. Beautiful walnut-finished wood cabinet, 25x12x 11¾ inches high. Complete with music book and new, patented "Magic-Organ" self-teach method that enables anyone to play almost immediately. UL approved 110–120 volt, 60-cycle AC. Shpg. wt. 30 lbs.
79 N 0539L—Only $5 down. **$49.95**

[2] Our finest .. Emenee decorator-styled grand console organ that makes a wonderful addition to any living room, den, or studio. Has 37 black and white keys .. 3 full chromatic octaves .. plays sharps, flats, and chords. Beautiful tones. Walnut-finished wood cabinet 31⅝x25x13¼ inches deep. *Matching bench.* Comes with music book and self-teach method booklet. UL approved 110–120 volt, 60 cycle AC. Shipping weight 61 lbs.
79 N M583—Only $8 down... **$79.95**

Emenee Electric Golden Table Model Organ

Here's an instrument so like a real electric reed organ it can be the basis for professional training. Beautiful full-bodied tone. Full 27 black and white keys include sharps and flats. Plays over 2 full chromatic octaves. Well-designed table model case of strong high-impact plastic has simulated mahogany finish. Comes with easy-to-read music book and key selection method. Safe on-and-off switch. 2½x9½x18 inches long. UL approved. 110–120-volt, 60-cycle AC.
9 N 621—Shipping weight 9 pounds 4 ounces..........................**$16.95**

Our Economy-priced Electric Console Organ

Youngsters will love learning to play on this rich-toned miniature. 30 plastic keys .. 18 white and 12 black are same width (⅞-inch) as large organs. 2½ octaves . . plays sharps, flats and chords. Brass reeds. Organ and matching bench are made of finest-quality plywood .. finished in walnut lacquer. Organ 19½x 11¾x16¾ inches high. Comes with music book and electric cord. UL approved for 110–120-volt, 60-cycle AC.
79 N 0536L—Shipping weight 18 pounds. $3.00 down......................Cash **$29.95**

SHIPPING NOTE: Item (2), 79 N M583, shipped by freight (rail or truck) or express

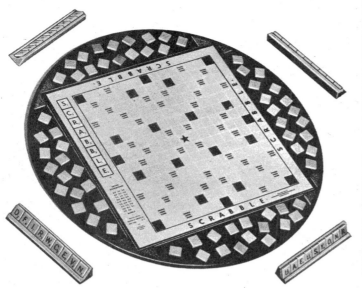

Scrabble® .. fascinating word game! Buy Turntable, too

Gives intriguing competition in building words, pitting your skill against the other players. Fun for 2 to 4 players. Build words with numbered letter tiles. High number score at end of game wins. 14½x14¼-inch playing board.
49 N 139—Game only, no turntable. Shipping weight 1 lb. 8 oz.............$2.37

Turntable of Masonite Presdwood. Rubber rim-edge and feet.
79 N 0462—Revolving Turntable only. Cork holders for board. Shpg. wt. 4 lbs.....$2.69

Carroms and 85 games on one board .. All equipment included $8.47

Play Carroms, Checkers, Backgammon, Crokinole and many, many more games on this big 28½-inch square board of 3-ply panel. Wood rim, reversible net pockets, 2 cues, 29 carrom rings, 15 discs, 10 tenpins, 3 tops, score tab, 2 dice, 18 flies. Instructions for all 85 games included. Here's fun that the entire family can enjoy, from little tykes to grandma and grandpa.
79 N 0481L—Complete outfit. Shipping weight 10 pounds............$8.47
49 N 480—29 extra Carrom Rings. Shipping weight 8 ounces............50c

It's Game Time .. TV Teasers, other Favorites

Scrabble® for Juniors. Famous word game, simplified for your youngsters. Double-sided board, one side has regular board, one has easy pictorial version of game. 100 lettered tiles and 33 counters. Board 18½ inches square.
49 N 235—Shpg. wt. 2 lbs. 2 oz......$1.69

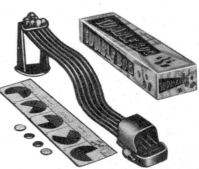

Tumble Bug. A game of action and thrills. 4 tricky and colorful Tumble Bugs hop, skip and tumble down the wavy runway. Place your bets .. watch the fun. Made of plastic. 21 in. long.
49 N 230—Shpg. wt. 1 lb. 4 oz.......$1.69

1. **The Price is Right.** Exciting version of the TV show. Set includes a mechanical bid recorder, price cards, prizes and 4 small bid recorders. For 2 to 4 players.
49 N 307—Shpg. wt. 2 lbs. 2 oz. ..$2.69

2. **Steve Canyon Air Force Game.** "Pilots" fly scale models of planes through maneuvers. Board, 4 planes, 4 control panels, playing cards. For 2 to 4 "pilots."
79 N 136—Shpg. wt. 2 lbs.......$2.69

3. **Name That Tune.** Non-breakable 33⅓ RPM record, playable on both sides .. 130 tunes. Music cards, dial with spinner. Wood covering pieces. For up to 10 players.
49 N 312—Shpg. wt. 1 lb. 6 oz. ...$2.69

4. **Concentration.** Based on TV game. Match hidden items, numbers to work out solution. Rollomatic puzzle box, 30 ft. of word-puzzles. Exciting suspense. 2 to 5 players.
49 N 298—Shpg. wt. 1 lb. 14 oz. ..$3.49

5. **Jan Murray's Treasure Hunt.** Includes category cards, treasure-cove, timing device, treasure cards, category bid selection, and play money. Any number can play.
49 N 344—Shpg. wt. 1 lb. 11 oz. ..$2.69

6. **Let's Build a Cootie.** Players race to assemble cooties ... head, body .. plastic pieces for 4 cooties. Die included. Lots of fun and amusement for up to 4 players.
49 N 176—Shpg. wt. 12 oz......$1.67

Fully Electronic, with Six Disney Records

Let's listen to music! Luggage-type portable electric phonograph plays all 4 record speeds . . 16 rpm, 33⅓ rpm, 45 rpm, and 78 rpm up to 12 inches. Six 10-inch Disney children's records. Hi-gain crystal pickup. Electronic amplification for deep, resonant tone reproduction. Wide range volume control. Lightweight tone arm with crystal cartridge and synthetic sapphire needle. One tube plus rectifier. Built-in 45 rpm centerpiece. Handsome plastic-coated fiber case . . brown and beige.

49 N 549—13x11¼x5⅞ inch. Shpg. wt. 6 lbs. 8 oz..... **$15.98**

NOTE: All electric phonographs described on this page are UL approved, 110–120-volt, 60-cycle, AC.

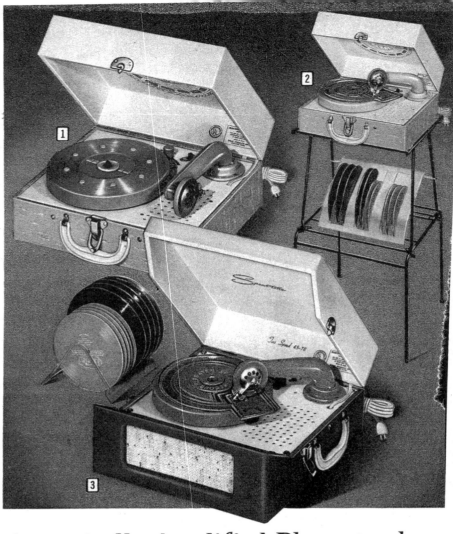

Acoustically Amplified Phonographs

2-speed Electric Portables play all 45 and 78 rpm records

[1] A phonograph of their very own for young music lovers! Wonderful tone reproduction . . . integral tone chamber amplification. Plays just like mom and dad's. Scuff-resistant fiber case . . blue and white pyroxylin-coated covering wipes clean. Plastic handle. Loud and soft needles included. 13x11¼x5⅞ in. high.

49 N 580—Shpg. wt. 8 lbs. . **$10.98**

[2] Something they'll never tire of playing. Combination phonograph and metal record rack-stand, plus 10 records (five 45 and five 78 rpm). Phonograph has integral tone chamber amplification. Blue and white fiber case . . pyroxylin covering wipes clean. Plastic handle. Loud, soft needles incl. 12x14x 28½ in. high.

79 N 0578—Wt. 16 lbs.... **$16.98**

[3] Tops with little listeners. Electric portable with metal rack that holds 35 records . . 10 children's records included. Automatic repeater attachment, built-in tone chamber amplification. Wood-frame case, wipe-clean pyroxylin covering. 13½x14x6 in.

79 N 0534—Wt. 19 lbs... **$14.98**

79 N 0564—Phono above without records, rack. Wt. 17 lbs... **$12.98**

Portable 4-speed Electric Phonograph with stand

A rumpus-room "must" for pre-teen parties. Stand holds up to 39 records . . 10 children's records included. Electronic amplifier . . full volume control. Plays 16, 33⅓, 45, 78 rpm records. Hi-gain crystal pickup, permanent type needle. Plastic-coated fiber case . . brown and beige. 12x14x 28½ in. high (on stand).

79 N 0569—Shpg. wt. 17 lbs.... **$19.98**

Order with or without metal racks, records

Electric portable . . plays 78 rpm records. Metal rack, 10 records incl. Integral tone chamber. Automatic repeater attachment. Fiber case.

49 N 570—11x11x6 in. Shpg. wt. 9 lbs......... **$9.98**

49 N 548—Phono above without rack, records or repeater attachment. Shipping weight 8 lbs................**$7.98**

Tear-drop design all-metal electric phonograph. Rigid inter-channel metal construction for extra durability. Comes with 35-record metal rack, 10 records. Blue, gray enamel finish. Needles.

49 N 591—13x8x7 in. Shpg. wt. 7 lbs...........**$8.98**

49 N 577—Phono, needles only. Shpg. wt. 6 lbs... **6.98**

4 speeds, 2 speakers, fully electronic!

Party-time Portable plays like a dream

Something special for the junior "social set" for dancing or listening. New 4-speed electronic portable features Tandemonic® sound . . a form of hi-fidelity. Two speakers are attached to either side of the case . . . open outward for playing. Speakers can be detached from the phonograph, too, and placed up to eight feet away from the center amplifier, which contains two separate output jacks. Separate volume controls for each speaker. Plays all 16, 33⅓, 45 and 78 rpm records up to 12 inches. Turnover cartridge with two separate synthetic sapphire needles. Two-tone green plastic-coated fiber case wipes clean in a jiffy with a damp cloth . . measures 18¾x 11¼x5⅞ inches high. Underwriters' Laboratories approved, 115-volt, 60-cycle AC. Order on Easy Terms . . only 10% down.

79 N 0550—Shipping weight 13 pounds. $2.50 down................Cash **$23.98**

Smart Santas order from Sears Christmas Catalog
. . it's the quickest, easiest way to take care
of their gift lists . . and the most economical, too!

They'll all want this Record Carrying Case

Easiest and best way to carry records to parties, school, beach, etc. without scratching or breaking them.
    Record index holds up to 50 records (7 inch diameter only). Sturdy fiber case . . pyroxylin-coated covering wipes clean with a damp cloth . . two-tone green. Plastic handle. Records are not included. 7⅞ x 8¾ x 5 inches high. Shipping weight 2 pounds 5 ounces.
49 N 582.....................**$1.98**

$2998

Roy Rogers
Stereophonic Phonograph

The new sound sensation in children's phonographs . . . a real stereophonic hi-fidelity instrument at a price so low you'll find it hard to believe. Brings out beautifully the high highs, the low lows, and the in-between shadings of tone on all recordings . . . and gives you the magic of stereophonic sound. 4-speed portable plays *both* stereophonic and regular records. Two speakers attached . . one to each side . . can be detached and placed up to 8 feet away. Two output jacks. Dual purpose stereo cartridge, two synthetic sapphire needles. Two channels . . volume control for each speaker for balanced tone. Plays all 16, 33⅓, 45, 78 rpm records up to 12 inches. Sturdy case of plastic-coated fiber, brown and tan. UL approved, 115-volt, 60-cycle AC.
79 N 0555—18x11x8 inches high. Shipping weight 14 pounds. $3.00 down....Cash **$29.98**

Use Sears Easy Terms . . . only 10% down on orders of $20 or more . . see page 294

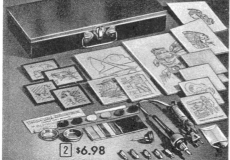

[1] $8.95

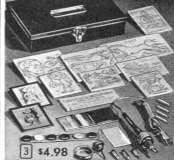

[2] $6.98 **[3]** $4.98

[4] [5] [6]

Woodburning Sets

Work on wood, leather, cork and foil!
UL-approved electric pens, 110-120-v. AC-DC

[1] Our Best Woodburning Set. Actually a combination of several hobbies! A wealth of things to do, all packed in good-looking, baked-on-enameled steel chest. Electric pen with one main point and 4 screw-on brass overpoints of different shapes, sizes. 4-piece book ends for woodburning, 6-piece book ends for woodcarving and 4 woodcarving plaques. 6 cork coasters, 3 leather bookmarks, ready-to-assemble tie rack with dowels and nails. Two carving tools (straight chisel and angle chisel), metal hammer, C-clamp, coping saw, colored leaf foil, 6 water color paints, artist's brush, craft pattern transfer sheet, sandpaper.
49 N 2209—Complete instructions. Shipping weight 6 pounds 4 oz.........**$8.95**

[2] Fine Woodburning Set. Electric pen and point with 4 extra points (not 5 as shown), paints, brush, tapping tool. 4 large wood plaques, 2 book ends, 4 foil and 2 wood plaques. In metal box with tray.
49 N 2178—Complete instructions. Shipping weight 3 lbs. 8 oz...........**$6.98**

[3] Good Woodburning Set. Electric pen and point with 3 extra points, paints, brush, tapping tool. 7 wood plaques, ready-to-assemble tie rack, 2 figured foil plaques, 6 leaf foil transfers. In metal box.
49 N 2177—Complete instructions. Shipping weight 2 lbs. 8 oz...........**$4.98**

[4] Economy Woodburning Set. Electric pen and paints. Wood, foil plaques.
49 N 2221—Complete instructions. Shipping weight 1 pound..........**$1.69**

[5] Woodburning Kit. 5-piece planter and 4-piece comb and brush shelf.
49 N 2213—Instruction sheets. (No pen.) Shipping weight 12 ounces....**$1.73**

[6] Big Craft Kit. 2 large and 2 small wood plaques, pair of flower boxes, 2 cork hot pads, 4 cork coasters, 2 cork bookmarks.
49 N 2217—Instruction sheets. Shipping weight 1 pound.................**$2.64**

Mr. Chips Woodcrafting Set

Carve and color fun for kids! Designed plywood to make 5-piece napkin holder, 2 designed wall plaques, 2 carving tools (straight chisel and angle chisel), metal hammer, C-clamp, coping saw with 2 extra blades, 6 water color paints, brush, sandpaper and practice board.
49 N 2218—Instructions. Shpg. wt. 1 lb. 10 oz...**$2.98**

Ben Franklin Print Shop Set

Sturdy steel press works like a real one! Automatic inking. Easy hand action. Print area 2½x4 in. for cards, tickets, envelopes, news, etc. Absorbing hobby—fun kit with full instructions. Ample supply of rubber type, type holder, tray, ink, non-flammable ink cleaner, tweezers, screwdriver, etc.
79 N 02199L—9½ in. high over-all. Wt. 17 lbs....**$19.95**

Build a real Clock!

All parts needed to assemble by hand a pendulum wall clock that *keeps accurate time!* No tools needed. Gears and pinions fit between brass plates. No springs . . movement works by hanging weight. Plastic housing, 4-color front.
49 N 2223—Full instructions. Wt. 2 lbs. **$3.98**

Soldier Casting Set

[7] *Make your own army!* 3-figure mold makes new commandos—rifleman, bayoneteer, bugler. Figures 2¼ in. high. Electric melting stove . . 110-120-volt, 60-cycle AC-DC. Ladle, mold clamp, handles, 18 pigs metal, mold-smoking candle, 2 bottles of paint and brush.
49 N 2039—Shpg. wt. 4 lbs. 4 oz....**$6.49**
49 N 2205—72 Extra Pigs of Casting Metal. Shipping weight 2 pounds 8 ounces....**$2.97**

[8] 49 N 2023—Extra Mold; makes three 2¼-in. high figures: submachine gunner and two different riflemen. Shpg. wt. 1 lb. 8 oz. **$2.37**

[9] 49N2208—Extra Mold; makes three 2¼-in. high figures: grenade thrower, flame thrower man, mortar man. Shpg. wt. 1 lb. 8 oz.. **$2.37**

Indian Beadcraft

Useful fun for boys and girls! Make your own beaded belts, bags, headbands, rings, bracelets, etc. Outfit includes bead loom, finished strip of beadwork, wrist strap, 10 bottles assorted seed beads, thread, needles, beeswax, wire, imitation jewels, and instruction booklet.
49N2175–Shpg. wt. 1 lb. 8 oz.....**$2.79**
49N2197–Extra beads. Shpg. wt. 12 oz... **89¢**

Happy Hands Assortment

Five popular hobby crafts! Indian beadwork, leathercraft, plexon braiding, "Suji" wire art and bamboo beadwork. Many projects of decorative beadwork; leather comb case, key case; lanyards, bracelets, etc.; small wire figures; bamboo-bead place mats. With all instructions and materials needed.
49 N 2227—Shipping weight 2 pounds. **$4.49**

The most popular and largest selling toy ever marketed to girls... if not the most popular toy of all time... quietly made its debut in the 1960 Christmas Wishbook. Barbie, "The Famous Model", made an inauspicious appearance in the back pages of the catalog's doll section. Although only the first, swimsuited Barbie was initially offered, Mattel would go on to make hundreds of variations on Barbie, Ken and their friends.

Some experts claim that Barbie's thin, busty, undernourished look (by 1959 standards) was what scared toy buyers away. But the buying public loved her and turned a toy into an industry.

Not yet ready to go full force selling Barbie, the 1960 Wishbook offered other, more realistic looking dolls to girls. Tiny Tears utilized water in every way -- drinking, wetting and crying (so did, for that matter, Betsy Wetsy); and a fashionable Betsey McCall wore a variety of gowns and costumes while proudly showing off her ability to walk, sit and kneel.

In these early days of the Civil Rights Movement, it is also worth noting that a Black doll makes her first appearance in these pages. Even for the smallest children, the world was beginning to change.

Sears Christmas
Wishbook

1960

I'm Toodles

and I can say "Mama", too!

22-inch Baby Toodles in Super Kart $17⁷⁷

She's vinyl plastic with jointed arms, legs . . head turns. Bathe her like a real infant . . brush and comb her curly rooted Saran hair. Coy rolling and sleeping glassene eyes with long lashes. Drinks from her bottle, wets . . has "Mama" voice. Wears cotton sateen romper, socks, sandals. Super Kart (18x 13x23 in. high) is all steel with wood handle . . use it as a high chair or stroller. Removable basket. Boxes of empty name brand foods included.
79 N 3203L—Toodles in Super Kart. Easy to assemble. Wt. 11 lbs......$17.77

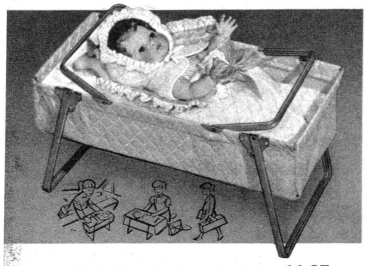

16-inch Infant Toodles in Car Bed $11.87

Baby Toodles is a great little traveler. Her quilted car bed has tufted air-filled mattress, sturdy metal frame. She nestles snugly in a glamorous lace-trimmed rayon satin bunting with matching bonnet on her curly rooted Saran hair. Underneath she wears a checked romper and knitted booties. Toodles has pretty sleeping eyes, jointed arms and legs, turning head to pose realistically. She coos happily when you squeeze her. See how many ways her car bed can be used in small views above.
49 N 3263—Infant Toodles in 20-inch Car Bed. Shpg. wt. 5 lbs. 10 oz....$11.87

I'm Tiny Tears..

Rock me and I slowly close my sleepy eyes
Squeeze me and tears roll down my cheeks
I drink from my bottle and wet my diaper

16-inch Tiny Tears in Crib $17.77

Tiny Tears snuggled cozily in her white plastic rocker-crib, ready for sleep. Washable molded vinyl body, fully jointed . . Saran hair to comb and care for. Eyes open and shut . . cry tears. She drinks, wets too! Dressed in cotton romper and bonnet . . nice and warm under rayon satin brocade quilt that zips to keep drafts out. Pouch at bottom holds Tiny Tears' bottle, diaper, booties, pins, sponge, bubble pipe, and pacifier. Fluffy cotton dress and panties included. Rocker-crib about 18x12x12 inches high.
79 N 3243C—Shipping weight 6 pounds............................$17.77

Betsey McCall walks, sits, kneels $1.97

1 Petite 8-inch doll of hard plastic with creamy bisque finish. Jointed arms, legs, knees and turning head. Lustrous Saran hair . . lashed sleeping eyes. Wears lacy chemise, socks and vinyl shoes. Buy other outfits separately below.
49 N 3002—Betsy McCall doll. Shipping weight 8 ounces..................$1.97

Wardrobe Outfits. Carefully sewn of fine fabrics. Shipping weight each 6 ounces.

Outfits may vary slightly

A **49 N 3820—Sweet Dreams.** Lacy-trimmed nylon tricot peignoir over nylon tricot nightgown. Dainty mules....$2.27

B **49 N 3824—Bridal Outfit.** Overskirt of rayon satin and lace. Taffeta slip, panties. Veil, bouquet, slippers.....$2.79

C **49 N 3821—Riding Habit.** Cotton blouse, cotton suede vest, brass-color buttons, kerchief, felt jodhpurs....$1.37

D **49 N 3823—On-the-ice.** Cotton felt skirt, jersey sweater, cummerbund, felt hood and ice skates........$1.79

E **49 N 3876—Sugar and Spice.** Evening gown with nylon net, tricot ruching. Slip, panties, shoes. Perky straw hat.....................$2.79

F **49 N 3873—Schoolgirl.** Cotton velvet skirt, blouse, panties....$1.37

with Rock-A-Bye Eyes®

I can blow bubbles, too. Bathe my molded vinyl body . . shampoo my rooted Saran hair. My plastic head turns . . is hard to break

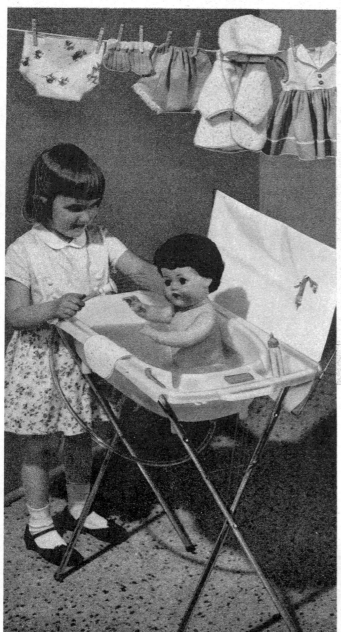

16-inch Tiny Tears with Case, Layette $11.87

Sweet little Tiny Tears with glossy rooted Saran hair for you to comb, brush and set over and over again. She comes in a de luxe case of fiberboard with plastic handle . . just what little girls need when they take dolly traveling or need a neat place to keep her layette. Nicely dressed in embossed cotton romper . . brings her own extra dress of cotton with matching panties, bonnet and booties. Care for her with diaper, bottle, washcloth, sponge, pins, clothespins; keep her happy with pacifier or bubble pipe. Instruction booklet is included for novice "mommies."

49 N 3239—16-inch Tiny Tears with case and layette. Shpg. wt. 5 lbs...........$11.87
49 N 3236—11½-inch Tiny Tears with case, layette. Shpg. wt. 3 lbs........... 8.98

20-inch Tiny Tears with De luxe Spra-Bath

$21.77 cash $2.50 down   Spra-Bath only **$9.77**

Little girls will love bathing Tiny Tears . . and giving her a shower rinse with the battery-operated spray attachment (uses 3 "D" batteries, not included). Water in tub is recirculated . . no need to attach anything to a water tap. And what fun it is to shampoo her rooted Saran hair . . rinse it and blissfully comb and brush back her curls. Life-size Tiny Tears drinks, and wets her diaper. Blows soap bubbles through her tiny bubble pipe. Terrycloth wrapper keeps her warm after bath.

Accessories include dress and pants, diaper, pins, sponge, booties, washcloth, pacifier, 2 clothespins and complete instructions.

The 26x14x5-inch deep tub is molded polyethylene plastic . . won't rust, peel or leak . . is puncture-proof, easy to clean. Tub sits on tubular metal legs; has fold-over dressing table top.

79 N 3232C—Tiny Tears with Spra-Bath. Shipping weight 10 lbs.. $21.77
79 N 3473C—Spra-Bath only. Shipping weight 7 pounds......... 9.77
34 N 4650—Batteries for above. Size "D". Wt. three, 12 oz. 3 for 44c

Tiny Tears, Accessories $13.57

All the true-to-life features of dolls above. Rooted Saran hair. Dressed in rompers. Has booties, diaper, bottle, pins, sponge, bubble pipe, washcloth, pacifier; also cotton dress and panties with the two larger sizes. All sizes come in gift box.

79 N 3240C—20-in. Tiny Tears. Wt. 7 lbs....$13.57
49 N 3235—13½-in. Tiny Tears. Wt. 3 lbs.... 7.98
49 N 3230—11½-inch Tiny Tears. (No dress or panties included). Shpg. wt. 2 lbs...... $5.98

Betsy Wetsy..drinks. wets
and cries real tears

12 to 22-inch Betsy Wetsy with bath tub, layette

[1] The famous, life-like baby doll .. always a favorite on Christmas day. She coos appealingly .. her vinyl plastic body is soft to the touch. Arms and legs are jointed, head turns. "Baby fashioned" rooted Saran hair .. lashed sleeping eyes. Betsy comes dressed in 2 piece romper, bib and booties. Layette has lace trimmed organdy dress, bonnet, slip, diaper, safety pins, powder puffs, bottle and nipple, soap, wash cloth, tissues, clothes pins. Her plastic bath tub (23x11x5 in. deep) has bracket to fit across standard tub.

79 N 3193C—12-inch Betsy. With layette and tub. Shpg. wt. 4 lbs........ $ 8.88
79 N 3194C—16-inch Betsy. With layette and tub. Shpg. wt. 5 lbs........ 11.97
79 N 3196C—22-inch Betsy. With layette and tub. Shpg. wt. 6 lbs........ 13.97

$13⁹⁷
22 inch

22-inch Betsy Wetsy in romper outfit

[2] Big Baby doll drinks and wets just like Betsy sold above. A delight for young mothers. Comb, brush, dampen and set her shining rooted, baby-like Saran hair. She's all vinyl plastic .. fully jointed to assume a number of life-like positions. Has sleeping eyes with long lashes. Dressed for play in perky lace trimmed cotton romper outfit and knit booties. Comes with her own bottle and nipple. Shipping weight 4 lbs.

79 N 3199C..............$9.98

[2]
$9⁹⁸
22-inch doll

Lots of fun to dress up all your baby and infant dolls, see below

Betsy Wetsy with layette as low as $4.57

Betsy Wetsy in shirt and diaper with pretty Layette all in a Gift Box. Same life-like vinyl baby as sold above, but with dress, bonnet, slip and accessories as shown. She drinks, wets, cries with coo voice as "tears" roll down her cheeks. Your choice of 2 popular sizes .. with lustrous rooted Saran hair or molded hair.

[3] Betsy Wetsy Baby Doll with Saran hair, layette, gift box.
49 N 3114—12-inch Betsy. Shipping weight 2 pounds 4 ounces.......... $5.33
49 N 3116—16-inch Betsy. Shipping weight 3 pounds..................... 7.88

[4] Betsy Wetsy Baby Doll with molded hair, layette, gift box.
49 N 3108—12-inch Betsy. Shipping weight 2 pounds.................... $4.57
49 N 3178—16-inch Betsy. Shipping weight 3 pounds.................... 6.99

Clothing for plump Baby Dolls .. Sizes 12 to 28 inches

[5] Baby Sleeper and Robe Set. Comfy cotton sleeper and pretty flannelette robe. Shpg. wt. 10 oz.

49 N 3403—Size 12 to 13 in.... $1.17
49 N 3405—Size 16 to 17 in.... 1.29
49 N 3406—Size 18 to 19 in.... 1.59
49 N 3407—Size 20 to 21 in.... 1.77
49 N 3423—Size 24 to 25 in.... 2.27
49 N 3438—Size 28 in.......... 2.57

[6] Coat and Bonnet Set. Rayon taffeta with dainty lace edging, for baby's "dress-up" wear. Nicely made with fine detail. Shpg. wt. 10 oz.

49 N 3411—Size 12 to 13 in....$1.47
49 N 3413—Size 16 to 17 in.... 1.57
49 N 3414—Size 18 to 19 in.... 1.77
49 N 3415—Size 20 to 21 in.... 1.87
49 N 3424—Size 24 to 25 in.... 2.37
49 N 3435—Size 28 in.......... 2.79

[7] Snowsuit and Bonnet. Cuddly outfit of cotton fleece with wool loop trim, knit cuffs. Shpg. wt. 10 oz.

49 N 3436—Size 12 to 13 in...... $1.69
49 N 3439—Size 16 to 17 in...... 1.77
49 N 3444—Size 18 to 19 in...... 1.89
49 N 3445—Size 20 to 21 in...... 1.98
49 N 3446—Size 24 to 25 in...... 2.57
49 N 3448—Size 28 in........... 2.98

[8] Baby Doll Layette. Lace-trimmed nylon dress and bonnet. Cotton slip; socks and shoes. Shpg. wt. 10 oz.

49 N 3418—Size 12 to 13 in.... $2.19
49 N 3425—Size 14 to 15 in.... 2.29
49 N 3426—Size 16 to 17 in.... 2.29
49 N 3427—Size 18 to 19 in.... 2.49
49 N 3428—Size 20 to 21 in.... 2.57
49 N 3429—Size 22 to 23 in.... 2.79
49 N 3433—Size 24 to 25 in.... 2.98
49 N 3434—Size 28 in.......... 3.57

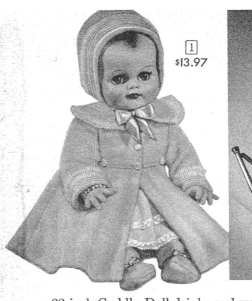

$13.97 ①

② $6.97

④ $5.87

⑤ $3.77

⑥ $2.87

③ $4.97

22-inch Cuddly Doll drinks and wets

① So like a real baby with her moving arms, legs and head . . "mamma" voice. Molded hair and go-to-sleep eyes . . soft, "easy-to-wipe-clean" vinyl body. Dressed for cold weather in rayon and acetate fleece coat, hood and leggings, all rayon taffeta lined. Underneath she wears cotton dress, shirt, diaper, I.D. bracelet. Has her own bottle . . young mothers will love caring for her.
79 N 3184C—Shipping weight 5 pounds...........$13.97

18-inch Baby Doll in her own rocker

② Huggable toddler wears adorable cotton jumper and knitted booties. 18-inch vinyl body, fully jointed to assume many positions . . big lashed go-to-sleep eyes . . molded hair. Rocker (15½ inches high, 20 inches long, 10 inches wide) has tubular plated steel frame, embossed vinyl fabric seat, plastic beads. Chair has glider-like action for rocking baby. Shpg. wt. 5 lbs.
79 N 3017C2—Doll and Rocker complete..........$6.97

17-in. Little Girl Doll is extra life-like

③ 17 inches tall and so perfect in detail even fingers and toes have distinct knuckles and nails. Jointed vinyl body has new "miracle" head that can be posed in practically any position. Rooted "Perma-curl" hair in tie-back style . . sleeping eyes. Wears print cotton dress, ruffled cotton bloomers, long cotton stockings, felt shoes.
49 N 3337—Shipping weight 1 lb. 10 oz............$4.97

Lovable Babies, attractively dressed

All three have easy-to-clean vinyl bodies, lashed sleeping eyes, turning heads. Comb and set their rooted Saran hair. Each wears lacy panties, socks and vinyl shoes.

④ 19-inch Baby. An older toddler, fully jointed, stands alone. Dressed in Sunday best . . a striped rayon taffeta dress, coat and matching bonnet.
49 N 3176—Shipping weight 2 lbs. 8 oz..............$5.87

⑤ 17-inch Baby. Drinks and wets . . has her own bottle. Pretty party dress is lace-trimmed polished cotton with matching bonnet brim. Jointed arms and legs.
49 N 3016—Shipping weight 1 lb. 12 oz.............$3.77

⑥ 15-inch Baby . . coos when gently squeezed. Cotton stuffed one-piece body. Cute cotton dress.
49 N 3014—Shipping weight 1 lb. 12 oz..............$2.87

These Dolls open and close their eyes

$1.94

$2.88

$2.98

$3.99

15-inch Cutie with soft "coo" voice. One-piece cotton-stuffed vinyl body, molded hair. In ninon dress, bonnet, half slip, knit panties, socks and shoes.
49 N 3112—Wt. 1 lb. 4 oz....$1.94

15-inch Toddler . . sure to win any child's heart. Jointed vinyl arms, legs, turning head . . stands or sits, assumes many poses. Molded hair. Stylish cotton dress, matching bonnet, knit panties, vinyl shoes and socks.
49 N 3015—Shpg. wt. 2 lbs...$2.88

17-inch Baby. Big, soft colored dolly. Cotton-stuffed one-piece vinyl skin body, turning head. Coos when squeezed. Rooted Saran hair topped with "bonnet-brim." Fluffy sheer ninon dress has attached slip. Panties, socks and shoes.
49 N 3507—Wt. 1 lb. 10 oz......$2.98

8-inch Drink-wet Baby. Adorable infant has all-vinyl jointed body. Comes with wardrobe of nylon dress and bonnet; flocked nylon dress with bonnet; cotton dress and bib; cotton sleeper; sunsuit; diaper bag; diaper; clothespins; blanket; 3 sponges; bottle; washcloth; shoes. Baby wears panties, eyes close.
49 N 3531—Shpg. wt. 1 lb. 8 oz........$3.99

15-in. Doll .. trunk full of clothes

An adorable vinyl toddler with jointed arms, legs, turning head . . . lashed go-to-sleep eyes and rooted acetate hair that's washable. Dressed in rayon taffeta dress, panties, socks and vinyl shoes . . and a complete wardrobe including coat, street dress, hat, pajamas, nightgown, housecoat. 3-piece vanity set, tissues, curlers, set of luggage, all packed in 16-in. fiberboard trunk with metal hinges, plastic handle.

49 N 3139—Doll, trunk, clothes. Wt. 4 lbs. 9 oz. **$6.88**

$6⁸⁸

Big-as-life Toddler

All dressed up for a party in dainty cotton organdy dress, with attached slip and panties. Her rooted Saran hair is swept into a ponytail, but you comb and set it any way you like. Appealing lashed eyes open and close. Hard-to-break vinyl body has jointed arms, legs, turning head. Wears socks and shoes.

79 N 3302C—31-in. doll. Wt. 6 lbs..... **$8.99**
79 N 3301 C—28-in. doll. Shpg. wt. 4 lbs.   **6.99**

$8⁹⁹
31-in.

17-inch Doll, Big Wardrobe, Trunk

Our best .. has trunk, will travel! Soft vinyl doll is dressed for visiting in lace trimmed polished cotton dress, undies, socks and shoes. Rooted Saran hair, jointed arms, legs, turning head with lashed, sleeping eyes. Her vacation wardrobe features cotton dress, robe, coat and bonnet, 2 pairs of shoes and socks and sun glasses. Sturdy, reinforced fiberboard trunk (18x9x9 inches) has big drawer, extra hangers, metal hinges and latches, plastic handle.

49 N 3338—Doll, wardrobe, trunk. Shpg. wt. 6 lbs... **$12.97**

$12⁹⁷

"Barbie," the famous model and her latest fashions

[1] An exciting new doll with fashion appeal for girls of all ages! So grown-up and life-like, she almost breathes. Flesh-toned vinyl plastic body has movable arms, legs and head making her easy to dress . . she poses on her plastic stand! Rooted Saran hair can be set and brushed to suit her outfit. Wears striped jersey swimsuit, sun glasses, earrings and shoes. From Japan.
49 N 3701—"Barbie" doll 11½ inches tall. Shpg. wt. 1 lb............. **$2.26**

Wardrobe for "Barbie" doll. From Japan. Shipping weight each 4 oz.
[A] 49 N 3702—Cotton sailcloth sundress, wedge-heeled white sandals........**77c**
[B] 49 N 3704—Glamorous party dress with velvet top, white rayon satin skirt and gold color belt. Matching gold color bag, stylish black shoes **$1.13**
[C] 49 N 3705—Zippered sheath dress of polished cotton, matching shoes.. **1.13**
[D] 49 N 3706—Dressy gold color brocade outfit. Accessories include imitation "pearl" jewelry, tricot gloves, velvet purse and shoes............... **1.57**
[E] 49 N 3707—Casual ensemble. Cardigan and slip-on sweater set, cotton flannel skirt, shoes. Also tiny knitting bowl, needles, yarn, scissors.... **2.27**

Collectors' Miniature Dolls

Exquisitely dressed Happi-time miniatures (just 7½ inches tall). Practically unbreakable plastic with jointed arms, heads, lustrous mohair wigs, open and shut lashed eyes. They all stand alone to model their gorgeous finery. Shipping weight each 14 oz.

[2] 49 N 3165—New Majorette. Rayon-satin costume, rick-rack trim, crinoline slip. Baton.... **$1.59**
[3] 49 N 3106—Nun dressed in black rayon taffeta. Crucifix, imported Italian rosary. No wig.... **1.69**
[4] 49 N 3101—Beautiful Bride. Rayon satin gown, flowing net veil and beribboned bouquet..... **1.69**
49 N 3102—Bridegroom (not shown). Wears traditional trousers, tails and high hat. Painted hair .. **1.59**

The 1961 Christmas Wishbook was dominated by toys bearing the Walt Disney trademark. Disney had always been an aggressive marketer of movie and TV-related merchandise and now there were toys connected to virtually every Disney film and character. A 10 1/2 inch tall Annette doll didn't much resemble the most popular Mouseketeer, but she came equipped with moving arms, legs and head and she had go-to-sleep eyes.

Mickey Mouse, Pinocchio and other Disney favorites existed as Marionettes, as hand puppets and as tiny, hand-painted "Disneykins." There was also a Mickey Mouse Music Box and a wind-up train called the Disney Express.

But the Wishbook featured plenty of non-Disney characters, too -- Shari Lewis's puppets Lamb Chop, Hush Puppy and Charlie Horse; and the Hanna-Barbera TV cartoon characters Huckleberry Hound, Yogi Bear, Jinx the Cat and Pixie the Mouse.

But for more Disney fun, the Wishbook introduced the Disneyland Playset, 95 pieces of fun that recreated the legendary theme park right there in a kid's home. Sure the rides weren't quite as thrilling, but the lines weren't nearly as long!

Sears Christmas

Wishbook

1961

$15⁷⁷

THE TOYS THAT WALT DISNEY BRINGS TO

[1] "The Princess" Doll .. famous Babes in Toyland ballerina in a regal pink rayon satin gown, royal blue cape. Silver-color crown. All plastic body, movable arms and legs .. stands by herself. Turning head, go-to-sleep eyes. Rooted acetate hair.
79 N 3606C—32-inch doll. Shpg. wt. 5 lbs...$15.77

[2] Gun Boat. Cannon "shoots" in any direction. Admiral's head bobs humorously up and down from smokestack as boat rolls along. Bright wood.
49 N 5322—7¾x7x5½ in. Shpg. wt. 1 lb. 2 oz..$1.79

[3] Jumping Jack. Crazy clown wildly waves his arms and head as toy rolls on two irregular wheels. Smooth wood, brightly finished.
49 N 5305—8x6x7½ in. Shpg. wt. 1 lb.......$1.99

[4] Hobby Horse. Spring neck lets head shake as wood horsie rides on 4 irregular wheels. Felt blanket, saddle and stirrups. Yarn mane and tail.
49 N 5321—7x6¼x4½ in. high. Shpg. wt. 14 oz.$1.69

[5] Soldier with Cannon. Moves arm to shoot captive out of cannon. Bright wood.
49 N 5307—10x9x4½ in. high. Wt. 1 lb. 8 oz..$2.69

[6] Soldier on horseback proudly displays American flags. Horse and rider go up and down as toy is pulled. Bright-finished wood.
49 N 5306—9x8x3¾ inches. Shpg. wt. 1 lb. ...$2.34

[7] Soldier and Guardhouse. Wooden soldier moves arms up and down to keep the "enemy" away. Stays "at ease" in hardboard guardhouse.
49 N 4521—Soldier, 9 in. high. Wt. 1 lb. 8 oz..$2.39

[8] Three Soldiers. Can twist into comic poses. Vinyl heads. Cotton uniforms, wire frames.
49 N 3716—About 12 in. tall. Wt. 1 lb.....Set $2.88

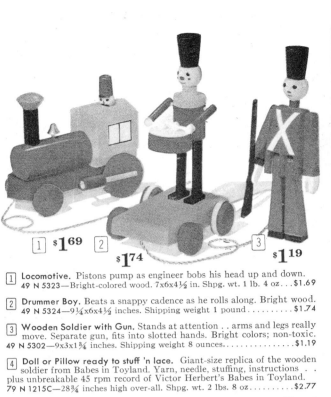

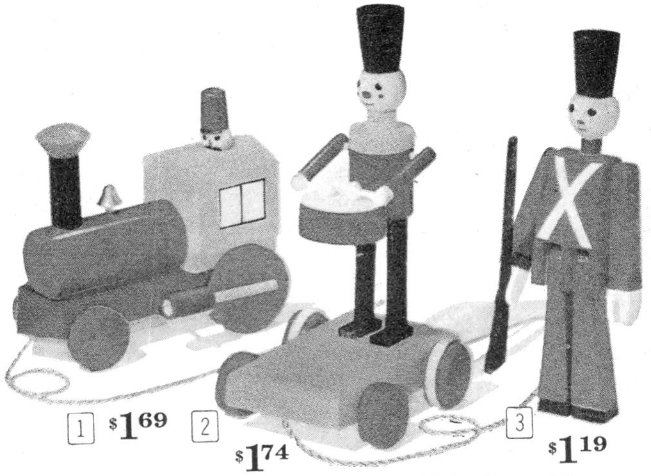
1 $1.69
2 $1.74
3 $1.19

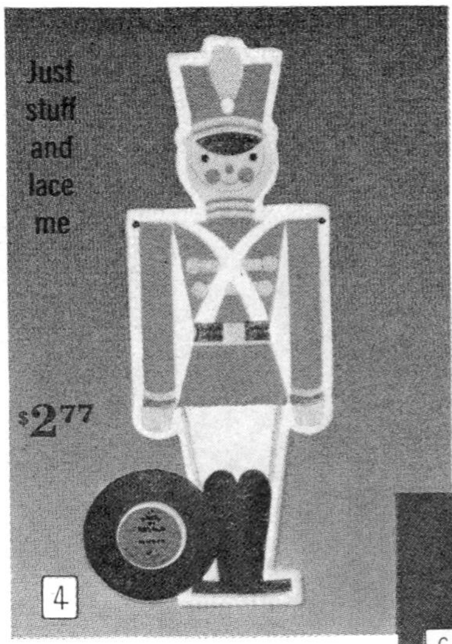
Just stuff and lace me
$2.77
4

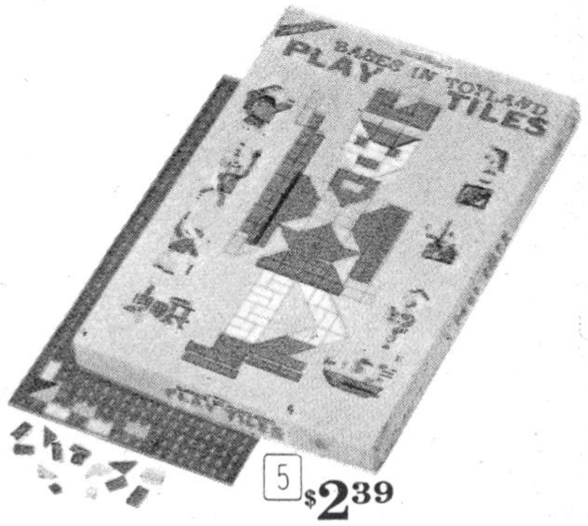
BABES IN TOYLAND PLAY TILES
5 $2.39

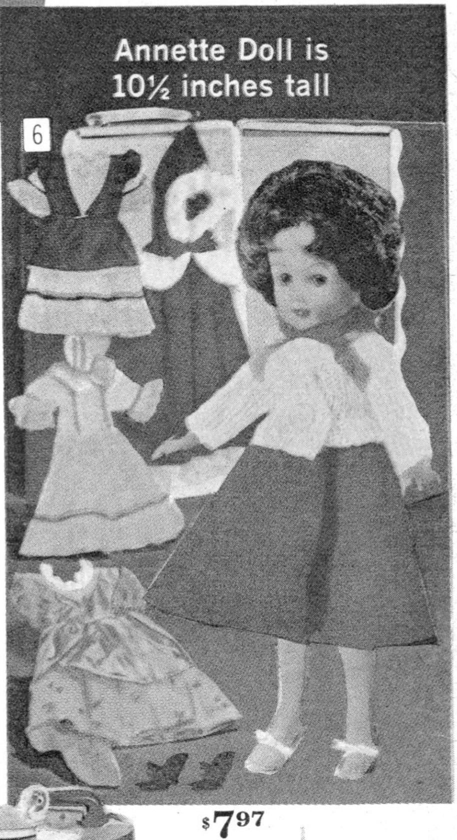
Annette Doll is 10½ inches tall
6
$7.97

1 **Locomotive.** Pistons pump as engineer bobs his head up and down.
49 N 5323—Bright-colored wood. 7x6x4½ in. Shpg. wt. 1 lb. 4 oz. . . $1.69

2 **Drummer Boy.** Beats a snappy cadence as he rolls along. Bright wood.
49 N 5324—9¼x6x4½ inches. Shipping weight 1 pound $1.74

3 **Wooden Soldier with Gun.** Stands at attention . . arms and legs really move. Separate gun, fits into slotted hands. Bright colors; non-toxic.
49 N 5302—9x3x1¾ inches. Shipping weight 8 ounces $1.19

4 **Doll or Pillow ready to stuff 'n lace.** Giant-size replica of the wooden soldier from Babes in Toyland. Yarn, needle, stuffing, instructions . . plus unbreakable 45 rpm record of Victor Herbert's Babes in Toyland.
79 N 1215C—28¾ inches high over-all. Shpg. wt. 2 lbs. 8 oz $2.77

5 **Pegboard Playtiles.** Capture the toy soldiers, admiral, battleship and many more Toyland favorites with these 336 colorful plastic tiles.
49 N 4517—18x9-in. Masonite Presdwood board. Shpg. wt. 2 lbs. 4 oz. . $2.39

6 **Annette and her wardrobe.** Charming 10½-in. vinyl doll with moving arms, legs, head and go-to-sleep eyes. Rooted acetate hair. She wears a felt skirt and turtleneck sweater; lace-trimmed panties; hi-heel shoes. Her wardrobe includes 3 party dresses with taffeta petticoats; full-length rayon cape and hood; nylon stockings and extra hi-heel shoes.
49 N 3412—All packed in sturdy fiberboard trunk. Shpg.wt. 1 lb. 12 oz. $7.97

7 **"Punch-me" Soldier.** Knock 'im down. Nose squawks . . comes back for more. Inflatable vinyl with weighted base. 31 inches high.
49 N 2569—Shipping weight 2 pounds $1.94

8 **Electric Portable Phonograph.** Comes complete with six 78 rpm records of Babes in Toyland and fairy tale music. Plays all 78 rpm records up to 12 inches. Sturdy fiber case . . colorful drum motif. 14x14x16 in.
79 N 663L—110-120-volt, 60-cycle AC. UL approved. Shpg. wt. 11 lbs. $13.99
79 N 652L—Phonograph only. Shipping weight 9 pounds 12.99

9 **Indian Skater.** Wind him up—he skates about with his bow and arrow.
49 N 5766—Bright lithographed steel. 6¼ in. high. Shpg. wt. 7 oz. . . . 89c

10 **Mechanical Soldier.** Really marches along floor beating his drum. Sturdy metal with clock spring motor, attached key. With brake.
49 N 5767—5¾ inches high. Shipping weight 6 oz 89c

11 **Wood Inlaid Puzzles.** Babes in Toyland soldiers with drum; gun boat.
49 N 4520—Each 7½x3½ inches. Shpg wt. 1 lb. 5 oz . . . . Set $1.97

12 **Magic Gun** shoots a roll of plastic coated paper 5 feet . . reloads automatically. Durable plastic.
49 N 2691—10 inches long. Shipping weight 6 oz. 89c

13 **Ball and Jumping Jack.** Hangs on crib or playpen. Arms and legs jump up when string is pulled. Bright wood. 7½-in. diam. vinyl ball.
49 N 4535—2-piece Set. Shipping weight 1 pound $1.89

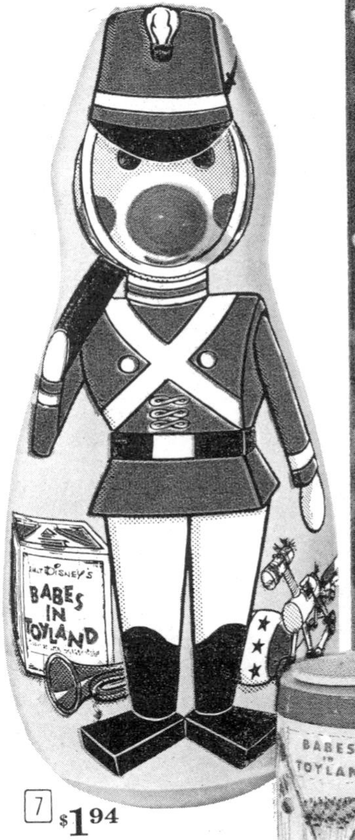
BABES IN TOYLAND
7 $1.94

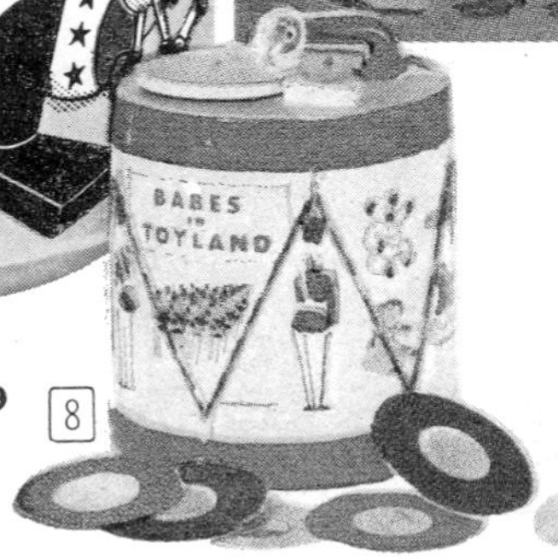
BABES IN TOYLAND
$13.99 8

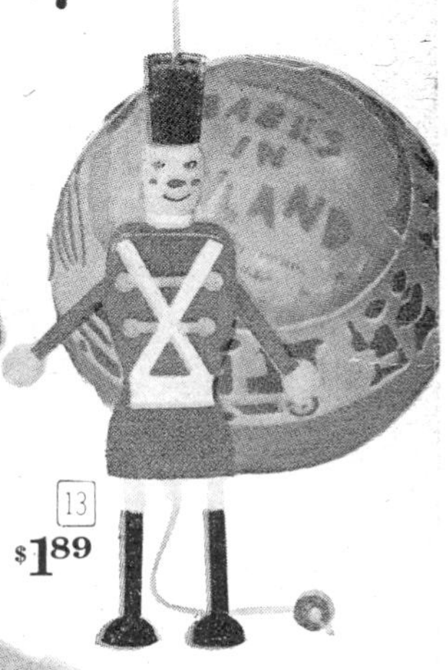
BABES IN TOYLAND
13 $1.89

LIFE IN BABES IN TOYLAND

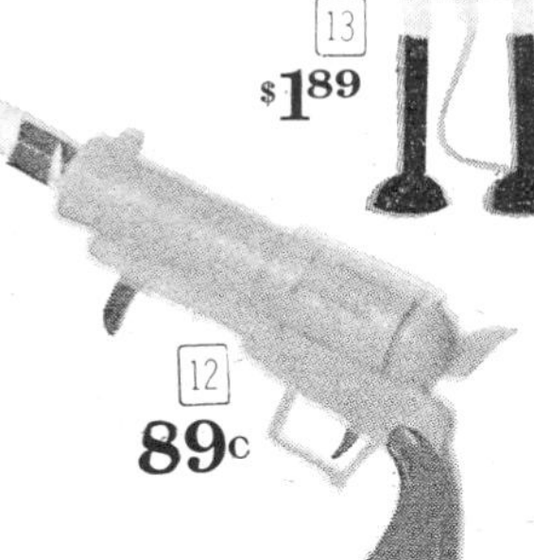
12 89c

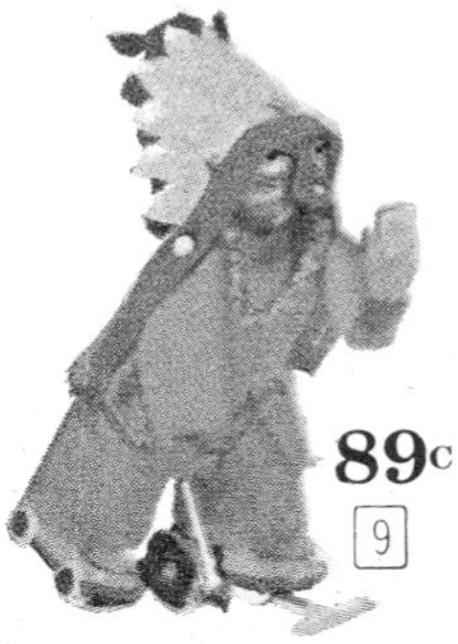
89c 9

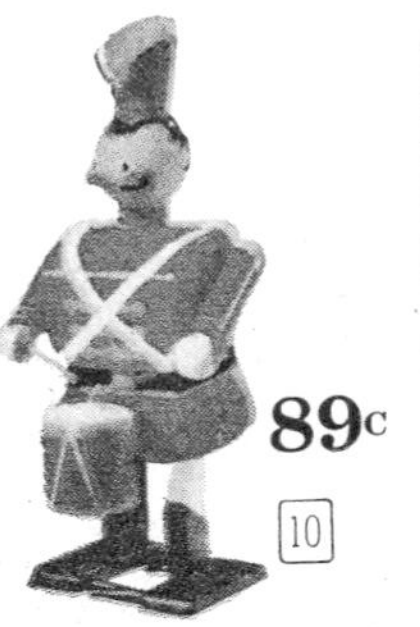
89c 10

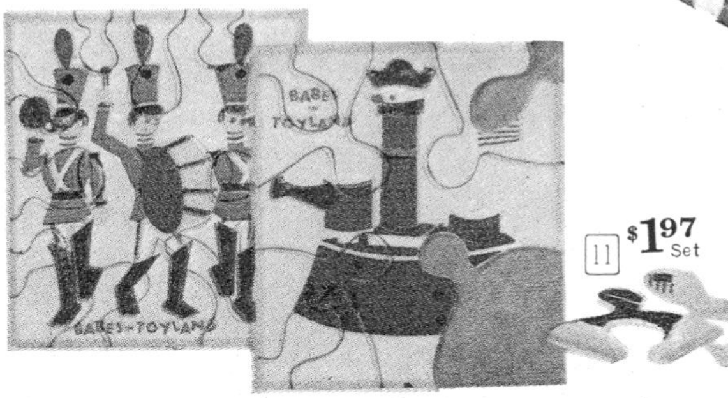
BABES IN TOYLAND
11 $1.97 Set

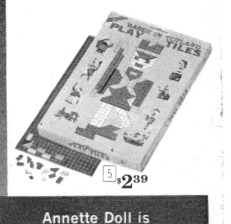

From the wonderful world of

WALT DISNEY

© 1961 Walt Disney Productions

[1] $1⁹⁷

[2] $2⁸⁹

Mickey Mouse Music Box

[1] Just turn the crank—plays gay tune, then up pops Mickey Mouse complete with bow tie and a mischievous grin. Metal box 5½ inches high and decorated with Disney characters.
49 N 4570—Shpg. wt. 1 lb. 2 oz. $1.97

Disney Scenic Express Wind-up Train

[2] Zips around its magic kingdom about 20 times on one winding! 22x13-inch metal base has attached grooved track, is decorated with Disney characters. 3-unit train has plastic engine with attached key, metal tender and car. 2 tunnels.
79 N 9510C—Shpg. wt. 3 lbs. . $2.89

Disneykins

[3] **Set of 34 Disneykins®.** The teeniest, weeniest, most lovable playthings in the whole wide world . . delightful as ornaments for a what-not shelf, too. Each is a character made famous by Disney, each is skillfully modeled in plastic and hand painted.
49 N 5998—Made in Hong Kong. Shipping weight 1 lb. $3.39

[4] **Three Disneykin Play Sets.** Each set's in its own miniature cardboard stage. First set stars Snow White and the 7 dwarfs; the second, Mickey and Minnie Mouse and 3 friends; the third, Pecos Bill and 4 others. Each set has 5 to 8 Disneykins.
49 N 5988—Made in Hong Kong. Shipping weight 10 oz. $2.57

Jack-in-the-Blocks $2⁴⁹

6 giant fiberboard nesting blocks topped by a plastic Donald Duck jumping from top box. 5 to 7-in. sizes. 35 in. high over-all.
49 N 4513—Assembled. Shpg. wt. 2 lbs. 8 oz. $2.49

Babes in Toyland GUNDIKINS

Each $1⁹⁹

Famous Toyland characters in colorful rayon plus. Cotton filled. Heads are soft vinyl. About 10 inches. Wt. each 8 oz.
49 N 4978—Clown
49 N 4979—Soldier
Each. $1.99

[5] $2²⁹

$9⁹⁹

[6] 89c

Walt Disney Xylophone

[5] Produces beautiful tones on the felt-cushioned, tempered-steel bars. Disney characters add to the fun. 13 in. long. 2 mallets, music book included.
49 N 606—Wt. 2 lbs. 8 oz. . $2.29

Disney Puzzles amuse and educate

[6] Four puzzles starring Donald Duck, Dumbo, Bambi, 3 Little Pigs. 13x10 inches.
49 N 4689—Wt. 1 lb. 8 oz. . . . 89c

Donald and Mickey

Both $1⁵⁷

Donald Duck's a handy soap boat and Mickey Mouse is a cute little squeaking squeeze toy. Soft, long lasting vinyl in non-toxic colors.
49 N 4463—Shipping wt. 9 oz. . $1.57

Donald Duck Electric Portable

Plays all 78 rpm records up to 12 inches. Includes ten 6-inch records and 24-record plastic rack. Blue and white pyroxylin covered fiber case wipes clean. Tone chamber is amplified. Sound head locks into playing and rest positions.
Replay attachment repeats 6 and 7-inch records automatically. Loud and soft needles included. 11 inches square, 6 inches high.
49 N 696—Shpg. wt. 7 lbs. . . . $9.99
49 N 676—Without rack, records, or repeater. Shpg. wt. 6 lbs. . . $7.99

BE A PUPPETEER

Pelham Marionettes

$4⁹⁹ each Any 2 for $9⁶⁶

Could be the start of a fun-filled profitable hobby. Designed by puppet master Bob Pelham of England. Complete with necessary controls for lifelike, tangleproof animation. Round wooden heads, bodies, metal joints. 12 inches tall. Instructions included. Shpg. wt., each, 1 lb.

1	49 N 5157—Clown	
2	49 N 5110—Fritzi	Each $4.99
3	49 N 5111—Mitzi	Any 2 or more
4	49 N 5152—Cowboy	each $4.83
5	49 N 5153—Cowgirl	

Starring Walt Disney's beloved characters

$6⁶⁶ each Any 2 for $12⁸⁸

Better quality Pelham marionettes. Each is an authentic reproduction of a well-known Disney or storybook character. Molded wood composition heads, more elaborate costumes than at left. Tangleproof animation. Each about 12 in. high. Age 8 and over.

6	49 N 5055—Minnie Mouse. Shipping weight 1 lb. 2 oz.
7	49 N 5054—Mickey Mouse. Shipping weight 1 lb. 4 oz.
8	49 N 5048—Gretel. Shipping weight 1 pound.
9	49 N 5050—Jiminy Cricket. Shipping weight 1 lb. 3 oz.
10	49 N 5056—Donald Duck. Shipping weight 1 lb. 8 oz.
11	49 N 5047—Hansel. Shipping weight 1 pound.
12	49 N 5049—Pinocchio. Shipping weight 1 pound.

Each $6.66 . . . . any 2 or more, Each $6.44

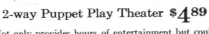

2-way Puppet Play Theater $4⁸⁹

Not only provides hours of entertainment but could also start a profitable hobby. Big 5-foot fiberboard theater converts from a marionette stage to a hand-puppet playhouse by shifting plastic curtain. Plenty of standing room for puppeteers. Folds flat.

79 N 4989C—Wt. 9 lbs. Puppets not incl. $4.89

13 **Shari Lewis Puppet Set.** Youngsters will enjoy imitating Shari talking to Lamb Chop, Hush Puppy and Charlie Horse. Heads have painted, washable vinyl faces, bodies are cotton.

49 N 5026—Shipping weight 1 pound. . . . . Set $2.77

Walt Disney Hand Puppet Sets. All have squeaker voices, soft vinyl heads, cotton clothes. Box can be converted to stage. Shipping weight, set, 1 lb. 12 oz.

14 49 N 5031—Mickey and Minnie Mouse, Donald Duck, Pluto. . . . . . . Set $3.57

15 49 N 4997—Babes in Toyland characters including the Cadet, Clown, Gonzorgo, Toy Maker. . . . . Set $3.66

"Billy Goon" Sock Puppets (left). Designed by famed puppeteer, Bill Baird. Includes Goony Bird and Alligator. Soft vinyl heads and cotton knit bodies.

49 N 5038—Shpg. wt. 1 lb. . . . . . Set $1.87

Huck Hound Hand Puppet Set. What a show they'll put on making believe they're Yogi Bear, Huckleberry Hound, Jinxie the Cat and Pixie the Mouse. Washable vinyl plastic molded heads. Bodies are brightly colored rayon plush with cotton felt trimming. Shipping weight, set, 2 lbs. 8 ounces. Set of four.

49 N 4984. . . . . . $6.49

Our Best 7-room House has a sunporch

70 pieces **$9⁹⁷**

Colonial-style mansion is extra roomy—over 3½ feet long. Plenty of space to occupy even the busiest little girl. Even has real draperies that can be removed, awnings for the second floor, towels for the bathroom, patio furniture for the sunporch, plus a family of 4 plastic figures. Big, corner jalousie windows light up the family recreation room. Each room completely furnished with high-impact plastic pieces . . all authentic-looking, scaled in proportion. Interior rooms include: family room, living-dining rooms, kitchen, utility room, bedroom, bathroom and nursery. Each room colorfully decorated from ceiling to floor. Exterior is "landscaped" . . portico has simulated wrought-iron decor. House is steel, 44x15x18 inches high. Easy to assemble, instructions included.

79 N 1412L—Shipping weight 10 pounds........**$9.97**

5-room House with pool that really holds water

35 pieces **$5⁹⁷**

Colonial-style residence is over 2 feet long . . almost 3 feet long with pool. Equipped to let your little homemaker enjoy suburban living. Hollywood-style pool has diving board, pool accessories . . holds 2 plastic children. Barbecue grille and umbrella table handle pool-side snacks. *There's even a sports car to park in the carport.* Each room completely furnished with high-impact plastic pieces . . all authentic-looking, scaled in proportion. Interior rooms include: kitchen, living-dining rooms, nursery, bathroom and bedroom. Colorfully decorated from ceiling to floor. Exterior is "landscaped" . . simulated wrought-iron pillars support front porch and carport, has posts with chain-link railing. House is steel, 26x15x16 inches high. Easy to assemble. For a family of 5 plastic figures to live in house, order 49 N 1413 on facing page.

79 N 1411C—Shipping weight 9 pounds..............................**$5.97**

Travel Chums for the young Miss

334 SEARS 2PCB

1   2   3   4   5

5-room ranch style House with patio

$3⁹⁷

One-story home is 2¾ feet long with patio . . over 35 pieces. All the joys of home-ownership! Your little miss can rearrange furniture to suit her whim. Completely furnished in modern style. Scaled-to-size, high-impact plastic furniture. Interior includes: master bedroom, bathroom, living-dining rooms, nursery and kitchen.

Patio features simulated flagstone floor, has chairs and play pen for relaxing in the sun. Exterior is "landscaped." House and base are steel, 33x9x10 inches high. Easy to assemble. Order the family of 5 plastic figures below to move right in.
79 N 1401C—Shipping weight 6 pounds....$3.97

Family of 5 figures 88c

All set to make themselves at home in any doll house listed on facing page or above. Mother, father, daughter, son and baby can sit, stand, "walk," crawl, etc. Jointed arms, bodies, legs. Durable polyethylene plastic . . practically unbreakable.
49 N 1413—Father is 6 in. tall. Shpg. wt. 4 oz.....88c

$3⁹⁷

Convert your card table into playhouse

Gaily printed, cotton cloth playhouse slips over any standard, 30-inch square, card table . . makes it a private hideaway. Fun for children from 2 to 9 years old. Use indoors or out. Side flap lifts for easy entrance and ventilation. Push wooden dowel into block, place in center of table to form peak in roof. Shipping weight 1 pound 8 ounces.
49 N 1414—Kiddy Kottage for girls.....................$3.97
49 N 1415—Fire House for boys....................... 3.97

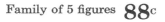

The Corner Store
Only $3⁸⁸

Shop, add up purchases, make change. Shelves hold tiny boxes of famous brand groceries. Cash register has sliding drawer with play money . . is mounted on movable check-out counter. Handy plastic phone hangs on store wall. Blue and gray fiberboard store folds flat for storage. About 32x17x64 in. high. Simple assembly.
79 N 1112C—Shpg. wt. 10 lbs....$3.88

Doll House Mansion
Only $4⁸⁸

Just open the twin doors . . little Miss Homemaker can stand up and play with this 4½-ft. tall house. 3 rooms equipped with fiberboard furniture. Living and bed rooms have 5-piece suites and simulated rugs. Kitchen has 3-piece set and complete appliances. Beautifully decorated corrugated fiberboard. Use as chest or book case. 27x13x53 in. high. Simple assembly.
79 N 1416C—Shpg. wt. 10 lbs....$4.88

Little girls love Luggage (ILLUSTRATED ON FACING PAGE)

1 **2-piece Weekender Set.** 14x10x5-in. Overnight Case *plus* 10x6x5-in. Train Case. Linen-grained vinyl plastic covering. Aluminum edges, wood frames. Plastic stitched bindings. Nickel-plated locks with keys. Plastic handles. Train Case has mirror. *State color* white or blue.
49 N 9219E—2-piece Set. Shpg. wt. 6 lbs.....$9.98
49 N 9221E—Overnight Case only. Wt. 4 lbs.. 5.98
49 N 9223E—Train Case only. Shpg. wt. 2 lbs... 4.79

2 **5-piece Bobbi-Sox Set.** White vinyl plastic with nifty, teen-ager scenes on each. 9-inch diam. Train-and-Plane Bag opens on 2 sides, plastic handle. 4-inch diam. Purse opens on 1 side, loop handle. 6½x4¼-in. Autograph Book has assorted color pages. 6x5½-in. Diary has ruled pages, padlock, 2 keys. 4½x4½x4½-in. Money Bank holds 4 separate funds, padlock, 2 keys.
49 N 9268E—5-piece Set. Shpg. wt. 3 lbs.....$4.99

3 **2-piece Travel Set.** 12x12x5-inch Suitcase plus 10x7½x5½-inch Train Case. Two-layered patent plastic resists scuffs. Lilac with pink-and-white butterflies. Zip open. Plastic linings have floral print. Plastic handles, ID holders.
49 N 9270E—Shpg. wt. 3 lbs..$4.79

4 49 N 9272E—Hat Box. As above. 11x12x4½-in.Wt.1lb.12 oz.$2.79

5 **Umbrella, Suitcase Set.** 12-in. vinyl plastic case with embossed tweed-look . . zipper, plastic handle. Rayon plaid umbrella, 30-in. diam. . . fits in holster on case.
79 N 9279CE—Shpg. wt. 2 lbs. $2.79

NOTE: Catalog numbers ending in "E" include 10% Federal Excise Tax in price

Miss Homemaker shops by phone $2⁹⁷ Set

Call the Corner Store (above) if that's where you shop. Just pick up replica of newest-style phone. Use the pencil to fill out shopping list on pad. Wire basket with plastic handles holds 4 Coca-Cola bottles in carrier and 30 name-brand packages.
49 N 987—Basket is 15x10½x5 in. high. Shpg. wt. 2 lbs. 4 oz...$2.97

Ivy Plastic Tea Set $3.97

Richly beautiful with 3-dimensional effect of white ivy on rich green. Clear plastic sugar plum tree plus ½ lb. candy gum drops. Metal plates, saucers. Service for 4 . . plates, cups, saucers, knives, forks, spoons, place mats. Also covered teapot, sugar bowl, creamer, 8x6-inch tray, salt and pepper shakers, napkin holder and 4 napkins.
49 N 988—43-piece Set. Shipping wt. 2 lbs. . . $3.97

Just like mommy's Russel Wright Set $4.44

Dinner Set for six created by a famous designer especially for little hostesses. Wonderfully tough plastic in mottled pottery colors that stay bright. Set includes 6 each turned-edge plates (6¼-in. diam.), cups, saucers, metallized cutlery, clear plastic goblets, napkins. Also sugar bowl with cover, creamer, teapot with cover, gravy boat with stand, large platter and casserole with cover.
49 N 944—58-piece Set. Shipping weight 2 lbs. 14 oz. $4.44

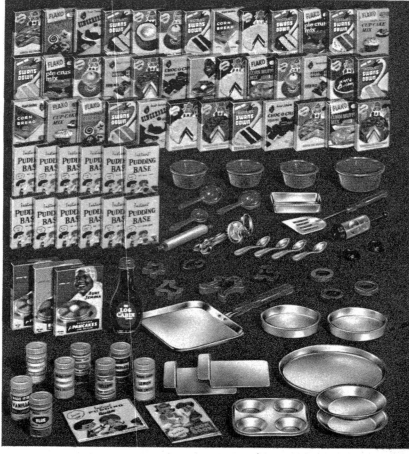

Tea Set, Play Food
$3.99

Authentic copies of colonial hobnail milk glass in detailed, white plastic. Tea set includes service for 4 . . 6-in. plates; cups; saucers; dessert dishes; tumblers; metallized forks, knives, spoons; pitcher, sugar bowl, creamer, bread basket, bud vase with bouquet.
Plastic play food includes turkey, corn, asparagus, jello, baked potatoes, slices of bread, 6 pie wedges. Paper napkins.
49 N 989—69-piece Set.
Shpg. wt. 1 lb. 12 oz. $3.99

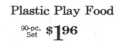

Plastic Play Food

90-pc.
Set $1.96

Roast beef, turkey or lobster entrees . . a loaf of bread and a cake for dessert. Also six individual servings of steak, 5 different vegetables, 2 different desserts, bacon 'n eggs, franks 'n beans. 6 gelatin molds, 12 dinner rolls. Plastic place mats, candle. Serves 6.
49N966—90-pc. Set. Wt. 6oz. $1.96
49N967—60-pc. Set. As above, but serves 4. Wt. 5 oz. $1.46

"Barbie's" own Tea Set $2.99

With Barbie doll's full length picture in a different costume on each plate—and her portrait on each saucer. Set includes service for 4 . . plastic plates, cups, saucers, soup-plates, goblets, knives, forks, spoons and paper napkins. Also modern 5⅛-inch teapot, sugar bowl, creamer, soup tureen with cover and ladle. Purple and white.
49 N 991—42-piece Set. Shpg. wt. 1 lb. 12 oz. . . $2.99

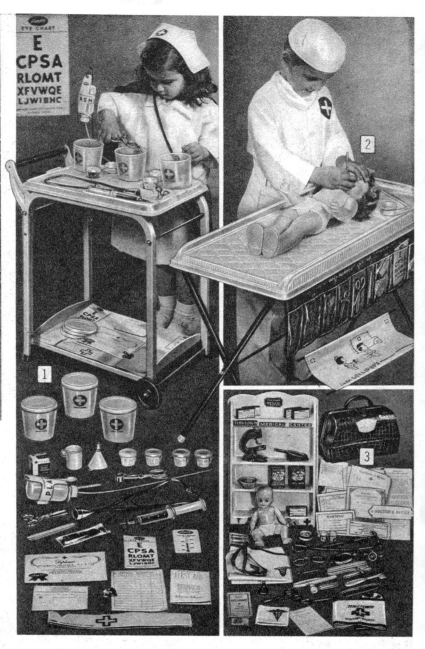

85-piece Nurse Kit
$3³⁴

Even if your professional nursing career is a few years off, you can get plenty of practice with this set. You'll wear an apron, cape and arm band .. carry a beautiful red plastic bag to hold your equipment: stethoscope, hypodermic, earoscope, microscope with slides, thermometer, medical forms, Diploma, and more. Shipping weight 1 pound 10 ounces.
49 N 1875. . . . . $3.34

85-piece Doctor Kit
$3³⁴

If you're a young man who's looking forward to being a doctor, you'll like this big kit. You'll get a complete set of professional-looking equipment to put in your sturdy black plastic bag.

Scale with weights, intercom, reflex hammer, microbe meter and slides, microscope, earoscope, stethoscope, candy pills, and lots more. Shpg. wt. 1 lb. 10 oz.
49 N 1874. . . . . $3.34

64-piece Jr. Nurse Kit
$2³⁴

Big enough to take care of office patients or emergency cases. The red plastic bag holds such equipment as a stethoscope, hypodermic needle, eye chart, microbe meter, vue-scope, films, and other plastic medical replicas. Also includes plastic wrist watch.
49 N 1860—Wt. 1 lb. 4 oz. $2.34

60-piece Jr. Doctor Set
$2³⁴

Young doctors will find this set especially handy for "house calls." Black plastic bag holds up under travel, holds thermometer, tongue depressors, adhesive strips, candy pills, microscope and slides, much more. For the office, there's a Diploma, shingle, medical forms.
49 N 1859—Wt. 1 lb. 4 oz. $2.34

Bring Dolly to your own clinic

[1] Like a real hospital, complete with easy-rolling cart (all steel) for patients' comfort. More than 30 pieces of equipment: stethoscope, forceps, plasma bottle, first aid supplies, life-size "Hypo-Phony" and still more. Shipping wt. 10 lbs.
79 N 1640L . . . $7.99

[2] Meet all doll emergencies with this fully-equipped checkup table .. steel frame, molded plastic top with blood-pressure gauge. Wrist watch, forceps, soap, hypo, scissors, band-aids, stethoscope, stretcher, much more. Doll not included. Shpg. wt. 6 lbs.
79 N 1641C . . $6.29

[3] Enough medical equipment to open a junior-scale clinic .. just look at all you get!

Doctor's bag and uniform, nurse's apron, wall-type plastic medicine chest, reflector, hypo, microscope and slides, earoscope, reflex hammer, thermometer, watch, tongue depressors, first aid supplies, medical forms, Diploma, eye chart, office sign, telephone, hot water bottle, nose shield, and more—even a doll "patient."
49 N 1639—Wt. 3 lbs. $4.39

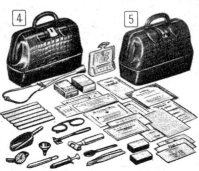

Low-priced Medic Kits
$1⁴⁴ each

Plastic bag holds stethoscope, hypo, earoscope, thermometer, watch, signs, Diploma, much more.

[4] 49 N 1889—42-piece Nurse Kit with red bag. Shipping weight 1 pound. $1.44

[5] 49 N 1888—42-piece Doctor Kit with black bag. Shipping weight 1 pound. $1.44

MATTEL TOYS

TOMMY BURST DETECTIVE SET
$4.66

Set includes 25-in. Tommy Burst Automatic cap firing gun; 7-in. Shootin' Shell snub-nose 38 pistol and holster set; 6 Shootin' Shell cartridges; 12 plastic bullet noses; wallet, badge, and I.D. Caps not incl.
79 N 2640C—Complete set. Shpg. wt. 3 lbs.... $4.66
79 N 2821C—Tommy Gun only. Wt. 2 lbs..... 2.66
49 N 2677—Snub-nose Pistol and Holster Set. Like above set but without Tommy Gun. Wt. 1 lb. 8 oz..... $2.99

You'll see these on TV ..priced low at Sears

CHATTY CATHY
$12.44

She really talks! Just pull the magic ring and she says 11 different phrases. Brush her rooted "hair", pose her movable head, arms and legs. Sturdy plastic, 20 inches tall. Wears a cotton dress (assorted styles), panties, knit socks and shoes.
49 N 3303—Shpg. wt. 3 lbs. 4 oz....... $12.44

CASPER THE GHOST
$6.66

POPZA-BALL
[2] $4.63

[3] $3.88
WINCHESTER SADDLE GUN

LIE DETECTOR GAME $3.88

BARBIE GAME $2.77

[1] He talks. He's the star of "Matty's Funday Funnies" TV show and says 11 different things like "I'm a friendly ghost" and "I like you-oo-oo" when you pull the ring on his neck. 15 in. high. Soft cotton stuffed terrycloth body, cute painted plastic face.
49 N 3559—Wt. 2 lbs. 3 oz. $6.66

[2] The fun's built right in. Just roll the ball in and it automatically pops right back to you. 50 throws per windup. Durable clock spring mechanism, 10-in. high plastic. With booklet on how to play many Popzaball games; 4 plastic balls and target.
49 N 121—Wt. 3 lbs...... $4.63

[3] Has secret rapid fire trigger and realistic lever action. Smokes, fires caps and ejects 8 metal play shells. Can also be fired single shot. Has front and rear sights, grained plastic stock and fore piece and blued steel barrel. 33 inches long. Caps not included.
79 N 2649C—Wt. 2 lbs.... $3.88

[4] Scientific crime detection game for 2 to 4 players. Includes mechanical lie detector; 24 suspect cards; secret testimony cards; subpeonas, warrants and guilty cards. Score is kept with pegged scoring board and colored pegs.
49 N 193—Wt. 2 lbs. 3 oz. $3.88

[5] Exciting new game is centered around teenage girl activities. Object of game is to be elected "Queen of the Prom". . and what young girl doesn't want that? For 2 to 4 players. Dice, cards, Barbie board and play money included.
49 N 454—Wt. 2 lbs..... $2.77

KENNER'S PRESTO-SPARKLE PAINT SETS
$2.24

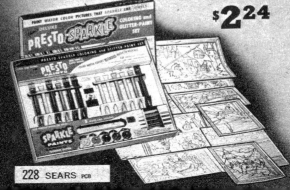

Paint water color pictures that sparkle like jewels. First paint picture with Presto paints (no water or brush needed) then add Sparkle paint. Includes 12 Presto paints, 5 Sparkle paints, 10 pictures and 6 greeting cards.
49N1667-Wt. 1 lb. 6 oz. $2.24

Popeye Presto Paint Set. Contains 12 Presto paints with 2 Popeye comic strips, 6 Popeye action characters.
49 N 1666-Wt. 14 oz...$1.49

Sparkle Paint Set. 10 colors, 10 brushes, 10 views.
49 N 1665-Wt. 15 oz...$1.49

$2.84

ELDON'S JUMPING JACK

Wind it up and start jumping . . just like you do with a rope. Spring-wound motor keeps it turning for four minutes while one to four kids jump at one time. Adjusts for speed and height, from 5½ to 11 inches. Made of rugged polyethylene. 10 different game ideas included. Easy to assemble.
49 N 2423—Shipping weight 1 lb. 7 oz.............. $2.84

TOYS BY IDEAL

KISSY DOLL $12⁴⁴

You'll see these on TV .. priced low at Sears

Patti Play Pal, 3 feet tall, the size of most 3 year olds. Walks when guided by her arms. Has rooted, washable, Saran hair. Plastic body, vinyl head; assorted style outfit, slip, panties, socks, shoes.
79 N 3366L—Shpg. wt. 9 lbs..........$18.88

Kissy Doll. Loves loving, will pucker up and make kissing sound when hands are pressed together. 22 in. high, has rooted, Saran hair, plastic body, vinyl head. Wears one-piece cotton playsuit, shoes.
79 N 3291C—Shpg. wt. 3 lbs.........$12.44

PATTI PLAY PAL $18⁸⁸

ROY ROGERS QUICK-SHOOTER HAT $3⁹⁹

As the villain approaches, you just remove hat, hold it in your hands . . then press release bar and zingo—gun pops out of its hidden pocket and fires caps. Black wool felt. Caps not included. *State size* small (17-18 inch); medium (19-20); large (21-22).
49 N 2672—Shpg. wt. 2 lbs......$3.99

SKIN-DIVER GAME $2⁸⁸

TRICK SHOT GUN $1⁹⁹

ROBOT COMMANDO $14⁹⁹ without batteries

The first player to have his diver "submerge," get the treasure and surface, is the winner. Each player strikes lever on Big Bopper which registers number of moves to make. Includes 4 plastic skin divers, gameboard, bopper.
49 N 187—Wt. 2 lbs...$2.88

This gun shoots over your shoulder! Unbreakable metal mirror is inserted in slot above grip, target is sighted and rubber-tipped dart is fired. Gun has another trigger for forward shooting. 27 in. long. Plastic. 4 darts, target.
79N2671C—Wt. 2 lbs. $1.99

Obeys spoken commands . . goes forward, turns right or left, fires rockets or throws missiles. 19 in. high. Plastic. 4 rubber tires. Play missiles, rockets included. Uses 3 "D" batteries; order below.
79 N 5802LM—Shipping weight 8 lbs...........$14.99
79 N 4662M—"D" Batteries. Wt. two, 8 oz....2 for 39c

HASBRO'S MAGIC CUTTER $2⁹⁴ without batteries

Art Linkletter toy. Jig saw cuts preformed styrofoam models electrically. Kit includes ready-to-cut model of locomotive, plastic paint and cement. Order 2 "D" batteries (49N4662M) on page 230.
49 N 1509M—Shipping weight 3 pounds......$2.94

Extra Models. Shpg. wt. each, 1 lb. 4 oz.
49 N 1527—Airplane and fire truck...$1.49
49 N 1528—Stagecoach, antique car.. 1.49

MR. MACHINE $7⁹⁹

MR. MACHINE GAME $3⁷⁷

Take-apart robot walks, swings arms, rings bell, opens and closes mouth, sounds siren. 18 in. high. Wind-up. Wt. 5 lbs.
49 N 5873........$7.99

Object of game is get Mr. Machine to factory. Gears in arm and head of indicator show moves. Movers, cards incl. Wt. 2 lbs. 3 oz.
49 N 188.........$3.77

The mystery of ADVENTURELAND

The fun of FANTASYLAND

The thrill of THE MATTERHORN

Enjoy all the fun of

Disneyland

Exclusive at Sears

© 1961 Walt Disney Productions

The excitement of TOMORROWLAND

95 pieces
$9⁷⁷

Once upon a time Santa journeyed to Disneyland and loved it so much he created this marvelous miniature model for girls and boys. If you look close, you'll see enchanting Fantasyland with its fairy castle; mysterious Adventureland with wild animals, jungle and boats; rip-roaring Frontierland with cowboys and Indians; Tomorrowland with spring-operated flying saucers and rocket laun- cher; revolving carousel and Dumbo Flying Elephant ride; station with train; Matterhorn mountain with bob-sled; the celebrated Professor Ludwig Von Drake and his nephew Donald Duck, and many other animals, people and machines. Easy to assemble on 30x 60-inch plastic layout sheet. Figures, buildings, etc. 3D plastic.
79 N 5995L—Shpg. wt. 6 lbs......$9.77

SEARS
ROEBUCK AND CO

Chicago 7, Illinois

The doll pages of the 1962 Sears Christmas Wishbook were dominated by Barbie, the perky, modern blonde and her dapper boyfriend Ken. They had been introduced only a couple of years earlier, but now they were without competition as the most popular dolls in the world.

The Wishbook offered not only a bewildering array of clothes, furniture, homes and automobiles for the glamorous duo, it also gave little girls the chance to dress up like Barbie themselves -- with prom gowns, blonde wigs and every conceivable kind of accessory. Presumably, boys who wanted to dress like Ken were on their own.

At 11 1/2 inches high, Barbie was too tall to fit into any of the doll houses offered in this year's catalogue. Too bad for her, because there were some stunning homes offered at prices ranging from $5.97 for a basic Colonial house (with fallout shelter!) up to $17.88 for an ultra-modern House of the Future, "inspired by the newest designs that drop the boundaries between in and outdoor living." In other words, the house had no walls.

Come to think of it, even if she could fit, Barbie wouldn't like such a house. If there are no walls, where is all the closet space?

SEARS
Christmas
1962

Sears Christmas
Wishbook

1962

It's a Barbie World...

Dress up like Barbie
Make 8 costumes from 1 set
$9⁴⁴ set

Bride
Prom Queen
Sugar Plum Fairy
Ballerina
Nurse
Fairy Princess
Drum Majorette
Royal Highness

Costume Set. 4 to 8-year olds can dress up as eight different heroines changing from nurse to princess at the drop of a cap for a crown. In set .. blouse; 1 long, 1 circle skirt; nurse's bib, cap, skirt; bridal cap, veil; wings; crown; wand; baton; sash; name plate; pink Barbie bow, wig, ballerina skirt. No shoes. *Sizes* small (4-6), medium (8-10). *State size 4 to 10.*
49 N 840F—Shipping weight 4 lbs.....Set $9.44

Barbie
QUEEN OF THE PROM
$5⁷⁴

Costume with Blond Wig. Prom queens 4 to 8 wear pretend roses, reign in a shimmering dress with bodice of pink rayon satin, puff sleeves and braid-edged midriff. Lacy over-skirt drifts over soft, pink rayon taffeta dance skirt. No shoes.
Sizes small (4-6), medium (8-10), large (12-14). *State size 4 to 14.*
49 N 817F—Shipping weight 1 lb. 4 oz....$5.74

Costume Jewelry Sets for you and Barbie
Barbie wears necklace, earrings, tiara. These, plus bracelet, pin, adjustable ring adorn you. Metal, "stones" gleam in diamond-like settings. 10% Fed. Excise Tax incl.
49 N 1311E—Shpg. wt. 8 oz. **$1.88**

Barbie 3-piece Dresser Set
For little girls who want their hair as pretty as Barbie's. Attractive pink plastic set has Barbie pictures on back of 9-in. mirror. Comb; nylon-bristled brush.
49 N 1383—Shpg. wt. 12 oz....**97c**

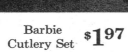

Smart little hostesses use Barbie 42-piece Tea Set **$2⁹⁹**
New Barbie pictures decorate each plate, saucer. Pink-white. 4 ea. glass goblets, plastic plates, cups, saucers, soup bowls, knives, forks, spoons. Teapot, creamer, sugar bowl, tureen, ladle, paper napkins.
49 N 942—Shipping weight 1 lb. 12 oz..........$2.99

Barbie Cutlery Set **$1⁹⁷**
Chest of wood-look cardboard has 6 each forks, knives, spoons, soup spoons; salad set. Butter knife, cake server, soup ladle, 2 candleholders. Gold-color plastic.
49 N 941—Wt. 1 lb. 4 oz...$1.97

Barbie Nurse Kit **$1³⁹**
Little nurse will proudly wear her "Barbie" autographed cap .. cure all her dolls with this set. Reflex hammer, forceps, stethoscope, utility jars, hot water bottle. All in pretty pink plastic bag.
49 N 1694—Wt. 1 lb. 8 oz.....$1.39

Barbie Game **$2⁹⁹**
Be elected Queen of the Prom when you win this game. You can do it if you play your cards right. Set also includes 18-in. Barbie board, dice, play money. 2 to 4 players.
49 N 454—Wt. 2 lbs......$2.99

Meet TV's Barbie and Ken

The teen-age sweethearts . . lifelike molded in fleshtone vinyl plastic with jointed arms and legs, turning head, painted features. They pose on removable wire stands. 11½-inch Barbie has rooted acetate hair, 12-inch Ken sports crew cut. Dolls and outfits made in Japan. Sorry, no choice of hair color.

[1] **Basic Ken Doll.** Wears cotton trunks, jacket and sandals.
49 N 3731—Shipping weight 12 oz. $2.38

Extra Ken Outfits. (Doll not incl.)

[A] **Yachtsman.** Blue denim slacks and knit-trimmed jacket. Striped T-shirt, socks, shoes. Yachting book.
49 N 3790—Shipping wt. 4 oz. . $2.19

[B] **Sportsman.** Bermuda shorts, sport shirt, socks and oxford shoes.
49 N 3789—Shipping wt. 4 oz. . $1.64

[C] **Campus Hero.** Includes pull-over sweater, duck slacks, socks and oxfords. Pennant, trophy, letter "U" for sewing.
49 N 3791—Shipping weight 4 oz. $2.19

[2] **Basic Barbie Doll.** Wears cotton knit swimsuit, sun glasses, earrings, shoes. Shipping weight 10 ounces.
49 N 3701—Barbie with bubble-cut rooted hair $1.97
49 N 3805—Barbie with ponytail rooted hair 1.97

Extra Barbie Outfits. (Doll not included.) Shpg. wt. each 4 oz.

(D) 49 N 3702—**Cotton Casual.** Full-skirt dress, sandals 79c

(E) 49 N 3779—**Movie Date.** Cotton dress with overskirt $1.29

[F] 49 N 3784—**Garden Party.** Cotton print dress, gloves, shoes 1.66

[G] 49 N 3734—**Singing in the Shower.** Cotton terry cloth robe, scuffs, towel, cloth; shower cap, brush, soap, puff 1.68

[H] 49 N 3785—**Mood for Music.** Cotton velvet capris, cardigan, sweater, gold-color banded wedgies, "pearl" choker. 2.47

[J] 49 N 3735—**Ballerina.** Black cotton leotard and tights; white tutu, tiara, ballet shoes; shoe bag, ballet program . . 2.27

[K] 49 N 3786—**Evening Splendor.** Metallic brocade dress, coat, simulated fur cuffs, hat, jewelry, purse, shoes, gloves 2.77

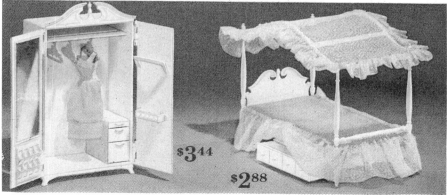

$3⁴⁴

$2⁸⁸

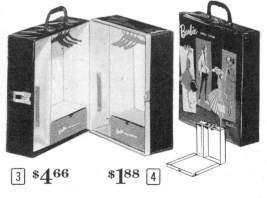

[3] $4⁶⁶ $1⁸⁸ [4]

Furnish Barbie's bedroom with her own Wardrobe and a 4-Poster Bed

Elegant Wardrobe is a wonderful showcase for Barbie's costumes. White high-impact plastic, wood-grain finish. Metal-hinged doors open showing hat rack and utility basket attached to one, shoe rack and long mirror on the other door. Has long shelf, 3 varied-size drawers, 6 plastic hangers. 5x15x16 inches. (Dress not included.)
49 N 9321—Assembles easily. Wt. 1 lb. 12 oz. $3.44

Graceful Canopy Bed made for fashion-plate Barbie. Carefully detailed, it boasts a molded plastic mattress, an under-bed chest with wood grain finish and sliding drawer. Spread and matching pillow cover are dotted, sheer pink muslin. High-impact plastic. 7x12x13 inches. Assembles easily.
49 N 9248—Shipping weight 1 lb. 6 oz. $2.88

Barbie takes a trip with Doll Cases her own size

[3] **Trunk** totes Barbie and Ken or 2 dolls their size. Hangers, 2 drawers. Black vinyl has a look of patent. 13x10x7 inches. Snaps shut.
49 N 9281—Shipping weight 4 pounds 4 oz. $4.66

[4] **Barbie Case** carries her (or Ken). Hangers and drawers. Black vinyl. 10½x12½x2¾ inches.
49 N 9309—Shipping weight 2 pounds $1.88

Barbie's Sports Car $3⁹⁹ Car only

Aqua bucket seats hold Barbie and Ken. Peach-tone plastic. Chrome-color grille, "lights", bumpers. 7½x18 in.
49 N 1405—Shipping weight 2 lbs. 10 oz. $3.99

Barbie's Portable House $4⁴⁴

Corrugated suitcase becomes Barbie's house just as fast as you unfold it. Pictures, pennants and rugs come attached to 3 walls, floor. Colorful chipboard furnishings include sofa, chair, ottoman, vanity, mirror, bench, pillow, coffee table, 2 book sets, record albums, Ken's picture, lamp, wardrobe, bed, TV-record player console. 26x14½x33 inches.
79 N 1429C—Shipping weight 8 pounds $4.44

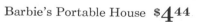

405 Bluebird Lane

Eight-room luxury house built of steel.
Two-story colonial style boasts these features .. ringing doorbell, living room light, vinyl-framed walk lined by plastic shrubs and a plastic picket fence around the swimming pool.

Colorful steel house has 22 plastic doll inhabitants. Scaled-to-size, they're made to be moved to any of the 8 rooms: bath, nursery, bedroom, family room, kitchen, laundry room, living-dining area. Attractive appointments include cloth draperies that frame 5 windows; 3 window awnings; plastic shutters and porch. Plus sports car. 52 plastic pieces furnish 8 rooms, include record cabinet, bed, buffet, tableware, washer, lawn pieces, etc. Unassembled. 44x14x18 inches high.
79 N 1424L—Wt. 17 lbs......$14.88
79 N 4660—"D" Batteries. Order 2 for house lights. Wt. 4 oz.. Each 16c

$14.88
without batteries

7-room Northern Colonial Metal House with sun porch
$9.97

Steel house is painted to look like red clapboard and white brick, with "landscaped" exterior. Portico has simulated wrought iron door. Rooms include family room, living-dining area, kitchen, utility room, bedroom, bath, nursery. Has 51 scaled-to-size plastic pieces. Awnings shade second floor. 4 plastic figures. Unassembled. 44x15x18 inches.
79 N 1412L—Shpg. wt. 10 lbs.....$9.97

Colonial Metal House has fall-out shelter
$5.97

Conversation-piece design has its own fall-out shelter! This 15x8x38-inch house makes one of the most up-to-date toys you can give little girls. They like the other special features, too, like the plastic Dutch door that opens as one piece or swings open only at the top or bottom, and the breezeway. There are eight more attractive rooms, including the patio, den, living and dining room, bedroom, nursery, kitchen and bath. Rooms are tastefully furnished with 35 plastic pieces including chairs, sofas, tables, beds, etc., all colorfully designed and each one scaled to size. Assembles easily.
79 N 1419C—Shipping weight 9 pounds....................$5.97

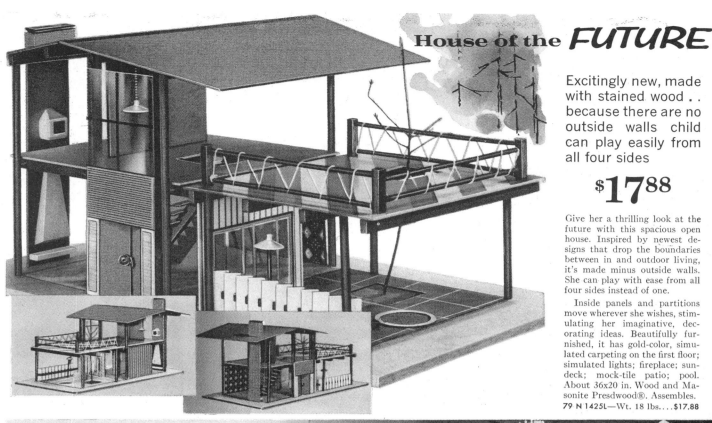

House of the FUTURE

Excitingly new, made with stained wood .. because there are no outside walls child can play easily from all four sides

$17⁸⁸

Give her a thrilling look at the future with this spacious open house. Inspired by newest designs that drop the boundaries between in and outdoor living, it's made minus outside walls. She can play with ease from all four sides instead of one.

Inside panels and partitions move wherever she wishes, stimulating her imaginative, decorating ideas. Beautifully furnished, it has gold-color, simulated carpeting on the first floor; simulated lights; fireplace; sundeck; mock-tile patio; pool. About 36x20 in. Wood and Masonite Presdwood®. Assembles.
79 N 1425L—Wt. 18 lbs....$17.88

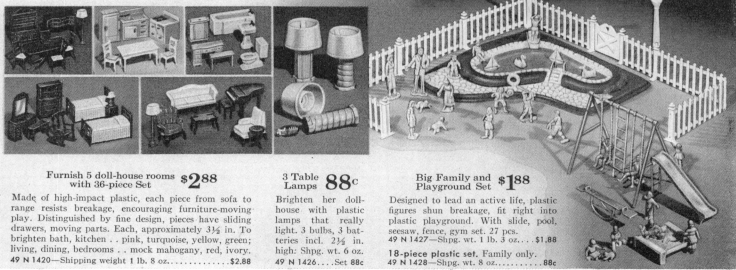

Furnish 5 doll-house rooms with 36-piece Set $2⁸⁸

Made of high-impact plastic, each piece from sofa to range resists breakage, encouraging furniture-moving play. Distinguished by fine design, pieces have sliding drawers, moving parts. Each, approximately 3½ in. To brighten bath, kitchen .. pink, turquoise, yellow, green; living, dining, bedrooms .. mock mahogany, red, ivory.
49 N 1420—Shipping weight 1 lb. 8 oz.............$2.88

3 Table Lamps 88ᶜ

Brighten her dollhouse with plastic lamps that really light. 3 bulbs, 3 batteries incl. 2½ in. high: Shpg. wt. 6 oz.
49 N 1426....Set 88c

Big Family and Playground Set $1⁸⁸

Designed to lead an active life, plastic figures shun breakage, fit right into plastic playground. With slide, pool, seesaw, fence, gym set. 27 pcs.
49 N 1427—Shpg. wt. 1 lb. 3 oz.... $1.88
18-piece plastic set. Family only.
49 N 1428—Shpg. wt. 8 oz...........88c

Doll Houses in pairs make friendly neighborhoods

Both Houses $7⁴⁴

Save 50 cents .. buy set of both houses below. Shipping wt. 13 lbs.
79 N 1431 C2....Set $7.44

6-room Colonial House. Has nursery, bedroom and bath upstairs; kitchen, living-dining area and utility room with sundeck on the second floor. This colorful steel model comes with attractive plastic furnishings. 25½x9½x15½ in. high.
79 N 1430C—Shipping weight 7 pounds.............$3.97

Either House $3⁹⁷ each

6-room Ranch House. Completely furnished bedroom, bath, living-dining area, utility room, plus patio. Durable, colorful steel .. designed to take lots of rugged play. 33x9x10 in. high. Plastic furnishings are scaled to size.
79 N 1401C—Shipping weight 6 pounds.............$3.97

VIDEO VILLAGE

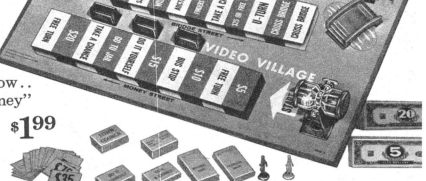

Video Village .. just like the TV show .. walk the magic mile and win "money"

The magic mile is paved with cash and prizes—but it's a hair-raising journey to get there. You may have to go to jail, do stunts and answer questions along the way. Takes luck with the dice to win the most "cash" and reach the finish line first. 18x13-in. board, with 3-D dice cage, jail, bridge. Chance cards, play money. 2 players, ages 10 to adult.
49 N 126—Shipping weight 1 pound 8 ounces........$1.99

$1.99

Seven Keys $3.22

Win the key that "unlocks" your favorite prize by answering questions on every subject imaginable—nicknames, historical figures, animals, sports. Includes question box, prize cards, prize board, many other items. For two players, ages 10 to adult.
49 N 132—Shipping weight 2 pounds.......$3.22

Camouflage $3.33

Hunt for each object camouflaged by a maze of see-through overlays. First one to pinpoint and trace object wins. There are 48 different objects. Takes sharp eyes to win. Includes spinner, tracing crayons, play money, question book, 9x9½-in. plastic holders. Two, three, or more players, ages 10 to adult.
49 N 110—Shipping weight 2 lbs. 3 oz.........$3.33

Charge Account $2.99

Just like Jan Murray's TV program. Build up a charge account—good for prizes—by making words out of scrambled letters. After 3 rounds, player with most money in prizes and cash wins. 2 charge account recorders, prizes, letters, revolving drum, word sheet. 2 or more players, all ages.
49 N 109—Shipping weight 2 lbs. 2 oz.........$2.99

Concentration $2.97

Match items hidden behind numbers to solve picture-word puzzles. Each match exposes more of puzzle. First to guess what picture says wins. Good memory is big advantage. Rollamatic changer with 60 puzzles, "cash," prize cards, plastic slides. 2 to 5 players, ages 10 to adult.
49 N 298—Shpg. wt. 1 lb. 14 oz..........$2.97

Password $1.44

Score points by guessing the correct password from one-word clues given by your partner. The more words you know, the easier it is to win. Red window in card holder reveals the password. Includes 24 password cards, 2 leatherette card holders, score pad. For 4 players, ages 10 to adult.
49 N 212—Shipping weight 12 ounces.........$1.44

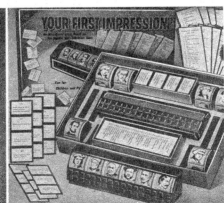

Your First Impression $3.44

Ask the MC questions to discover which of six famous historical figures he is representing. His answers provide the clues. 10 points for every right identification, 100 to win. Includes questions, answers, 24 figures on 6 drums, cylinder. For 3 or more players, ages 10 to adult.
49 N 174—Shipping weight 2 lbs. 4 oz.........$3.44

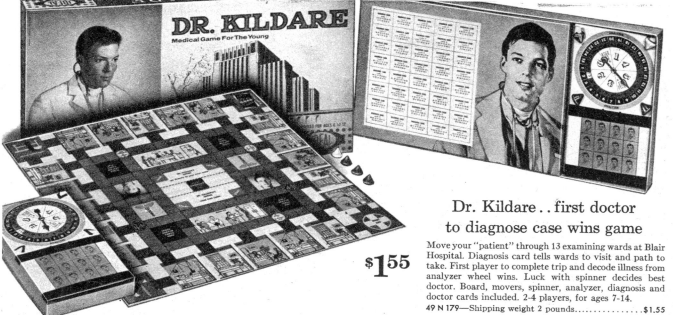

DR. KILDARE
Medical Game For The Young

$1⁵⁵

Dr. Kildare .. first doctor to diagnose case wins game

Move your "patient" through 13 examining wards at Blair Hospital. Diagnosis card tells wards to visit and path to take. First player to complete trip and decode illness from analyzer wheel wins. Luck with spinner decides best doctor. Board, movers, spinner, analyzer, diagnosis and doctor cards included. 2-4 players, for ages 7-14.
49 N 179—Shipping weight 2 pounds...............$1.55

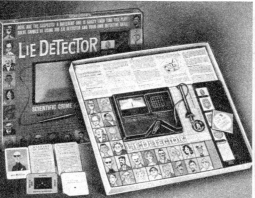

Dick Tracy $2⁶⁶

As one of Tracy's deputies, you must recover stolen goods and capture the crook. Loot hidden in 28 different places—find it before villain does. When villain is caught—or skips the country—game ends. Playing board, characters, spinner, loot card. 2-5 players, ages 7-15.
49 N 123—Shipping weight 2 lbs. 4 oz.....$2.66

Mattel's Lie Detector Game $3⁸⁸

Calls for razor-sharp powers of deduction. Examine conflicting testimony of suspects with lie detector. Discover whether answers are true or false. Gain promotion by exposing the real criminal. Get to be chief-of-police and you win. Mechanical lie detector, suspect and guilty cards, subpoenas, warrants, scoreboard. 2-4 players.
49 N 193—Shipping weight 2 lbs. 3 oz............$3.88

Surfside 6 $2⁴⁹

A murderer is on the loose! Locate the scene of the crime .. study clues under a magnifying glass .. accuse another player of the crime and prove you are correct. Takes great powers of observation to win. Game board, pawns, pencils, clue cards, die, 4 magnifying glasses. 2-4 players.
49 N 127—Shpg. wt. 2 lbs. 10 oz..........$2.49

Topper $5⁹⁹

Each section of the playing surface has 12 holes. With each spin of color wheel underneath, the holes change colors. All players place topper pieces in their section after each turn of the spinner. First to peg all 12 wins. Plastic case with color wheel, 48 topper pegs, 4 players, all ages.
49 N 190—Shipping wt. 2 lbs. 8 oz........$5.99

Play It Cool $7⁷⁷

Leap-frog 2 penguins up the mountain, using 1 hand only. When light's green, everybody scrambles. When light's red, everyone stops. Buzzer signals every light change. (2 flashlight batteries make it all automatic, order below.) 8 plastic penguins included. 2-4 players.
49 N 192—Shipping weight 3 pounds.............$7.77
49 N 4660—"D" batteries. Wt. 4 oz. Each 16c; 4 for 60c

Go to the Head of the Class $2⁵⁹

Answer questions correctly and move from desk to desk, grade to grade. First player graduated to college wins the game. Knowledge of all subjects counts most, luck helps. Includes game board, 792 questions and answers, dice, 6 moving pieces. 2 to 8 players, for ages 8 to 80.
49 N 388—Shipping weight 2 pounds.......$2.59

Make sundaes, sodas and soft drinks with your own Fountain Center

without batteries **$9⁹⁹**

Watch spray action in see-through bowl that holds 1½ quarts of your favorite drink; 20½-in. blue and yellow base. Includes 2 banana split and 2 sundae dishes; ice cream scoop; 4 spoons; 12 paper cups; 4 soda cup holders; 24 straws; 3 packages Kool-Aid. High-impact plastic. Sears exclusive, lab tested. Uses 2 "D" batteries (order below).
79 N 1106C—Shipping weight 3 pounds.... $9.99
"D" Batteries
79 N 4660—Shpg. wt. 4 oz....Each 16c; 4 for 60c

Sno-Cone Maker

$3⁸⁷

Shaves ice cubes into snow. Snow fills cup. Top with fruit syrup—delicious! Syrup dispensers, paper cups, funnel, shovel, 4 packages of syrup. 9½ in. high. Plastic, with a metal grinder.
49 N 1629—Shipping weight 3 pounds..... $3.87

Ice Cream Machine **$2⁴⁴**

Fill with ice and make tasty ice cream or sherbet in just a few minutes. Hand-operated plastic set is compact 11½x5¾ in. high. Junket ice cream mix, cups, spoons, recipes included.
49 N 1741—Shipping weight 2 lbs........ $2.44

The Flintstones Refreshment Bar **$2⁹⁹**

Fruit juice, pop or milk taste zingier pumped from 4 bottles with labels like "brontosaurus orange". 4 cups, 4 straws, bar. All are plastic. 16½x8¾x5 inches.
49 N 1719—Shpg. wt. 1 lb. 14 oz.....$2.99

Coca-Cola Dispenser **$1⁹⁹**

Double the fun of drinking a "Coke" at party or play time . . pour it from 10¾-in. dispenser of red and white plastic. Put in regular-size "Coke" bottle, pull handle, fill 4 plastic "Coke" glasses.
49 N 1819—Shipping weight 2 lbs. 1 oz.......$1.99

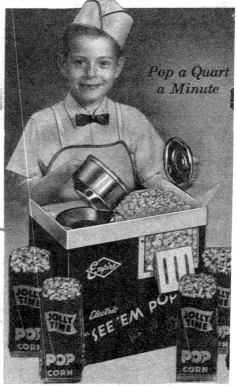

Pop a Quart a Minute

Electric Corn Popper **$5⁹⁹**

See corn pop, empty into hopper, then pour from spout, filling Gay pop corn bags. Red enameled steel; 14 in. high. AC-DC. 110–120 V. UL listed. Corn incl.
79 N 1669C—Shipping weight 8 pounds........$5.99

Kool-Aid Kooler

$2²⁹

Set up your own Kool-Aid stand. Mix the 2 packs Kool-Aid (1 gallon) add ice cubes, serve in the 20 paper cups. Red and white plastic Kooler; 6¾x 10¾x5¼ inches. Shpg. wt. 2 lbs. 2 oz.
49 N 1720.......$2.29

Cotton Candy Machine **$9⁹⁹** without batteries

Spin a froth of cotton candy in minutes with rust-proof, aluminum machine. All you need do is to heat some sugar. 2 plastic holders, scraper. About 16 in. diameter. Order 2 "D" batteries above.
79 N 1787C—Shipping weight 7 lbs........ $9.99

If you thought that Barbie's life was one of endless glamour and wardrobe possibilities, the 1963 Christmas Wishbook offered a glimpse at the other side of her existence. Turns out that Barbie had to cook and clean just like less fashionable dolls. Fortunately, she had some very stylish appliances to help her out -- vacuum cleaners, dishwashers, rotisseries and every other household item the Blonde One might need.

For little human girls living the Life of Barbie, there were also new combination washer-dryers, coffee percolators, sewing machines and looms. And for dolling up when the workday was through, a Budding Beauty Vanity by Marx ($9.88) with "everything a young beauty could want."

On rainy afternoons, girls could relax with the Modern Miss Play Box...featuring Barbie and Ken paper dolls, coloring books, crayons and other fun things, all for $3.67. Disney fans had a similar -- but much bigger -- "TV Clubhouse" for $5.87 with books, paper dolls, jigsaw puzzles, crayons and much more, featuring every Disney star from Goofy to Annette.

Sears Christmas
Wishbook

1963

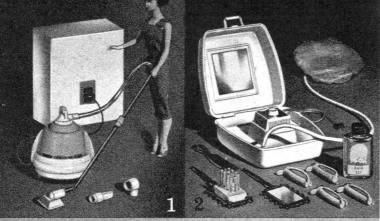

3-piece doll-sized Metal Kitchen Set

$5⁹⁷

Young homemakers appreciate this beautiful kitchen. Lustrous enamel finish in popular coppertone and ivory on sturdy heavy-gauge steel. 11-inch high stove has "see-through" oven window, sliding shelves. Faucet control on sink has shut-off. 15-inch high refrigerator. Pots, pans included.
79 N 1016C—Shpg. wt. 10 lbs.....Set $5.97

KIDDYPLIANCES® for fashion dolls like Barbie, Tammy

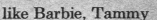

Styled in miniature . . .
powered by a tiny motor . . .
act like big appliances

Each **$2⁴⁹** without batteries

All are plastic . . 2 to 5 inches long. All except Starter Set require Power Pack listed below. Accessories as shown.

1 **Vacuum Cleaner Starter Set.** Picks up dust from dolly's carpet. Power Pack included. Order 2 "D" batteries below. Doll not included.
49 N 1019—Shpg. wt. 5 oz..... $2.49

2 **Hair Dryer.** Blows air from cap. Portable. 8-piece vanity set.
49 N 1024—Shpg. wt. 5 oz.... $2.49

3 **Dishwasher.** Hear it "play wash" a full service for 4 plus cutlery.
49 N 1025—Shpg. wt. 5 oz.... $2.49

4 **Rotisserie.** Make-believe turkey turns on spit. Red light goes on to pretend the right temperature.
49 N 1034—Shpg. wt. 5 oz.... $2.49

5 **Washer-Dryer.** Drop in Barbie's clothes . . see tumbler rotate.
49 N 1035—Shpg. wt. 5 oz.... $2.49

Power Pack. Operates 2 Kiddypliances at once. Order 2 "D" batteries.
49 N 1036—Shpg. wt. 3 oz.... 79c

"D" Batteries. Shpg. wt. each 4 oz.
49 N 4660 ..... Each 16c; 4 for 60c

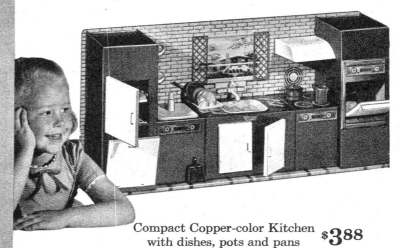

Compact Copper-color Kitchen with dishes, pots and pans $3⁸⁸

Help dolly do the "cooking" with this all-in-one metal and plastic kitchen set. Coppertone-color finish, white trim. Refrigerator has two compartments . . shelves with plastic food. Dishwasher has agitator for make-believe washing of many plastic dishes . . strainer for drying on sink. Cabinet space under sink. Hood over range. Wall oven has see-through door. 23x5x11 in. high.
79 N 1115C—Shipping weight 5 pounds..........................$3.88

SEE SUDS IN MAGIC ACTION WINDOW

No water, no fuss with Laundra-Magic Washer

$5⁹⁷ without batteries

Little girls marvel at this realistic, fun-to-operate toy. Looks like it's washing dolly's clothes. Just open the door, put in clothes. Set automatic timer for 3-cycle washing. Machine whirls, tumbles and builds up real soapsuds in the specially sealed "magic action" window. 21x15x9 inches high. Uses 2 "D" batteries (not included, order from listing above). Wt. 3 lbs. 8 oz.
49 N 1043........$5.97

10-pc. Laundry Set with hand-operated wringer-washer

$2⁹⁷

Just add soap and water and let the agitator do the scrubbing . . all you do is turn the crank. Adjustable rubber roller wringer helps you wring clothes damp-dry. 12 inches high. Metal. White with turquoise and pink trim. Hang clothes on revolving dryer, plenty of line. Woven basket, 6 pins.
Shpg. wt. 3 lbs.
49 N 1030 . . . $2.97

CAN-O-MATIC
Opens cans automatically
Safe .. no sharp edges

$3⁹⁷ without batteries

Place can into Can-O-Matic, press the lever and watch it revolve .. lid simply pops off. Won't scratch little home-makers because cans are plastic, lids pre-cut. Lids fit back on cans .. use them over again. Eight cans of different Libby's foods contain built-in plastic food. Plastic and metal opener is 6 in. high. Order 2 "C" batteries below.
49 N 1040—Shipping weight 1 lb. 2 oz $3.97
49 N 4665—"C" Battery. Wt. ea. 2 oz..Each 16c; 4 for 60c

Watch it perk $1⁷⁴

Just add water .. no batteries or winding necessary. Actually perks water without heat or wiring. Air pressure draws water up the spout in the center of the Wonder Perk pot. Comes complete with play stove. Both of white plastic with black trim. 6 in. high. Sized just right for little girls.
49 N 1042—Wt. 12 oz..$1.74

Really cleans clothes, spins them dry for ironing

Combination Washer-Dryer $9⁸⁸

Just turn crank and agitator churns water like a real washer. For spinning, turn a knob and agitator shifts into high. "See through" plastic lid lets you watch the whole operation. Easy loading, unloading from top. Sturdily made of heavy-gauge steel. Easy emptying with drain hose. Holds up to 1 quart of water. Measures 23½ inches high to the work surface, 18x15x27½ inches high over-all.
79 N 1060L—Shpg. wt. 19 lbs...... $9.88

13-piece Laundry Set $6⁸⁸

Store entire set in 3¼-ft. high simulated wood closet .. easy-to-reach shelves. Adjustable ironing board in pink, turquoise .. has pad and cover. Big 7-inch chrome-plated electric iron. Endboard hamper, 6-ft. clothesline, plastic clothespins, apron.
79 N 1027C—Shpg. wt. 7 lbs... Set $6.88

5-piece Power Sweep Set $3⁹⁹ without batteries

Sweeper actually cleans at flick of switch. Empties easily. Rose-colored metal .. tubular steel handle. 31 in. high. Brillo, apron, dust cloth, mop. Uses 3 "D" batteries.
79N1150C—Wt. 2 lbs... Set $3.99
"D" Battery. Shpg. wt. each 4 oz.
79N4660.... Each 16c; 4 for 60c

5-piece Cleaning Set $1⁹⁷

Pick up hard to get at dirt with metal sweeper's fiber brush. Bottom opens for emptying. For hard to reach corners .. 24-inch wood handled broom with plastic bristles, dust mop and pan. Plastic apron. Shpg. wt 2 lbs.
79 N 1302C.......... Set $1.97

"Friction" Vacuum Cleaner $1⁹⁷

Run it across floor .. motor hums, draws in air; brush revolves to pick up dirt. No batteries. Bag inflates.. slips off to empty. Metal, 27-inch wood handle.
49 N 1203—From Japan. Shipping weight 2 lbs..$1.97

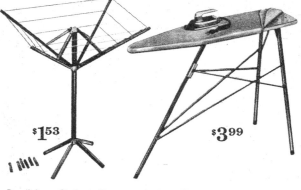

$1⁵³

$3⁹⁹

Revolving Clothes Dryer. Almost 20 feet of cotton clothesline—gives plenty of drying area. Sturdy metal and wood stand is 25 inches high. Six plastic clothespins included. Folds compactly for easy storage.
79N1058C—Wt. 2 lbs.$1.53

4-piece Electric Ironing Set. 22x30-inch steel table with pad, cover .. pink trim. About 6¼-inch chrome-plated iron.
79 N 1056C—Wt. 6 lbs.$3.99
Ironing table, pad, cover only.
79 N 1021C—Wt. 5 lbs.$2.58
Ironing table only.
79 N 1002C—Wt. 5 lbs.$1.99

$1⁹⁷

88ᶜ

De luxe Electric Iron. Chrome-plated metal base, hood. 6¼ in. long. Plastic handle. Shpg. wt. 1 lb. 4 oz.
49 N 1038........$1.97

Non-electric Toy Iron. Chrome-plated metal base with plastic handle. Imitation cord, plug. 6½ inches long.
49 N 1039—Wt. 12 oz... 88c

NOTE: Electric irons on page are UL approved for 110-120-volt, 60-cycle AC

She gets everything a young beauty could want..
cosmetics by TUSSY, a brush and comb set,
a hand mirror and costume jewelry in the

Budding Beauty Vanity
by MARX
$9⁸⁸

Dresser and Bench Set is just her size
$3⁶⁰

Plenty of room for all her beauty aids and even room for books. Helps her keep things neat and orderly. Center cosmetic shelf, two drawers and 4 open shelves. 37x33x11½ in. deep with plastic framed mirror. In dainty pink and blue provincial pattern to brighten any room. Sturdy pieces made of reinforced, corrugated fiberboard. Easy to assemble .. parts lock together. Accessories not included, see below.
79 N 1113C—Shipping weight 8 pounds.........................$3.60

Dresser Set $1⁸⁷

Teach good grooming. Delicate pink set includes plastic comb, brush, 2 jars, mirror, tray, picture frame. Shipping weight 1 lb. 3 oz.
49 N 1322.........$1.87

Make-Up Kit $2⁸⁷

Save raids on mother's cosmetics. Includes 18 pcs. .. lipstick, rouge, powder, puff, 4 nail groomers, bubble bath, mirror, etc. Vinyl case. Shipping weight 1 lb. 8 oz.
49 N 1371............$2.87

Jewelry and Chest $2⁵⁷

Vinyl chest (5x7x2¾-in. high) with tray. Metal jewelry includes necklaces, earrings, rings, charm bracelet. 10% Fed. Ex. Tax. incl.
49 N 1387E—Wt. 1 lb.....$2.57

Sewing Basket $2⁴⁴

Fiber quilt-lined basket (9x6x5 in. deep) has plastic lift-out tray. Needles, thimble, 8 spools thread. Made in Japan.
49 N 1223—Wt. 1 lb. 8 oz. $2.44

What a luxurious way to "pretty up." Provincial-style vanity is beautifully shaped and delicately detailed. Makes any young miss feel like a queen. Sturdy plastic construction. Compact center compartment has flip-top mirror .. holds brush and comb, mirror, jewelry (bracelet, ring, and locket). Cosmetics include lipstick, 2 beauty soaps, 3 bubble baths, after-bath powder, toilet water and hand lotion. Nail polish and remover for manicures. Informative booklet of "Beauty Hints." 23x24 inches wide. "Tufted" plastic hassock also has storage compartment inside .. stands 12½ inches high.
79 N 1304L—Shipping weight 14 pounds..........................$9.88

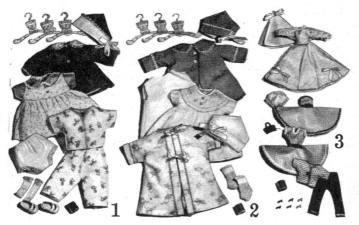

It's Sew Simple . . to make your own doll clothes

$1⁹⁹ for 12-13 in. Baby doll   **$2⁴⁴** for 12-13 in. Newborn doll   **$2⁴⁴** for 11½ in. Fashion doll

Ready to sew . . materials are pre-cut so there's no cutting. Detailed illustrated instructions are easy for little girls to follow. Complete with coordinated accessories. Trimmings, notions, and hangers included.

1 Baby Doll Wardrobe. Fits Tiny Tears, Betsy Wetsy, many other baby dolls. Makes a dress, panty, pajamas, coat and bonnet.
49 N 1449—(12 to 13-inch baby doll) Shpg. wt. 1 lb. 2 oz........$1.99
49 N 1450—(16 to 17-inch baby doll) Shpg. wt. 1 lb. 2 oz........ 2.44
49 N 1451—(20 to 21-inch baby doll) Shpg. wt. 1 lb. 2 oz........ 2.88

2 Newborn Baby Doll Layette. Fits Thumbelina, Baby Dear, many other newborns. Makes a dress and bonnet, slip, kimono, coat and bonnet.
49 N 1452—(12 to 13-inch newborn baby) Shpg. wt. 1 lb. 2 oz....$2.44
49 N 1453—(14 to 15-inch newborn baby) Shpg. wt. 1 lb. 2 oz.... 2.88
49 N 1454—(18 to 20-inch newborn baby) Shpg. wt. 1 lb. 2 oz.... 3.33

3 Fashion Doll Trousseau Wardrobe. Fits Barbie, Midge. Makes a play dress, party dress, pajamas, panty and bridal gown.
49 N 1455—(Fits all 11½-inch fashion dolls) Wt. 1 lb. 2 oz.......$2.44

Electric Sewmaster $14⁹⁷

Plug it in and start sewing . . steady stitches make it easy to do better work every time

Little girls feel a true sense of accomplishment as they develop their sewing skills on a deluxe electric machine. They learn to sew at a faster speed with steady, even power . . gain control with safety on-and-off switch. Machine refuses to start until wheel is turned by hand. Rubber-covered cord and plug.

Well-built hardwood base makes it easier to sew sleeves and collars . . has drawer for accessories. Streamlined contour of stamped steel head allows generous movement of fabric . . just what you need for larger, more complex patterns. Thread tension adjusts to fabric thickness . . holds firm with pressure foot. Makes a strong chain stitch. Uses standard 12x1 size 14 needles. Extra needles and thread included. For girls 8 years and older. Operates on 110-120-volt, 60-cycle AC. Measures 9¾x5x7½ inches. Made in West Germany.
49 N 1299—Shipping weight 4 pounds............................$14.97

MARX E-Z Weaver Loom $7⁹⁷

Make novel gifts for friends or many useful items for yourself with this real yet easy, modern handloom. Made of strong plastic in wood grain . . complete with shuttle, harnesses, warp strings and spacing wires.

Simple instruction book contains many suggestions. Over 400 feet of red and white "Bernat" banded yarn included. 12x13x13 inches high.
Shipping weight 4 lbs..
79 N 1372C................$7.97

REMCO Spinning Wheel $4⁹⁶

What fun pioneering with this wonderful, old-fashioned method of spinning. Turn the wheel, loop the wool, pull, and out comes finished braid. Sew together to make hats, rugs, pocketbooks, etc. 4-ply red wool yarn, 2 needles, 3 spinning heads included. 18 inches high. Red plastic. Assembled.
79 N 1243C—Wt. 4 lbs.......$4.96
Extra Yarn.
100% virgin wool, 105 yards. Red.
49 N 1274—Shpg. wt. 6 oz.....88c

Both hands are free to control fabric . . with battery-powered Sewmaster

$8⁹⁷ Without batteries

Sewmaster provides constant power . . has safety guard to protect little fingers. Raised base . . streamlined stamped steel sewing head. Converts to hand operation when wanted. Thread tension adjusts to fabric thickness, pressure foot adjusts to fabrics. Chain stitch.

Uses 12x1 size 14 needles. Thread, needle, clamp included. 8½x4⅝ inches wide. Order 2 "D" batteries below. Made in West Germany.
49 N 1202—Shipping weight 3 pounds 3 ounces.................$8.97
49 N 4660—"D" Batteries. Shpg. wt. each 4 oz.... Each 16c; 4 for 60c

$3⁸⁷   **$6⁹⁷**

Beginners' Hand-operated Machine. Safety guard. Thread tension; pressure foot. Enameled steel, die-cast head, plated trim. Uses standard 12x1 size 14 needles. Extra needle, thread . . clamp included. 8x4 inches high. From West Germany.
49N1250—Wt. 1 lb. 14 oz...$3.87

Advanced Hand-operated Machine. Extension table for more complex, larger patterns. Hardwood base has drawer for accessories. Enameled steel. Uses standard 12x1 size 14 needles. Extra needle, thread, metal clamp. 12 x 5 inches high. West Germany.
49N1221—Wt. 2 lbs. 8 oz...$6.97

Make farm family and animals
PLAY-DOH FORGE PRESS
$2⁹⁹

Just insert Play-Doh compound into 1 of 6 molds and press down handle of forge press. Forms 3-D figures that dry hard in 24 hours. Animals are horse, pig, turkey, lamb, dog, cow. 6x5x8½-in. plastic forge press, 4 cans Play-Doh, instruction booklet. Order extra Play-Doh compound below at right.
49 N 1784—Shipping weight 3 pounds 7 ounces.....Set $2.99

Build a city, planes, trains, ships $3⁵⁵
Play-Doh Fun Factory

This 30-die set lets you build everything from airports to shopping centers . . even create your own navy. Set includes 12 basic-form dies plus 6 dies each for planes, trains, ships; plastic trimmer; 4 cans of Play-Doh; city map (to help you plan a town); 36x36-in. plastic sheet to cover tabletop; instructions.
49 N 1783—Shipping weight 4 pounds 15 ounces....Set $3.55

Jr. Fun Factory

Tot-size high-impact plastic extruder for 3-D creative modeling with clean, soft, colorful Play-Doh. Includes dies to make 10 different shapes, trimmer, three 2-oz. cans of Play-Doh. Wt. 1 lb. 2 oz.
49 N 1728.........Set $1.49

Make rings, bracelets, pins you can really wear
Play-Doh Jewelry Maker
Includes forge press, 4 sets of molds, 4 cans Play-Doh, 130 jewelry fittings $3⁷⁷

Form gem-like shapes that attach to any of the 130 fittings for rings, necklaces and other jewelry items you can design. Just insert Play-Doh modeling compound into 1 of 4 color-keyed matching molds . . place it in the Jewelry Maker forge press, and press down handle. Dries hard in 24 hours, so you can wear your own personal jewelry next day. Set contains 6x5x8½-inch plastic forge press, 4 sets of plastic molds, 130 jewelry fittings (all non-metallic), four 7-oz. cans of Play-Doh (red, yellow, blue and white). Idea book included.
49 N 1727—Wt. 3 lbs. 14 oz..... Set $3.77

Play-Doh Modeling Compound 4-Pack

Use as refills for our Play-Doh kits or for hand-modeled objects you create. 7-oz. cans. Red, yellow, blue, white.
49 N 1871—Shipping weight 2 lbs. 4 oz........Pkg. 72c

MAGNETIC BOARDS
For busy fingers and minds . . reverse to wipe-off crayon boards

1 Deluxe 73-piece Spelling and Numbers Board. Extra-large 20¼x23-in. wood frame securely holds durable metal board. Letters, numbers, arithmetic signs are colorful 3-dimensional polyethylene with built-in permanent magnets. Wipe-off crayons and sponge eraser included.
79 N 1772C—Shipping weight 5 lbs.....$3.55

2 37-piece Numbers Board . . the fun way to learn all the important basics of arithmetic . . encourages solving problems in addition, subtraction, multiplication, division. Colorful numbers and symbols have built-in permanent magnets. Metal board has strong plastic frame . . 14x20 inches. Wipe-off crayons included.
49 N 1750—Shipping weight 2 lbs. 8 oz....$1.94

3 36-piece Alphabet Board . . easy, enjoyable way to learn words, sentence structure and spelling. Gaily colored letters have permanent, built-in magnets. Metal board, plastic frame . . 14x20 inches. Wipe-off crayons.
49 N 1730—Shipping weight 2 lbs. 8 oz....$1.94

Mold and paint Disney favorites with Mickey Mouse Modelcast
$1⁵⁹

Cast the characters in plaster simply by using the colorful plastic molds and special modelcast plaster. Then, just color the 3-dimensional plaques and hang them on the wall. Set includes 4 molds, 2 bags plaster, paints, brush, plaque hangers.
49 N 1855—Shipping weight 1 lb. 12 oz.......$1.59

24^{88} cash without battery

27^{77} cash without battery

2 19^{97} cash without battery

Sears puts at your fingertips more of what America's children want most

BATTERY-POWERED MARX RIDERS

They stop easy, turn, go into reverse . . . and a safe 5 MPH is top speed!

TONY-THE-PONY . . is saddled-up and ready to gallop when you step on the stirrup. It's his starter, speed control and reverse pedal all in one. Pull on the reins and he'll turn right or left . . and take you round in a circle. For a wonderful, fun-packed ride, just hop on and go.

This rollicking sidewalk hobbyhorse is heavy-duty plastic, an exciting palomino equipped with foot and handle bars. Motorized and with extra-wide wheels for sure-footed going. It works on a 12-volt hot-shot battery (not included, order below). 33x16x23 inches high with 12½-inch saddle height.
79 N 8610NM—Shipping weight 30 pounds $24.88
79 N 8611M—12-volt Hot-shot Battery. Shipping weight each 10 pounds. 4.44

The Stutz Bearcat—red, racy, realistic

1 Looks like it roared in from the 1920's. Bucket seat, running boards, horn, back mount spare tire . . even a noise-making crank in front. Steel chassis. Heavy-duty plastic body with gold-color trim. The foot pedal is on the fender and controls both forward and reverse. Handbrake for quick stops. Measures 42x15 inches with 5½-inch wheels. Order 12-volt battery at left.
79 N 8609NM—Shipping weight 20 pounds $27.77

Marx-A-Kart, plus helmet and racing goggles

2 It's made to order for you junior "Hot-Rodders." Scaled down in size . . hugs the ground on curves. Foot pedal controls both forward and reverse. Hand brake on rear wheel. Strong polyethylene body on strong steel frame with 5½-inch plastic wheels. Size: 14¾ inches wide; 37 inches long. Uses one 12-volt battery (not included, order at left).
79 N 8608LM—Shipping weight 19 pounds $19.97

NO MONEY DOWN on Sears Easy Terms

49^{99} cash without battery

Heavy-duty Electric-Drive Kart

A boy-sized version of a regular racing go-kart. It has car-like stick shift and link steering . . a hand brake . . even deep tread rubber tires . . and it scoots along at an easy-going 5 MPH

So whisper-quiet, it just purrs along. Rugged tubular steel frame: 27 in. wide and 46 in. long. Rubber tire wheels: 8 inches high; 2 inches wide. Plus foam seat. Uses one 12-volt storage battery (order below). To keep battery power at capacity, order 12-volt battery booster 28G7167 from Sears General Catalog.
79 N 8916N—Shipping weight 45 pounds . . . . Cash $49.99
28 N 349N—12-volt Battery. Shipping weight 41 pounds 7.95
NOTE: Items with suffix "N" (as 79 N 8916N) sent freight (rail or truck) or express.

ACTIVITY SETS for boys and girls

Now .. *You are a doll!*

Imagine how excited your little girl will be when she finds this 16-inch doll whose face *is her very own!*

My Fun-filled Playhouse of Stars $3.99

Make *your* little girl the top star of this exciting playhouse: We'll include with your order a special self-addressed envelope in which you enclose a color snapshot or negative. Face will be enlarged, adhesive applied and returned to you within 5 days so you can stick right over doll's face .. *all included in price of set!* Complete set includes the following:

1 "You Are A Doll" board doll over 16 in. tall with lovely costumes
1 Large-size Shari Lewis statuette board doll with beautiful dresses
1 Shari Lewis 24-page coloring book with 16 stencils; 1 box 8 crayons
1 Shari Lewis lacing fun sheet with yarns, costumes; 1 paint palette
2 Sheets of Shari Lewis finger puppets, 2 sheets of sticker pictures
1 Angela Cartwright super treasure slate with stylus, 8½x13½ in.
1 Board doll over 9 in. tall with wavy hair, colorful costumes
1 "Once Upon A Wedding Day" 80-page coloring book, 8x11 in.
1 Book of ballet paper dolls with complete wardrobe, 8¾x11¾ in.
3 Games in one box: "Storm the Castle," "Splash" and "Bunny-Ho"
4 Color-by-number pictures with printed frames, ready for hanging
4 Easy-to-assemble die-cut puzzles in full color, 7x10½ in.; 1 brush
5 Sewing tards, 4 plastic-tipped yarns, 1 pair 3-in. plastic scissors
3 N 517—Shipping weight 3 pounds......................$3.99

Space Age Set featuring Jetsons $3.93

Ready on the launch pad! Your junior astronaut will go "into orbit" when he opens up this big box. It's just loaded with popular "out-of-this-world" TV characters from his favorite programs. Here's what he'll find:

1 Jetsons coloring book, 128 pages of space scenes to color or paint
5 Jetsons board dolls featuring George, Jane, Judy, Elroy and Astro with over 50 push-out costumes for outer space; packed in big 10x13-in. portfolio
1 Jetsons jigsaw puzzle; 100 interlocking pieces .. makes 14x18-in. picture
1 Flintstones magic slate with plastic stylus, size 8½x13 in. Just lift the film and everything written on slate disappears like magic!
7 Flintstones magic rub-off cards with wipe-off crayons and cleaning cloth
1 Top Cat sticker fun book, size 10x12 inches. Push out, stick on and color such scenes as Top Cat eating in a restaurant, visiting in a hospital, etc.
1 Yogi Bear picture story book with hard cover, 28 pages, size 5½x6¼ in. Funny story about Yogi and his super scooter .. with all pictures in full color
1 Huckleberry Hound picture story book with hard cover, 144 pages, 5⅝x7⅞ in.
1 Pair of 3-inch plastic safety scissors; 1 package of drawing paper
1 Paint and crayon set with plastic tray; 1 package of paper play money
1 Paint-with-water paint book, 64 pages. Brush water on .. watch colors appear!
3 N 514—Shipping weight 4 pounds 4 ounces..................$3.93

New Ark Full of Fun $1.27

A boat-load of activities! 14 coloring books, each 7¼x5½ inches, 16 pages. 6 paint-by-number animal pictures, 5½x8 inches. Wood stylus, 8-color paint palette, brush, self-erasing slate, 4 assorted crayons. Daisy-chain gummed sheets .. make 88 colorful chain links. Safety scissors.

3 N 556—Shipping weight 1 lb. 2 oz......$1.27

Rainy Day Box 86c

Lots to do on sunny days, too. Set includes large 8½x11-in. 32-page coloring book, 28-page full-color picture story book, 16 sheets of drawing paper, magic slate with plastic stylus, 4 straws and plastic-tipped yarn, package of daisy chains, colorful sticker construction sheets, 4 weaving strips, box of 6 crayons in assorted colors. Shipping weight 1 pound.

3 N 557..............................86c

New Pop-up Books $1.67 set

Turn the page and POP! .. a full-color scene springs to life. Eight dramatic 3-D scenes in each book .. complete with small plastic props. Heavy paper with plastic spiral bindings. 2 books in each set.

Farm and Doll's House Set.
3 N 519—Shipping weight 1 pound.....Set $1.67

Wild West and Garage Set.
3 N 520—Shipping weight 1 pound.....Set $1.67

3 to 8 years . . jam-packed with fun things to do

TV CLUBHOUSE

starring

★ Mickey Mouse ★ Mouseketeers
★ Annette ★ Donald Duck

Exclusive at Sears! $5⁸⁷

It's our finest assortment of activities to help keep the "little ones" busy with interesting things to do. Here's what they get:

1 Mouseketeer 28-page book showing how Mousketeers are picked
1 Mouseketeer 36-piece jigsaw puzzle with Walt Disney characters
2 Mouseketeer stand-up board dolls featuring Karen and Cubby with 28 colorful costumes . . packed in handy portfolio
4 Walt Disney starlet board dolls, including Annette, each standing 9 inches tall . . with 45 costumes, accessories; in sturdy carrying case
1 Annette 256-page coloring book showing her dancing, modeling, dressing, camping, etc., 1 box of 16 assorted crayons
1 Donald Duck 28-page picture story book in full color
1 Lady and the Tramp 65-piece sticker fun book
1 Lady and the Tramp 70-piece jigsaw puzzle measuring 14x18 in.
1 Lady and the Tramp 128-page coloring book of favorite scenes

Plus—1 zoo-animals punch-out book, 6 coloring books, 12 picture story books, 1 deck of animal rummy cards, 1 tracing and coloring book, 4 sewing cards with yarn, 1 paint and crayon set, 1 magic play slate, 1 safety scissors, 4 sheets of 20 stencils with paper, 4 weaving strips, 4 straws with lace, daisy chains, play money.

3 N 518—Shipping weight 8 pounds......................$5.87

Modern Miss PLAY BOX
. . featuring Barbie and Ken

Complete with 9-in. tall Barbie and Ken board dolls!

Exclusive at Sears! $3⁶⁷

Popular Barbie and her friends, Ken and Midge, will almost come alive in your little girl's eyes . . 'cause there's so much to do! You get:

1 Barbie and 1 Ken 9-inch stand-up board doll with 40 costumes, accessories; packed in attractive suitcase-styled box with plastic handle.
1 Barbie, Ken and Midge 128-page coloring book showing Barbie walking under the stars with Ken, taking a plane trip, modeling a formal, etc.
1 Barbie 52-page push-out, stick-on and color activity book showing Barbie and Ken on a date, Barbie studying in school, Barbie's sister, etc.
1 Barbie 84-page color-by-number book showing Barbie at an outdoor barbecue, skiing, listening to records, dancing with Ken, etc.

Plus—2 paint and coloring books, 2 cut-out paper doll books, 6 sewing cards with yarn, 1 pair of plastic safety scissors, 1 magic slate with stylus, 1 deck of hearts card game, 1 paint and crayon set, 1 package of four-color gummed sheets, 1 package of daisy chains with gummed backs.

3 N 593—Shipping weight 4 pounds 5 ounces $3.67

PCBKM
AEDSLG SEARS 117

Here Barbie can put on a fashion show in her own new shop $3⁹⁹

It's over 3 feet long and really elegant. Mannequin with movable arms poses in showcase window. Shelves and built-in cabinet adjoin display alcove . . hang fashions here. Display case. Note curtained stage . . use it as dressing room, too. Model's entrance is in back. 3-way mirror. 2 arm chairs assure "customers'" comfort. Coffee table. Chipboard fashion shop stands 17½ in. high. Carrying handle. Folds compactly for easy storage.

79 N 1408L—Shipping weight 8 pounds. . . . $3.99

NOTE: *Dolls and clothing not included with any Doll House on these 2 pages. All assemble easily.*

Barbie's Dream House

Barbie relaxes in her furnished Studio $4⁴⁰

A small girl's delight. Unfold the corrugated suitcase . . it's Barbie's colorful chipboard home. Easy-to-assemble furnishings include sofa, chair, ottoman, vanity, mirror, bench, pillow, coffee table, 2 book sets, record albums, Ken's picture, lamp, wardrobe, bed, TV-record player console. Pictures, pennants and rugs attached to 3 walls, floor. 26x33x14½ inches high.

79 N 1429C—Shipping weight 9 pounds. $4.40

Tammy's Dream House

Tammy entertains in her Playroom or Patio $4⁴⁰

Has soda fountain, juke box, TV set, table tennis table, shuffleboard, built-in desk, closet. Pictures, dart board game on wall. Patio has chaise lounge, side table, barbecue pit. Chipboard. Folds, with handle. 26x33x14½ inches high.

79 N 9361L—Shipping weight 8 pounds. $4.40

In 1964, Beatlemania was sweeping the nation, bringing an onslaught of collarless jackets, Beatle Boots, Beatle Wigs, board games, magazines, trading cards and a plethora of other items related to the Liverpool Mop Tops. But you wouldn't have known it from the 1964 Wishbook. One set of 4 1/2 inch tall Beatle dolls, at $1.65 each, was the only suggestion that John, Paul, George and Ringo were the most popular humans on Earth.

But little girls who were buying their Beatles records elsewhere, looked to Sears for the new breed of talking dolls: Little Miss Echo, who repeated everything you said to her; Scooba-Doo,the beatnik doll who said eleven different "far-out" things, such as, "Play it cool...don't be a square"; and -- the most prominent of all -- Chatty Cathy, who could say *eighteen* things (take that, Scooba-Doo!) at random. Although it must be admitted that Chatty Cathy's "Where are we going?" wasn't nearly as "far-out" as the counter-culture remarks Scooba-Doo had to say.

Sears Christmas
Wishbook

1964

"Talk or sing to me.. I'll repeat everything word for word"

Little Miss Echo

Actually 30 inches tall

Now just **$14.99** without batteries

Can you imagine anything more fun than a doll that repeats everything you say to her? She has a magnetic tape recorder built right in. Plastic . . jointed arms, legs and head. Her rooted blonde hair can be combed. Order 2 "D" batteries and one 9-volt battery below.
79N3665CM–Shipping weight 8 pounds $14.99

"D" Batteries. Shipping weight each 4 oz.
79 N 4660 . . . . .2 for 32c; 4 for 60c

9-volt Battery. Shipping weight 4 oz.
79 N 6417M . . . . Each 35c

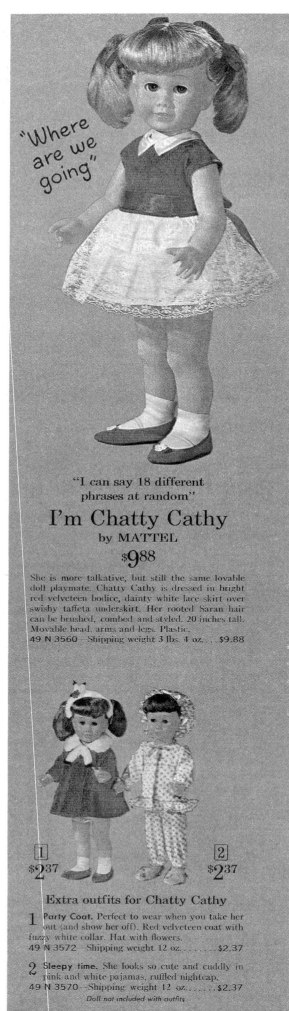

"Where are we going"

"I can say 18 different phrases at random"

I'm Chatty Cathy
by MATTEL
$9.88

She is more talkative, but still the same lovable doll playmate. Chatty Cathy is dressed in bright red velveteen bodice, dainty white lace skirt over swishy taffeta underskirt. Her rooted Saran hair can be brushed, combed and styled. 20 inches tall. Movable head, arms and legs. Plastic.
49 N 3560 - Shipping weight 3 lbs. 4 oz. . . . $9.88

[1] $2.37   [2] $2.37

Extra outfits for Chatty Cathy

1 Party Coat. Perfect to wear when you take her out (and show her off). Red velveteen coat with fuzzy white collar. Hat with flowers.
49 N 3572 - Shipping weight 12 oz. $2.37

2 Sleepy time. She looks so cute and cuddly in pink and white pajamas, ruffled nightcap.
49 N 3570 - Shipping weight 12 oz. $2.37
Doll not included with outfits

"I dig That crazy beat . . . . yeah!"

Scooba-Doo
by MATTEL
Says 11 different things
$8.97

She's the singin' swinger doll . . just pull her Chatty-Ring and she says far-out things like "Play it cool . . don't be a square." She's 23 in. tall with a soft, cotton-stuffed body, sculptured vinyl head. Rooted hair.
49 N 3634 – Shipping wt. 3 lbs. $8.97

LOOK-ALIKES "My baby and me"
$8.97

Big doll is 27 in. tall and wears cotton Cordana dress. She carries her own 8-in. drink and wet doll. Hold her hand, she'll walk with you. Has rooted hair, sleeping glassine eyes with lashes. Wears size 1 clothes.

Baby dressed in matching cotton Cordana overall outfit. Nursing bottle. Rooted hair. Both plastic.
79 N 3410C–Shpg. wt. 5 lbs. $8.97

Fiberboard Play Luggage. Fashionable matching set, in favorite colors, with room to take everything you want when going on short play trips. Just right for dolly's clothes. 4 pieces, 1 each: 8-inch, 9-inch, 10-inch and 11¾-inch cases. Nest for easy storage when you and your dollies are in a stay-at-home mood. From Spain.
49 N 8444—Shpg. wt. 1 lb. 5 oz....Set $1.66

Beatle Dolls. Made of life-like vinyl plastic with rooted hair in the famous Beatle mop cut. Each caricature is 4½ inches tall.
49 N 8445—Ringo Starr
49 N 8446—Paul McCartney
49 N 8447—John Lennon
49 N 8448—George Harrison
Shipping weight each 8 oz......Each $1.66

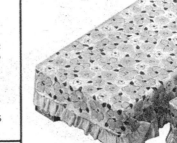

Fashion Doll Boudoir Set. Thoroughly feminine 3-piece matched set fits Barbie, Tammy, Tressy and other dolls to 12 inches. Includes bed upholstered in floral printed plastic with pillow and spread; skirted dressing table in modern kidney shape and matching hassock.
Shipping weight 1 pound.
49 N 8449.......................Set $1.66

Barbie and Midge Travel Case. Holds everything a doll needs for an overnight trip. Smooth black vinyl with zipper top and handle. 6x10x7½ in. high. Shpg. wt. 1 lb. 6 oz.
49 N 8451 ..$1.66

Bendee Quintette Doll Set. 4 girls in pink bunting, 1 boy in blue. 3 have open eyes, 2 are sleeping. Vinyl faces with blond bangs. Each 7 in. long. Shipping weight 6 oz.
49N8450-Set $1.66

Wonder Corn Popper. Sounds real . . crackles, pops. Acts like a real corn popper. No batteries, no heat, nothing to wind. Real kernels, popped corn included. Shpg. wt. 11 oz.
49 N 8452...$1.66

BIG TOY VALUES

The kind you expect at Sears

$166 EACH

Tiny Tot Toy Set. All colorful wood. Has 7½-inch long pounding bench with hammer. 4½-inch stack, 8-inch roller, 14 beads with cord to string them on. Shpg. wt. 1 lb. 4 oz.
49 N 8453...$1.66

Fantabulous Paint Box Set. Includes 100 watercolors, good quality brush. Beautifully designed box 14¾x9¼ in. Mixing instructions. From England. Shpg. wt. 1 lb. 8 oz.
49 N 8455...$1.66

Wind-up Tractor. Climbs easily over obstacles, shooting off harmless sparks. Steel body, rubber treads. Clock-spring motor. Big key. 9½ inches long. Shipping wt. 1 lb. 4 oz.
49 N 8454...$1.66

Slinky Toys. Colorful items are made of flexible spring steel and styrene. Dog is 10 in. long. 12-in. long train has whistle. With pull cords.
49 N 8456—Slinky Dog. Wt. 1 lb......$1.66
49 N 8457—Slinky Train. Wt. 12 oz. .. 1.66

Amsco's Magic Gas Pump. Attach suction cup nozzle to car or truck. Turn handle and pump appears to feed gas into car. Pump refills automatically. Break-resistant plastic. 6½ in. high. Car not included. Wt. 12 oz.
49 N 8458...$1.66

Fill 'er up! Attach suction cup nozzle to car or truck

Fireman Set. Red fire hat with emblem; 12-in. extinguisher. 14-in. fire axe, siren whistle . . all flexible plastic. 6 "Fire" signs. Shpg. wt. 1 lb. 6 oz.
49 N 8459...$1.66

Card Table Tent. Fits all 30-inch square card tables. Made of embossed vinyl with green camouflage print. Front entrance flap forms canopy (canopy wood bracing incl.). Pyramid top. 30x30x36 inches high. Shpg. wt. 2 lbs. 4 oz.
49 N 8461......$1.66

Combat Soldier's Outfit. Cleverly camouflaged helmet; machine pistol, 7¾ in. long; 12 play bullets. Also canteen with cup; mess kit, knife, fork, spoon. All sturdy plastic. Shpg. wt. 1 lb. 2 oz.
49 N 8460....$1.66

*Build and move furniture,
design room settings
to suit your own taste*

INTERIOR
DECORATOR
SETS

Just for play, or for budding architects
and decorators . . hundreds of combinations
limited only by your imagination

Simply move wall panels to enlarge a room, put
cushions on benches or in chairs, combine chair
base with table top to have a coffee table . . it's
all up to you. Furniture is accurately scaled,
beautifully styled. Included are floors, paintings,
sculpture, lamps, even towels for the bathroom
. . all in House and Garden coordinated colors.
Every homemaker, be she six or sixty, will enjoy
letting her imagination run free to create her
dream rooms. A gift to delight the entire family.

5-piece
Doll Family
$1 33

This happy family is
designed to live in the
beautiful rooms on this
and facing page. Moth-
er, father, brother, sister
and dog are in correct
scale for rooms and
furniture. Colorful plas-
tic. From British Crown
Colony of Hong Kong.
Shipping wt. 3 oz.
49 N 1476. Box $1.33

236 separate pieces . .
enough furniture for 5 rooms
$7.99

Five rooms with furniture, all in coordinated colors from House and Garden magazine. Decorate rooms, design furniture in combinations you alone dream up. Interlocking plastic parts are interchangeable . . no glue or tools needed. Make tables, chairs, cabinets, fixtures. Decorated cardboard wall panels and floors, even fabric rugs, 5-piece doll family. About 39x10x6 inches high. Accurately scaled.
49 N 1469—Shipping weight 5 pounds 6 ounces.......................Set $7.99

Individual Room Sets

68-piece Dining Room Set. Ready to be transformed into a room handsomely furnished for dining. Has dining table with centerpiece, comfortable chairs and storage cabinets. About 10x 10x6 inches high.
49 N 1471—Shpg. wt. 1 lb. 11 oz... Set $2.99

64-piece Kitchen Set. With sink, range, refrigerator and cabinets . . even dishes and utensils to combine, interchange and enjoy. Set is excellent for pre-planning your real kitchen. About 10x 10x6 inches high.
49 N 1472—Shpg. wt. 1 lb. 11 oz... Set $2.99

62-piece Bedroom Set. Watch room take shape before your eyes . . with cabinets, shelves, beds that can be varied, even stacked to form bunk beds. Includes walls, floor, lamps, too. About 10x10x6 inches high.
49 N 1473—Shpg. wt. 1 lb. 12 oz... Set $2.99

43-piece Bathroom Set. A fabulous family-size bathroom in minutes. Has basin, tub, shower and dozens of other pieces—all in House and Garden magazine colors. Walls and floor included. About 10x10x6 inches high.
49 N 1474—Shpg. wt. 1 lb. 10 oz... Set $2.99

94-piece Living Room Set. Has a fireplace, modern chairs, wall cabinets, tables and 6x10-in. step-up floor. About 19½x10x6 in. high. Wt. 2 lbs. 1 oz.
49 N 1470.... Set $3.33

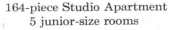

164-piece Studio Apartment
5 junior-size rooms $4.99

Lovely, livable studio apartment designed in scale . . walls, floors, furniture and accessories of great charm. Dozens of different arrangements possible as many pieces interlock . . no tools or glue needed. An exciting lesson in color, taste and homemaking for future decorators. About 19½x10x6 in. high. Architectural scale ¾ inch equals 1 foot.
49 N 1475—Shipping weight 3 lbs. 6 oz...... Set $4.99

Up to five can talk on the new Multi-phone operating Switchboard

Dial numbers .. ring bells .. plug in phone-to-phone calls
Board automatically lights to show which phone is calling

A Sears exclusive **$11⁴⁴** without batteries

Talk room-to-room. As operator, you can plug in and connect any extension phone with other extensions. Signal and ring any extension phone just by pushing the proper switchboard key.

Operator's phone with removable headband, plus one extension pink dial phone included with 11x9x6-inch switchboard. All sturdy plastic. Order 4 "D" batteries below. (For extra extensions, order any of the dial phones at bottom of page.)

49 N 2275—Shipping weight 3 lbs. 10 oz...$11.44

$6⁶⁶ without batteries

Play Switchboard

Press button on phone to talk .. pull switch to ring bell on board

Phone a friend in another room .. or un-plug both phones from switchboard and use outdoors as Walkie-Talkies. 4 bell-ringing switches, 4 dummy plugs on 11x9x 5¾-in. plastic switchboard. Message pad, operator's dial. Order 2 "D" batteries below and 2 "C" batteries at right. (Extra phone can be used; order 49N2091 at right.)

49 N 2276—Wt. 2 lbs. 14 oz..... $6.66

Hand Phones for 2-way talking

$3⁷⁹ without batteries

High-impact plastic receivers really work. Push button to buzz for attention. Both 8 in. long. 2 wall hangers, 25-ft. wire. Order 2 "C" batteries below. Shipping weight 1 pound.

49 N 2091........ Set $3.79
"C" Battery. Shpg. wt. each 2 oz.
49 N 4665—2 for 32c; 4 for 60c

Walkie-Talkie for 2-way secrets

$2³⁷

Great way for friends to keep in contact from room to room or attic to basement in your own home. The 25 feet of wire allows "long distance" calls. Two red plastic receivers are each 8½ inches long. No batteries needed. Wt. 1 lb. 1 oz.

49 N 1967........ Set $2.37

Remco's 2-way Wrist Radio

$3⁴⁴ without battery

Important messages come in loud and clear. Two-way voice plus 1-way secret code buzzer and click transmission. Order 1 "C" battery at left. Includes 2 plastic wrist radios, and 25 feet of wire.

49 N 1955—Wt. 1 lb.$3.44

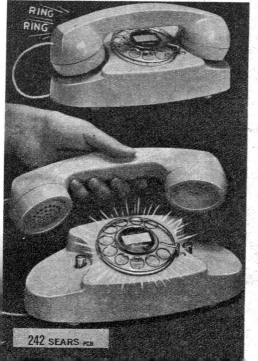

Have your own Private Phone System

Set of two, pink or blue **$6⁸⁸** without batteries

Lift receiver .. dial lights up. Dial number .. other phone rings.

Now your little girl can talk for hours with her friends on her very own phone set—without tying up your line. No extra phone bills to pay, either. These authentic-size phones come in charming pastel colors. Voices transmit clearly, loudly. You get 2 plastic dial phones with 8½-inch receivers, 30 foot communication wire. Order 4 "D" batteries below.

Shipping weight 2 lbs. 4 oz.
49 N 6320—Pink......... Set $6.88
49 N 6321—Blue......... Set 6.88

"D" Battery. Shpg. wt. each 4 oz.
49 N 4660........2 for 32c; 4 for 60c

Gay red or blue as well as black

$6⁶⁶ without batteries

Send your voice over 30 feet .. other phone rings, light comes on

Such distinct, loud voice transmission over long distances .. you'll be amazed. These colorful sets let you talk between offices or rooms, indoors or outside.

Other phone rings as you dial. Push button, light goes on. Set consists of two phones (receivers 8 in. long, plastic bases 4 in. high), plus 30 feet of connecting wire. Batteries not included; order 4 "D" batteries at left.

49 N 6383—Black   49 N 6386—Red   49 N 6358—Blue
Shipping weight 2 pounds 6 ounces............Set $6.66

Set type, print your own newspapers, signs, posters, cards

BIG PRESS
by IDEAL
$9⁹⁹

Have your own printing shop. The Big Press is simple to operate . . just set up your type and place it in the press. Then turn the crank and the type becomes inked. Push the lever and the paper moves into the press to become imprinted—like on a real shop press. Ruggedly built of sturdy plastic . . beautifully designed to turn out printed materials of all kinds.

Prints on 5x8-in. paper. Comes complete with all the equipment you need . . 2 sets of type, tweezers for setting type, a typeholder, ink, blank paper, three 6x6-in. printing plates for comic illustrations. Machine is 19x10x11 in. high.

Shipping weight 7 pounds.
79 N 1648L $9.99

All Metal Printing Press $3⁶⁶

Prints red and black programs, ads, notices, etc. 3½x5½ in. long. 200 pieces of rubber type, red and black inks, tweezers for type-setting, 25 postcard-size sheets of paper, additional ink cylinder with ribbon attached, 2 rubber picture dies, tools.
49 N 1713—Shpg. wt. 2 lbs...$3.66

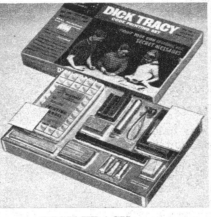

DICK TRACY Code Printing Set $4⁹⁹

Devise your own secret code. Metal printer's type to print stationery, notices, badges in black, red or invisible ink. Wood code-maker, type case, roller, paper, cards, manual.
49 N 1816—Wt. 4 lbs. 6 oz. $4.99
49 N 1834—Small letters. Wt.1 lb. Pkg. 1.99
49 N 1835—Extra Ink. Wt. 9 oz. 99c
49 N 1840—3 photo dies. Wt. 8 oz. Pkg.69c

Make the news yourself with EMENEE'S
HEADLINE PRINTER $4⁴⁴

Put out your own special newspaper edition. Announce birthdays, school or sports events. Type, type case, headline printer frame, type press, ink applicator, ink, 20 pre-printed 11x15-inch newspaper sheets with headlines blank.
79 N 1642C—Shipping weight 5 pounds $4.44
49 N 1643—Extra ink, 20 newspapers. Wt. 1 lb. 2 oz. Pkg. 88c

Artist's Easel $4⁹⁹

1 Red and black Mickey Mouse Art Easel grows with young artist . . all the way up to 69 in. high. Sketch board doubles as blackboard. Steel tripod. Brush, board clip, 6 bottles water colors.
79 N 1823L—Wt. 8 lbs.$4.99

Water Colors 97ᶜ

2 Learn to blend colors. 80 quick-drying colors; brush.
49 N 1619—Wt. 1 lb. 3 oz. . .97c

Crayons $1.29

3 64 in colorfully decorated 4x6-in. steel box.
49 N 1684—Wt. 1 lb. 8 oz.$1.29

Colorola $1⁶⁹

4 Keeps youngsters busy, at home, in car, in sickbed. Color, wipe off, color again. 3 re-color rolls, each with 8-panel story. Crayons and sponge eraser. Red plastic case with handle. 9½x11 in.
49N1689—Wt.1 lb.6 oz.$1.69

Melt 'n Color $3⁹⁹

5 Applicator melts crayons to finish outline pictures included. Crayons, 3 plastic frames. UL listed, 110–120 v, 60-c. AC. Wt. 2 lbs. 10 oz.
49 N 1859 . . . .$3.99

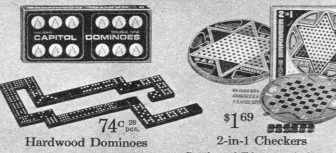

Hardwood Dominoes

74c 28 pcs.

28-piece set. Plays up to double 6's.
49 N 361—Shpg. wt. 11 oz. . . .74c

55-piece set. Plays up to double 9's.
49 N 398—Shpg. wt. 1 lb. 4 oz. .$1.44

91-piece set. Plays up to double 12's.
49 N 323—Wt. 1 lb. 8 oz. . . .$1.95

2-in-1 Checkers

$1.69

Regular and Chinese . . paired in one 2-sided metal board. Thin as a magazine. Packs its own playing pieces right inside. 60 marbles, 24 checkers. 15½-in. diam. For 2 to 6 players. Shipping wt. 2 lbs. 14 oz.
49 N 399 . . . . Set $1.69

Bridg-It

$1.77

Fast-moving game for two, with the fun and skill of chess and checkers. Build a bridge across board; your opponent tries to block your moves. Ages 6 to adult.
49 N 373—Wt. 1 lb. 4 oz. . . $1.77

Stadium Checkers

$1.99

Marbles shift as players spin plastic rings. First to sink 5 marbles in center wins. Takes skill to move without helping opponents. Stadium, 20 marbles. 2 to 4 players. Ages 8 up.
49 N 156—Shpg. wt. 1 lb. . .$1.99

Fascination

$2.96 without batteries

Get through maze, light up towers first. 2 double-sided mazes, 6 steel balls. Order 2 "C" batteries below.
49 N 106—Wt. 2 lbs. $2.96

"C" Battery. Shpg. wt. ea. 2 oz.
49 N 4665 . . .2 for 32c; 4 for 60c

High Gear

$3.97

Teaches simple principles of gear mechanics. First player advancing all 4 of his pegs from low to high gear wins. Includes 16x16-in. plastic board with colorful gears, 20 plastic pegs. Shpg. wt. 3 lbs. 12 oz.
49 N 290C $3.97

Kookie Chicks game

$2.29

Exciting action for ages 5 to 12. Maneuver plastic chickens with magnetic wand . . they twirl and wobble, bumping plastic eggs all around 14x 11-in. board and into nest. 2 players.
49 N 431—Shpg. wt. 1 lb. . .$2.29

POW! Cannon game $2.32

Game of skill for ages 5 to 12. Toy soldiers on either side of barrier, moved forward, backward as spinner directs. Spring-loaded plastic cannons knock down opponent's soldiers.
49 N 416—Wt. 2 lbs. $2.32

crazy clock game
by Ideal

Wackiest way to get a man out of bed .. clock starts all the crazy action

$3.87

All-time record for generating amusement and amazement. 2 to 4 players play with a deck of cards that indicate which part each player is to assemble. Player who holds the last card wins the chance to snap the key on the clock . . the clock pushes the broom into the cat . . on and on in a wacky series of crazy happenings . . until the sleeping man leaps out of bed. All plastic pieces.
79 N 231C—Shipping weight 4 pounds $3.87

mouse trap game
by Ideal

Catch "mice" with wildest trap ever

$3.87

Dice determines move. Land on white, add part to plastic trap. When built, turn crank, ball rolls down into plumbing to make men dive into pool, and drop trap. Last mouse left wins. 2 to 4 players. Ages 7 and up.
79 N 293C—Wt. 4 lbs. . .$3.87

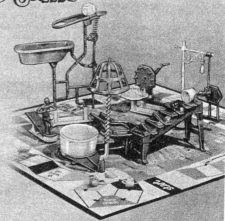

Time Bomb creates excitement as players try to get rid of it before it goes "bang"

$2.27

Try a fast game of "catch" with this exciting toy. One player sets timer, tosses Bomb to next player. Get rid of it before it goes BANG! Player holding bomb is eliminated. 5-inch black plastic bomb is break resistant.
49 N 206—Wt. 1 lb. $2.27

By 1965, nearly every TV show and movie with any kind of kid appeal had a board game designed after it. The 1965 Wishbook offered a "Mary Poppins" game, as well as games based on "Bewitched" and "The Patty Duke Show." There was a Barbie board game, too, as well as one based on The Beatles which promised "lots of swingin' action!"

If you wanted to spin some platters while playing your board games, a fully transistorized record player was only $19.66 and it came with five hit records..."all big names, all teen favorites."

Since the fifties, the Sears Wishbooks had offered toy ovens that actually worked, but several improved items came along in 1965. The Jr. Chef Cookie Factory baked cookies on a conveyor belt, and the Big Electric Oven baked "bigger cakes than other ovens." But the big seller that year was Kenner's Easy-Bake oven. It not only baked cakes, cookies and candy, it popped corn, too!

And in the most bizarre addition to the world of Little Girl Fashion, were four plastic wigs. Selling for $1.88 each, these "wigs" offered four different styles in four different colors in molded plastic. "Ready to wear," the copy said, rather unnecessarily, "without combing."

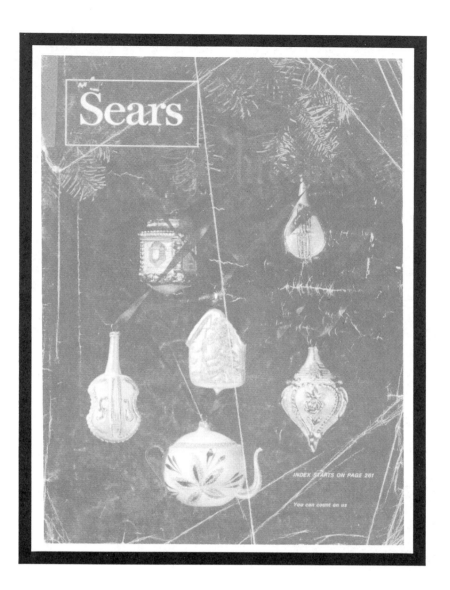

Sears Christmas
Wishbook

1965

Let magic spinner direct your play. Stop at carpetbags, umbrellas, as you race from Cherry Tree Lane to Park

Save this catalog . . you can order toys on pages 441 to 673 from now until Sept. 1, 1966

$1⁹⁷
Mary Poppins Game

Bert and Mary team up on opposite ends of Magic Spinner to guide you along this fantasy path. Simply ask one or the other directions, then make move indicated. Beware of delays caused by Birdwoman, Uncle Albert and such. Includes board, magic spinner, 4 plastic playing pieces and full instructions for 2 to 4 players.
49 N 460—Shpg. wt. 1 lb. 10 oz. $1.97

Patty Duke Game $1⁸⁹

Join TV's look-alike cousins in this contest to match the Patty and Cathy cards as you travel round the board. All it takes is a little luck, skill and memory. Ages 7 to 14.
49 N 458—Shpg. wt. 1 lb. 12 oz. $1.89

Barbie Game $2⁸⁶

Play your cards right and you, as Barbie, can be elected Queen of the Prom. You'll shop, spend play money, have parties to win title. Includes board, dice, cards. 2-4 players.
49 N 222—Shpg. wt. 1 lb. 12 oz. $2.86

The Beatles $2²²

Be John, Paul, George or Ringo and race around the board trying to be first to acquire game cards associated with your Beatle. Lots of swingin' action as you gain, lose, trade cards. For 2 to 4 players, 7-14 yrs., who like the "yeah, yeah" fun of Beatles.
49 N 387—Shpg. wt. 1 lb. 9 oz. $2.22

Bewitched $1⁵⁷

Ever found a tiger at your door? It can happen when you play this bewitching game. As you're trying to reach Vacation Land first, you'll have to watch out for the antics of Samantha and Endora. 2 to 4 players, ages 6 to 12.
49 N 389—Shpg. wt. 1 lb. 12 oz. $1.57

Game of Life $4³²

With car and $2000, start up 3-D road of life. Make the right decisions, and the "Wheel of Fate" may spin you into Millionaire Acres as winner. 24-inch board, 8 cars, $7 million in play money, cards, certificates. 2 to 8 players, ages 10 years and up.
79 N 169C—Shpg. wt. 4 lbs. $4.32

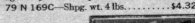

Concentration $2⁹⁷

A real memory-tester of a game. Match items behind numbers to solve picture-word puzzles. Each match exposes more until you guess what picture says and win "cash" cards. 60 puzzles, 30 plastic slides. 2-5 players, age 10-adult.
49 N 298—Shpg. wt. 1 lb. 12 oz. $2.97

The Match Game $2⁹⁹

Extra-sensory perception would really come in handy to win this fun game. Write down most likely answer to questions with many correct answers . . only a match wins. 550 questions in all. For 3-7 matcher-uppers, ages 10 to adult.
49 N 283—Shpg. wt. 1 lb. 12 oz. $2.99

Tripoley $1⁸⁸

Red, white and green vinyl plastic layout turns any table top into perfect base for Hearts, Poker or Michigan Rummy. It's 27x27 inches. Keeps 2 to 9 players interested for hours. Cards and poker chips not included.
49 N 358—Shpg. wt. 1 lb. $1.88

4 push buttons switch cars to inner or outer lanes . . think fast or the gangsters will be chasing you

Tip-It

$2⁷⁷

Remove discs for points but don't topple man on the

The most fantastic, most breathtaking game of balancing skill. Watch the man balance on his nose as he weaves back and forth 2 feet high. Spin the dial to learn which color discs to remove . . use "scooper" to slip them off peg—without upsetting the little man. Get discs totaling 100 points to win. For 2 to 4 players. Ages 7 and up.

Shpg. wt. 1 lb. 8 oz.
49 N 158......$2.77

$7⁸⁸ without batteries

Good guys chase bad guys in motorized cars

Getaway Chase Game

Battery-run 1932 Ford police car races full tilt after gangsters in a 1931 Duesenberg. They speed through city streets, take shortcuts by zipping around buildings. Each player controls his car by pressing buttons on panel. Just tag bumper of other car to score. 32x24-in. plastic layout snaps together. 3-dimensional cardboard buildings. Plastic cars about 4½ inches. Order 2 "C" batteries.

79 N 159C—Shipping weight 6 lbs.....$7.88
"C" Battery. Shipping weight each 2 oz.
79 N 4665.............Each 16c; 4 for 60c

$1⁶⁷

Road Race Skill Drive Game
with magnetic remote steering

Dare-devil thrills . . compete with opponents . . race against time. Operate car by magnetic remote control . . steer it over 2 different courses. 21 pieces including cars, road blocks, bridges, tunnels. Course about 15x11 in.

49 N 305—Shpg. wt. 1 lb. 8 oz.......$1.67

$5⁹⁷

Cars vibrate around this
4-lane Electric Road Race

Thrills . . chills . . spills as plastic cars race on vibrating track . . through tight turns and crossovers. Hardboard base, steel frame. 28x15 in. wide. Plugs into any 110-120-volt, 60-cycle AC outlet. UL listed.

79 N 417C—Shipping weight 5 lbs.....$5.97

$1⁶⁶

NFL Football Game

All the excitement of "Pro" football strategy . . quarterback each play, spin dial and move as yardage chart directs. "Pro" rules and scoring. 18x18-inch board, 3 pawns, 10-yard marker.
49 N 242—Shpg. wt. 1 lb. 12 oz.......$1.66

$1⁹⁷

Magnetic Pee Wee Hockey

Players use two magnetic hockey sticks to shoot or block puck that's enclosed in 17x10 inch plastic rink. 10 goals win. Keep score with magnetic balls.
49 N 258—Shpg. wt. 1 lb. 8 oz.......$1.97

$4⁶⁶

Bats fly out without warning . . catch 'em in your monster claw

Bats in Your Belfry

Wait in spooky suspense for bats to fly out of castle tower . . steel ball drops into belfry to trigger mechanism. Confuse your opponents by pressing your "skunker skull" . . repeats or changes action. 15-in. sturdy castle, 10 bats, tokens, 2 claws. For 1 to 4 players. Ages 6 to 12.
49 N 238—Shpg. wt. 3 lbs. 8 oz.....$4.66

Come Alive!

You're in the swingin' generation with Sears own

Fully Transistorized Record Player

Leather-look plastic case goes everywhere in style

$19⁶⁶

Electronic amplifier and top-mounted speaker fill the room with lively music. Tone control and volume control let you tune in the sound you like best. Dual, permanent-type synthetic sapphire needle and high-gain crystal pickup to give you the truest tones. Tone arm balanced and turntable rubber cushioned to assure "kid-glove" treatment for all your 16, 33⅓, 45 and 78 RPM records. Super-silent motor. Break-resistant polypropylene case 14x13x7 inches.
49 N 680—Shpg. wt. 7 lbs. 10 oz.......$19.66

plus 5 Hit Records ..
all big names, all teen favorites

Wow! Wait till you hear these 45 RPM discs cut by Herman's Hermits, Dion, The Beatles, Gene Pitney and The Four Seasons .. all included with above phonograph.

NOTE: Both phonographs on this page UL listed for 110-120 volts, 60 cycle AC.

THE BEATLES

GENE PITNEY

HERMAN'S HERMITS

DION

THE FOUR SEASONS

Instant play .. no warm-up needed ..
4-speed, solid state Portable Phonograph

Fully transistorized so there are no tubes to replace.
Full-range sound delivered by front-mounted speaker

$23⁹⁹

Set the Dial-O-Matic speed selector to play any 16, 33⅓, 45 or 78 RPM record. Heavy-duty amplifier, high-gain crystal pickup and permanent-type synthetic sapphire needle to give you a true, clear tone. Volume and tone control knobs let you set the sound to get ear-pleasing music that you and your friends like best.

Precision tone arm with flip cartridge expertly balanced for delicate record treatment. Whisper-quiet motor. Scuff-resistant pyroxylin-coated case elegantly styled in yellow and sandalwood shades. Smart inverted-design front-mounted speaker. Case 14x13x6 inches high.
79 N 672C—Shipping wt. 10 lbs...$23.99

No Money Down on anything Sears sells

Add water to mix, fill cookie press . . . and bake golden brown heart, star or animal cookies . . then frost and decorate them

..Eat 'em up

Jr. Chef Cookie Factory with electric oven and moving conveyor belt $9⁸⁸

When you turn the sand timer, conveyor automatically moves cookies through steel oven. With 8 mixes, cookie press, cookie decorator, 14 utensils, easy-to-read recipe book. Plastic, 20x7½x5 inches.
79 N 1131C—Shipping weight 6 pounds. $9.88
49 N 1138—12-pc. Cookie Mix Refill Set. Wt. 1 lb. 2 oz. 1.97

Whip up drinks,
cake batters
Electric Mixer
$6⁸⁸

Works like a big portable mixer. Makes frothy milk shakes . . beats cake and cookie batters. With mixer blade, 2 egg-beater blades, bowl, measuring spoon, recipes. 8 in. high with blades. Wt. 2 lbs. 10 oz.
49 N 1268. . . . . . . $6.88

Soft plastic blades are safer

Food Mix Set $2⁹⁹

From 16 individual box mixes you can bake and frost 3 cakes, make pancakes, cookies, pudding, gingerbread, pie, lots more. Also 16 baking utensils including pans, cookie sheets, cutters. Recipes.
49 N 1214—Shpg. wt. 2 lbs. $2.99

Extra Mixes $1⁴⁹

Re-stock the junior pantry with 12 refills—2 cake and frosting mixes, pancakes, pie, biscuits, gingerbread, and cookies. Wt. 1 lb. 2 oz.
49 N 1249. . . . . . $1.49

$9⁷⁷

Magic-Cool Electric Oven

Knobs move pan to oven—hands stay away from heat. Takes pans up to 4 inch

Put pan in open-loading chamber . . it automatically feeds into oven. Child never touches heated portion of oven (outside temperature never exceeds a warm 100°F.) Double window lets cook watch foods. When done, twist knob and pan slides into cooling chamber. Heavy gauge metal with porcelain ceramic and wire heating element. 11x10x6 inches deep. With 6 food mixes, 8 utensils and cook book.
49 N 1222—Shipping weight 8 pounds. $9.77

Easy-Bake Oven . . now with corn popper
$13³³

Pour corn in popper, push in knob. Corn pops in enclosed oven (window lets you watch the action). Pull knob out, corn empties automatically into bowl. Oven and cooling chamber takes pans up to 4 in. Bakes cakes, pizza, candy, etc. With 12 mixes, 3 bags of popcorn, 2 caramel syrup mixes, 3 baking pans, 4 utensils, recipe book. High-impact plastic, 14x12x7 in. deep. Uses two 100-watt bulbs, not included. Shipping weight 9 lbs.
79 N 1186L $13.33

Big Electric Oven with thermostat .. takes pans to 7 in.

$14⁹⁹

Bakes bigger cakes than other ovens. Heats from 200° to 400°. Fiber glass insulation. Double glass window. Steel, 11½x12 x13 in. high. Shipping weight 18 lbs.
79 N 1226L . . $14.99

You can order toys from pages 441 to 673 from this catalog until Sept. 1, 1966

NOTE: *Electrical items on page UL listed, 110- 120-volt, 60-cycle AC.*

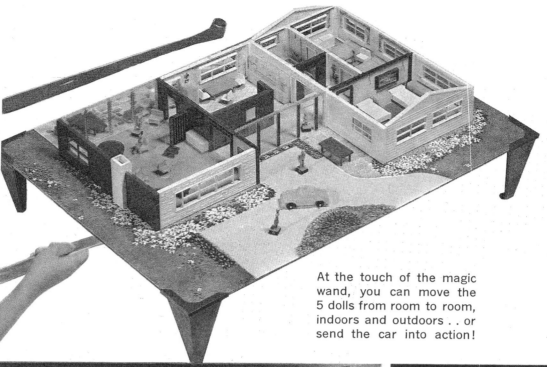

Magnetic Doll House
$3⁸⁴

Point a Magic Mover wand, and the magnetized doll family glides into motion without being touched. Open roof lets you watch the action. Modern 5-room house with over 40 pieces of furniture and accessories can be arranged many ways. Set includes 15 walls, 5 dolls and a snappy little car. 36x20-inch Masonite Presdwood base, colorfully decorated with driveway, walk, landscaping. 4 sturdy plastic legs. Two plastic wands included. Partly assembled. Easily sets up on table or on floor. Shipping weight 6 lbs.
79 N 1433C..........$3.84

Save this catalog . . . you can order toys on pages 441 to 673 from now until Sept. 1, 1966

At the touch of the magic wand, you can move the 5 dolls from room to room, indoors and outdoors .. or send the car into action!

Spacious fully furnished Colonial Doll House with electric light, front door that opens ..

$5⁹⁷ without battery

Admire simulated wrought iron grillwork, porch. Open door, flick on living room light, see enchanting interior. Rumpus room with table-tennis set and TV, living-dining room, kitchen, bathroom and 2 bedrooms. 32 pieces of plastic furniture; 4-doll family. Steel house, about 26x14½x15½-in. high. Unassembled. Uses one "D" battery, order below.
79 N 1410C—Shipping weight 8 pounds.......................$5.97
79 N 4660—"D" Battery. Shipping wt. each 4 oz..Each 16c; 4 for 60c

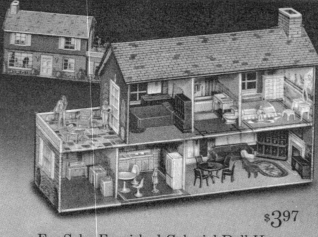

For Sale: Furnished Colonial Doll House with sundeck. The purchase price is low

$3⁹⁷

One of the best buys in toytown real estate. Classic Colonial house has a spacious living-dining room with stereo set, fully equipped kitchen and utility room with appliances, 2 bedrooms, bathroom .. even a sundeck. Complete with 30 pieces of plastic furniture and accessories. 4-doll family eager to move in. Tastefully decorated house, of steel, is about 24¾x8x16 inches high. Unassembled.
79 N 1458C—Shipping weight 7 pounds.................$3.97

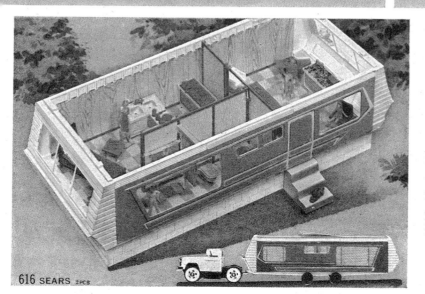

You're free to roam in this furnished MOBILE HOME with truck tractor

$8⁹⁹ Fully assembled home and tractor | $6⁹⁹ Mobile home only (unassembled)

Travel the countryside or set up housekeeping in a trailer court with this modern mobile home. Free-wheeling polyethylene truck tractor moves the trailer wherever you like. Colorful plastic furniture can be taken apart and rearranged in designs you alone dream up. You can make various style chairs, tables, stools .. parts interlock; no glue or tools needed. Frames for walls can be moved to vary the size of rooms. Roof with skylight removes for playtime. Transparent plastic windows give the doll family (included) a view of the outdoors. Tiny flowerpots add cheer to the front windows. Trailer with tractor about 38½x10x9 in. high. Trailer is brightly decorated, high-impact plastic and heavy paper chipboard.
79 N 1412L—Shipping weight 8 pounds.................$8.99
79 N 1480C—Mobile home only. (28 in. long). Wt. 4 lbs... 6.99

Just say "Charge it" when you phone your order

Show movies again and again .. no threading, no rewinding

Set includes movies of Casper, Popeye, Bozo, Dick Tracy, Alvin, Mr. Ed

Just snap in cartridge and turn handle to show movies anywhere

Kenner's EASY-SHOW MOVIE PROJECTOR

$4⁶⁹ without batteries

High impact plastic, precision lens, crank. 9x6x2 in. Incl. 6 black and white movies on 3 continuous-loop snap-in cartridges. *Order 3 "D" batteries below.*
49 N 1656—Shipping weight 2 pounds...........................$4.69

4 Extra Films. Magoo, Munsters, Lone Ranger and Superman.
49 N 1748—Wt. 6 oz..Pkg. $1.69

4 Extra Films. Lassie, Roy Rogers, 3 Stooges, Rocky and Bullwinkle.
49 N 1753—Wt. 6 oz....Pkg. $1.69

112 glorious-color slide scenes

Kenner's GIVE-A-SHOW $3⁸⁸ without batteries

Laugh at the antics of your cartoon friends in 16 all-new shows with top TV stars including the Flintstones, Yogi Bear, Magilla Gorilla and many more. Each show complete on strip of seven 35mm. slides. Projects a picture 5 feet square. Projector measures about 9x2x6 in. Ages 3 to 8. *Order 3 "D" batteries.*
49 N 1842—Wt. 1 lb. 11 oz.... $3.88

Extra Kenner Shows. Each set has 84 color slides for 12 shows.
49 N 1830—Flintstones, etc.
49 N 1831—Roy Rogers, etc.
49 N 1832—Huckleberry Hound, etc.
49 N 1833—Popeye, etc.
Shpg. wt. each 8 oz....Set $1.66

"D" Battery. Shpg. wt. each 4 oz.
49 N 4660.........16c; 4 for 60c

Save this catalog .. you can order toys on pages 441 to 673 from now until Sept. 1, 1966

Dim lights, aim and "shoot" color pictures of comic strip adventures on most any surface

Flashy Flickers by MARX $3⁸⁸ without batteries

"Shoots" big 4x4-foot pictures. Includes 4 color film strips with 29 scenes in each. Projector 15x7 in. *Order 3 "D" batteries below.*
49 N 1640—Shipping weight 1 pound 9 ounces..........$3.88
49 N 1757—Six Extra Film Strips. Shpg. wt. 5 oz....Pkg. 1.09

$6⁷⁴

Show 3 Mary Poppins and 7 Disney favorites with Tru-Vue Electric Projection Theatre

See 70 color pictures on 11x14-in. screen or up to 3-ft. wide image on wall. Plastic viewer to preview shows, 6x4x5-in. projector with 30-watt bulb, F3 focus lens. 110–120-v., 60-c. AC-DC UL listed.
49 N 1758—Shipping weight 2 pounds..................$6.74

Pkg. of 70 Disneyland Pictures.
49 N 1759—Wt. 4 oz.. $1.66

Pkg. of 70 Casper Pictures.
49 N 1771—Wt. 4 oz... $1.66

Project your own shows without slides or film

Super Show by Kenner

$5⁸⁸

Now you can enlarge small objects like butterflies, seashells, coins, pictures to a big 4x4-foot projection. Make up your own shows .. inspect stamp collections. Just slip objects onto 36-in. square playing area. See them magnified in full-color detail. Uses one 100-watt bulb (not incl.). 110–120-v., 60c. AC. UL listed.
49 N 1733C—Shipping weight 4 pounds.................$5.88

See famous TV characters "come alive" in full color

Stereo Slide Viewer

$1⁴⁸

Alvin and the Chipmunks, Dennis the Menace, Linus and his friends and many more of your favorite TV cartoon characters seem to pop into life in full-color 3-dimensional pictures. 15 complete shows . 105 stereo scenes. Viewer 4x2x2 in. Ready to go—no bulb or battery needed. Wt. 8 oz.
49 N 1801....... $1.48

Dress like
Mary Poppins
of movie
fame

$4⁸⁹

$4⁸⁹

$3⁷⁹

$4⁸⁹

$5⁸⁹

Visiting Nurse. Styled for the "pretend" nurse who travels. Crisp cotton belted uniform shrinkage controlled. Cotton cape with insignia. Shoulder bag. State S, M, L; see size chart on opposite page. Wt. 1 lb.
49 N 799F...... $3.79

Drum Majorette .. lead the way in high-stepping costume of rayon satin as the band marches on. Hat, baton, belt, tasseled boot tops. State S, M, L; see size chart on opposite page. Wt. 1 lb. 12 oz.
49 N 829F.... $4.89

Evening Gown. Brocade-look rayon taffeta with sheer nylon yoke. Stole, tiara, evening bag. Elegantly styled for important occasions. State S, M, L; see size chart on opposite page. Shpg. wt. 1 lb.
49 N 813F.... $4.89

Dance, Ballerina, Dance in elasticized acetate satin outfit. 3-tier nylon tutu overskirt. State S, M, L; see size chart on opposite page. Shpg. wt. 12 oz.
49 N 820F...... $5.89

Dance, sing, even look like Mary Poppins. Perky rayon dress with ruffles, bodice-effect, print skirt. Bonnet, parasol. Makes you want to fly and fly .. all the way to Cherry Tree Lane. Carpetbag (not included) sold on page 621. State S, M, L; see size chart on opposite page. Shpg. wt. 1 lb. 4 oz.
49 N 819F............. $4.89

"It's SUPERMAN!"

$4⁸⁹

$6⁸⁹

$5⁹⁹

$4⁸⁹

Marine Sergeant. Shrinkage controlled cotton. Includes cap, belt, insignia. Elastic back on trousers. State S, M, L. Wt. 1 lb. 7 oz.
49 N 837F...... $6.89

Highway Trooper. Shrinkage controlled cotton. Plastic cap, gun, goggles. Metal badge, whistle, handcuffs. State S, M, L. Wt. 1 lb. 12 oz.
49 N 827F......... $5.99

Superman .. no mistaking him as he speeds to the rescue in his suit and cape of Sanforized® cotton, max. shrinkage 1%. A real trim, ready-for-action look. State S, M, L; see size chart on facing page. Wt. 1 lb. $4.89
49N730F—Wt. 1 lb. $4.89

Batman .. comes alive and ready to fight crime when he wears this washable cotton outfit. Shirt, pants, cape, hood, mask. State S, M, L.
49N807F—Wt. 1 lb. $4.89

Elegant "dress-ups" made just for her

Magnificent 40-inch Stole and 3-piece dress-up Set

$2⁶⁶

Every little girl adores jewels and the fur look. Grant her wish with this elegant stole of deep-pile rayon and cotton with rayon lining. Plastic ring, simulated pearls and orchid pin add glamour.

49 N 1360—Shpg. wt. 1 lb. 2 oz...$2.66

Muff, Headband, Jewels .. little girl luxuries

$1⁷⁷

Prettiest dress-ups ever .. deep pile printed plush fabric headband made of rayon and cotton and matching muff look like fur. Rayon satin lined. Simulated pearls, matching bracelet, poodle pin.

49 N 1430—Shpg. wt. 6 oz.....$1.77

Little girls love to wear Wigs, too

Look like real hair $2⁹⁷

Pixie-type styles of Saran and acetate feel like real hair, have soft luster and sheen. She'll love combing, setting and restyling her wig. Elastic band inside for snug fit. With red bow. Shpg. wt. 8 oz.

49 N 1353—Platinum blonde.....$2.97
49 N 1358—Ginger blonde.......2.97

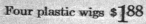

Four plastic wigs $1⁸⁸

A change of a wig .. she can be a top-knotted brunette, a sophisticated blonde, a dramatic redhead, or Cleopatra with jet black hair. Styled in soft plastic, ready to wear without combing, fit smoothly on girls 3 to 8.

49 N 1356—Shpg. wt. 12 oz. Set $1.88

Waiting for her car and escort

Formal Outfit **$2⁹⁹**

For those "formal" dress-up occasions every little girl loves, a long flame red acetate taffeta gown with matching bag. Pretty hat, artificial orchid corsage, ring and necklet complete the outfit. Shoes not incl. Dress sizes S(1–4), M(5–7), L(8–10). *State size* S, M or L.
Shipping weight 8 oz.
49 N 1281F...Set $2.99

Here comes the radiant bride

Bridal Outfit **$3⁹⁷**

A costume to dream about. Acetate taffeta gown, long nylon net train with a finger loop to hold, and a luxurious lace-trimmed nylon net veil. Extras too .. glitter mitts, wedding band ring, corsage, bridal bouquet, a lacy hanky. Dress sizes S(1–4), M(5–7), L(8–10). *State size* S, M or L. Shpg. wt. 8 oz.
49 N 1431F......$3.97

Musical Purse $2⁹⁷

A love of a handbag in patent-leather-like plastic, with a Swiss music box to play a delightful tune when the purse is opened. Has snap closing. 6½x4½x3 inches wide.

49 N 1432—Shpg. wt. 1 lb..$2.97

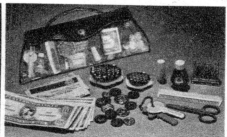

Mommy's Purse $2²²

All the things that make mommy's purse so interesting. Play money, pill box, credit cards, cosmetics, and more. Black patent-look vinyl, 15x5¾ inches, with clear front, gold-color metal chain.

49 N 1306—Shipping wt. 15 oz...$2.22

High-heeled Shoes

$1⁹⁹

Made extra strong with steel shanks in arch. Shoe sizes S (8–10), M (11–13), L (1–3). *State* S, M, L. Wt. pr. 12 oz.

1 Red straps, flower center.
49 N 1388F......$1.99
2 Red-tipped rayon plush.
49 N 1389F......$1.99
3 Striped, with red heel straps.
49 N 1391F......$1.99

Our strongest Shoes

$2⁹⁹

4 Gleaming gold and silver color. Strong steel shank arch plus thick innersole and arch liner. *State size* S, M, or L (see above).
49 N 1365F—Shpg. wt. 12 oz. $2.99

Ready-to-Sew Wardrobes

Sew a wardrobe for your favorite doll .. the easy way. Each outfit is pre-cut and ready to sew. Even buttons, thread, trim are included with all these sets

54-piece Fashion Set for Barbie, Tammy, Mary Poppins, 12-in. dolls

It's more fun to dress a doll in clothes you make yourself. Set includes school, party and holiday dresses, blouse, skirt, pajamas, panties, shoes, belts, gloves, other accessories, plus needles, thread, instructions. Easy to sew.
49 N 1262—Shipping weight 6 oz.... Set $2.44

Dolls not included with wardrobes

44-pc. Trousseau Set

Sew for Barbie, Tammy, Tressy, Midge, other 11½-in. dolls. Taffeta and flocked nylon net bridal gown, veil, two dresses, panties, shoes, belt, gloves, purse. Needles, thread and instructions.
49N1455—Wt. 6 oz...Set $2.44

80-pc. Boy doll Set

Makes wardrobe to fit Ken, Alan, other 12-inch dolls. Sport shirt, jacket, tuxedo with accessories, pajamas, shoes, more. Needle, thread, instructions included. Wt. 7 oz.
49 N 1263......Set $2.44

71-pc. Pre-teen Set

Fit 9-inch dolls: Skipper, Cricket, others. School, dress-up, play clothes, shoes, purse, more, needle, thread, instructions.
Shipping weight 8 oz.
49 N 1483......Set $2.44

74-pc. Little Girl Set

Fit Penny Brite, Pepper, Dodi and other 9-inch dolls. Dresses for every occasion: blouse, skirt, panties, pajamas, shoes, belt, purse, hangers, needle, thread, instructions and much more. All ready to sew. Shpg. wt. 9 oz.
49 N 1484........Set $2.44

62-pc. Baby Set

Make pretty things for 9-in. baby dolls like Teenie Weenie Tiny Tears, Tearie Dearie and others. Sew dresses, panties, pajamas. Accessories, needle, thread, instructions.
Shipping weight 9 oz.
49 N 1485......Set $2.44

66-pc. Baby Set

Cute outfits for 7½ to 8-inch baby dolls like Susie Cute, Baby Ginger, Marie, others. Dresses, a play set, pajamas, shoes, socks, hangers. Needle, thread, instructions included. Wt. 9 oz.
49 N 1486......Set $2.44

$4⁹⁷

E-Z Weaver Loom by Marx .. with shuttle and harness

Just like a big loom, with shuttle, harness, warp strings, spacing wires .. makes simple or complex weave fabrics 10 in. wide. Plastic, with wood-grain finish, 19x13x13 in. A fascinating .. and useful hobby. With 400 ft. of colorful Bernat yarn, instruction book.
49 N 1372C—Shipping wt. 4 lbs........$4.97

Make hats

Make scarves

Make purses

$2⁴⁷

Pom Pom Pets

Create animals, decorations with automatic pompon makers in 3 sizes. Yarn, chenille stems, felt included. Knitting spool, too. Instructions. Wt. 13 oz.
49 N 1487....$2.47

$1⁷⁷

Knitting Set

A beginning knitter can make pretty things right away. Set has two knitting spools, pair of wooden needles, 12 skeins of colorful wool yarn. Easy-to-follow instructions. Shpg. wt. 1 lb.
49 N 1488......Set $1.77

The make-believe homemaker of 1966 could now have a better stocked, more luxurious kitchen than ever before. A Kenmore Classic Range came in coppertone or white enamel finish; a four-piece kitchen set came with matching range, sink, cabinet and refrigerator; and a double sink boasted a working faucet.

To stock the shelves of this dream kitchen, there were colorful plastic vegetables, fruits, dairy products and meats... not to mention empty cans and grocery packages.

If 1964 was the year of the Talking Doll, 1966 was the year of the Walking Doll. Mattel's Babystep walked -- and even roller skated -- all by herself. Another one, simply called Walker, came in 16 inch, 18 inch and "life size." These walked only when held by the hand.

Little girls who felt like dancing instead of merely walking could trip the light fantastic with a "Go Go" doll, whose feet strapped onto a girl's shoes, and so kept up with even the most complicated step.

And Twister, "the game that ties you up in knots", immediately became a Sixties bestseller.

Christmas 1966 Sears

INDEX STARTS ON PAGE 255

SEARS, ROEBUCK AND CO. / CHICAGO, ILLINOIS 60607
Satisfaction guaranteed or your money back...You can count on us

Sears Christmas
Wishbook

1966

For the cute little cook at your house . .

ALL STEEL MAKE-BELIEVE KITCHENS

Built of heavy-gauge steel with metal handles . .
Rigid-Lock construction makes them easier to assemble

Buy Sets and Save $2.66 to $4.64

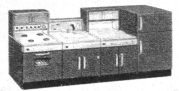

4-piece Set—Range, Sink, Cabinet, Refrigerator $39.99

Separate prices total $44.63. Shpg. wt. 70 lbs.
79 N 1169L4—Coppertone.....Set $39.99
79 N 1180L4—White.........Set 39.99

3-piece Set . . Range, Sink and Refrigerator $29.99

Separate prices total $33.64. Shpg. wt. 53 lbs.
79 N 1168L3—Coppertone.....Set $29.99
79 N 1178L3—White.........Set 29.99

2-piece Set . . includes Range and Sink $18.99

Separate prices total $21.65. Wt. 30 lbs.
Coppertone. Set.
79 N 1149L2–$18.99
White. Set.
79 N 1176L2–$18.99

She'll love this double-oven range with see-through doors, 6 control knobs to turn . . burners look so real

Kenmore Classic Range
Durable enamel finish in coppertone or white

Completely stocked $14.99

Save $1.86. Range plus 22-pc. food set (49N1132) and 34-pc. cook set (49N938) both shown below. 18x15x36 in. high. Unassembled.
79 N 1198L3—Coppertone
79 N 1199L3—White
Shpg. wt. 18 lbs.....Set $14.99

Unstocked $11.99

Just the right size for your little miss. Plated steel handles; upper oven doors have plastic handles. 18x15x36 in. high. Unassembled.
79 N 1163L—Coppertone
79 N 1170L—White
Shpg. wt. 16 lbs.....Set $11.99

A WELL-SUPPLIED KITCHEN IS A HOUSEWIFE'S BEST FRIEND . .

34-piece aluminum Cook 'n' Bake Set $2.99

She can whip up a fast snack or an 8-course dinner with this set. Includes whistling teakettle, roaster, double boiler, saucepan, colander, fry pan. Also measuring cup, spoons, cookie cutters, pie pan, cake pans.
49 N 938—Shipping weight 1 pound 8 ounces...............Set $2.99

"Perishables" to refrigerate

22 dairy delights, meats and vegetables . . so realistic and so-fresh-looking she'll want to pop them right into her refrigerator. Use them over and over . . plastic is so practical!
49 N 1132—Wt. 9 oz.... Set $1.87

Plastic Foods to serve

Delectable foods fully molded of plastic to give her table a real, full-dimensional look. Set of 44 items includes fruits, vegetables, meats and tempting gelatin desserts.
49 N 1136—Wt. 13 oz....Set $2.99

**Double Sink
. . water flows
from faucet**

$9⁶⁶

Water stored in reservoir flows into twin basins
when you turn on chrome-plated swivel faucet . .
empties when you pull stoppers. Colorful counter
top. Chrome-plated steel handles. Storage cabinet
below is so handy. Unassembled. 18x15x28 in. high.
79 N 1164L—Coppertone 79 N 1171L—White
Shipping weight 14 pounds.........Each $9.66

**Large Cabinet
. . sliding doors
in storage top**

$10⁹⁹

Cabinet comes stocked with 6 food cartons. Cutlery
drawer holds kitchen odds and ends. Colorful counter
top. "See-through" doors at top, storage below.
Chrome-plated steel handles. Unassembled. 18x15x36
in. high. Buy it the easy way—order by phone.
79 N 1166L—Coppertone   79 N 1173L—White
Shipping weight 17 pounds...........Each $10.99

**Refrigerator
. . well-stocked
with play food**

$13⁵³

Save $1.50, Separately $15.03. Get 22 foods, 40
grocery boxes shown below. 18x15x36 in. high.
79 N 1174L3—Coppertone 79 N 1181L3—White
Unassembled. Shpg. wt. 25 lbs......Set $13.53
Stocked with 12 food boxes only. Unassembled.
79 N 1165L—Coppertone 79 N 1172L—White
Shipping weight 23 pounds.........Set $11.99

You can order toys from this catalog, pages 467 to 638, from now until August 1, 1967.

STOCK UP ON ACCESSORIES, GROCERIES, APPLIANCES

**Battery-
Operated
Mixer**

$2⁹⁷ *without
batteries*

Flip switch and
metal beaters whirl,
light glows. 8-in.
high plastic mixer
has removable,
tilting head and
mixing bowl. Order
2 "D" batteries on
page 482.
Shpg. wt. 1 lb.
49 N 1143. $2.97

Farm and Dairy Foods

So fresh-looking and realistic . .
look good enough to eat! 22 items
including meats, eggs, dairy and
bakery treats . . all of molded
plastic to stay "fresh."
49 N 1182—Wt. 1 lb.. Set $1.57

Packaged Groceries

Groceries just like the real ones
Mom buys from your grocer's
shelf. 40 unfilled boxes in small
scale size. All are colorfully printed
and carefully labeled.
49 N 1102—Wt. 1 lb. Set $1.47

Popular Canned Goods

All the name brands that Mom
always insists on buying. All the
trimmings for a perfect meal in 2-
dozen empty, 3-in. high cans in
small scale. Shpg. wt. 1 lb. 2 oz.
49 N 1101............Set $1.87

PC [Sears] 599

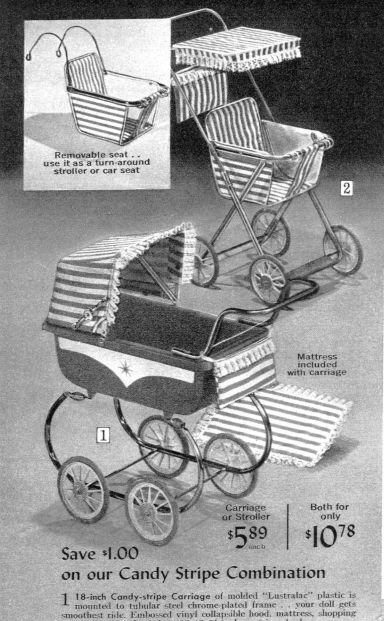

Removable seat .. use it as a turn-around stroller or car seat

Mattress included with carriage

17½-inch Doll Carriages

Sturdy sculptured steel .. name plate kit is included so you can put Dolly's name on her carriage

$5.99 each

(3 thru 5) She'll push dolly along proudly in one of these little beauties. So dainty, so brightly-colored .. yet they're built to **stay** beautiful. Welded steel body finished with high-gloss baked enamel. Chrome-plated tubular gear. Coil spring suspension. Strong, 6-inch plastic wheels roll smoothly, easily. 3-bow hood. 17½x9½x21 in. high. Name kit included. Partly assembled.

3 Red body with matching vinyl hood fabric. No doll.
Shpg. wt. 7 lbs.
79 N 8209C...$5.99

4 Blue body with matching vinyl washable fabric hood.
Shpg. wt. 7 lbs.
79 N 8211C...$5.99

5 Yellow body has washable yellow and gold print vinyl hood.
Shpg. wt. 7 lbs.
79 N 8212C.....$5.99

Carriage or Stroller	Both for only
$589 each	**$10**78

Save $1.00 on our Candy Stripe Combination

1 18-inch Candy-stripe Carriage of molded "Lustralac" plastic is mounted to tubular steel chrome-plated frame .. your doll gets smoothest ride. Embossed vinyl collapsible hood, mattress, shopping bag trimmed in plastic lace. 18x10x21 in. long. 6-in. wheels.
79 N 8207C—Partly assembled. Shpg. wt. 6 lbs..............$5.89

2 Candy-stripe Stroller with plastic footrest, play rings and lock clip. Chrome-plated tubular steel handle. Embossed vinyl canopy, shopping bag with plastic lace trim. 10½x11x29 inches high.
79 N 8208C—Partly assembled. Shpg. wt. 6 lbs..............$5.89

Candy-stripe Combination 2-pc. Set .. Carriage, stroller listed above.
79 N 8217C2—Partly assembled. Shpg. wt. 12 lbs.......Set $10.78

So wonderfully soft and cozy .. 3-piece Bedding Set **$1**99

All dolly's dreams will be sweet when she's tucked into this cuddly set of printed rayon crepe. Dainty ruffle edge. Soft cotton filling. 22x18 inches. Sun yellow.
Shpg. wt. 2 lbs.
79 N 8204C..........$1.99

Child-size, 3-piece Supermarket $6 69

6 Fill your shopping cart from shelves of make-believe groceries. Pay bill at check-out counter. Sliding drawer in cash register holds play money. Handy plastic wall phone. Store counter and cart of corrugated fiberboard (not wood, hardwood). Market 20x47 inches high. Counter 24x27x15 inches high. Cart 20x8 inches wide.
79 N 5002 C—Unassembled. Shpg. wt. 10 lbs..... .$6.69

Ringing Cash Register $2 99

7 Ring up every sale with this precision-action steel cash register. Handy side arm holds pad of paper and pencil so cashier can give each customer a Sears sales check with every purchase. Push one of the 13 numbered keys .. amount pops up to show in window and bell rings. Push lever and drawer slides open to bank of plastic coins and paper money. Red enamel finish. 8 inches high.
49 N 1751—Shipping weight 3 pounds. 12 ounces. $2.99

RING RING

SAVE THIS CATALOG. You can order toys on pages 467 to 638 from now until August 1, 1967

Removable front seat
converts to car seat

Stroller fun for 2 dolls at once $9.69

Tandem stroller for the little mother with "twins" . . or carries one doll and lots of packages. Frame and adjustable footrest are chrome plated. Washable vinyl seat and fringed canopy. 23x11x31 in. high. Dolls shown not included. Plastic tires. Buy it the easy way—order by phone.
79 N 8216C—Red plaid   79 N 8215C—Blue solid
Partly assembled. Shipping weight 7 pounds.............Each $9.69

Name plate kit lets you personalize Dolly's own carriage

DOLLY

Sculptured Steel
20-inch Doll Carriages

. . with vinyl lining and name plate kit $10.99 each

(1 thru 3) She'll really pamper her doll in one of these handsome, 2-tone carriages. Steel body has high-gloss baked enamel finish. Shiny, chrome-plated gear and wire wheels. Hand brake. Spring suspension for smooth ride. Name kit. 20x11x24½ in. high. Partly assembled.

1 Navy and white body with vinyl hood and lining. Wt. 12 lbs. No doll.
79 N 8210C-$10.99

2 Peaches 'n cream body with print vinyl hood, lining. Shpg. wt. 12 lbs.
79 N 8213C-$10.99

3 Maroon and white body, vinyl lining, quilted hood. Shpg. wt. 12 lbs.
79 N 8214C-$10.99

17½-in. Doll Carriage $2.89
in pert rosebud print

Bright as a summer afternoon is this blossomy print on washable vinyl. Strong steel frame with aluminum-colored enamel finish. 5-in. plastic wheels. 17½x8x21 in. high. Foldable. Partly assembled.
49 N 8205—Wt. 3 lbs. 8 oz. $2.89

Perky Stroller $2.89
in rosebud print

Flower motif covers vinyl. Sun shade canopy, shopping bag. Steel frame with aluminum-colored enamel. 9½x8x23 in. high. 5-in. plastic wheels. Partly assembled. Wt. 2 lbs. 8 oz.
49 N 8206.............$2.89

FUN WITH PHONES . . plug 1 to 4 phones into Switchboard below. Select these extensions from Princess-style color Phones at right. BE A RECEPTIONIST!

$7.99
switchboard without batteries

What a busy operator you'll be . . answering calls, plugging in extensions. Plug in phones at right for real calls, room-to-room conversations. Sturdy plastic set includes operator's phone, headband. 11x 9x6 in. high. Order 2 "D" batteries on page 482. Wt. 2 lbs. 12 oz.
49 N 6419....$7.99

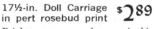

Lift receiver . .
dial lights up.

Dial number . .
other phone rings.

You can talk for hours on $3.77 each without batteries
your Princess-style Phone

Mom won't mind a bit because you'll be practicing telephone manners and how to take messages for her on the real phone. Buy 2 phones and you can call Sis, Brother or your friend . . 30-foot wire lets you place "long distance" room-to-room calls. Receiver is 8 in. long. Plastic. Order 2 "D" batteries on page 482.
49 N 6420—Pink   49 N 6429—Aqua
Shipping weight ea. 1 lb. 6 oz.....Each $3.77

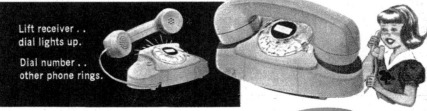

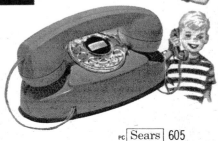

Mattel's Babystep

$12⁷⁷
without batteries

Bright, bouncy and so energetic she walks and even roller skates by herself

New Babystep takes each little step carefully and perfectly all by herself. Just by turning her hidden switch, you'll send her walking or skating—balloon in hand—all the way across the room or down the sidewalk. Plastic, 18-in. high, with soft rooted synthetic hair and big painted eyes that always seem to be smiling. She arrives in a perky little outfit that matches her own sparkle . . she looks out for Mother's floors with skates that won't scuff. Uses 2 "D" batteries, order on page 482.
49 N 3019—Wt. 3 lbs. 8 oz.. $12.77

For Babystep and Baby First Step $2⁹⁹

5-piece clothing ensemble includes coat, hat, 2-piece pajama set and sunsuit.
49 N 3048—Shipping weight 7 ounces.....Outfit $2.99

"Can we take a walk and talk together?"

Mattel's Talking Baby First Step

$19⁷⁷
without batteries

Baby First Step's grown up just a little so she can now talk, walk and even skate by herself. Pull Chatty Ring® for 10 phrases. 18 in. of plump plastic with rooted hair, moving eyes and her own red no-scuff skates. Order 2 "D" batteries, page 482. Wt. 4 lbs. 2 oz.
49 N 3406......$19.77

Baby Stroll-A-Long $7⁶⁶ without battery

Walks by herself. Her sparkling eyes close when you lay her down. Plastic body, 14 in. tall; rooted hair. Order 1 "C" battery, pg. 482. Wt. 1 lb. 12 oz.
49 N 3027..........$7.66

18-inch Walker $4⁹⁹

1 Take her hand in yours, lift her arm and you're all set for walking in the park. Her red velveteen outfit is perfect for home or visiting. Rooted hair, moving eyes, plastic body. Wt. 2 lbs. 6 oz.
49 N 3517.....$4.99

16-inch Walker $3⁹⁹

2 A long-haired little lass who needs someone to walk with her. Plastic body; vinyl head, arms; jointed arms, legs. Wears neatly trimmed shift over dainty lace panties. Has moving eyes. Wt. 1 lb. 6 oz.
49 N 3187.....$3.99

Dolls who stroll hand-in-hand with you

"Let's play school"

Life-size Walker brings her own Poodle along

$9⁸⁸

Carry the plush pup, take your 32-in. walker by the hand, and you're set for strolling fun. Doll and 14-in. dog in matching outfits. Doll has plastic body, moving eyes, rooted hair and can wear a child's size 3 clothing. Wt. 6 lbs.
79 N 3504C..........$9.88

20-inch Terry Talks $9⁸⁸ without battery

A lively girl who's always ready to walk and talk with you. Press her talking button for 11 different phrases. Plastic doll, dressed for walking in a red paisley white trimmed dress. Order 1 "D" battery, pg. 482. Wt. 2 lbs. 10 oz.
49 N 3408..........$9.88

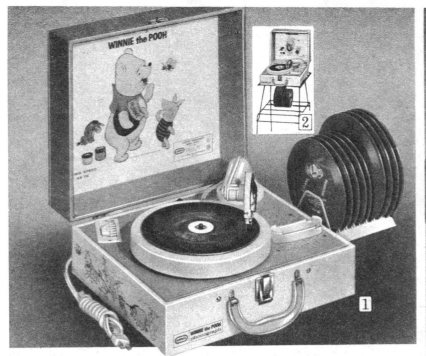

New .. WINNIE-the-POOH Electric Phonograph

- Two speeds—plays all 45 and 78-rpm records
- Built-in 45-rpm record adapter—pops up for use
- Ten delightful children's 45-rpm records
- Sturdy plastic rack has space for 24 records

All this for only **$12⁷⁹**   With metal stand **$15⁷⁹**

1 Dial-A-Matic speed selector with neutral position helps prevent damage to drive wheel. Tone arm locks in place when not in use. Acoustical-type volume control .. just switch needles (included) to make loud or soft. Integral tone chamber gives clear sound. Scuff-resistant pyroxylin-coated case, 13x11x5 inches high. UL listed for 110–120-volt, 60-cycle AC.
49 N 682—Shipping weight 8 pounds..........................$12.79

2 As above, but with 14x12x21-inch metal stand.
79 N 683 C—Shipping weight 13 pounds 15.79

*Save this catalog .. you can order toys
on pages 467 to 638 until August 1, 1967*

Grab a Dolly and dance!

They follow your every move because you strap their feet to yours

New "Go Go" Doll
$5⁹⁹

Dressed in colorful discotheque outfit. So authentically styled—all the way from "pop art" cotton print dress (that's removable) and "lace" stockings to hair curlers and sunglasses. "Bleached blonde" hair of acrylic fabric can be combed and set. 36 inches tall.
Shpg. wt. 4 lbs.
79 N 3625C.....$5.99

Musical Raggedy Ann Doll
3 Built-in music box plays a gay nursery tune. Giant 39-inch size. Red wig and locked-in eyes. Multicolor print dress, pretty white apron.
79 N 3662C—Shpg. wt. 5 lbs.. . $9.99

Musical Raggedy Andy. (Not shown.) Blue pants, red-and-white checked shirt, cap. 39 in. tall. Red wig.
79 N 3663C—Shpg. wt. 5 lbs.. . $9.99

Patti, the golden haired Doll
4 A full 39 inches from head to toe. Cotton print skirt. Painted plastic face, cotton yarn hair.
49 N 3530—Wt. 3 lbs. 8 oz.... . $3.47

$9⁹⁹ $3⁴⁷

Just slip a record in slot .. it plays instantly

$21⁶⁹ without batteries

MAGIC PHONO plays anywhere .. it's battery-powered

So easy to operate that even a preschooler can play it alone. All he has to do is slip record in and it starts to play. When through, it shuts off automatically. Side-mounted volume control. Fully transistorized .. no tubes to replace. Plays 7-inch 45-rpm records. Tough plastic case measures 10x8x5 inches high. 45-rpm record included. Needs 6 "D" batteries; order from page 482. Gives about 24 hours of continuous play. So easy to buy when you just use the phone.
49 N 640—Shpg. wt. 5 lbs. 10 oz....$21.69

$9⁹⁹

Mickey Mouse 78-rpm Electric Phonograph, 10 records, rack

Loud and soft needles give acoustical-type volume control. Integral tone chamber for a clear sound. Tone arm locks into cup for traveling. Scuff-resistant pyroxylin-coated case, 11x 11x6 inches high. Includes 10 children's records and 24-space plastic rack. UL listed for 110–120-volt, 60-cycle AC.
49 N 651—Shpg. wt. 6 lbs.... . $9.99

No Money Down on ANYTHING Sears sells

12-button Electric Organ in case **$44⁹⁵**

Boasts stainless steel reeds, 30 keys, 6 pre-set chords, 6 bass tones. Volume-control slide bar. Number system simplifies playing. Vinyl-coated wood veneer cabinet, 22x11x8 in. high. Book of 22 songs. From Italy. 110–120-v., 60-c. AC.
79 N 603L—Shipping weight 18 lbs. *$5 monthly*. Cash $44.95

8-button Electric Organ **$31⁹⁵**

Play 4 cords, 4 bass notes with left hand .. melody with right. 25 keys. Stainless steel reeds. Volume-control slide bar. Walnut-grain vinyl over wood veneer cabinet, 18x9x7 in. high. Book of 22 songs. 110–120-v., 60-c. AC.
79 N 602C—Shipping weight 11 lbs. *$5 monthly*. Cash $31.95

Play 12 different games

Including Skee Ball and Bowling with automatic pin setter $12⁸⁸

The fast, competitive sport of bowling is fun with two 5-inch balls. Automatic pin setter saves time, keeps the game going at a lively pace. Plastic Skee Ball attachment, "Bounce the Checker" game. Play Shuffleboard with 4 pushers, 8 discs, Tic-Tac-Toe and golf. Three racing games with 4 each of racers, horses, jet planes. Dart toss with 4 darts and target. Printed linoleum strip measures 2x12 feet long. With sturdy plastic parts.
79 N 2548L—Shipping weight 18 pounds........$12.88

Automatic Pin Setter

Skee-Ball unit

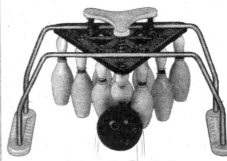

Automatic Pin Setter with 2 bowling balls

$6⁸⁸

Hit pins, they flip up . . push down lever, they reset automatically. Plastic pins and parts; steel tubing. Two 5-inch injection molded balls. 30x14x14 inches deep.
Shipping weight 10 pounds per postal regulations.
79 N 2549L....................$6.88

HUCKLE-CHUCK 3-in-1 Game

$3⁶⁶

Play ring toss, bean bag and darts. Head swings sideways . . snag it with 3 plastic rings, land 3 vinyl bean bags in mouth or hit target with 3 rubber suction-cup darts. Pressed wood. 32 in. high, 15 in. wide.
79 N 466C—Shpg. wt. 4 lbs...... $3.66

TWISTER . . the game that ties you up in knots! $3⁸⁸

Twister has to be the greatest fun game of our time! Youngsters, teens, adults can play it indoors or out in bare or stocking feet. Big spinner points to color on which you place your hand or foot.

As players move into each other, it's harder to keep balance . . first one to fall loses. 24-spot washable vinyl playing sheet (6x4½ feet) can be folded up or rolled.
49 N 207—Shpg. wt. 2 lbs. 8 oz.... $3.88

MB MILTON BRADLEY

Inflatable Court
for a good game of marbles indoors or out

Complete with big bag of marbles $3⁴⁹

Big 45-in. court of smooth fabric has no lumps or hollows to spoil good shots. Marked off for regulation play, court surrounded by lightweight, easily inflated and deflated ring. Instruction book included. Use your phone if you want to order it the easiest way of all. Shipping weight 1 pound 12 ounces.
49 N 2493....................$3.49

574 Sears PC

By 1967, bikes were getting snazzier all the time. Spyders -- low-riding bikes with banana seats and high handle bars -- were available in one - and three-speed models. The girl's Spyder came with a white plastic basket, decorated with a (plastic) floral garland.

The artistically inclined girl could make "Now-Wow" jewelry out of papier mache, or could paint Early American pictures on wood via paint-by-numbers. Or she could collect and mount butterflies or manage either a cricket or ant farm.

With sexism becoming a relevant issue of the late 1960's, lo and behold a boy is pictured cooking beside a girl at the $12.99 Cook-N-Snack Center!

Everyone wanted to be as modern as possible in 1967, and even toys started to look toward the cutting edge of technology. The Think-a-Tron was a toy computer that answered questions fed to it on a punched card. Wheels turned, lights flashed -- just like a real computer. Ah, but did it come with a fax modem?

Sears Christmas
Wishbook

1967

Bendable, Twistable Lovable Gumby

Gumby's Western Marshal Set

Only at Sears $4.89 Set

Frontier town, plastic horse and 10-inch wagon .. everything Gumby needs to be a lawman

Gumby turns Western Marshal with 10-gallon hat, double holster with pistols, lasso, guitar, badge. 7-in. horse hitches to wagon and Gumby takes the reins. Stand-up cardboard scene of 3 buildings, wagon. Plastic Gumby takes any position you set.
79 N 4779C—Shipping weight 6 lbs. Set $4.89

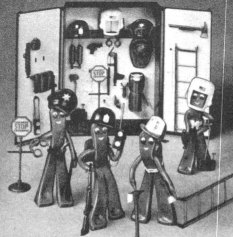

Set of 4 Gumby Outfits $3.88 without Gumby

Dress Gumby as spaceman, fireman, policeman or soldier. Gumby's own wardrobe closet holds costumes and accessories. Space suit with helmet, oxygen tank, ray gun, walkie-talkie. Fireman—hat, axe, ladder, extinguisher, flashlight. Policeman—hat, stop sign, holster, gun, badge, handcuffs, night stick. Soldier has helmet, rifle, field pack, canteen, walkie-talkie.
49 N 4781—Shpg. wt. 1 lb. 3 oz........ Set $3.88

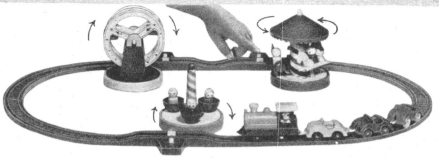

Child Guidance Kiddieland

Has 3 working rides .. train stops at each ride .. ride goes into action .. push button and train goes to next ride $7.99 without battery

Colorful kiddie-rides .. twirling teacups spin on revolving platform, Ferris wheel and candy striped merry-go-round with jogging horses. Ferris wheel has swinging bucket seats. Child directs Joy Ride express with "engineer."

Plastic. Takes 1 "C" battery, order below.
49 N 4494—Shpg. wt. 4 lbs.....$7.99
"C" Batteries. Package of 2.
49 N 4665—Wt. 4 oz...... Pkg. 36c

You're invited to Mr. Potato Head's Picnic .. where the food has all the fun

$2.88 Set

Mr. Potato Head goes on a picnic with Frankie Frank, Frenchy Fry, Willy Burger, Mr. Ketchup Head, Mr. Soda Pop Head and Mr. Mustard Head. You can make funny faces with pickle, onion ears, eyes, mouths.
49 N 4765—Shpg. wt. 12 oz. Set $2.88

Gumby and Pokey have their own Jeep $2.99

Gumby's off on another adventure in his own jeep with Pokey sitting right next to him. Jeep of high impact plastic is a replica of the one Gumby uses on his own TV cartoon show. Free-rolling jeep has folding windshield and heavy-duty tires .. 10 inches long. Gumby is a flexible 6 in. tall; Pokey is 4½ inches tall. Both plastic, can be bent in hundreds of hilarious positions. For even more fun with Gumby, order outfits above.
49 N 4780—Shipping weight 1 pound 10 oz. . $2.99

NOTE: Gumby outfits from British Crown Colony Hong Kong, Jeep from Japan.

450 Sears PC

[1] [2] [3]

Mattel's Ge-tars play a happy tune with the turn of a crank

$1.69 each

Whistle and sing along as these tuneful Ge-tars play along. Just turn the crank as you plunk the nylon strings. Plastic body with cartoon figures. 14 in. long. Shipping weight each 10 ounces.
(1) 49 N 532—Flipper........$1.69
(2) 49 N 588—Bugs Bunny...... 1.69
(3) 49 N 557—Tom and Jerry ... 1.69

Single-speed Spyders—sharp and sporty . . boy's and girl's models

Deluxe 20-inch Spyder. Vinyl tiger-print bucket banana saddle, chrome-plated scoop fenders and rich gold-color frame highlight sportster styling. Highrise handlebars, rims, hubs, sprocket—all with chrome-plated finish. Reflector mounted below seat. Convenient, dependable coaster brakes. Knobby tread 2.125-in. rear tire; 1.75-in. front tire. Leg reach adjusts from 23 to 28 inches.
6 N 47786N—Wt. 44 lbs. *$5 mo*....Cash $38.85

SHIPPING NOTE: Bikes on this page are sent via freight (truck or rail) or by express.

Pre-stripped 20-inch Spyder. Brilliant flamboyant green frame. Chrome-plated highrise handlebars, rims, sprocket and hubs. Quilted banana seat—black top, contrasting white sides. Surestop coaster brake. Knobby tread 2.125-in. rear tire for fast starts; 1.75-in. front tire. Leg reach adjusts 23 to 28 in. Ready to customize with Spyder-style accessories (see page 358 selection).
6 N 47761N—Wt. 44 lbs. *$5 mo*...Cash $33.99

CUSTOMER CONVENIENCE—the Sears way. These bikes are sent with frame and wheels completely assembled. All you have to do is install seat, handlebars, pedals and any accessories.

Single-speed, 20-inch Girl's model. We've tamed a tiger . . almost . . made him tame enough for a sweet lass' Sunday cruise—yet kept him ready for sassy Saturday Spyder fun. White banana saddle. Highrise handlebars. White plastic basket and colorful floral garland. Flamboyant turquoise, white trim. 1.75-in. whitewall tires. Chrome-plated rims, fenders. Leg reach adjusts 23 to 28 in.
6 N 47777N2—Wt. 47 lbs. *$5 mo*..Cash $38.85

"NO DOWN PAYMENT AT SEARS? BOY, I CAN HANDLE *THAT* PART!"

3-speed Girl's 20-inch Spyder with front and rear hand-grip brakes

Designed for tomboy fun, yet full of feminine appeal with a bold new racing color frame—candy apple red (raspberry). Quilted bucket banana seat matches frame. Power-grip highrise handlebars with twist-grip speed control, white grips. Gleaming chrome-plated fenders. Sporty 2.125-in. knobby tread rear tire; 1.75-inch front tire. Leg reach adjusts 23 to 28 inches. Why not pick up the phone and order it?
6 N 47776N—Shpg. wt. 45 lbs. *$5 mo*...Cash $52.95

'TWAS THE NIGHT BEFORE CHRISTMAS AND VISIONS OF SPYDER BIKES RACED IN THEIR HEADS

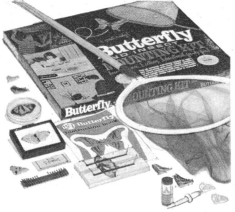

Catch and mount Butterflies $3⁹⁹

Start a fascinating hobby with 10 ready-to-mount specimens, net, insect pins, display mount, relaxing and dispatching fluids, jar, wing-pin strips, manual.
49 N 2196—Wt. 1 lb. 8 oz...... Set $3.99

Cricket Farm $2⁹⁹

Watch the cheerful, chirping crickets as they live in their specially made farm. You can watch their funny antics as they play with the plastic horse and carriage.

Feed with special food from eyedropper feeder. Educational fun. Instruction manual, food and cricket coupon* included. Clear plastic form 8x4x3 inches high.

Shipping weight 1 pound.
49 N 2151........................$2.99

Giant Ant Farm $5⁴⁴

Follow the labors of ant "engineers" as they dig tunnels, build rooms, erect bridges and store away food.

Escape-proof, break-resistant plastic case, 15x10 in. high. Year's supply of ant food, liquid feeder, sand, handbook and ant stock certificate* included.
49 N 2302—Shipping weight 3 lbs. .$5.44

*Mail coupon and/or certificate to receive crickets and/or ants from factory.

Make NOW-WOW Jewelry

Shape instant Paper Maché, fun to wear .. great to give

$3⁹⁹ kit

Each kit has enough materials for:
• Necklace and Leaf Pin
• 2 Brooches, Ring, 2 Necklaces
• Dangle and Snap-on Earrings
• 2 Bracelets

Now you can create sleek, chic, mod-looking jewelry that is all the rage today. Instant Paper Maché needs only to be mixed with water then spread on the decorative flex-a-form shapes.

When dry, paint with any of the 10 vivid colors. Glaze and sealer included for a choice of finishes.

You don't have to make all your jewelry at once. Left-over Paper Maché can be stored and used again later. Is nonsouring, nonfermenting and nontoxic. Includes re-usable forms, jewelry backs, glue and instructions.
49 N 23980—Shpg. wt. 1 lb. 8 oz.... Kit $3.99

SAVE THIS CATALOG . . you can order toys on pages 433 to 609 until August 1, 1968

You can re-create charming primitive wood paintings in the style in which they were done by early American artists. Each one sure to be a conversation piece.

You paint each easy-to-follow numbered panel with premixed oil paints. Finished painting is easily antiqued with a special solution to give it a mellow, aged look—as though it were painted 2 centuries ago.

Complete kit includes instructions, paints, brush and gold colored fob-type hanger. No framing needed.

PAINT ON WOOD

Early American Art-by-Numbers Kit includes premixed paints, all the materials you need to
paint it! antique it! hang it!

$2⁴⁴ 14x10-inch panel

9 Two Farm Scenes: Summer and Wintertime. Each panel is 16x12 inches high.
79 N 2306C—Shipping wt. 4 lbs... Kit $4.88

10 Two Sea Scenes: The Whalers. 16x12 in.
79 N 2357C—Shpg. wt. 3 lbs... Kit $4.88

11 Early American Eagle. 14x10 in. high.
49 N 2370—Wt. 1 lb. 12 oz..... Kit $2.44

PC Sears 459

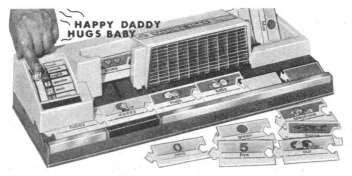

HAPPY DADDY HUGS BABY

Mattel's new Talking Tiles Learning Machine

Teaches English, foreign words and phrases with sound effects and music **$19.99** without batteries

Children begin a delightful new adventure as they see, hear, learn words, phrases, numbers in English, French and Spanish. Just feed colorful talking tiles into machine, set 6-position selector bar to choose language, question, sound effect or music. 36 two-sided tiles. Guide book. Transistorized. Plastic, 25x12½x5 inches high. Uses 4 "D" batteries, order 2 pkgs. below.
79 N 1681C—Shipping weight 7 pounds.................$19.99
79 N 4660—"D" Battery. Package of 2. Shpg. wt. pkg. 8 oz..Pkg. 36c
Alphabet Zoop Talking Tiles Accessory Set. 18 more two-sided tiles.
49 N 1756—Shipping weight 1 pound 3 ounces........Set $4.49

Puzzle reverses from World to U.S.A. map **$1.97**

Children 7 to 13 learn names and locations of foreign lands and all 50 states by putting the puzzle together. Fiberboard pieces with wood centers. About 14x20 in.
49 N 406—Shipping weight 1 lb. 4 oz.........$1.97

Styled like a Whaling Captain's Desk and Chair, this Set makes homework much more fun **$18.99** set

Pretend you're in the captain's cozy cabin writing logs on the high sea . . or do geography and math on this fun desk and chair set. The top is set at just the right angle for reading and writing. Opens to inner storage compartment. Desk front has 2 built-in book shelves. Walnut finish pressed wood with super hard melamine surface . . resists stains, ink, heat. Desk legs, chair frame tubular steel. Chair 23 in. high, desk 21x25x32 in. high. Partly assembled.
79N9049N—Freight (rail, truck), express. Wt. 31 lbs. Set $18.99

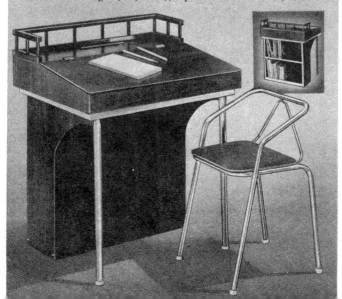

Learning facts is fun when you feed question card into

THINK-A-TRON

Toy computer gives answer on lighted screen
300 questions cover broad subject range

Available only at Sears **$7.99** without batteries

Realistic, dramatic . . wheels turn, lights flash as you push a button and almost instantly the answer to your question lights up on the screen. Just select a data card that has the question you want answered and feed it into computer. Answers are coded A,B,C, or T,F depending upon the type of question you choose.
Fun to play with a group of friends . . try and guess the answer to the question before the computer tells you. 150 question cards each with 2 questions, 3 stack-up card holders. Plastic, gray with blue trim. 8½ inches high. Operates on 2 "D" batteries, order 1 package below.
49 N 1679—Shipping weight 2 pounds 9 ounces.............$7.99

"D" Battery. Package of 2.
49 N 4660—Shipping weight package 8 ounces........Package 36c

Be an architect with Etch A Sketch®
Just turn the 2 knobs to design and draw **$2.77**

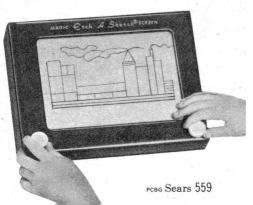

Lines, circles and diagonals appear under frosted glass base. You can form anything from basic geometric shapes to pictures and very intricate designs. Use it again and again . . erases itself with just a shake. Plastic, 9½ in. long.
Shipping weight 1 lb. 7 oz.
49 N 1878............$2.77

Little Girls adore Luggage of their very own

Deluxe 2-piece Vinyl Luggage Set

Open vanity . . there's an extra compartment and a handy mirror

$7⁹⁹ set

What little girl wouldn't love to go visiting with this matched vanity and tote bag set? 16½-in. plywood vanity has molded side panels, washable vinyl cover. Easy action nickel-plated locks, molded plastic handle. Plastic interior has ruffle trim, mirror in lid. 12½-inch teardrop design tote bag . . vinyl cover, washable interior. Loop handle. Blue color.
49 N 1446—Shipping wt. 4 lbs. 12 oz. . . . . Set $7.99

Fashion Floral 2-piece Set $5⁹⁹

She'll love this pretty blue floral patterned set. Practical vinyl covers a wood frame, has matched and stitched bindings and a colorful lining. Neatly finished with metal tongue and groove closures, nickel-plated trim. 12½, 14 in. long.
49 N 1496—Shpg. wt. 5 lbs . . . Set $5.99

Our finest set of Child Luggage nests for storage $9⁹⁹ set

3 travel cases of simulated leather-grained sponge vinyl. Full width outside zipper pockets, long pull tabs, locks, key. Molded handles, inside pocket, tie-tapes. Cases 14, 15, 16 in. long. Avocado green.
49 N 1447—Shpg. wt. 7 lbs . . Set $9.99

Snow White Overnighter $2⁵⁹

Snow White and the 7 Dwarfs are screened in full color on this 14-inch white vinyl case. Easy to keep clean, just wipe with a damp cloth. Lined in vinyl, with nickel-plated hardware and a plastic strap.
49 N 1498—Shipping weight 2 lbs . $2.59

Mary Poppins Carpetbag $1⁹⁹

Pack this "magical" bag full of the things you'll need for a day's adventures or a visit to Grandma. Tapestry print vinyl wipes clean, metal frame snaps shut. Perfect size to carry . . about 12x6x10 inches high.
49 N 1046—Shipping weight 1 lb . . $1.99

Luggage with umbrella $3⁹⁹ 3-piece set

Rain or shine, she'll be prepared. 21-in. umbrella fits into holder at side of 12-in. case. 8-in. shoulder bag. Lam. vinyl.
49 N 1091—Wt. 2 lbs . . . . Set $3.99

Snow White Umbrella $1³⁹

White vinyl with colorful decorations. 8 steel ribs, opens to 24-inch width. Secret compartment in handle holds plastic rainhood. Steel shaft, safety tip.
49 N 1477—Shipping wt. 13 oz . $1.39

Little Girls love to help Mommy iron

Deluxe 4-piece Ironing Set $6⁴⁹

Electric iron really works. 4-position ironing board adjusts to 22-in. height . . silicone coated cover and Tuflex® pad.

Everything to do up handkerchiefs, doll clothes, or what have you. Steel ironing board, avocado green enamel . . 30 in. long, 8 in. wide. Aluminized, silicone coated print cover with Tuflex® cellulose fiber pad, clothespins. 10-watt iron, green-plastic handle, gold-color plated base, simulated heat control buttons. UL listed for 110–120 volt, 60-cycle AC.
79 N 1077C—4-piece Set. Shipping weight 6 lbs . . . Set $6.49
49 N 1079—Electric Iron only. Shpg. wt. 1 lb. 10 oz 2.99
79 N 1081C—Board, pad, cover only. Shpg. wt. 5 lbs . . 3.49

4-piece Set with Toy Iron $3⁹⁹

Turquoise non-electric iron, yellow enameled steel 27-in. perforated top board. Pad, cover, clothespins.
79N1076C-Shpg. wt. 5 lbs. Set $3.99
3-piece Set. Board, pad and cover.
79N1080C-Shpg. wt. 4 lbs. Set $2.29

10-watt Electric Play Iron $1⁹⁹

Nicely styled iron with avocado color steel base, sole plate, yellow plastic handle. UL listed. 110–120-v., 60-c. AC. Buy it the easy way, order by phone.
49 N 1078—Wt. 1 lb. 3 oz . . $1.99

Little Girls Love to help clean house

Clean all around the house with this big 9-piece Cleaning Set $3.99

Nine pieces of deluxe housecleaning equipment give your junior-size clean-up squad lots of help. She'll be sure to keep her room neat with this pressed steel carpet sweeper that really works and self-squeezing sponge mop. There's a plastic fiber broom for fast sweep-ups and a cotton floor mop that gets down and under where the dust is. The standup dustpan has a wood handle just like mother's. A filled Brillo box, plastic apron, sponge and dustcloth included. Partly assembled (just insert handles).
79 N 1303C—Shipping weight 3 pounds...................Set $3.99

5-piece Cleaning Set $1.99

Metal carpet sweeper with fiber brush . . bottom opens for emptying. The 24-inch wood-handled broom has plastic bristles, and there's a dustmop, dustpan and plastic apron too. Buy it the easy way—order by phone. Shipping weight 2 pounds.
79 N 1302C........Set $1.99

Electric Plug-in Vacuum Cleaner for Mother's Little Helper.. *it really works!*

$14.95

Big 5-inch turbine motor cleans powerfully. Removable cleaning bag. dust-finding light. Sears price includes . . broom, dustpan, apron!

Here's a real electric vacuum cleaner that works just like Mom's. It's styled just like the full size models and powered by a strong induction motor with 12 feet of electric cord. Operates on 110–120-volt, 60-cycle AC. UL listed. It's made of heavy duty, high impact plastic. Orange color. 30 in. high. Turn the on switch and a light goes on, to track down that elusive dust. The bag is removable for easy cleaning. Partially assembled. Also included . . a plastic broom, dustpan and apron.
79 N 1068C—Shipping weight 4 pounds.................$14.95

Battery Powered Cleaners
Conventional "heavy-duty" floor model or tank type

Your choice $4.99 *without batteries*

"BOY! YOU'RE AS FUSSY AS MY MOM!"

$2.49
Friction motor hums

Just push cleaner over the floor and friction motor drags in dirt, makes humming sounds as it moves along . . front window shows harmless sparks and plastic dustbag inflates. Zipper makes it easy to empty. Metal body, plastic handle. 25 in. high. Blue. Partly assembled. Japan.
49 N 1280—Wt. 1 lb. 5 oz..$2.49

$8.99 *without batteries*
Battery powered Cleaner

This brightly styled vacuum really works . . just press the foot switch to turn on motor. Green plastic body, red, easy to empty bag. Operates on 3 "D" batteries, not included. Order 2 packages separately below.
79 N 1228C—Wt. 5 lbs..$8.99
"D" Batteries. Package of 2.
79N4660—Wt. pkg. 8 oz.Pkg. 36c

Floor model
No cord to come between a lady and her cleaning

Just flick switch . . fan motor starts cleaning, light turns on. Easy to empty vinyl bag inflates as it picks up dirt. Steel body and handle. 39 in. high, 8½ in. wide. Beige and brown. Made in Japan. Partly assembled. Uses 3 "D" batteries. Order 2 packages at right.
49 N 1301—Wt. 2 lbs. 6 oz..$4.99

Tank type
Handy shoulder tote with 5 attachments

Has a really powerful suction motor, and 5 attachments to clean rugs, upholstery, radiators and so forth. High impact plastic case with 21½-in. flexible tube and 12-inch extension. Aqua color. Operates on 4 "D" batteries. Order 2 pkgs. below.
49 N 1305—Wt. 2 lbs. 8 oz.....$4.99
"D" Batteries. Package of 2.
49N4660—Shpg. wt. pkg. 8 oz. Pkg. 36c

Gelatin Mixes and Molds
$2⁷⁹

Delicious fruit gelatins packaged in child-size boxes. Just the right amount in each box fills the molds. Plastic molds shape gelatin into dog, clown, boat, car, airplane and kitty cat.

Set includes 6 assorted fruit flavored gelatins. 6 molds, recipe book and measuring spoon.
49 N 1066—Wt. 14 oz. Set $2.79

Mix .. Bake .. Eat .. Most any kind of treat
Fully insulated Coppertone Magic-Cool Oven bakes so well yet the outside is always cool to the touch

$14⁹⁹

Complete set includes 13 utensils, 22 mixes

With the Magic-Cool oven child never touches a hot pan because just a turn of a knob moves pan from oven to cooling chamber. Nichrome wire, porcelain ceramic heating element (not light bulb) provides even baking temperature. Set includes mixes to bake 6 cakes, 4 packages frosting, 2 pie, 2 biscuit, 2 gingerbread mixes plus brownie and fortune cookie mixes.

All the utensils you need are included: aluminum cake pan, bread, muffin and pie pans; plastic cookie cutters, spoon, bowl, wood rolling pin. Cook book. Oven made of heavy gauge steel, 11x6x10 in. high; has double-glass "peek-thru" window so child can watch cake rise. Oven takes pans up to 4 in. UL listed. 110–120 v., 60-c. AC. 79N1067C-Shpg. wt. 9 pounds. Set $14.99

Set of 12 Food Mixes
$1⁹⁹

This set has all the ingredients to bake 3 yummy cakes, 2 batches of cookies, gingerbread, biscuits, brownies and an apple pie. Also 2 packages of frosting mix.
Shipping weight 1 lb. 4 oz.
49 N 1071 . . . . Set $1.99

Kids' Cook-N-Snack Center
Make your own hamburgers, shakes, hot dogs
Cook all the drive-in treats right at home
Bake your own hot dog and hamburger buns, too

Sears Exclusive **$12⁹⁹** set without batteries

Shakes and grilled treats ready in a jiffy with the Cook-N-Snack Center. Metal grill has protective see-thru plastic cover .. cooks with a 150-watt light bulb (not incl.) Light glows when grill is on. UL listed, 110–120-v. 60-c. AC. Portable mixer whips up shakes. Includes 6 add-water shake mixes, 12 pancake mixes, syrup, buns; bun molds, spatula, spoon and 2 plastic glasses. Grill and grease trap remove for easy cleaning. Mixer uses 2 "D" batteries, order 1 pkg. below.
79N1257C-Cook-N-Snack Center. Wt. 7 lbs. Set $12.99
79N4660–"D" Batteries. Pkg. of 2. Wt. 8 oz. Pkg. 36c

576 Sears PCBKM AEDSLG

Nineteen sixty-eight was a tumultuous year for the United States; the country was rocked by assassination, riots and civil unrest.

But everything was just fine in Barbie-land; in fact, the Blonde One had more features, more accessories and more friends than ever before. New Talking Barbie said thought-provoking things like, "I love being a fashion model!" and could drive around in a Swinging Sports Car -- a bargain at $2.97. Barbie -- talking or otherwise -- could also pal around with chums Francie, Stacey and Christie. In fact, they could talk, too!

While Flower Power ruled the streets of America's cities, it only appeared in the Wishbook in the form of Flower Pow sleeping bags, "for those pajama parties where the girl-talk is as groovy as these flowery bags." Before slipping into those bags, though, a slumber party could be enlivened by The Game of Love, a "Twister"-like floor game, or the ever-popular Mystery Date.

Sears Christmas
Wishbook

1968

"I love being a fashion model"

The spotlight is on New

TALKING BARBIE

in a fur-trimmed dinner suit that's a Sears exclusive

Also has a swingy swimsuit

8-piece Gift Set $7⁹⁷

Elegant lamé suit accented with sumptuous fur collar. Hot pink taffeta blouse has ruffle trim and rhinestone buttons. Shoes and stockings complete the outfit. Talking Barbie says many long phrases...just pull the cord. Vinyl, 11½ in. tall with bendable legs. Swimsuit, plastic stand and hanger included.
49 N 30088—Shipping weight 1 pound........Set $7.97

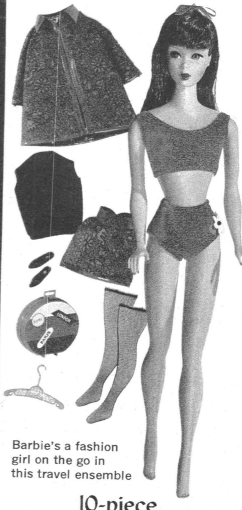

Barbie's a fashion girl on the go in this travel ensemble

10-piece Barbie Gift Set
$4⁹⁷

Barbie goes cosmopolitan with this stylish floral print coat, matching mod-length skirt, knit shell, sheer blue hose and shoes. The fashion hat box adds a finishing touch to the outfit. 11½-inch vinyl Barbie wears a sporty swimsuit. Clothes hanger and clear posing stand included.
49 N 30086—Shpg. wt. 1 lb...Set $4.97

FASHION DOLL ACCESSORIES

SWINGING SPORTS CAR
Riding fun for slim 9 to 11½-inch dolls
$2⁹⁷

A sleek sports car for the teen-age dolls. Plastic body with clear windshield. Bucket seats. Whitewall tires with silver-color hubcaps. Steel axles. Silver-color decorated grill. Bumper and headlights. 7½ x 18 inches long. Doll not included.
49 N 9320—Shipping weight 2 pounds..............$2.97

Barbie Hair Fair $2⁹⁷
New hairdos for Barbie and friends with braided switch, crown-ette, wiglet, fall. All Saran. One Barbie head with rooted hair, hair accessories. Wt. 6 oz.
49 N 3561....$2.97

Barbie Flats 'n Heels 97¢
A complete shoe wardrobe for Barbie and her 11½-inch friends. Set includes flats, slip-ons, open-toes, high and low heels. 13 pairs of plastic shoes in a rainbow of colors to match any outfit.
Shpg. wt. 2 oz.
49 N 3559......97¢

Barbie Accessories 97¢
"Change-abouts" for 11½-inch fashion dolls. Includes: um-brella, net stockings, long braided hair-piece, and two purses with matching pairs of shoes. A real addi-tion to any outfit.
Shpg. wt. 2 oz.
49 N 3560...97¢

Francie's fashions fit Casey. Barbie shares her clothes with Stacey and Christie. Dolls not included.

The Mod Look for Francie .. a Sears exclusive

5-piece Outfit $2⁴⁹

1 Orange Zip. Day coat with the look of leather. Dress has matching orange skirt and a striped knit top. With hanger, shoes.
Shpg. wt. 7 oz.
49 N 30091 . . $2.49

Francie Outfits with slippers

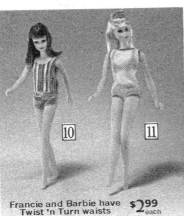

2 Slumber Number. Nylon nightgown with a sleep shade. Shpg. wt. 4 oz.
49 N 34351 . . $1.29

3 Hill-Riders. Ribbed knit sweater and rayon slacks. Wt. 6 oz.
49 N 30098 . . $1.99

4 Night Blooms. Filmy negligee and gown. Wt. 7 oz.
49 N 34321 . . $2.69

Glimmer Glamour
A Sears exclusive **$2⁹⁷**

Fashion Favorites for Barbie and Stacey

5 Sparkly blue dress and fully-lined lamé coat. Gold-color hose, clear shoes. Hanger.
49 N 30089—Shipping weight 8 ounces. $2.97

6 Knit Hit. Dress in two colors with accent on the top. Hanger and footwear included.
49 N 34371—Shipping weight 5 ounces. $1.49

7 Trailblazers. A corduroy pantsuit with blouse and sunglasses. Hanger and shoes included.
49 N 30104—Shipping weight 7 ounces . . . $2.69

8 Wedding Wonder with train, ribbons and flowers. Satin slip, sheer veil. Hanger, shoes.
49 N 34387—Shipping weight 10 ounces . . $2.99

9 Jump into Lace. Elegant hostess pajamas. Plastic hanger and shoes included.
49 N 34375-Shipping weight 6 ounces $1.97

STRIPES
are happening

Only Sears combines this super new outfit with

Twist'n Turn Stacey

8-piece Gift Set $5⁹⁷

Stacey loves this madly mod sports ensemble. Wide striped shell, skirt and socks. Jacket top and matching ankle boots. Vinyl, 11½-in. Stacey doll has twist 'n turn waist and bendable legs. Rooted hair, "real" eyelashes. Clothes hanger and a clear plastic posing stand included. Stacey comes dressed in a fashionable 1-piece swimsuit.
49 N 30087—Shipping wt. 1 lb. $5.97

Francie and Barbie have Twist 'n Turn waists $2⁹⁹ each

10 Francie with a striped knit swimsuit and long, bouncy rooted hair. Plastic stand included. Vinyl, 11½ in. tall with bendable legs, "real" lashes.
49 N 3550—Shpg. wt. 11 oz. $2.99

11 Barbie in a luscious swimsuit. Long, rooted hair. Plastic stand. Vinyl, 11½ in. tall with bendable legs.
49 N 3549—Shpg. wt. 11 oz. $2.99

"Stacey and I are having tea"
"Let's have Barbie over for tea"
"Let's visit Barbie and Stacey"

Barbie, Stacey and Christie TALK $4⁴⁴ each

(12 thru 14) Listen in on the gabfest. Each doll says many full-length, teen phrases . . all at random. Stacey has a British accent. Just pull the talking ring, no batteries needed. Clear stand combines with box cap to form a chair. Vinyl dolls are 11½ in. tall. Rooted hair, "real" lashes and bendable legs. Shipping weight each 12 ounces.
(12) 49 N 30015—Talking Barbie $4.44
(13) 49 N 30014—Talking Stacey 4.44
(14) 49 N 30072—Talking Christie 4.44

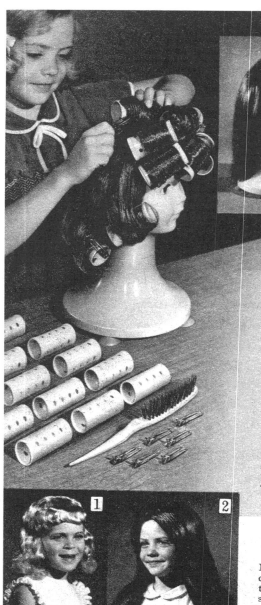

Beauty School..
all the tools you need for teaching yourself to set and style hair like a professional

$8.99 set

Learn hair care this fun and easy way. You can wash, comb, set, brush and tease the rooted nylon hair on the mannequin head.. get ideas for your own hair styles. Start with straight, wet hair.. design your own styles as you go along. Roll hair on rollers or use clips for a firmer set. Soft, vinyl head has moving eyes, lashes.. head swivels. Rubber suction cups hold plastic base firmly. 12 plastic rollers, 6 metal clips and a hairbrush. Head is 13 inches high.

49 N 1361—Shpg. wt. 2 lbs. 8 oz..... Set $8.99

High fashion Wigs and Falls for little girls

Now your little girl can have a wig or fall of her very own that she can set and style. Washable nylon hair takes a curl easily. Wig only is mounted on head-shaped form ready for styling; fall is unmounted.

1 Wig. About 18 inches.
49 N 13631—Blonde
49 N 13633—Brunette
Shpg. wt. 1 lb...... $5.97

2 Fall. About 22 inches.
49N13661—Blonde
49 N 13663—Brunette
Shpg. wt. 10 oz... $3.97

3 $4.97

4 $3.27

Musical Jewelry Boxes

Winsome and modern teen doll on top bends to almost any position.. looks so graceful when snapped to top of box. Open it and a music box plays as a pretty ballerina twirls in time to the tune. Every little girl would love such a keepsake. And your little one will enjoy having a place to put her own special trinkets. Sturdy wood box covered with simulated white leather in a modern design. Rayon satin lining keeps her jewelry in a queenly setting. Petite mirror in lid. Brass-finished snap lock. From Japan.

3 **Large.** About 9x5x4 inches high.
49 N 1375—Shpg. wt. 1 lb. 8 oz.... $4.97

4 **Regular.** About 6x4x3 inches high.
49 N 1378—Shpg. wt. 14 oz....... $3.27

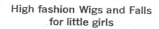

You'll go "out" looking glamorous with these "Dress-up" accessories $3.99 set

The best dressed little lady in town wears a rayon plush stole that looks like mink and a fashion-right "wig" of plastic. Step out in high heels with adjustable pop-it beads. Your pretend diamond fingers glisten when you wear fingernails with paste-on color. And ring flashes in the light. Other accessories include a plastic orchid corsage for those very special occasions and a lorgnette.

49 N 1349—Shipping weight 1 pound 6 ounces.. Set $3.99

Your very own Purse filled to the brim $2.97 set

Leather-look vinyl "Mini" bag has an adjustable shoulder strap. Inside you can put your lipstick, play powder and compact with your comb, brush and mirror set. You'll love wearing modern accessories such as make-believe glasses with eyelashes, link belt with medallion, and bangle bracelets. Set also includes play nail polish, play polish remover, applicator brush, 3 manicure aids, and polyurethane puff.

49 N 13037—Shpg. wt. 1 lb...... Set $2.97

Pretty Girl Travel Case filled with cosmetics $3.97 set

Washable vinyl "hatbox" style case. And it's filled with famous brand cosmetics just like Mom's. Tray inside contains flower shaped soap, Pacquins® hand lotion, Chap Stick®, Shower to Shower powder, lipstick, rain bonnet with case, hair clips, hair combs, 2 small barrettes and 1 large barrette and 2 hair rollers. Case is about 10x10x3½ in. deep with handy carry strap.

49 N 1333—Wt. 1 lb. 12 oz..... Set $3.97

Flower *Pow*

Take Along Slumber Bags

Really "in" for those pajama parties where the girl-talk is as groovy as these flowery bags

$14.99

Flower-fields shimmer in blues, pinks or greens. "Slumber" comfortably while you talk about school news, latest movies. Quilted, washable cotton shell, liner with matching tote. 2 lbs. of long-lasting bonded Vycron® polyester fiber fill. 75x34 in. 100-in. separating zippers . . zip two bags together.

Shipping weight 5 pounds 4 ounces.
(1) 6N70316 — Blue on blue.........................$14.99
(2) 6N70317 — Blue, pink and orange................14.99
(3) 6N70318 — Green, yellow and pink...............14.99

Bag can open as comforter

The Game of LOVE
$3³³

Twist and turn .. but don't fall down .. as you try to spell LOVE. A great party game .. can be played in stocking feet. Colorful vinyl sheet is placed on floor .. spinner stops at letters L, O, V or E. Use your hands and feet to spell LOVE .. the first to spell it is the winner. Large sheet is 54 inches long, 48 inches wide. 2 to 4 people can play. Age 6 to adult. Instructions included.
49 N 65123—Wt. 2 lbs. 8 oz..... $3.33

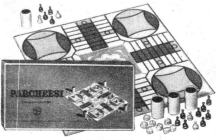

BOY, LOOK AT THE GAMES! HOW 'BOUT ASKIN' SANTA CLAUS FOR ONE OF EACH!

FEELEY MEELEY $3⁷⁷

The game that gives you a funny feeling—by testing your sense of touch. Find objects you can't see. Box holds plastic objects .. spider, frog, ring, car, dog, spoon, rooster and more. A card is turned signaling players to find item shown .. by feel! Winner is player who finds the most objects. For 2 to 4 players, ages 10 to adult.
49 N 65166—Shipping weight 3 lbs. 8 oz.. $3.77

Deluxe **MONOPOLY** with tray $5⁹⁹ deluxe

For 2 to 10 players, ages 10 to adult. Deluxe edition contains enough "money" and equipment for 10 to play at once, or for 2 to play almost indefinitely. Plastic banker's tray keeps deeds, money and buildings in order. Board is strongly reinforced to last.
79 N 6501C—Shipping weight 4 pounds........$5.99
Standard Monopoly. For 2 to 8 players. No tray.
49 N 65039—Shipping weight 2 pounds 8 ounces.$3.99

PUZZLES IN ROUND $2⁷⁹ set

Beautiful full-color reproductions of ancient works of art .. in round jigsaw puzzles. Set contains 3 antiquities .. Aztec Stone Calendar, Ching Dynasty Chinese Porcelain depicting courtyard scene of 1662, and Embroidered Antique American Textile of 1700. 19x19 in.
49 N 6528—Wt. 3 lbs. 1 oz..Set $2.79

ELECTRIC FASCINATION $3⁹⁹ without batteries

Get three metal balls through the maze before your opponent does—and light up the tower. 2 double-sided mazes about 8 in. long. 8 balls. Uses 2 "D" batteries, order 1 pkg. below.
49 N 65117—Shipping weight 2 lbs..........$3.99
49N4660-"D" Batteries. Pkg. of 2. Wt. 8 oz. Pkg. 38c

SQUARESVILLE $3⁹⁹

Make the right connections in this game of skill and strategy. Place your sticks strategically and complete as many squares as possible while keeping your opponent from doing the same. Markers show your progress. For 2 to 4 players, ages 10 to adult. Plastic gameboard with raised squares to hold wooden sticks and markers. 18x14 in.
49 N 65281—Shipping weight 2 lbs. 5 oz..$3.99

PARCHEESI $2⁵⁹

The original backgammon game of India. Throw dice to get your 4 men "home" before your opponent. Delightful fun for 2 to 4 players, ages 10 to adult. Set includes 4 sets of dice, 4 dice cups, 16 polished wood pawns and a colorful board.
49 N 65054—Wt. 2 lbs. 2 oz....$2.59

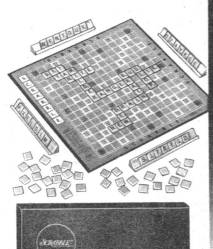

SCRABBLE® ... great word game $3⁷⁷

The crossword game that increases your word power. Accumulate points as you build words on board . . high score wins. 2 to 4 can play, ages 8 to adult. Game includes board, 100 word tiles with scoring numbers in corners and 4 letter racks.
Shipping weight 1 pound 11 oz.
49 N 65053 . . . . $3.77

You play checkers to capture card symbols and add up points. Capture only symbols that will make up a gin rummy hand. When your checkers cross into enemy territory, choose a symbol from the special cards on the board. Plastic marker shows symbol has been "captured". Winner is one who has the most points after last checker has been captured. Set includes board, plastic checkers, markers, cards. For players aged 12 to adult.
79N65082C–Wt. 3 lbs..$5.95

AVANTÉ
Combination Checker-Gin Rummy Game
$5⁹⁵

SCRABBLE® for Juniors $2⁴⁴

One side has easy picture identification words . . advance to harder words on other side. Player spelling the most words wins. Helps build vocabulary, makes spelling more fun. New 3rd edition has board, 100 letter tiles, instructions. For 2 players, age 6 and up.
49 N 65055—Wt. 2 lbs. 4 oz...$2.44

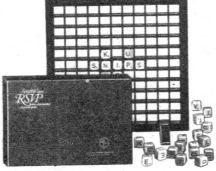

RSVP . . crossword game $4⁶⁹

3-dimensional game is played on both sides of an upright grid by individuals or teams. The object . . to form words horizontally or vertically by placing letter cubes crossword fashion on your side of board while blocking formation of words on opposite side. Game, in handsome leatherette (imitation leather) box, includes grid, 75 polished hardwood cubes and directions.
49 N 65168—Shipping weight 2 lbs. 2 oz. $4.69

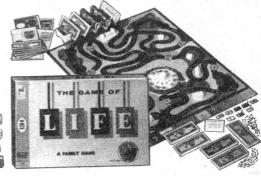

THE GAME OF LIFE $4⁸⁹

Start up 3-dimensional road of life with car and $2,000. Run into snags and good luck as you go through college, business and married life. Make the right decisions and Wheel of Fate may spin you into Millionaire Acres . . as winner. Game includes 8 cars, $7,000,000 in play money, cards and certificates, board. For 2 to 8 players, age 10 to adult.
79 N 65034C—Shipping weight 4 pounds. . . . $4.89

GRAB A LOOP . . action game $4⁴⁴

Attach belts with loops . . object of game is to grab as many loops of the right color from other participants as you can without losing any of yours. Player with most loops at end wins. 36 plastic loops, 6 belts and bases. Age 8 to adult.
49 N 65309—Shipping weight 3 lbs. $4.44

MYSTERY DATE GAME $2⁸⁹

Girl players (2 to 4) try to collect the right combination of cards to complete their date-time outfits. Dates include dance, skiing, bowling or beach party. Player wins if she has right outfit.
49 N 65035—Wt. 1 lb. 12 oz. . . . $2.89

RISK! Game of War Strategy $6⁵⁹

Place armies on 42 territories. Each roll of dice pits army against army. Win by occupying every territory on board. 450 army pieces, cards, 6 dice. For 2 to 6, age 10 and up.
79 N 65147C—Shipping weight 4 pounds. $6.59

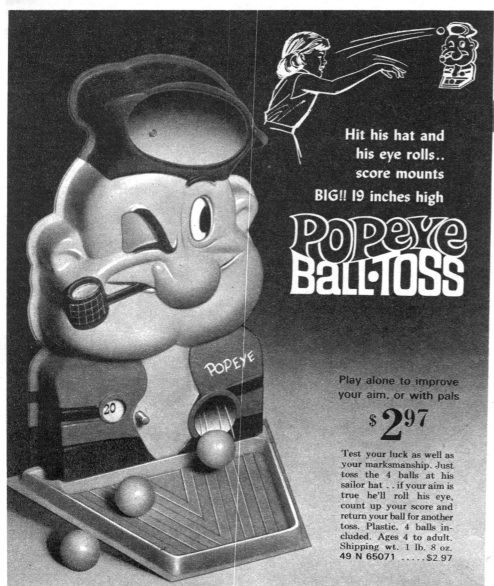

Hit his hat and
his eye rolls..
score mounts
BIG!! 19 inches high

POPeye BALL·TOSS

Play alone to improve
your aim, or with pals

$2⁹⁷

Test your luck as well as
your marksmanship. Just
toss the 4 balls at his
sailor hat .. if your aim is
true he'll roll his eye,
count up your score and
return your ball for another
toss. Plastic. 4 balls included. Ages 4 to adult.
Shipping wt. 1 lb. 8 oz.
49 N 65071 .....$2.97

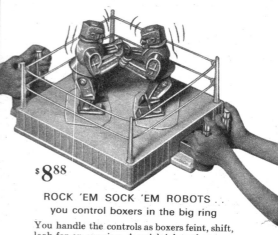

$8⁸⁸

ROCK 'EM SOCK 'EM ROBOTS ..
you control boxers in the big ring

You handle the controls as boxers feint, shift,
look for an opening. A quick jab to the opponent's jaw sets off a spring mechanism that
pops his head up . . you're the winner by a
KO. Press his head down to begin a new bout.
12½ in. tall plastic boxers, 20x17-in. ring.
79 N 65119C—Shipping weight 6 lbs. $8.88

$3⁹⁹

HANDS DOWN .. the slap happy game
.. you just might win by bluffing!

Pick a card, match a pair. Quick! Hit the
"hand". Last hand down loses a card. High
score in points on matched pairs win this
game, but if your bluff is called the joker's
on you. Plastic. 3 to 4 players. 7 to adult.
49N6507–Shipping weight 1 lb. 12 oz..$3.99

$3⁸⁹ without batteries

OPERATION .. you're the
Doctor .. remove parts with
electric probe .. gently.

'Doctors' operate on patient with hilarious ailments. Pick a card to determine
operation and fee. If you goof, nose lights
up, buzzer sounds. Ages 6 to 14. Uses 2
"D" batteries, order 1 pkg. below.
49N65028—Shpg. wt. 1 lb. 12 oz..$3.89
"D" Batteries. Package of 2.
49 N 4660—Wt. 8 oz............38c

KA-BOOM! Pump up
balloon .. carefully.
If it pops, you lose

$3⁹⁹

First player puts balloon on
machine, then picks a number from 1 to 10. Pump that
number, then next player
takes over. Tension mounts
as balloon grows .. Ka-
Boom! Plastic. Balloons included. 2 to 6 players, ages
5 to 12. Wt. 1 lb. 4 oz.
49 N 6503 ....$3.99

$2⁴⁷

Score mounts as
stack shortens, but
don't topple it.

Bash the funny man with
the hammer .. add points
as you strike out sections.
Careful! Game ends when
he topples. 2 or more players, 5 to 12. Shpg. wt. 1 lb.
49 N 65025 ......$2.47

Play catch with
the TIME BOMB ..
you're out when
it goes off.

$2⁹⁹

Toss it away before it
goes "Bang" or you're
out of the game. Plas-
tic. For all the family.
Shipping weight 1 lb.
49 N 65026 ....$2.99

Blaze Ponderosa trails with the Cartwrights and their versatile 4-in-1 Bonanza Wagon

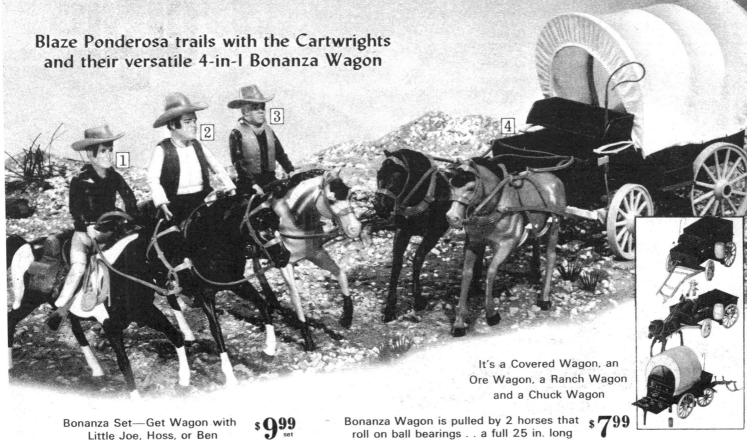

It's a Covered Wagon, an Ore Wagon, a Ranch Wagon and a Chuck Wagon

Bonanza Set—Get Wagon with Little Joe, Hoss, or Ben $9⁹⁹ set

The Cartwrights are fully jointed . . take any pose for lifelike action. Each 9 in. tall and comes with his own horse, saddle and cowboy accessories. Horses have ball-bearing hooves. Plastic. Wagon (2 horses included) is described at right.

(1) 79 N 59032L—Joe, horse and wagon. Wt. 10 lbs..Set $9.99
(2) 79 N 59033L—Hoss, horse and wagon. Wt. 10 lbs.Set 9.99
(3) 79 N 59034L—Ben, horse and wagon. Wt. 10 lbs..Set 9.99

Cartwright Family only. Joe, Hoss and Ben, each with horse.
79 N 59035C—Wagon not included. Shpg. wt. 4 lbs..Set $12.88

Bonanza Wagon is pulled by 2 horses that roll on ball bearings . . a full 25 in. long $7⁹⁹

4 Convertible wagon rolls across the Ponderosa. Blaze new trails across the West in the covered wagon. Change to ranch wagon to haul supplies from Virginia City. Or use it as a chuck wagon on a tough 'n rough cattle drive. Even converts to an ore wagon when you're ready to inspect the mines.

Wagon is fully equipped with camping gear . . for cooking, prospecting or carrying cargoes. Converts easily and quickly without cutting or gluing. It's made to scale for the Cartwrights. Has 65 authentic-looking scaled pieces in all. Wagon and horses are 25 inches long overall. Fully detailed plastic. Wagon has fabric cover.

79 N 6088L—Allow 10 pounds per postal regulations....................$7.99

JANE WEST AND HER DAUGHTER, JOSIE

Each has her own horse, dog, corral and carry case

Johnny West and his horse "Comanche" $3⁴⁴ each

5 **Johnny West** is ready for any kind of rugged action. He's 11½ inches tall, fully jointed to stand, "run," sit and ride. Completely outfitted in western gear. Plastic.
49 N 6015—Wt. 1 lb. 6 oz...$3.44

6 **Comanche.** Johnny's faithful horse. Fully jointed to "gallop" or "trot." 11½ inches tall. Plastic.
49 N 6037—Wt. 1 lb. 5 oz...$3.44

Jane West Set $7⁷⁹

Lovely and lifelike Jane West stands 11½ inches tall, fully jointed for action. She rides in corral or on the range with "Flame" . . 13 inches tall with saddle and bridle.

Includes 4 changes of clothes, range gear for Jane. "Flick" dog, 5½-inches tall. Plastic figures and paperboard carry case.
79 N 6025C—Shpg. wt. 5 lbs.....Set $7.79

Josie West Set $5⁹⁹

Have fun with Josie the teen-age cowgirl as she rides the trail on 11-inch tall "Poncho," protected by her 5-inch dog "Flack." She's 9 inches tall, fully jointed for action. Includes a set of accessories including clothes, corral and saddle. Plastic figures. Paperboard carry case.

Shipping weight 5 lbs.
79 N 6017C.........................Set $5.99

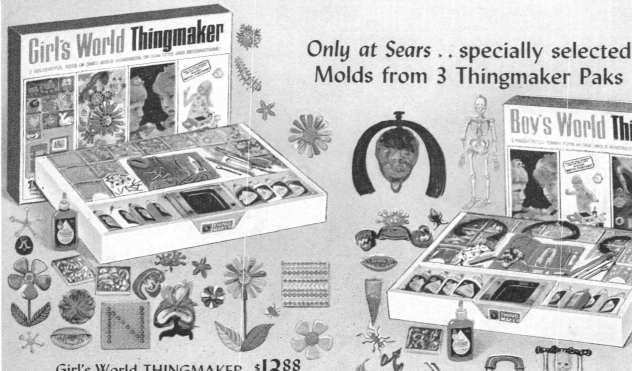

Girl's World Thingmaker

Only at Sears .. specially selected Molds from 3 Thingmaker Paks

Boy's World Thingmaker

Girl's World THINGMAKER $13.88

Outfit contains molds from Picadoos (3), Mini-Dragons (5) and Fun Flowers (6)—14 molds in all—to help sugar 'n spice young ladies make all the colorful, creative things they want.
Here's what they'll get:
14 specially selected molds; 8 bottles of Plastigoop; heating unit; cooling tray; mold handle; prying tool; 2 bundles of wire; plastic knife; tube of cement; flower arranger; bobby pins; plated mold guide; pattern pack guide; backup board; 2 strip packs; foil pack and full operating instr.
49 N 20023—Wt. 5 lbs...$13.88

Fun Flowers Thingmaker Set: heater, molds; Plastigoop; cooling tray; accessories.
49 N 2226—Wt. 4 lbs.....$8.94

Jumbo 12-ounce size Plastigoop

There are hours of fun in these king-size plastic bottles.
49 N 20051—White
49 N 20052—Red
49 N 20053—Flesh
49 N 20054—Nite-Glo
49 N 20055—Fluorescent Green
49 N 20056—Fluorescent Blue
49 N 20057—Yellow
49 N 20058—Fluorescent Orange
Shipping weight 12 ounces each............... Each $1.99

Boy's World THINGMAKER $13.88

14 frightfully funny molds selected from Mini-Dragons (5), Creepy Crawlers (5), Fright Factory (4) to make all the icky things that boys like.
Here's what they'll get:
14 molds; 8 bottles of Plastigoop; heater; cooling tray; mold handle; prying tool; bundle of wire; plastic knife; 2 strip packs; 3 hairpieces; 8 pieces of colored yarn; ¼-ounce bottles blue, red paint; ¼-ounce bottle cement; a brush; 5 pieces clear plastic, and complete instructions.
49 N 20022—Wt. 5 lbs... $13.88
Mini-Dragon Thingmaker Set. Incl. heater, molds, Plastigoop, accessories.
49 N 20094—Wt. 3 lbs. 8 oz. $8.94
NOTE: Thingmakers, Vac-U-Form UL listed, 110–120-v, 60-c A.C.

doodley-doo
.. colorful, squiggly plastic things you can trace or design $2.66

It's easy! Make all the wiggly-plastic things you want. Just trace a flower, a clown or write your name on a foil sheet, place in mom's oven for 10 minutes (at 300°), remove and let cool. That's all there is to it. Set contains 7 assorted tubes of colored plastic fluid and 3 different aluminum-foil sheets with printed patterns or design your own—no molds required.
49 N 20024—Shipping weight 1 pound 4 ounces.....$2.66

Vac-U-Form .. make toys, jewelry, lots more from plastic sheets $11.88

Mattel's sturdy metal machine forms permanent plastic sheets into exciting toys, comic buttons and signs from more than 60 forms. Unit is 9½x4x4½ in. high and comes with 65 plastic sheets plus everything you will need including instructions. Order extra refill below.
49 N 2261—Shpg. wt. 6 lbs.....$11.88

Vac-U-Form Refill Pack. 45 assorted colored plastic sheets.
49 N 2221—Shpg. wt. 4 oz...Pkg. 99c

Thingmaker Molds for Vac-U-Form $1.99

Note: Both Skeleton and Squirtles Accessory Kits can be used with Thingmaker or Vac-U-Form machines.

Squirtles .. make black bugs that squirt water.
49 N 20048—Shipping weight 8 ounces......$1.99

Skeleton .. jiggly, monstrous .. **GLOWS** in the **DARK**.
49 N 20049—Shipping weight 8 ounces......$1.99

Explore outer space indoors . . learn the stars and constellations with Sears Home Planetarium and Dome

Planetarium projects over 250 stars and all major constellations . . BIG 4-foot dome simulates the sky

Planetarium $14.99   Dome $17.99

Lightweight Plastic Dome

Sturdy Plastic Planetarium

Extraordinary Home Planetarium. Makes the sky as familiar to you as the ceiling of your room. Learn to recognize over 60 constellations as seen from any geographical location in the Northern Hemisphere. Use the pointer to identify specific stars and constellations. Planetarium plugs into any AC outlet . . the pointer operates from planetarium current. Dimmer control increases or decreases star brightness. Instructions, star charts included. 7 inch diameter. Planetarium is 14 inches tall. UL listed for 110–120-volt, 60-cycle AC.
49 N 1959—Shipping wt. 3 lbs. 12 oz. . . $14.99

Plastic Dome. Gives the same visual effect as planetarium domes many times its size, such as those used in schools and colleges. For ideal results use dome with planetarium (above) so that stars and constellations are projected in correct proportions. Only a dome-shaped surface gives a realistic representation of the sky. Smooth white surface for excellent projection results. Lightweight, high-impact styrene. 4 feet wide, 2 feet high. 6 sections. Unassembled. Freight (rail or truck) or express.
79 N 1960N—Shipping weight 6 pounds. $17.99

BLAST OFF! 3 rockets soar 150 to 300 feet on water-power thrust

2-stage Apollo

2-stage Gemini

Anti-ballistic missile

$7.66

Watch the scale model Apollo zoom to 150 feet, separate, go 150 feet more. Gemini climbs 200 feet and releases a capsule that floats down by parachute. Anti-ballistic missile shoots 300 feet. Launch all 3 rockets by remote control. Fuel the control center with water, pump handle until gauge shows proper altitude. Pressure pumped through 8-ft. hose. Count down by turning knob. Zero hour! 14-in. gantry swings out to release rocket. All plastic.
49 N 1963—Shipping weight 3 pounds 12 ounces. . . . Set $7.66

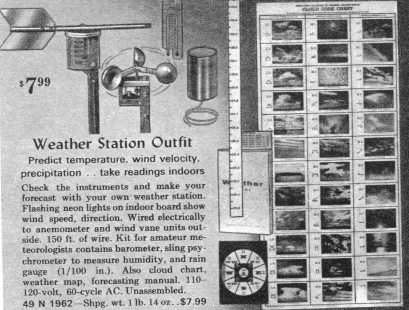

$7.99

CLOUD CODE CHART

Weather Station Outfit

Predict temperature, wind velocity, precipitation . . take readings indoors

Check the instruments and make your forecast with your own weather station. Flashing neon lights on indoor board show wind speed, direction. Wired electrically to anemometer and wind vane units outside. 150 ft. of wire. Kit for amateur meteorologists contains barometer, sling psychrometer to measure humidity, and rain gauge (1/100 in.). Also cloud chart, weather map, forecasting manual. 110–120-volt, 60-cycle AC. Unassembled.
49 N 1962—Shpg. wt. 1 lb. 14 oz. . . $7.99

STAR FINDER

Locates constellations . . tells time and position by the stars

Plot the rising and setting of the sun and moon, identify constellations, galaxies and clusters; use the stars for time, direction, and position. No mathematical computations required. This sturdy, metal based, multiple use instrument easily explains movements of the stars and planets. Can be mounted on a tripod. Includes star chart, manual and instructions. Star finder is 7¼x10¼ in. wide, 10½ in. high.
79 N 1964C—Shpg. wt. 5 lbs. . . . $13.66

$13.66

PC Sears 541

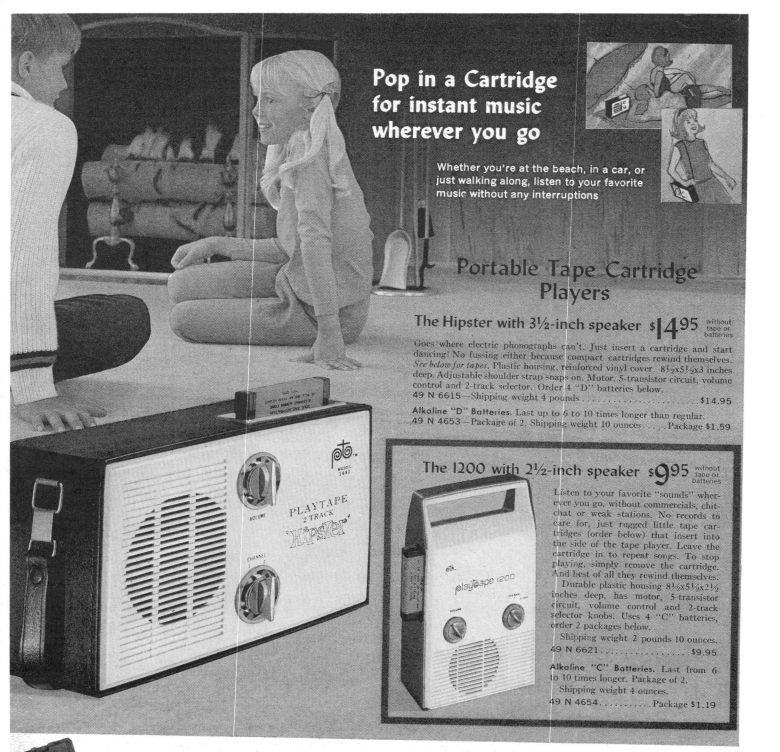

Pop in a Cartridge for instant music wherever you go

Whether you're at the beach, in a car, or just walking along, listen to your favorite music without any interruptions

Portable Tape Cartridge Players

The Hipster with 3½-inch speaker $14.95 *without tape or batteries*

Goes where electric phonographs can't. Just insert a cartridge and start dancing! No fussing either because compact cartridges rewind themselves. *See below for tapes.* Plastic housing, reinforced vinyl cover. 8½x5½x3 inches deep. Adjustable shoulder strap snaps on. Motor, 5-transistor circuit, volume control and 2-track selector. Order 4 "D" batteries below.
49 N 6615—Shipping weight 4 pounds $14.95

Alkaline "D" Batteries. Last up to 6 to 10 times longer than regular.
49 N 4653—Package of 2. Shipping weight 10 ounces . . . . . Package $1.59

The 1200 with 2½-inch speaker $9.95 *without tape or batteries*

Listen to your favorite "sounds" wherever you go, without commercials, chit-chat or weak stations. No records to care for, just rugged little tape cartridges (order below) that insert into the side of the tape player. Leave the cartridge in to repeat songs. To stop playing, simply remove the cartridge. And best of all they rewind themselves.
Durable plastic housing 8½x5½x2½ inches deep, has motor, 5-transistor circuit, volume control and 2-track selector knobs. Uses 4 "C" batteries, order 2 packages below.
Shipping weight 2 pounds 10 ounces.
49 N 6621 . . . . $9.95

Alkaline "C" Batteries. Last from 6 to 10 times longer. Package of 2.
Shipping weight 4 ounces.
49 N 4654 . . . . Package $1.19

Pre-recorded Magnetic Tapes

$1.29

Play for 10 to 12 minutes. Sealed in durable plastic. Cartridge 3½x3x½ inches thick. Shipping weight 2 ounces . . . . . . Each $1.29

49 N 66149—**Herb Alpert.** *Lollipops and Roses; Tangerine; Love Potion No. 9; 1 more.*

49 N 66151—**Herb Alpert.** *Shadow of Your Smile; It Was a Very Good Year; 2 more.*

49 N 66021—**The Animals.** *It's My Life; Gonna Send You to Walker; 2 more.*

49 N 66208—**Eric Burdon and the Animals.** *Help Me Girl; A Girl Named Sandy; 2 more.*

49 N 66205—**The Beatles.** *Help, I Need You; The Night Before; Another Hard Day's Night.*

49 N 66206—**The Beatles.** *Lucy in the Sky; A Little Help from My Friends; 2 more.*

49 N 66213—**The Beatles.** *Hello, Goodbye; Flying; Magical Mystery Tour; Penny Lane.*

49 N 66204—**The Beach Boys**—*Don't Worry Baby; Fun, Fun, Fun; 2 more.*

49 N 66011—**The Righteous Brothers.** *Soul and Inspiration; Hey Girl; 2 more.*

49 N 66154—**Petula Clark**—*Downtown; In Love; You Belong to Me; Music.*

49 N 66207—**Herman's Hermits.** *Upstairs, Downstairs; Moon Shine Man; 2 more.*

49 N 66029—**Herman's Hermits.** *Hold On; I Got a Feeling; A Must to Avoid; 1 more.*

49 N 6603—**Herman's Hermits.** *Leaning on a Lamppost; Gotta Get Away; Wild Love; 1 more.*

49 N 66155—**Trini Lopez.** *Lemon Tree; Michael; This Train; Puff (the Magic Dragon).*

49 N 6617—**Trini Lopez.** *You are My Sunshine; The Saints; Smile; Sweet Georgia Brown.*

49 N 66198—**Dean Martin.** *The Door's Still Open; Gonna Change Everything; 2 more.*

49 N 66197—**Sandpipers.** *Strangers in the Night; Angelica; Cast Your Fate to the Wind.*

49 N 66199—**Frank Sinatra.** *I Concentrate on You; Baubles, Bangles, Beads; 2 more.*

49 N 66202—**The Supremes.** *Nothing but Heartaches; He Holds His Own; 2 more.*

49 N 66209—**The Supremes.** *You Can't Hurry Love; Back in My Arms; 2 more.*

49 N 66017—**Fantabulous Strings.** *Thunderball; What's New Pussycat; Pink Panther.*

49 N 66212—**Four Tops.** *Baby I Need Your Loving; It's the Same Old Song; 2 more.*

49 N 66201—**Jr. Walker and All Stars.** *Cleo's Mood; Shotgun; Shake and Fingerpop; 1 more.*

49 N 66203—**Stevie Wonder.** *Bang Bang; A Place in the Sun; Hey Love; 1 more.*

49 N 66211—**Stevie Wonder.** *A Fool for You; I Was Made to Love You; 2 more.*

As this century's most chaotic and exciting decade came to a close, great changes were taking place at every level of society. The struggle for Civil Rights and Women's Rights gained new prominence, but ideas like these took a great deal of time to settle into the minds of Middle America. In the costume pages of the 1969 Sears Christmas Wishbook, boys could choose from any number of active personalities -- astronaut, Marine, Highway trooper, Batman or Superman. But girls had only the old stand-bys -- ballerina, nurse, princess, bride.

True, there were also a number of gender-neutral toys available, as always -- three different farm playsets, pogo sticks, magic tricks, "world's tiniest record player" -- but little girls were still primarily being offered only the options of glamour, beauty and parenthood as the stuff of their fantasies.

But the imagination is a powerful thing. And throughout the years the Sears Christmas Wishbooks have given both boys and girls plenty of dreams to dream, and plenty of possibilities to contemplate -- and those are more durable, and more fun, than any toy could ever be.

Sears Christmas
Wishbook

1969

Heavy-gauge Steel Sets

5 animals travel first class in this Cattle Truck and Horse Trailer
$6⁹⁹

Everything you need to take prize livestock to the fair. Covered horse trailer has gate that lowers to form ramp. Horse and colt fit easily inside. Ford pickup farm truck has removable stake sides for transporting bull, cow and calf. Drop-down tailgate helps in loading. Also trailer hitch, non-marring tires. Heavy-gauge steel construction with tough, baked enamel finish. Plastic animals. 19½ in. long, overall.
49 C 54075—Shipping weight 4 lbs. 14 oz.... Set $6.99

SAFARI HUNT .. herd 9 "wild" animals into cage, then crank it onto trailer $6⁹⁹

Cage these "wild" animals and bring 'em back alive to your "game ranch" or "zoo." Elephants, giraffes, lions and camels .. even a monkey .. fit in the cage. Just turn the winch to bring the cage up onto trailer .. hitch it up to safari wagon .. and you're off! Sturdy steel construction. Slide-out metal ramp and lift-up door on cage to make loading easy. Plastic animals. 24½x5x6½ inches high overall.
49 C 5522—Shpg. wt. 5 lbs. 5 oz. .. . . Set $6.99

Die-cast Metal Sets

Mini Farm Set with all 1/32-scale models $4⁷⁹

Implements really work .. so you can plow, plant and cultivate just like a real farmer. Die-cast metal and steel set has 8-in. GMC truck, 4½-in. wagon, 5¼-in. tractor, 6⅛-in. spreader, 3¾-in. disc, 4¼-in. harrow, and 7 plastic animals. Farm implements have rubber tires; truck has non-mar plastic tires. Fun for the youngest "farmers."
49 C 54071—Shpg. wt. 2 lbs. 8 oz... Set $4.79

Deluxe Farm Set with all 1/16-scale models $6⁴⁹

These large-scale replicas of International Harvester equipment let you plant, plow and cultivate like a real farmer. All implements really work. Die-cast metal set with rubber or non-mar plastic wheels: 8-in. long tractor, 8-in. long wagon, 5½-in. wide 3-bottom plow, 8½-in. wide double disc, 6½-in. wide harrow.
79 C 54072C—Shipping wt. 6 lbs... Set $6.49

Transportation Set .. a fleet of 4 large die-cast metal vehicles $9⁹⁹ set

These are heavyweights. Each boasts clear plastic windshield, beautifully detailed interior. 6-inch beetle-bug car even has a sun-roof. 11-inch pick-up, 11-inch dump truck and 12-inch tow truck are finished in two-tone enamel .. have heavy-rib whitewall tires. Operating crane on tow truck, dump body on dump truck. Pick-up has stake sides.
49 C 54102—Shipping weight 9 pounds............ Set $9.99

A whole country world right inside the case

50-piece Farm Set centers around spacious barn with built-in silo .. plus you get plenty of farm implements, even a family of five to help with the work

$5⁹⁹ Corgi vehicles not included

1 Open the side of the handsome barn to find silo, hayloft, stalls, corral doors that really open. Be greeted by life-like horses, cows, ducks, other barnyard animals. Combine, tractor and stake truck mean chores go fast on this modern farm. Plastic parts.
Vinyl barn is 14x9½x11 in. high. Animals from Japan.
Shipping weight 3 lbs. 8 oz.
49 C 59057.........Set $5.99

2 Corgi Farm Vehicles. 27-pc. set. Fully described on opposite page.
49 C 54086—Wt. 1 lb. 14 oz. $9.99

Barn is a carrycase, too

SEARS CUTS PRICES on this 89-piece Livestock Farm Set

Move "crops" up and into barn on sturdy crank-action pulley .. truck, 28 animals, 6 farmhands included

$4⁴⁴

Save 10%. Was $4.94 last Christmas. Activity centers around all-steel open back barn. Freight traverse rod moves litter carrier in and out. Tractor has harrow, plow, corn planter, stone boat and 3 other accessories. Pick-up truck. Farm tools, vegetables, milk cans, feed box, bales of hay. 20x9x9 inches high. Plastic parts. Unassembled.
79 C 59773C—Shipping wt. 4 lbs.....Set $4.44

Whopping 214-piece Farm Set

42 lifelike animals .. tractor with plowing accessories .. handy haylift you can operate

$8⁹⁹

Big 22-inch platform supports all-metal barn and silo. Chicken coop houses the fowl; birds perch on board and barbed wire fences that hold the stock. Pick-up truck and jeep simplify your chores. 6 farmhands help you load produce into 3-level, open back barn .. hitch up rake, disc and harrow. Other accessories, including crops are 3-dimensional plastic. 22x17x12 inches high overall. Unassembled. Buy it the easy way—order by phone.
79 C 59779C—Shipping weight 9 pounds.........Set $8.99

PCBKN | Sears | 509

11 Games in all . .

everything from Darts to Golf to Shuffleboard to Bowling with an automatic pin setter

$13⁹⁹

The whole sports-minded family will enjoy this set. Play Shuffleboard with 4 pushers, 8 discs. Dart toss has 4 darts and target. Bowling set has two 5-inch plastic balls and time-saving automatic pin setter that anyone can operate with little effort. Try out "Bounce the Checker," Tic-Tac-Toe, Checker-Pitch and even golf. Also 3 racing games with 4 racing cars, horses and airplanes. Printed linoleum flooring is 12 feet x 2 feet wide. Plastic parts.

79 C 29113L—Shipping weight 15 pounds.............Set $13.99

Push down lever to set pins

Bowl a great game in your living room, basement or rec room . . no pins to pick up

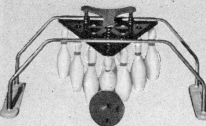

Automatic Pin Setter Game with 2 bowling balls.
$8⁹⁹

The steel and plastic pin setter holds 10 regulation-size pins in place. Hit pins, they flip up . . press-down action resets them. 5-inch plastic balls. Unit 30x14x14 inches deep. Great sport for bad weather days. *Allow 10 lbs. postage per postal regulations.*

79 C 29086L $8.99

Tall-up with Pogo Sticks or walk tall with Steel Stilts

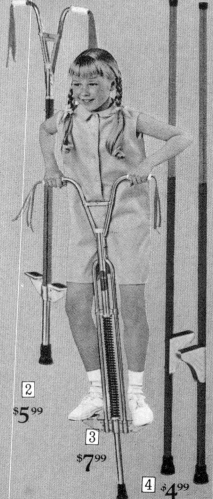

1 Pogo Stick with new count-meter. Accurately records each jump. Sturdily constructed with chrome-plated tubular steel frame. Tough nylon bearing with adjustable spring for long life. Grooved rubber foot pads and tip. 60 inches high. Holds up to 200 lbs.

79 C 29236C—Wt. 8 lbs. $10.99

2 Pogo Stick for weight up to 100 lbs. Designed for ages 6 to 12. It's 45 inches high. Spring tension adjusts. Baked enamel finish on sturdy steel tubing. Vinyl handle grips with plastic streamers for a racy look. Slip-resistant foot pads and tip.
Shipping weight 5 pounds.

79 C 2908C $5.99

3 Pogo Stick for all ages holds up to 180 lbs. Slip-resistant foot pads and tip; vinyl handle grips with plastic streamers. High tension triple tubular steel construction with friction-free spring for sturdy support. 48 inches high.

79 C 29059C—Wt. 8 lbs.. $7.99

4 Strong steel Stilts have adjustable footrests. Can be raised from 10 to 16 inches off floor. 5 feet high. Rubber tips help prevent sliding and floor scratches. Finished in red, white, blue enamel. For ages 6 to 14 years.

79 C 2916C—Wt. 5 lbs. Pr. $4.99

1 $10⁹⁹

JUMP COUNTER

7814

Automatically counts to 9999. Reset to 0 any time . . just twist dial.

2 $5⁹⁹

3 $7⁹⁹

4 $4⁹⁹

"Hey, hey! Somebody ate my porridge today"

Play 'n Show Phono-Projector .. $12.99 without batteries
insert picture platters and close lid

Color slides are firmly attached to each phonograph record. As story progresses, picture changes. Needle sets automatically when lid is closed. See and hear Yogi Bear and the Flintstones. Use also as a 45 RPM record player. Plastic projector measures 12x11x10¼ in. high. Uses 3 "D" batteries, order pkg. below.
79 C 16285C—Shipping weight 6 pounds...........................Set $12.99

Set of 2 Picture Platters. See and hear Mr. Magoo in 2 different episodes.
49 C 16286—Shipping weight 14 ounces......................Set 2.49

Set of 2 Picture Platters. See and hear Mr. Magoo and Yogi Bear. 2 shows.
49 C 16287—Shipping weight 14 ounces......................Set 2.49

"I'll huff and I'll puff and I'll blooow"

My-Books That Talk with Record Player .. $7.99 without batteries
press button to start hidden needle

Put book on player and turn page. Press talk button and record begins to play. 16-page books are fully illustrated, written for child-reading exercises. At end of each 2 pages player stops .. child turns pages and presses button to restart. Plastic 12x9x3 inches high. Uses 1 "D" battery .. order pkg. below. Set includes 2 talking books, the "Three Little Pigs" and "Chicken Little."
49 C 16288—Shipping weight 2 pounds 9 ounces.....................Set $7.99

Refill Set. Includes "Jack and the Beanstalk" and "Billy Goats Gruff."
49 C 16289—Shipping weight 12 ounces..........................Set 2.49
49 C 46606—"D" Batteries. Package of 6. Shpg. wt. 1 lb. 8 oz........Pkg. 1.19

MIGHTY TINY

World's Tiniest RECORD PLAYER
Fits in pocket or purse .. plays anywhere

With 24 records, each in its own colorful record jacket, so you can carry them all easily .. fun for school, outdoors, club meetings

$3.99 without batteries

Imagine carrying your very own record player and records around in your pocket. Plastic player operates on 1 "AA" battery .. order package below. Only 2¾x4¾x2 inches high with 2⅜-in. diameter records. Needle plays record automatically .. starts and stops by itself when lid is closed.
49 C 16291—Shipping weight 12 ounces.......................Set $3.99

"AA" Batteries. Package of six.
49 C 46666—Shipping weight 6 ounces.....................Package 99c

GEE, NO... I CAN'T MAKE MYSELF DISAPPEAR! I'M NOT THAT GOOD YET!

Semi-professional $9.99 MAGIC CHEST

Set includes 11 tricks with full instructions: Chinese linking rings, card locator, cigarette through handkerchief, dice cup, genie bottle, money maker, mystic smoke, nickel-to-penny-to-dime (coins not incl.) magic wand, book of 102 tricks. 18x10x6-in. heavy paperboard.
49 C 16121—Wt. 3 lbs. 4 oz. Set $9.99

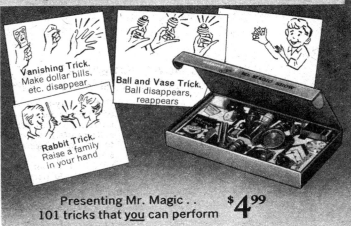

Vanishing Trick. Make dollar bills, etc. disappear

Ball and Vase Trick. Ball disappears, reappears

Rabbit Trick. Raise a family in your hand

Presenting Mr. Magic .. $4.99
101 tricks that you can perform

You'll learn to make play rabbits appear and disappear, turn a penny into a dime and dozens more baffling tricks. Magic show box includes all the props you'll need (except coins) for 18 special fun tricks, plus the famous book of 101 Magic Tricks .. even a mustache.
21x11¼x2½ inches thick.
49 C 1703—Shipping weight 1 pound 12 ounces..........Set $4.99

1 **Superman.** He "flies" to the rescue in his authentic costume of red and blue shrinkage-controlled cotton with sweeping cape. *State S, M or L.*
49 C 7747F—Shipping weight 1 lb. 2 oz.......$5.99

2 **Bride.** Long, brocade-like rayon taffeta gown. Net veil falls from lace-trimmed satin headband. Pretend pearl necklace and ring set; tiny bouquet included. *State S, M or L.* Shipping weight 13 oz.
49 C 7751F....................................$4.99

3 **Princess with light-up wand.** Starry gown of rayon acetate. Sparkling headpiece; detachable wings have translucent glow. Bulb and battery for wand included. *State S, M or L.*
49 C 77024F—Shipping weight 1 lb. 2 oz.......$5.99

4 **Ballerina.** Dance and twirl in elasticized acetate satin bodice trimmed with shimmery edging. Frothy nylon tutu over-skirt. *State S, M or L.*
49 C 77025F—Shipping weight 12 ounces......$5.99

5 **Drum Majorette.** Be the hit of the parade in your bright red and white outfit of shrink-controlled cotton and rayon satin. Set includes hat, belt and high-rising "spats" that slip over shoes. Fancy, gold-color decorations on visored hat and shoulder epaulets. *State S, M or L.*
49 C 7748F—Shipping weight 1 lb. 8 oz.....$4.99

6 **Astronaut Helmet.** Designed to look like a real outer-space helmet. Made of strong plastic with tinted, transparent lift-up face shield. Pretend microphone mouthpiece included.
49 C 77029—Shipping weight 2 lbs. 2 oz....$3.59

7 **Astronaut Uniform.** Dress for a pretend world of rocket launching, space walks and lunar exploration . . . it looks so real. One-piece silvertone cotton twill (fabric shrinkage controlled to 1%) suit has large pockets, zipper front for quick changes. Overseas cap and badge included. Order astronaut helmet above. *State S, M or L.*
49 C 77028F—Shipping weight 1 lb. 2 oz....$5.99

8 **Fatigue Outfit.** Green Sanforized® cotton (maximum fabric shrinkage 1%). Jacket has insignia, stripes and tab to write your name on. Trousers have bellows pockets, zipper. Cap is included. *State S, M or L.*
49 C 77021F—Shipping weight 1 lb. 8 oz....$6.99

9 **Highway Trooper.** Be on patrol and make travel safer in your outfit of gray and red cotton (fabric shrinkage controlled to 1%) shirt and pants. Plastic cap and goggles. Set includes metal badge and handcuffs *plus* plastic whistle to direct traffic. *State S, M or L.*
49 C 77022F—Shipping weight 1 lb. 12 oz...$6.99

10 **U. S. Marine.** There's no mistaking this dashing Marine sergeant as he marches briskly along in his regulation-type uniform. Made of 1% shrinkage-controlled cotton. Includes cap, belt and insignia. Pants have elastic back. *State S, M or L.* Buy it the easy-way—order by phone.
49 C 77035F—Shipping weight 1 lb. 7 oz. ..$6.99

FAVORITE?
costume of your choice

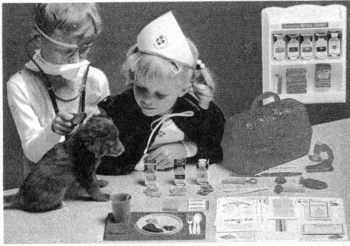

"Take blue pills on rainy days, orange ones on sunny days" . . prescribe 8 different candy pills in all, but first listen through real heart-beat stethoscope

Deluxe Nurse and Doctor Kits $4.99 each

Patients will get the best of care from nurse or doctor. Each kit contains over 70 pieces of "medical equipment," including thermometer, microscope, X-ray viewer, records and charts, in plastic bag. Hanging medical cabinet with each kit stores tasty Dr. "B" happy candy pills. 18-inch long stethoscope, designed like the one a doctor uses, amplifies sound so that you actually hear heartbeats. Nurse kit has apron, cape, sick tray with play food and plastic utensils. Doctor kit (not shown) has sleeveless medical jacket. Little "patient" not included.
49 C 1647—Deluxe Nurse Kit. Shipping wt. 2 lbs.................$4.99
49 C 1646—Deluxe Doctor Kit. Shipping wt. 2 lbs.............. 4.99
Extra Dr. "B" Happy Candy Pills. Package of 10 boxes.
49 C 16326—Shipping weight 12 ounces...............Package 99c

SEARS CUTS PRICES 14% on these popular Doctor and Nurse Kits $2.99 each

A great buy last Christmas at $3.49. Young doctor reaches into his plastic medical bag, carefully takes out and puts on "glasses," mask, stethoscope to examine his "sick" patient, then prescribes one of four Dr. "B" happy candy pills. Over 50 pieces in each kit, including microscope, thermometer, plastic syringes. Nurse kit (not shown) includes cap and apron. Order extra candy pills above.
49 C 1648—Doctor Kit. Shipping weight 1 lb. 4 oz.............$2.99
49 C 1653—Nurse Kit. Shipping weight 1 lb. 4 oz............... 2.99

11 Batman. Pow . . biff . . crack . . zowie, it's Batman to the rescue. With a mask over his eyes and Batsign on his chest, he is ready to fight crime everywhere in the world. Outfit of cotton shirt and pants (fabric won't shrink over 1%); plastic belt with buckle, cape, hood and mask.
State S, M or L.
49 C 7746F—Shpg. wt. 1 lb. 2 oz. $5.99

12 Spiderman. Crime is on the wane after the super-hero, Spiderman, appears on the scene in his scary play-suit of shrinkage-controlled cotton (max. fabric shrink. 1%). Authentic-looking outfit includes shirt with official "Spiderman" insignia, trousers, plastic hood and full-face mask.
State S, M or L.
49 C 77027F—Wt. 1 lb. 2 oz. $5.99

13 Bozo Outfit for Boys and Girls. Authentically-styled playsuit of Bozo the Clown made of 1-pc. acetate satin with contrasting white pompons. Wide neck ruffle has colorful braid trimming. Long sleeves have wide white cuffs with Bozo name stenciled on them. Comes with full-face plastic mask, fake red hair, rubber head band.
State S, M or L.
49 C 77036F—Wt. 1 lb. 2 oz.......$5.99

14 Visiting Nurse. Designed just right for the little "pretend" nurse who goes out to treat her "patients." White belted uniform is crisp cotton (fabric won't shrink over 1%). Includes blue cotton cape with insignia, perky little cap and handy plastic shoulder bag. *State S, M or L.*
49 C 7749F—Shpg. wt. 15 oz.....$4.99

SIZE CHART for all costumes on these two pages			
Size is	Small	Medium	Large
Height inches	35-42	43-51	52-60

FASHION DOLLS
"Mommy, these must be the

Two 15-inch Italian Beauties with skin
that feels like real .. waists that
twist 'n turn .. and limbs that
pose any way you want them to

Valentina

Vittoria

Each $6.99

Spirited, stylish and beautiful—they've captured the look of today! With gently curved arms and
shapely legs .. bright, clear eyes shining from beneath their long, long lashes .. and silky, rooted
hair you can comb and style again and again. Made by Furga of a new, supple vinyl that's softer,
more bendable than ever before. Dressed in mini wrap-arounds fastened with an initial pin; sandals.
49 C 30369—Brown-haired Vittoria. Shipping weight 1 pound 8 ounces.................... $6.99
49 C 30368—Blonde Valentina. Shipping weight 1 pound 8 ounces...................... 6.99

Italian-inspired Outfits ..
designed to turn Vittoria and Valentina
into the prettiest swingers to hit any scene

1 Elegant blue velvet evening dress with
organdy ruffles on collar, sleeves, hem.
Gold-color chain belt and sandals.
49 C 30642—Shpg. wt. 8 oz......... $6.99

2 Leather-look vinyl coat has plush orange
pile front lining, matching hat. Boots.
49 C 30639—Shpg. wt. 8 oz......... $5.99

3 Lounging pajamas in a pretty cotton
print with contrasting band trim. Sandals.
49 C 30637—Shpg. wt. 8 oz......... $4.99

4 Delicious apricot velvet evening pants
and tunic with long sleeves edged in
marabou, gold-color chain belt. Sandals.
49 C 30641—Shpg. wt. 8 oz......... $6.99

5 Perky linen dress has a painted daisy ..
contrasting collar, cuffs. Boots, purse.
49 C 30638—Shpg. wt. 8 oz......... $3.99

Note: Dolls not included with items 1 through 5.

most beautiful Dolls in the whole world!"

From Italy . .
lavishly gowned Dolls
she'll remember
a lifetime

3 Paola

2 Sophie

1 Vince

4 Simona

Magnificent in every detail. Each doll has delicate features . . long, thick lashes . . rooted hair that's been hand-arranged into the most romantic style . . and breath-taking clothes of the finest fabrics. Vinyl; jointed.

1 Vincé looks marvellously chic in her vibrantly patterned cotton dress accented with pure white organdy bell sleeves and a tucked bib and ruffled collar in the same crisp organdy. Her deep pink velvet cape has a marabou-edged hood. Crisp petticoats, cotton panties, socks, black "patent" shoes help make this doll a dream come true. 15 in. tall.
79 C 30371C—Shipping weight 3 pounds....$19.99

2 Sophie is a real enchantress in her romantic lavender blue gown with its ruffled organdy sleeves and bodice. Hem and matching wide-brimmed hat are trimmed in luxurious marabou. Fancy undergarments are petticoat, hoop skirt, organdy pantaloons, cotton pants, socks, "patent" shoes. Organdy parasol; chain necklace. 18 in. tall.
79 C 30372C—Shipping weight 3 pounds....$24.99

3 Paola looks absolutely enchanting in her tiered cotton gown with its swirl of rainbow stripes and lace trim. Her wide-brimmed hat is decked with flowers and ties with a lovely sheer veiling. Matching parasol, flouncy petticoat, panties, socks and "patent" shoes complete the outfit. 17 in. tall.
79 C 30108L—Shipping weight 4 pounds....$17.99

4 Here Comes Simona the Bride in a long white satin gown bordered with silk embroidery and detailed in back with a flowing train and bow. A matching satin headpiece catches the fingertip length, daisy appliqued veil. Lace gloves, cotton panties, white shoes. Bridal bouquet incl. 18 in. tall.
49 C 30123—Shipping weight 2 pounds....$14.99

French Provincial Styling
Snowy white with elegant blue or gold-color accents

1 Frilly Canopy Bed for your loveliest dolls. Hardwood construction with beautifully decorated panels. 25x15x32 inches high . . . ideal for dolls up to 23 inches. White plastic-covered mattress, canopy with ruffles. Unassembled. Doll not included. Bedding set sold at bottom of page.
79 C 92031C—Shipping weight 9 pounds......$12.99

2 Bunk or Twin Beds. For more "grown up" dolls. Ladder included. Padded mattress and pillows in lovely floral print cotton. Hardwood construction. 21x12x22 inches high as bunk. Holds dolls up to 20 inches. Unassembled.
79 C 92083C—Shipping weight 6 pounds......$10.99

3 High Chair. Has smartly turned legs, teddy bear screen design. Lift up tray. About 8x12x22 inches high. Hardwood construction. For dolls up to 20 inches. Shipped fully assembled.
79 C 92033C—Shipping weight 3 pounds........$6.99

4 Rocking Cradle. White enamel finished hardwood cradle has beautifully turned corner posts, dowel sides, steam-bent rockers. 26x14x18 in. high. Floral print cotton mattress and pillow. Unassembled.
79 C 92084C—Shipping weight 9 pounds........$8.99

Dolly's Bath or Feeding Time

$5.99

Bath and Dydee Set
Dolly loves her bath . . . water recirculates from vinyl tub to shower spray. Top flips down for dressing table. Steel tray holds soap, clothespins and line, diapers, tongs, sponge . . . all included. 21x13x24 in. high. Doll not included. Buy it the easy way—order by phone.
79 C 92086L—Shpg. wt. 4 lbs...$5.99

$4.99

Crib and Bath Set
A portable crib that doubles as an after-bath playpen. Tubular steel frame, nylon net siding. 21x12x17 inches high. Bath set has soap, a sponge, a rattle, a clothes line and 6 clothespins, 2 nursing bottles. Unassembled. For dolls to 20 in.
79 C 92085C—Shpg. wt. 3 lbs...$4.99

$3.99

High Chair, Feeding Set
Everything you need for dolly's feeding time. 24½-in. high chair has tubular steel legs, molded plastic seat, back and tray . . for dolls up to 18 inches. Bottle, "bottle warmer," spoon, dish, empty cereal box, cup and rattle included. Unassembled.
49 C 92087—Wt. 2 lbs. 8 oz....$3.99

Luxury Bedding Set
Only **$1.99**
Soft, smooth, pretty and dainty . . just what you want to show off your dolls. White rayon satin pillow and cover accented with yellow ruffle and bow. For all doll carriages, cribs, cradles and beds. The cover measures about 18x22 inches long.
49 C 92038—Wt. 8 oz....$1.99

She'll go "out" looking glamorous with these Dress-up Accessories $3.99 set

The best dressed little lady in town wears a rayon plush stole that looks like mink and a fashion-right "wig" of plastic. She will step out in high heels and wear an adjustable set of snap beads. Her finger tips will glisten with paste-on color plastic nails as she flashes her pretend diamond ring for her friends to admire.

Other accessories include a plastic orchid corsage for those very special occasions and a lorgnette so she can watch the opera or ballet with play sophistication.
49 C 1349—Shipping weight 1 lb. 4 oz.........Set $3.99

Suzy Homemaker Hair Dryer and Manicure Set $4.99 without batteries

Dry your hair just like Mom. Includes pretty beehive bonnet, plastic curlers. Grooming brush runs air through your hair. 4 utensils for nails. Plastic. Uses 2 "C" batteries, order package below.
49 C 1365—Shipping weight 2 lbs. 4 oz.........Set $4.99
49 C 46656—"C" Batteries. Pkg. of 6. Wt. 12 oz. Pkg. 1.19

Your very own Purse $2.99 set filled to the brim

Vinyl "mini" bag looks right in step with fashion. Inside put lipstick, play powder, compact, comb, brush and mirror. Set also includes glasses with fake lashes, belt, bracelets, manicuring aids. Strap adjusts.
49 C 13054—Shipping weight 1 pound 4 ounces. .Set $2.99

SEARS ROLLS BACK PRICES
Beauty School Set
Cut $1 $7.99
All the tools you need to set hair like a professional

Last Christmas Was $8.99. Learn hair care this fun and easy way. You can wash, comb, set, brush and tease the rooted nylon hair on the mannequin head to get ideas for your own hair styles.

Soft vinyl head has moving eyes, lashes . . head swivels. Rubber suction cups hold plastic base firmly to table or desk top. 12 plastic rollers, 6 metal clips and hairbrush included. Head is 13 inches high.
49 C 1361—Shpg. wt. 2 lbs. 10 oz. . .Set $7.99

High-fashion Hairpieces for girls

Now even little girls can have stylish hairpieces to set and style and wear anywhere. Washable nylon hair . : easy to curl. Wig (only) is mounted on head-shaped form. Fall is unmounted.

1 Wig. About 18 in.
49 C 13631—Blonde
49 C 13633—Brunette
Shpg. wt. 15 oz. . $5.99

2 Fall. About 22 in.
49 C 13661—Blonde
49 C 13663—Brunette
Shpg. wt. 9 oz. . . $3.99

Light-up Makeup Mirror $3.99 without batteries with accessories

Daisy-shaped mirror with sturdy plastic carrying case comes complete with bulbs, cosmetic aids, brush, comb, lipstick, apothecary jar. Uses 2 "D" batteries . . order pkg. below.
49 C 1362—Shpg. wt. 2 lbs. 1 oz.......$3.99
"D" Batteries. Package of 6.
49 C 46606—Shpg. wt. 1 lb. 8 oz... Pkg. 1.19

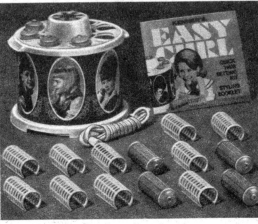

Easy-Curl Hairsetting Kit $6.99 sets hair in minutes

All you do is set hair on plastic rollers that have been warmed in plastic roller-warmer. Wait just 10 minutes, comb out. Warmer operates on one 60-watt light bulb (not incl.). UL listed for 110–120-volt, 60-cycle AC. Includes 8 rollers, clips, and styling booklet.
49 C 1364—Shpg. wt. 2 lbs........Kit $6.99

Exciting sights and sounds from The Windmill Group

BOYS' TOYS OF THE FIFTIES & SIXTIES

If you were a boy growing up in the Fifties or Sixties, you'll surely remember these wonderful old Sears catalog pages from 1950-1969. Chock-full of classic toys like G.I Joe, Lionel Trains, Marx playsets, James Bond spy gadgetry, Erector sets, Matchbox racers, slot cars, Tonka trucks, Roy Rogers pistols and more... with their original prices! 192 pages with thousands of illustrations.

$19.95

GIRLS' TOYS OF THE FIFTIES & SIXTIES

Destined to bring back happy childhood memories! This exciting book includes the best Sears Wishbook pages of toys and dolls from 1950 through 1969. Jammed with such classic toys as Barbie and Ken, Kenner's Easy Bake Oven, luxurious Marx dollhouses and kitchen sets, Twister, Mystery Date, Mouse Trap, Chatty Cathy and more with their original selling prices! 192 pages.

$19.95

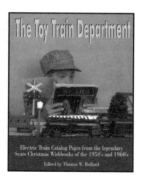

More BOYS' TOYS OF THE 50's AND 60's

By popular demand! A terrific sequel to BOYS' TOYS, featuring the very best boy toy pages from the great Montgomery Ward Christmas Books from 1950 through 1969. 192 pages jammed with illustrations and original prices of favorites like Marx playsets, American Flyer and Lionel trains, Davy Crockett and Lone Ranger toys. A fun book for any collector or just for happy memories.

$19.95

THE DOLL AND TEDDY BEAR DEPARTMENT

A "Must Have" book for anyone interested in the wonderful dolls and teddy bears sold by Sears from 1950-1969. This book is packed with great catalog pages of such classics as Barbie & Ken, Tiny Tears, Shirley Temple, Betsy McCall, Mme. Alexander, Betsy Wetsy, Miss Revlon, Chatty Cathy, Raggedy Ann, Kiddles and more. Cute teddy bears too, with original prices! 192 pages.

$19.95

THE TOY TRAIN DEPARTMENT

Electric trains were high on any boy's Christmas list during the Fifties and Sixties, and Sears sold the finest. This neat book contains *every* catalog page of toy trains sold by Sears from 1950 through 1969. The best and rarest are here, and beautifully illustrated: Lionel, Marx, American Flyer, Tyco and Revell trains and accessories in all gauges. 160 pages with the original selling prices!

$19.95

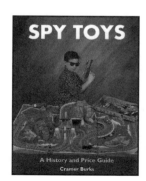

SPY TOYS
A Pictorial History and Price Guide

The hottest collectibles around... spy toys from 1962 to present. Spies were the superheros of their day. Hit movies and TV shows like James Bond's 007, *OUR MAN FLINT, MAN FROM U.N.C.L.E., MISSION: IMPOSSIBLE, THE WILD, WILD WEST, GET SMART, HONEY WEST* and *THE AVENGERS* ignited kid's imaginations. The Cold War brought us hundreds of neat toys too, all pictured in this big book with background data, old catalog pages and current valuations. 160 pages.

$19.95

THE TOY TRAIN DEPT. VOLUME TWO

By popular demand! This new book contains *every* electric train page from the great Montgomery Ward Christmas catalogs from 1950 through 1969. Thousands of trains, sets and accessories in all gauges are beautifully illustrated, including such great brands as American Flyer, Lionel, Marx and others. A superb reference book. 160 pages with original selling prices!

$19.95

Compact Disc $12.98
Stereo Cassette $8.98

TOY TRAINS - THE SOUNDTRACK

This incredible collector's volume contains 33 rare electric train audio treasures from such great toymakers as Lionel Trains, Gilbert's American Flyer, Erector Set and Marx Toys. Packed with original promotional records, talking train stations, radio and TV commercials, sound effects records from the 1940's, 50's and 60's. Great for train buffs *but kids love it too!*

EACH BIG BOOK ONLY $19.95

PLUS $4.00 SHIPPING PER ORDER AND SALES TAX IF APPLICABLE
Offers may be limited. Non-U.S.A. orders add postage.
Satisfaction Guaranteed

CREDIT CARD ORDERS
VISA **(800) 470-5540** MasterCard

Order by Credit Card or send Check or M.O. to:
THE WINDMILL GROUP
P.O. Box 56551
Sherman Oaks, CA 91413